Me & Others

Other books by Michael Smith

Eight Plays from Off Off-Broadway (editor, with Nick Orzel)
Theatre Journal, Winter 1967
Theatre Trip
The Best of Off Off-Broadway (editor)
More Plays from Off-Off-Broadway (editor)
American Baby
A Sojourn in Paris
Near the End
Automatic Vaudeville
Every Day Arising
A Cat's Tale
Johnny!
Rhapsodic Photography
Plays I & II
Names and Events
Theatre Journal: Reviews from The Village Voice, 1960–1974
Six Stories
Play Work
How to Be Funny

Michael Townsend Smith

Me & Others

an American life

FAST BOOKS

For all my loves

ISBN 978-0-9982793-3-6
Revised 2020

Fast Books are edited and published by Michael Smith
P. O. Box 1268, Silverton, OR 97381
Catalog at fastbookspress.com

Contents

Holy Memory

1935–1956

Master Michael

MICHAEL SMITH

IMMIGRANTS WAY BACK, my ancestors moved west to settle in the heart of America. My father, Lewis Motter Smith Jr., grew up in St. Joseph, Missouri, where his family's wholesale dry goods business, Smith McCord Townsend, supported a prosperous capitalist lifestyle. Graduating from Culver Military Academy in 1918, he just missed serving in World War I, traveled in Europe instead of going to college, and returned to St. Joe. His father's early death left Dad running the business when it failed in the Depression. His first wife, daughter of his late father's partner, divorced him and moved to Santa Fe with their two young children, Virginia and Lewis.

Mother's first husband fell ill on their wedding night and, so the story goes, they never consummated the marriage. Dorothy Pew, called Dot, was always nostalgic for the six months she and Johnny Townley spent in Europe before she went home to Kansas City, divorced him, and married Dad.

After a honeymoon in Nassau, the newlyweds moved to New York, but Mother, pregnant with me, was not happy living so far away from her family. They moved back to Kansas City, where Dad had inherited a house. I was born on October 5, 1935.

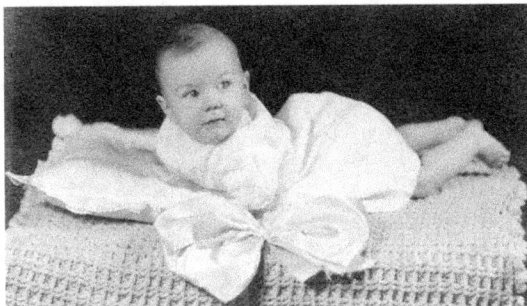

Left: 4400 Warwick Boulevard (1935–1937) Above: 814 West 59th Street (1937–1940)

With Mother

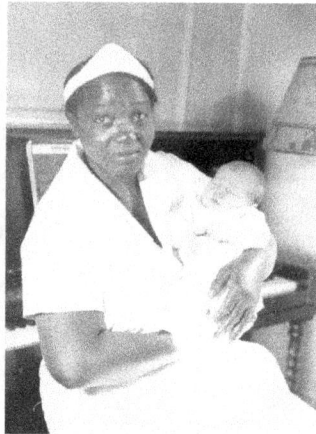

With Daisy

With Miss Scanlon

MICHAEL SMITH

With Uncle Alfred

James R. Scarritt's nanny and mine took us for walks in our baby carriages; we are friends to this day.

I still wear a beret.

Father and son

My father's family: front, Uncle John, my grandmother Dee Dee, Dad; rear, Aunts Bickley, Anne, and Sarah.

Mother's family on the Fourth of July, 1936. Front row: Aunt Viv with my cousins Ann, Francis Jr. (Bud), and Helen, seated between Boppo and Grammie, Mother with me on her lap. Back row: Uncle Fos, Aunt Ginny, Uncle John and Aunt Wig, Uncle Alfred, and my father.

MICHAEL SMITH

Oout of the collapse of the family business, my father salvaged a chain of four department stores in small towns in eastern Kansas, running them from an office in Kansas City. In September 1940, the year I started kindergarten, we moved to Ottawa, Kansas, sixty miles southwest of Kansas City, so he could save a manager's salary by running the store himself. Mother walked me to school until I was old enough to walk on my own. Here I am (second from right) making a maypole outside Hawthorne School

in Ottawa. At five I began taking piano lessons from Myra Adler. I learned to swim in the municipal pool. I learned to ride a bicycle. In December 1941 my parents called me indoors to listen to the radio, and we heard President Roosevelt announce the Japanese attack on Pearl Harbor and the declaration of war. Dad wanted to serve, but he was too old and had a family to support. Gas was rationed so travel was limited during the war years. We planted a victory garden, saved tinfoil and rubber bands, and knitted squares to be sewn into blankets for the soldiers.

My sister Bickley was born in Ottawa on October 21, 1942, when I was seven, ending my privileged status as an only child. (Virginia and Lewis, whose mother had remarried, lived with her in Santa Fe and were seldom seen.) War stimulated the economy. In 1943 we moved back to Kansas City and a roomy, comfortable house with a big yard on a leafy street in the Country Club District. Mary Spring came with us from Ottawa to look after Bicky and lived with us for several years.

Mary Spring on
my bike

Mother looked after my
cocker spaniel, Snappy.

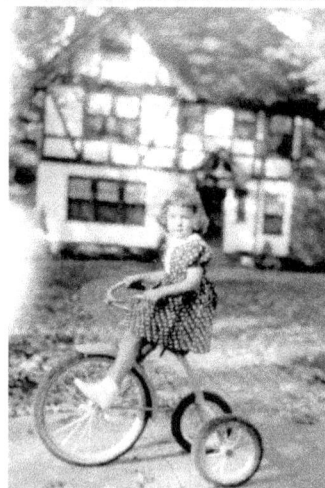

Bicky in front of our house
at 818 West 56th Street

MICHAEL SMITH

Boppo and Grammie with seven of their grandchildren, my cousins Bud, Helen, and Ann Foster, Mary and John Mitchell Lucas, me next to Grammie, Bicky on her lap.

Mother's father, John B. Pew, was an attorney, civic official, Baptist, and paragon of respectability. Maisie, her mother, loved poetry and music, played the piano, and lived by Coué's mantra, "Every day in every way I am getting better and better." Grammie passed on her generous spirit, sunny disposition, and love of beauty to my mother, who did her best to pass it on to me.

Uncle Alfred, my Mother's baby brother, would be a significant figure in my life. After studying piano and composition at Juilliard, Al became a Broadway dancer (which was hushed up in the family until much later). Serving in the Army Air Force in World War II, he staged musical shows for the troops. After the war, he married Maxine Munt, also a dancer, and they started a modern dance studio and company in New York. Al and Max inspired me with their example of a life in art and steadily encouraged me to follow my dreams.

Uncle Alfred as a boy, in the army, with his mother in New York, with Maxine in Paris.

MOTHER AND I had a special rapport. Dad taught me to shoot and often took me with him when he drove out to Kansas to visit his stores. They were a glamorous couple when they dressed up, Dad slim and severe, as handsome as Tyrone Power, Mother sparkling, fragrant, leggy and curvaceous like Betty Grable, with smiling, pouting lips and soft wavy hair grazing her shoulders. Like Proust I recall the dreamy sound of animated voices from downstairs when they had company and Mother's giddiness when she came up to kiss me good night. We had a wonderful life. We went to the circus, horse shows, rodeos, the Ice Capades, Blackstone the Magician, Roy Rogers and Dale Evans's stage show, outdoor operettas, and touring Broadway musicals. Mother wanted me to play the piano, insisted I practice., and took me to concerts when Dad didn't want to go.

Family vacations were high points of my early years. The summer I was six we joined Boppo and Grammie and assorted aunts, uncles, and cousins in Green Mountain Falls, Colorado. I drove out with Dad, who taught me to manage the accelerator crossing the rolling prairie. Mother, pregnant with Bicky, came with her parents on the train. Other summers we drove up to Minnesota to spend some weeks with Dad's mother, Dee Dee, at her capacious cottage on Lake Miltona. Mary Spring played with Bicky while Mother and Dad were out on the lake fishing. I had my own boat with a small, hard-to-start outboard motor. I liked taking machines apart and figuring out how they worked. In the polio epidemic of 1944 the Kansas City Country Club pool was risky so I went to stay with Dee Dee at Lake Miltona by myself. My cousin Jessamine was there, and we organized a carnival in the backyard, with Japanese war leader Tojo as the target for dart-throwing and a spook house in the shadowy passages underneath the cottage. My brother Lewis was with us at Miltona when Japan surrendered. Thirteen at the time, he remembers Mother running out of the bedroom in her underwear to announce the end of the war. We paraded up and down the lakefront banging on pots and pans. Later, while the grownups drank cocktails and highballs, we children invaded the cottages and pied their beds.

MICHAEL SMITH

Several winters we spent the month of February at Remuda Ranch in Wickenburg, Arizona. I kept up my lessons at a little schoolhouse on the ranch in the morning, rode through the beautiful desert landscape in the afternoon, and learned to play pool and ping-pong after dinner in the lodge.

After the war we took longer trips eevery summer in my father's big Chrysler. Dad drove, and Mother entertained us with games. I was intrigued with maps and acted as navigator, keeping track of our gas mileage and average speed. One summer we went to Small Point, Maine, where I took sailing lessons from a cousin, Sewall Williams, who was just back from the war. The ocean was too cold for swimming. The next year we rented a house in La Jolla, California. I enjoyed tennis lessons at the Beach and Tennis Club but avoided going into the ocean because of the stingrays.

In summer 1950 we went to C Lazy U, a dude ranch in Colorado, where my sister Virginia came to join us. Dinny had studied acting at the University of Iowa and was moving to New York to do theatre. Bicky was growing up, and so was I. My Kansas City friend Bill Evans happened to be staying nearby with his grandmother. I went over to visit, and we took our pants off and ran around in the woods, showing our virgin stiffies to the Colorado air.

Michael Smith

Big Wolf Lake in the Adirondacks, surrounded by miles of timber land owned by the Lawrence family of Bronxville, had a clubhouse and a score of private "camps" spaced well apart around the densely wooded shoreline. It was a very special place. Three summers we rented one of the camps for a month, sponsored by a friend of Dad's from Bronxville (who later would masturbate me in a Florida motel room, with my parents' unwitting complicity). I spent many days out on the lake on my own. There was a fleet of sailing canoes, with regular races. Or I sped around in my little boat, thrilled when Dad got me a 10-horse motor. One of the Lawrence family camps had a tennis court in the woods where I sometimes played. We were outsiders, but the natives were friendly. Mother and Dad went to cocktail parties. I was shy and self-conscious, but I loved being there and did my best to fit in with these sophisticated Eastern kids.

I went to segregated public school when we moved back to Kansas City, then from sixth grade on went to a private school, Pembroke Country Day. Jimmy Starr and James R. Scarritt (front left above) were my best friends. Pamela Morgan (above right) was my girlfriend: we danced romantically close, shyly held hands, and carefully kissed good night. I took three years of Latin and three years of French. I liked school and did well, always near the top of my class. My English teacher, Virginia Scott Miner, a poet, gave me a lifelong love for words and interest in grammar and writing.

I played the First Citizen in *Julius Caesar*, but I was happier as a backstage helper, pulling the curtain and running the lights. I was the boy who ran the movie projector for school assemblies.

Jimmy and I were the best students of our piano teacher, Mrs. Blim. He could play flashy crowd-pleasers; I took refuge in sensitive expression. In one recital we teamed up on the Arensky Waltz, a sparkling piece for two pianos in which the players take turns starting variations. I abruptly went blank. We looked at each other down the length of the matching Steinways. The audience tittered. Then Jimmy picked it up and we were off again. He remembers it the other way around.

MICHAEL SMITH

MY PARENTS WENT TO NEW YORK once or twice a year all through my childhood, Dad on buying trips for his stores, Mother to visit her baby brother, bringing me matchbooks from famous restaurants and night clubs. Mother brought home sheet music and played the songs from the latest shows. Dad, who always thought the East was superior to the Middle West, accordingly sent Lewis and then me to Hotchkiss, a high-class all-boy prep school in Lakeville, Connecticut. I resisted until I was fifteen and went for the last two years before college. At Hotchkiss, as it turned out, I came into my own as an artistic person. I took piano lessons and played in front of the whole school. I wrote a story for the literary magazine. I sang in the choir and glee club and turned pages for the organist. A fellow student, Griffith Rose, introduced me to the Bartok quartets. My English teacher, Charles Garside, taught me how to write a critical essay. And I acted in several plays. I played the Earl of Stanley in *Richard III* in a gray wig. As Sidney Carlton, the Noel Coward character in *The Man Who Came to Dinner*, I sat down at the piano and sang a Coward song. I was Queen Guinevere (some boy had to be) in *A Connecticut Yankee*, with my roommate Hugh Madden in a tuxedo as the visitor from modern times and that year's English exchange student as Sir Lancelot. Much as I was attracted to the theatre, acting made me unbearably nervous and gave me nightmares—wrong play, no pants.

Dad took me with him to buy Mother a new car, and we came home with this beautiful light green Chrysler convertible. The summer after I graduated from Hotchkiss, they let me drive it by myself from Kansas City to Santa Barbara, California, where my father had bought a store across the street from the Art Museum. Before long Mother and Bicky joined us, and we moved to a cabin at San Ysidro Ranch. Mornings I worked in the basement stockroom at Dad's store, receiving merchandise and putting on price tags. Another boy who was about to go to Yale, Peter Morse, looked after me when I got drunk for the first time. The house in Kansas City was sold, we went back to pack up, and they moved to Santa Barbara just as I left for the East: we parted at Union Station. It was hard for Mother to leave her family and friends, but it worked out well. Dad was happier in California, spending a few hours at the store in the morning, afternoons at the beach. Mother made new friends and did significant work in Santa Barbara as a volunteer and board member for Planned Parenthood, the Visiting Nurses Association, and the Music Academy of the West.

MICHAEL SMITH

MY FATHER TOOK ME AROUND to look at colleges. Cum laude at Hotchkiss, I assumed I could get in anywhere, and he was ready to pay. I floated the idea of going to Cal Tech. Good at physics and math as well as English; I could see myself as an architect or civil engineer and would have liked to be near my family. It was Dad who decided I should stay in the East. I rejected Williams and Amherst, was drawn to Hamilton and Harvard, hated Yale but somehow wound up going there anyway. Both my grandfathers had gone to Yale, and Hotchkiss was Yale-oriented. I did well at first, although my classes were disppointing: the teaching was better at Hotchkiss. Rejected by the glee club, I joined the Dramat and was taken under the wing of Bob Leach, the Dramat's lighting designer, launching me

Bob Leach, my lighting mentor, in my room on Chapel Sreet

on a lifelong interest. I soon made a number of interesting and cultivated new friends. Some of them were homosexual, whatever that meant. One of them kept me up late listening to Beethoven quartets, wrote poems to me, and wanted to get in bed with me, but I wasn't ready for that. Sex was something you did with women. I had gone out with some friendly girls, liked them, but couldn't figure out how to get anything started. As freshman year went on I gradually fell apart, slept through early classes, failed philosophy and math, though I had won a math prize at Hotchkiss, and flunked out. My parents were shocked; Mother cried. Taking summer courses at Occidental in Los Angeles. I got back in, a freshman again, required to live off-campus. I had better courses the second year at Yale, including color with Josef Albers and history of architecture with Vincent Scully. A friend and I started a little poetry magazine called *Voices*. I helped with lights for *Sweeney Agonistes* by T. S. Eliot and Ezra Pound's *Women of Trachis,* performed in the round in one of the college dining halls, my first close encounter with modernism. In the spring I designed the lighting for a major musical in the big university theatre.

Visiting from Yale: my perfect family

Academically redeemed, I rejoined my class as a junior and moved into Saybrook College but soon was losing my grip again. I took my confusion to the university health services and arranged a medical leave of absence. My dashng roommate Denis Deegan threw a party for our brilliant friends to see me off. Dad sent me to the Austen Riggs Center, a Freudian sanatorium in Stockbridge, Massachusetts, headed by his former psychiatrist from Meninger's. At Riggs I met two interesting older women: Elizabeth Hawes, a leftist writer, the first person to take me seriously as a writer; and Janet Stewart, a sophisticated New Yorker with many friends in the theatre. I stayed for nine months without making any progress in therapy. What did help was that Dick Spahn, the activities director, mentored me in directing a production of *A Sleep of Prisoners* by Christopher Fry and a Saroyan one-act by Saroyan. I had found my calling. If I wanted to get into the theatre, Dick said, I would have to go to New York. And so I did.

MICHAEL SMITH

When I Was Gay

1956–1974

On stage at the 1964 Obie Awards with Ellen Stewart and Joe Cino

MICHAEL SMITH

1

JANET STEWART INVITED fellow patient Hod O'Brien and me to stay with her for a week while we found ourselves an apartment in the city. Her thirteen-room co-op at 60th and Park was as big as the houses I had grown up in and seriously elegant, with a Rodin bronze on a chest in the hall, Dufys in the living room, and a Steinway grand in a corner of the dining room. I could have settled in, but Janet meant it about our only staying a week; her teenage daughter Serena and housekeeper Nona were coming back from Canada, where Serena had been figure-skating. Hod and I moved to a gritty two-room furnished apartment in a rundown brownstone on West 85th Street off Central Park.

Dick Spahn had advised me to study acting, saying it would help me to direct actors. My father would pay for acting school, in addition to giving me an allowance to live on for a time. It never even occurred to me to go back to Yale. I didn't know there were directing programs. Dick recommended Sanford Meisner at the Neighborhood Playhouse as the best acting teacher, but I was late applying and not prepared with an audition scene. I enrolled instead at Stella Adler's acting academy, which had its own small building at 77th and Lexington. Stella, a glamorous and charismatic teacher, offered direct transmission from Stanislavski as well as the more flamboyant acting tradition of the Yiddish theatre. The first day, when she had us count the blood vessels in each other's eyeballs, my partner was a starlet, Rita Gam. As one of sixty students in Stella's famous acting class, I would rarely or never have to expose my quivering self-consciousness to scrutiny. Other students were eager to show what they could do and take their chances with her sharp critique. I sat in the back, satisfied to listen and watch.

In addition to acting with Stella, we had classes in dance, speech, and singing. Warren Beatty and I played the piano for each other to practice our songs. I sang "On the Street Where You Live" from *My Fair Lady*, feeling ardent and romantic when I was by myself but stiff and nervous when I performed. Speaking lines and pretending to be someone else, I was hopelessly inept. I didn't want to be an actor.

Dance took the form of ballet classes with Nina Fonaroff, a former Martha Graham dancer who had reverted to classical technique. In her studio on lower Park Avenue, she worked us hard. It was bracing to be stripped to the physical, no psychological excuses entertained. Under our tights we boys were instructed to wear a strange, stiff piece of underwear called a dance belt to manage any bulge in the crotch; the City Ballet boys, it was rumored, stuffed theirs with socks. Ballet class was strict, positions and movements right or not. I enjoyed it despite the pain and frustration. I was no dancer but liked making the effort, becoming aware of my body, regarding my form in the big mirrors, gaining strength, learning to stand up straight and carry myself confidently.

On Sundays I walked across the park, ate a late breakfast at the counter in a Madison Avenue drug store reading the *Times*, and often spent the afternoon and evening at Janet Stewart's, watching the Ed Sullivan show, playing the piano, doing the crossword puzzle with Janet, seeing who else turned up. She was a famous beauty. Widowed, divorced, living well on her own, Janet had been working as a volunteer secretary at the Actors Studio; she'd had an affair with Tony Franciosa. Friends and admirers often dropped by in the early evening for a drink or picked her up for a date. I met Bill Inge, Bill Saroyan, Errol Flynn, Oscar Pettiford, and Randolph Churchill at her house. Once or twice I joined Janet and Hod, a jazz pianist, to hear Pettiford play. Billy Rose asked her to marry him, but she liked her life too much the way it was.

I played chamber music for the first time with two friends of Janet's, David Amram, a composer and horn player, and Frank Corsaro, a director and tenor, reading through Benjamin Britten's "Serenade." Playing with others was a revelation. The main thing was not to stop. My sight-reading immediately improved.

Janet invited me into her dressing room to watch her dress, letting me see and once even touch her small white breasts. I was tired of being a virgin and wished we could have an affair, à la *Rosenkavalier*. (I learned

MICHAEL SMITH

only much later that she was sleeping with Hod.) Janet maintained that I was destined to be homosexual, which had some advantages. Homosexuals were allowed to be sensitive, interested in art, classical music, and pretty things, encouraged to act silly and have fun. Queers could be theatrical. And nothing else was happening. Yet far from fantasizing about sex acts with another man, I could not begin to imagine what one would actually do. Ass fucking? You have to be kidding! I was so squeamish I had never touched my own asshole, just washed in that general direction. It was definitely not a turn-on. Female anatomy, meanwhile, was mysteriously dark and gooey. It was too ridiculous.

Alone in my West Side room I sat at my typewriter and tried to write—stories imitating Hemingway, Saroyan, and Gertrude Stein, fragments of dialogue and description. Janet predicted that in five years I would have my first play on Broadway. I loved the idea. But I had not written a play.

Serena, the younger of Janet's two daughters and a freshman at Sarah Lawrence, refused to "come out" in the debutante season that first winter, but she was invited to the parties anyway, and I was her escort, a role I had practiced in Santa Barbara. Janet let me wear jeweled studs and cuff links from Serena's deceased father's collection. At the St. Regis Roof and other swank party rooms we danced to the music of Lester Lanin or Peter Duchin, who had been in my class at Hotchkiss.

I FLEW OUT TO SUNNY CALIFORNIA to spend Christmas with my family and relaxed into the familiar warmth, going along with everything Mother had arranged. They were living in a glamorous rented house with swimming pool looking out to the ocean over the Montecito Country Club golf course, but it was too cold to swim. When asked, I said everything was going fine.

A different set of feelings emerged when I talked to Liz Hawes, my writer friend from Riggs. She invited me to dinner at her apartment in Hollywood before my night flight back to New York, and everything I had not said at home came flooding out. I did not like living in New York. The acting classes were a joke. I wanted to be a writer. If you want to be a writer you have to write, she told me, not waste your time doing other things. She said I should go to Ensenada, where life was cheap, and write. Liz, who had written a number of books, had an idea for a project we could do together, contrasting the views of two people a generation apart. I scarcely had any views, barely aware of political ideas or social issues, but I liked the idea of writing a book.

Postponing my flight till the next day, I spent the night on Liz's sofa. In the morning I called my father, who thought I was already in New York. He was far from pleased to hear that I wanted to give up on acting school and go to Mexico to write. I needed to learn to finish what I started, he said, not quit again in the middle. Unless I stayed in school, he would end his support. I felt completely powerless. I had never worked, never earned any money, had no idea how to support myself. So I went back to New York. Writers can write anywhere, I reminded myself—that's part of the charm.

I QUIT STELLA'S ANYWAY soon after that, it was too ridiculous, and Dad gave me a few more months while I set about learning to make a living. Janet's older daughter, Nancy Ryan, was going out with Alan Brien, an English writer then on assignment in New York as a correspondent for the *London Evening Standard*. Alan gave me my first job, working mornings at the office of the Beaverbrook newspapers in Rockefeller Center. I generally had nothing to do but read the New York papers and update a huge, never-used clipping file. Alan was rarely there but might phone to have me line up tickets for a show or locate a book, or a Telex might come from London requesting some tidbit of information. At the end of the theatre season, Alan went back to London and was not replaced, and I moved across the room to the *Sunday Express*—an office boy, though it was never quite put that way.

I soon parted ways with Hod; we had never been friends. Denis Deegan too dropped out of Yale and moved into the city, and we sublet an apartment together in the far depths of the Lower East Side, several plainly furnished rooms with a distant view of the Empire State Building. It was a longish

Denis Deegan

walk to the subway. I had the inspiration to buy a Vespa, which made commuting to midtown a lark.

I was still visiting Janet and going out with Serena, who touched my stiff penis through my flannels one time when we were lolling around on her bed. We were too ignorant and timid to go any further, although we were both fed up with being virgins. Denis solved that problem for her. In the early summer the three of us spent hot, sensual hours sunning on our asphalt rooftop, where the heat gave me a hard-on in my trunks while Denis and Serena went downstairs and fucked, she said.

Denis, who also wanted to be a director, departed to work as John Houseman's assistant at the American Shakespeare Festival in Stratford, Connecticut. Serena went to Canada one last time to figure-skate. I stayed alone in my airy rooms. On weekends I rode my Vespa out across Brooklyn to the beach at Riis Park or Coney Island. I was not making any progress with my ambition to become a director, but Janet had set me up to read scripts for a Broadway producer, producing a page of summary and comments for ten dollars a play. That was something.

WORKING IN ROCKEFELLER CENTER, the closest I could park on the street was east of Third Avenue. I would park my scooter perpendicular to the curb between parked cars, but inattentive drivers too often backed into it and knocked it over. On the north side of 53rd Street,

Serena by candlelight at P. J. Clarke's

toward the Second Avenue end of the block, I noticed a narrow house with a tiny fenced-in yard paved with slate that would be a perfect place to park my scooter. The ground floor, down a few steps, was the office of a telephone answering service, a friendly, fun-loving group of women called the Belles. I knocked and not only arranged to park my Vespa in the yard, I moved into the house. The owner worked in Philadelphia and was almost never there. She rented me a small back bedroom on the top floor, and I pretty much had the run of the house.

Serena quit Sarah Lawrence after a year and enrolled at the Neighborhood Playhouse. We went to the theatre, the new French movies, the ballet, hung out at P. J. Clarke's, and it was inevitable that we would go to bed. It happened in a curious way. A British explorer with rooms on a lower floor in my house went to Africa and left me his key. One night Serena and I let ourselves into his place and discovered slides he had taken of circumcision rites among the Ubangi, tall, black young men with long, bloody penises. Turned on and eager to fuck, we called up her sister for birth-control advice. Nancy said to be careful and pull out before I came, for now; in fact I was afraid to come, and didn't that time. Still, we had done it—what a relief! The next day I found a ten-dollar bill in a letter from my mother and gave it to Serena, who went to Planned Parenthood and had herself fitted with a diaphragm. After that we fucked whenever we liked, in my little room or at her place, once she moved out of her mother's. Sex at last: I loved it!

ICONTINUED TO TAKE DANCE CLASSES, which felt good and kept me fit, switching from ballet to classes in "modern" with Uncle Alfred and Aunt Maxine. Mother had taken me with her to see Al and Max's new loft on Sixth Avenue and 43rd Street when they were first moving in. I was shocked at the grime and decrepitude. They had cleaned it up and made it into a handsome dance studio with a comfortable small apartment at the back, decorated with books, art by friends, and angular modern furniture. Mother adored Al and Max and visited them whenever she was in New York and could get away from my father, who thought art was frivolous and disapproved of their impractical idealism, suspicious of their influence on me—a silent battle for my soul that went on for years.

Maxine Munt

Al and Max were dedicated modernists, their lives all about art. The big studio in the front had a gleaming maple floor, Chinese drums for beating time, a small piano, and a wall of mirrors. They worked hard. Every day before the first class one of them wiped down the whole floor, folding and refolding a moist towel around a wide broom and systematically pushing it up and down the long room. I took class from them twice a week for several years, enjoying the stretches and jumps and complex "combinations" taken diagonally across the floor. I was never good enough nor did I want to perform with their small company, but I went along to performances in gyms and auditoria in Long Island and New Jersey, helping them set up, running the lights and sound, pulling the curtain if there was one. Al and

Max were extraordinarily kind to me, inviting me to dinner and encouraging me to play the piano in the studio. I missed having a piano.

2

THE BEAVERBROOK OFFICE subscribed to Celebrity Service, which kept the press informed about who was in town and where they were staying. My ground-floor neighbors the Belles turned out to be the central switchboard of the Manhattan celebrity circuit. (They were the inspiration for Adolf Green's 1956 musical *The Bells Are Ringing*.) Answering machines, voicemail, and the rest had not yet been invented, and the Belles did more than any machine could, discreetly facilitating arrangements, sympathizing with the special needs and woes of their famous clients.

Richard Baldridge

I often stopped off in the Belles' dark, low-ceilinged den late at night on my way home to bed, chatting with Mary Printz and the other women between calls, listening to one side of their conversations, feeling I was getting to know their clients. Richard Baldridge, an opera director who lived in the building next door, also dropped in, and we came to be friends. Red-headed Richard was a dandy, discreet about his homosexuality, as one had to be in those days, but quite queeny, come to think of it.

Richard was acquainted with one of the Belles' famous clients, Anthony Perkins, the handsome young star of stage and screen. I had admired Tony's acting in *Tea and Sympathy* and the movie *Friendly Persuasion*, and I had something of a crush on him, loving the characters he played. We even looked a bit alike, tall and lanky. He was the image of me perfected. Tony was beautiful, with the extra glow of makeup, and artful lighting, and the glamour of fame.

Richard told me where Tony lived, in a floor-through apartment in a brownstone on West 56th Street, across the street from the stage door of the City Center, home of the New York City Ballet. Star-struck, I took to cruising by on my Vespa hoping to catch a glimpse of him.

As it turned out, Richard was friends not with Tony but with Helen Merrill, a portrait photographer Tony lived with when he was in New

Helen Merrill

York. Richard mentioned that Helen needed someone to paint her kitchen, and I persuaded him to take me to meet her. Tony was in Philadelphia, acting in the pre-Broadway tryout of *Look Homeward, Angel*.

Helen was a small, brisk, witchy woman nearing forty. Born in Berlin, she had a strong German accent and a European sense of culture. She was smart and articulate and made her living doing head shots of actors, many of whom kept in touch and valued her advice. She liked gay men.

After I finished painting the kitchen, Helen put me to work laying a floor of cork tiles in her office and studio. Further back was a dark, narrow, book-lined hallway leading to the private rooms. Helen had a Blüthner piano in the living room that I loved to play. An archway opened into her bedroom. Beyond was Tony's tiny boy's room with its narrow built-in bed.

Helen fed me, took me to the theatre, and I helped her with chores such as walking Punkie, Tony's dog, taking him out many a night to "do his duty," often walking him up Sixth Avenue into the park. Helen taught me to develop film and make prints and took me on as her darkroom assistant, sending me out on a few photography jobs of my own. I became an intimate of Helen's house as I had been at Janet Stewart's and sometimes still was—but this household was all about work.

Look Homeward, Angel was a hit on Broadway and ran all winter. Tony was brilliant as Thomas Wolfe's sensitive alter ego, Eugene Gant, his finely tuned performance reflecting a craftsmanship inherited from his father, Osgood Perkins, a Broadway matinee idol of the thirties, as well as his own bright, quirky character. He had already made three movies that year, *Fear Strikes Out, Desire Under the Elms* opposite Sophia Loren, and *The Matchmaker.*

Helen kept life going on around him normally. Tony accepted me as one of her several minions, calling me "Smish," mocking her accent. It was a thrill to go out in public with them: everybody recognized Tony, and we were the center of a buzz. Most nights he came straight home after the show, and we made grilled cheese and bacon sandwiches, eaten with butter and Grey Poupon. Then I buzzed off home on my Vespa. Tony was gentle and generous with me, fun to know.

Denis came back to town and rented a different room in my house. A very pretty girlfriend of his, the Honorable Sarah Rothschild, moved into the owner's big bedroom for a few weeks. Sarah took me to bed too once or twice, exposing me to a bolder, more driving sexuality.

There was zero overlap between the Helen-Tony scene and the Janet-Serena-Denis scene. That was the great thing about city life: I could live in several different worlds at once, close to the center of multiple circles, which suited my protean and open-minded nature.

Betty Rollin, a friend of Serena's from the Playhouse, came over to Helen's studio so I could practice my photography. Recognizing that I wanted to be a writer, she took me downtown to meet the editor and publisher of a new weekly newspaper in Greenwich Village, *The Village Voice.* Dan Wolf and Ed Fancher had started *The Voice* with $10,000 in seed money from Dan's friend Norman Mailer, who wrote a column for the paper that made it a magnet for hip writers and readers. Mailer quit after a few

Ed Fancher and Dan Wolf outside the first *Village Voice* office at 22 Greenwich Avenue

months, but by then the paper had an identity, a cadre of talented writers, and a small but significant readership. I volunteered to write whatever they needed, which turned out to be a sports car column, my main qualification being that I car-crazy as a kid and had always wanted a sports car. I wrote a column every other week called "Hubcaps." I covered the press conference at the Waldorf-Astoria at which the Edsel was unveiled.

The Voice would not start paying its writers for several more years, but they paid me for proofreading. I kept working more hours, and my father phased out my allowance.

3

MY STUDENT DEFERMENT HAVING LAPSED when I left Yale, the draft board summoned me to a pre-induction physical. There was no war going on, and I sensed that two years in the Army might be good for me—expose me to types I might otherwise never encounter, push me out of my narrow, elitist comfort zone, help me to grow up and face reality. I feared it, too, of course, knowing the experience would be alien to my values, uncomfortable, and a waste of precious time. Like all my friends, I tried to think how to get out of it. My feet were flat but not flat enough. Butch athletic coaches had made me feel like a ninety-seven-pound weakling; in reality I was a strapping if skinny six-footer. Saying you were homosexual was cause for rejection, but I was a bad liar. Two years in the army was a train bearing down on me; it did not seem right to jump out of the way.

In the event, there was a question on a form asking if I had homosexual impulses, and thinking of my fixation on Tony, I hopefully checked the yes box. That earned me an interview with a psychiatrist. He was interested to hear that I had spent nine months in residence at Riggs, but I failed to make a case for homosexual inclinations.

I passed the physical and received my induction notice. I had registered at my parents' address in California and opted to turn myself in out there, where I thought boot camp might be pleasanter. Dan List, the circulation manager at *The Voice* and a gung-ho rallyist, was eager to take over my car column. I sold my Vespa, gave up my little room upstairs from the Belles, and wrapped up my New York life.

Helen and I drove across the country in Tony's sky-blue Thunderbird, which he wanted in Hollywood, where he was making another movie. We camped out along the way, Helen cooking us suppers on a little stove.

We were not lovers—she was more like a godmother, fond of me but not expecting much. She had lined up gigs along the way: we stopped in Aspen to photograph the music festival and Santa Fe to photograph the opera.

Arriving in Los Angeles, we went directly to MGM, where Tony was shooting *Green Mansions* with Audrey Hepburn as Rima the Bird Girl. A fantastically detailed jungle set had been built on one of the sound stages. We watched the slow progress of a couple of shots, then went out for dinner with Tony and his friend Tab Hunter. It was my first night in Hollywood. To be with these two dreamboats was beyond wonderful. After dinner we went back to Tony's rented house and frolicked in the pool. Helen and I spent the night in Brentwood with Dorothy Jeakins, who had designed the costumes for *Friendly Persuasion*. Her elegant modern house, hidden behind hedges, smelt of a Guerlain soap called Fleurs des Alpes, which I used for years afterwards. She had an Oscar as a doorstop.

Mother drove down from Santa Barbara to collect me for the week before my induction into the Army. Helen kept nagging me to take action to avoid being drafted, averring that the Army would "destroy" me. So I made an appointment with a psychiatrist my parents knew and asked him to write a letter to get me out. He took me seriously, wrote a letter to the draft board, and recommended that I seek psychiatric help. He gave me a copy of the letter, which said I had a "personality disorder": I was "passive-aggressive," which sounded like a joke at the time. (Later I came to see what he meant.) He predicted that I would be "more of a liability than an asset" to the Army. Surely not!

The night before I was due to report, Tony took Dorothy, Helen, and me to see a sneak preview of Tab's new movie, *Damn Yankees*, at the Westwood Theatre. We slipped in unrecognized and sat in the back row. After a time I noticed that Tony's leg was touching mine. Could it be accidental? Our arms were touching too; I felt his warmth. Then he stopped pretending nothing was happening and held my hand.

After the movie Tony announced that he would drive me home. He drove to a secluded place, parked, and embraced me. It was awkward, two big guys in a little car. He felt different from a girl, shoulders broad, lats firm. He asked me a peculiar question: "Are you projective or receptive?" I pretended not to know what he meant: fuck or be fucked was beyond me, either one. Tony kissed me and tried to push his tongue into my mouth. I had heard of French kissing but it did not appeal to me. "I don't like that," I said, pulling away. He gave up on me as hopelessly backward and took me home.

I have always wondered what prompted Tony to move on me at that particular moment. Far-fetched as it may seem, I suspect that Helen had put him up to it to accomplish her intention of keeping me out of the Army— she could be ruthlessly manipulative. I was blown away. I had no idea what to think, no model for homosexual relations. Was Tony proposing some kind of an affair? How could I possibly resist?

Early the next morning, Helen drove me downtown to the induction center with my little bag, ready to be processed onto a bus to Fort Ord. Still expecting me to get out of it, she told me to call her when I was ready to be picked up. I joined the line and went through the routine. Before long I came up to a counter where a uniformed clerk gave my papers a final once-over. After him, the bus. He glanced at me, confirmed my identity, picked up a large rubber stamp.

"Did you find the letter from the psychiatrist?" I asked. "Is that in there?"

The clerk put down the rubber stamp, found the letter, and read it. He looked at me and said I would have to speak to the Army psychiatrist. I had to see Tony again! Last night had been so inconclusive!

This psychiatrist was more formidable. I told him I was not sure it was true that I was not homosexual, even though I still had not had sex with a man. I told him what had happened the night before, although of course not who it was, which was what had made it so exciting. It must have been obvious that something was going on; and he had the cautionary letter from a professional colleague. He deferred me for a year, advising me to seek treatment. I could go. I never heard from the draft board again.

I called Helen, who picked me up and took me to the back lot at MGM to share the good news with Tony. On a break between shots he took me for a stroll through the dusty old sets. We entered through a door in a western façade into a jumble of stuffed bison—creepy! We boarded a pirate ship moored in a river, went below, kissed, hugged, pressed together. I felt Tony's body long against me, the bulge in his crotch pressing against mine.

That night we had a date. Tony picked me up at Dorothy's and took me to his favorite hamburger place, the Dolores Drive-In, then back to his house for a swim. Undressing, alone together, we sat on the floor and looked at each other's penises. Tony's seemed quite long. I was thrilled to be with him but not impelled by instinct or fantasy toward any particular action, and Tony let the moment pass. He had a later date with Tab, who phoned.

4

EXPECTING TO BE RELIEVED of all responsibility for myself for the next two years, I had no backup plan, really no idea what to do next. Back in Santa Barbara, my mother took me to the Lobero Theatre to see *Der Rosenkavalier*, directed by the great Lotte Lehmann with students from the Music Academy of the West. Tony had instructed me to call him that night at nine-thirty so at intermission I excused myself and ran off into the streets looking for a phone. Everything was closed. Why am I not in New York, I thought, where there are phone booths everywhere? I ran back to the theatre, an oasis of light, where the second act had started. An usher showed me a tiny green-walled phone room off the lobby. Tony had little to say. How are you doing? What are you going to do? He was busy, working hard, and did not invite me to visit. I had to keep my voice low because of the opera. Undone, I went outside and walked around, smoking cigarettes, until the opera ended and my beautiful mother came out, sorry I had missed the second half.

My father took me to lunch at the Santa Barbara Club. I kept thinking he should take me into his business, which would solve the livelihood problem, but he said I would hate it: retail was a misery, he insisted, he would not want me to be stuck in it like him. He was sweet to me but unsure what to make of me. I was not convinced he wanted me around.

Liz Hawes, now living in her ex-husband Joe Losey's beach house at Trancas, still wanted to write a book with me, and I spent a week with her trying to get something started. Nothing came. I felt empty, lost, undefined. I could not stay still: I had to do something about my life. We could collaborate by mail.

So I went back to New York, where I had the beginnings of a life. Helen let me stay in Tony's room temporarily and found me a job at Charter Oak Films, a movie studio in upper Manhattan that made a weekly religious show for television. I learned the rudiments of editing, helped in the studio with the camera and lights, tried writing a script, and drove around the city in the company station wagon doing pickups and deliveries.

Proofreading for *The Village Voice* a couple of nights a week, reading scripts for an agent, working at my day job, I put together enough income to rent an apartment of my own, two rooms on the third floor of a small building on Third Avenue near Grand Central Station. Painting the walls the whitest of whites, I began to acquire a few pretty things. I bought myself a brass-trimmed three-quarter-size antique iron bed, built a sofa out of a hollow door and foam rubber, made bookcases out of cinder blocks and boards, sewed curtains, rented an upright piano. A woman with the lovely name of Tensie Spinner came down from Harlem one morning a week and cleaned. I bought a new Vespa.

Serena and I were pretty much over, but we had one more night of love after she came home from Canada, which made her pregnant. Janet arranged an abortion on condition that I have a session with her famous analyst, Dr. Lawrence Kubie. What could I say? How was I to know Serena hadn't put in her diaphragm? I hoped everything would work out all right. It was not really an issue of my mental health.

The Voice WAS STRUGGLING, issuing paychecks postdated to the following week, still not paying writers. I wrote a few interviews and features,

MICHAEL SMITH

Jerry Tallmer (with Julie Harris)

psyched to see my byline in the paper. I reviewed Jack Kerouac's *On the Road,* which had just come out, in the car column; and the following week waxed equally enthusiastic over James Gould Cozzens's *By Love Possessed.* I started helping Jerry Tallmer, the associate editor and drama critic, with the copy-editing as well as proofreading, and he began assigning me to write short reviews of plays he did not have time or desire to see.

The first play I reviewed was *Macbeth* in a church basement. Almost immediately it was obvious that this was something I could do. Reviewing plays came naturally to me, just as directing did. I was interested in what I saw, had thoughts I wanted to express, and loved seeing my name in print. Jerry was a serious critic and set me an excellent example, teaching me sound principles of journalism and forcing me to write to the subject: for months he had me start every piece with the title of the play. My early reviews were brief, two or three inches long; as the paper expanded, there would be vastly more space.

My interests in theatre and writing had converged. I was writing and being published, being read and scratching out a living, starting to be someone in a tiny way, part of the cultural fabric. After a couple of failed attempts to leave New York, it seemed I was there to stay. The city was unnatural, stressful, harsh, but also uniquely stimulating, with the best and most of everything I was interested in, all of it magically accessible to me. New York was the intellectual, cultural, and financial capital of the United States at a time of enormous national confidence and dynamism, the place where the liveliest, brightest people came together, ideas were born and standards set, a cauldron of ambition and desire in which a New Age seemed to be brewing, cosmopolitan, linked to Europe and beyond, acknowledged center of the post-war art world. There was exhilaration in the sheer grittiness and scramble of city life, the space and very air shared with multitudes, the range of possibilities unlimited. It was a tremendously exciting place to be twenty-three.

5

Serena and I felt bad about the abortion, but we were still friends and continued to go about together. Denis introduced us to Arthur Loeb, a scholar, wit, and bon vivant who came down from Cambridge and surrounded himself with pretty people in his apartment off Madison. Arthur was rich but sad. His body was slightly crooked, for one thing, one side weak, and he was homosexual, which was considered to be a mental illness. His parents kept threatening to have him committed. Arthur was smart and up-to-date, brilliantly knowledgeable about books and art. Many nights he wound up getting drunk and hostile or unbearably maudlin, but that was after hours of fun.

I couldn't afford dinner at Orsini's but joined Arthur's party afterwards at the Blue Angel to hear Mabel Mercer or the Baq Room to hear our new favorite, Janice Mars, sing "Fly Me to the Moon." After another summer at Stratford, Denis had new theatrical friends to add to the mix, and Arthur's boyfriend, Donny Nardona, knew the kids from the City Ballet. Arthur was often happy and magnanimous; in other moods he could withdraw into nastiness or take Donny into the bedroom and never reemerge.

By December 1958 I was hanging out at Arthur's on my own. I was drawn to Donny, but we didn't get much chance to know each other. Arthur, no fool, kept drinking and outwaited me or vanished with his prize behind a blank closed door, leaving me with the bit players or alone. I still could not imagine sex with a boy, but I was intensely smitten with Donny's darkly seductive Italian looks and powerfully attracted to him. He liked me too. Whatever had started with Tony Perkins needed to play out.

One cold winter night Donny told me to go, saying he would meet me on the corner in ten minutes. I drove around the block on my Vespa. Donny appeared, jumped on the back, wrapped his arms around me warmly and nuzzled my neck, and I whisked us down to my cozy apartment.

Making love with Donny was not like sex with a girl, where it was pretty much obvious what to do, and limited to that if you were as inept and squeamish as I was at this point. Mechanics aside, for the first time I felt myself merging with another person, body and soul, reaching for union as if Plato's theory that each of us is half a person were true. For a blissful moment out of time I was whole. The sensuality of his skin was a revelation. I marveled at how our bodies fit together. I held his heavy head in my hands and gazed ecstatically into his beautiful dark eyes.

Donny Nardona

Overwhelmed by Donny's melting, tender, generous sweetness and the delectable warmth of his body, I wanted to be with him all the time. There was no doubt in my mind that we loved each other. The obvious next step would have been for him to move in so we could sleep together every night. (I was so pleased to have my own apartment that I hardly noticed the obvious contrast with Arthur's.) Donny came again to make love with me, but afterwards got up and went home. He had no intention of leaving

Arthur, who Denis maintained was "keeping" him. Donny denied it: he had a job in a gallery and a real relationship with Arthur. He must have loved him or he would never have put up with him.

Our bliss tarnished, things got complicated and uncomfortable, and Donny left to spend Christmas with friends in Florida. The idyll was over. I was devastated. Arthur took me to lunch at the Oak Room at the Plaza and blathered on about how much he missed Donny. His drunken self-pity seemed grotesque: I was the one with the broken heart.

EMOTIONALLY SHATTERED, at the same time I felt liberated into a more interesting world of potential new experiences beckoning me to be brave, and I took up the homosexual life wholeheartedly, restrained by timidity and inhibitions but not too much.

In the fifties "coming out" meant doing it, not telling your parents or announcing it to the world. I may not have said I was now gay, but I hardly made a secret of it. It was amusing, for instance, to pick up an adorably available college boy at a party at Arthur's in the spring, right in front of Donny, who had cut me off, though we stayed friends. After an exchange of looks, I crossed the room to sit on the arm of the boy's chair, openly held his hand, took him home with me. He stayed for days, until he had to go back to Florida to school. Silly me, imagining a lasting liaison: I wrote him long, intense letters, only slowly realizing the protocol of such encounters.

I gave a cocktail party for my mother when she came to town, showing off my new apartment and friends. Most of the guests were gay young men, two or three of whom I had been sleeping with. Mother could hardly have missed what this cast implied and managed to suggest, delicately, that she didn't disapprove.

It was rare for me to go home with strangers. One exception was Bob Crewe, a sexy guy who picked me up in a gay bar. He was a record producer, he said, which meant nothing to me: I was entirely ignorant of popular music. He took me back to his apartment, a sleek duplex in the East 50s. His bedroom was designed for sex, with a big low bed in the middle surrounded by mirrors.

He knew exactly what he wanted—to fuck me—and paid little attention to my reluctance. It hurt but I somehow managed, and I spent the night, assuming this was the beginning of some kind of "relationship." He politely gave me breakfast on the balcony, but that was obviously the end of it. I realized with a shock that it was nothing personal: he did this all the time.

I wanted love, not one-night stands. I liked to get to know people, first find out if I liked them, then have sex with them as a way of making friends. Beyond that the aim was unclear. Heterosexual romance led to marriage, children, a life together. Where did gay romance lead? I was looking for a lover, not just sex, but had no model for gay coupledom. Was such a relationship possible?

I had a brief, hot, tender affair with a beautiful young actor named Frederick Combs, who was later in the original cast of *Boys in the Band*. He had the keys to an elegant house around the corner from me in Turtle Bay, where we lolled naked on a fur rug in front of a blazing fire listening to Johnny Mathis. It was outrageously romantic. Frederick fell in love with me, but I didn't take him seriously. I had discovered an ugly sense of power

Frederick Combs

in making people want me, playing with them, then rejecting them, and thoughtlessly broke his heart.

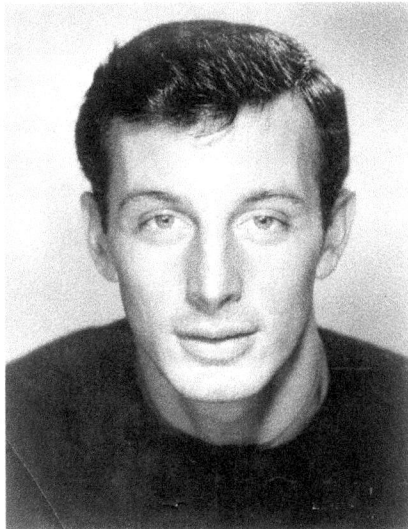

The gay theatre world was small and easily penetrated by someone like me. I met the English playwright Peter Shaffer at one of Roddy MacDowell's at-homes on Central Park West. Peter was the author of *Five Finger Exercise*, a play I loved, then playing on Broadway. I was in awe of him but conscious of being younger and cuter. In the elevator hall, as I was about to depart, he asked me to call him. I airily replied, "You'll have to call me, I never call people." He said, "Forget it, then," turning away. I felt like an idiot.

With Doon Arbus, Punkie, and another dog on the beach at Truro

6

HELEN AND TONY RENTED A HOUSE for the summer in Truro, on the outer end of Cape Cod, and I spent three weeks there with them. The setting was blissful, a short walk through cranberries over the high dunes to a wide open ocean beach we had entirely to ourselves. Tony's new boyfriend, elfin Teno Pollick, made Helen crazy with jealousy. Doon Arbus was there, an enterprising teenage girl who had waited on the stoop outside Helen's apartment after school every day for a year collecting glimpses of Tony. Eventually he invited her in, and now, like me, she was a member of the family. Other interesting people came and went. A brooding young actor brought me his crooked hard-on in the middle of the night in my cot on

MICHAEL SMITH

the porch. I peeked out the attic window on Teno naked taking an outdoor shower, and he saw me looking. I had several love scenes pending in the city.

Helen's friend Ted Thieme, a former boyfriend of Tony's, was undergoing psychoanalysis, which Helen kept urging on me as well. Did she think I was too scattered, moving in too many worlds? Or what? Guilty about being homosexual? Moody? My inner distress had more to do with the ruination of the world. Our whole civilization was about to be wiped out by nuclear war, collapsing any imaginable sense of meaning. I did not want to be well adjusted to evil or buy into the economy of death.

Helen was a Freudian true believer, though, I was not really happy, and ultimately analysis was too à la mode to resist, though I was not encouraged by my previous brush with it. Finally I yielded and went into treatment with Ted's analyst, Dr. John Cederquist, in his office at 68th and Madison. It was classical Freudian psychoanalysis, with me on the couch, him out of sight behind me, five sessions a week at $25 a session, and no credit for missed appointments. It was a lot of money, but my father agreed to pay for it. He too must have thought I was "sick."

ONE WINTER NIGHT, AFTER DAYS OF RAIN, a tremendous noise jolted me awake. I jumped up and looked out my bedroom window. The low buildings next door had been demolished for an office tower, and our whole backyard had collapsed into the excavation. The next day visible cracks zigzagged up the facade of my building. Diagonal timbers from deep in the pit propped up the side wall beside my bedroom; steel cables cinched the structure to the building on the other side. I was not as scared as I should have been, but the owners, who ran an Italian restaurant at street level, decided to tear off the top two floors: I would have to move.

I found a new place on the fifth floor of a tenement on 64th Street off Second Avenue, a cold water flat modernized into one irregular long room with an exposed brick wall and a new bathroom and kitchen in the middle. The main attraction was the light: the big corner lot next door was vacant, and the windows, originally facing an air shaft, let in the whole eastern sky.

I liked reviewing plays for *The Village Voice*, but it did nothing to satisfy the drive to pursue my own writing. Once I was settled I began a novel about a young man very much like myself doing very much what I had been doing since I came to New York, striving to convey the intensity of the journey from virgin solitude into sexual being, which seemed central, amid several swirling circles of friends and potential lovers. I put everything into the book, hopefully calling it *Getting Across*, trying to embody the delirium of hidden streams converging, transfigure my confusion into art, connect my sensations and sensibility with history and social reality, and generally figure out what was going on. My inner experience did not line up with any fiction I had read, which forced me to experiment: I needed new form and diction to convey the evolving subjectivity I was striving to write about.

Writing was wretchedly difficult. A beginner with no technique, I knew my personal work was awkward and naïve and rarely let anyone read it. I felt miserably lonely sitting there struggling to put intangible thoughts and feelings into words, pulling sentences up from inside, doubtful that anyone would ever read what I was writing. If I did not do it, though, I felt incomplete. It was a great feeling when the words flowed. The hard part was staying in the chair.

I TOOK OFFENSE when Janet Stewart asked me not to come by without a jacket and tie. What would the doormen think? Serena had a new boyfriend. I was still a regular at Helen and Tony's, walking Punkie around the Central Park lake late of an evening, helping Helen in the darkroom, playing her piano, working on the curtain of glass beads we had made for the doorway to the living room, which constantly broke as Punkie scampered through it and constantly had to be repaired. Tony finished shooting *Psycho* and came back to New York to star in the Frank Loesser musical *Greenwillow*, which opened in January in Philadelphia and ran all spring on Broadway. Helen set up a few photography gigs for me, photographing Albert Fuller's harpsichord, photographing Tony for fan magazine stories and a record jacket. He had me shoot a picture of his name up in lights.

Tony listening to playback in a recording studio

I finally had sex with Tony à trois with Teno. After a birthday party for Doon at her mother's carriage house in the Village, we three guys went back to Teno's mother's empty apartment across from a gloomy church on 16th Street, ostensibly to watch television. As we sat gazing at the tube in the dark I felt Tony's hand creep slowly, secretly up my leg. Tony liked this sort of pseudo-stealth; I'm sure he and Teno had planned the whole thing. Sex was initiated without anything actually being said: it was a very buttoned-up time. We did it again at Helen's. It felt oddly impersonal to be part of a threesome, when any actual love was between the other two.

Mischievous Teno visited me privately and shamelessly seduced me, persuading me to take off my clothes so he could sketch me, inviting me to inspect an itch high on his inner thigh. Gay sex was highly titillating though it was still not clear what I really wanted to do, how to turn it from boyish naughtiness into love-making, and be satisfied. I was too squeamish to like fucking and too tense to enjoy being fucked, I choked on cock and never came from being sucked. Jacking off together seemed a little puerile.

It was intensely rewarding, though, to push through conventional propriety into intimate physicality and naked contact with another person.

In a pool hall on Sixth Avenue, Tony suggested we play for a blow-job. I didn't quite understand. Was the winner to receive or give the blow-job? Which was more desirable? Was the loser to suffer somehow? Humiliation? So the moment passed.

Filming Serena in *Washday*

A BASIC COURSE IN FILMMAKING at City College introduced me to montage theory. For our assignment to make a five-minute silent movie, I filmed Serena and an actor friend on my rooftop in *Washday*, a tiny domestic drama. Artily panning around the cityscape, the camera discovers a moody young woman hanging up laundry, a guy comes up from below, they start to have a fight but wind up letting it go, laughing, and making up, love in the offing. Either I was copping out on expressing what I really felt or I was basically pretty cheerful.

I had a day job now at PRAids, a public relations mailing house near the U.N. The gay owner, Richard, took an avuncular interest in my well-being.

Ostensibly his assistant, I spent most of my time coding Addressograph plates with little metal tabs, which was pleasant enough: I always liked machines. Richard and I played tennis together on a rooftop under the towering Con Edison smokestacks on First Avenue. He invited me to decorous gay parties in his apartment, showing me off to his thirty-something friends, but we never "did anything." Richard encouraged me to write blurbs and short puff pieces for public relations clients. A bit about the soprano Anna Moffo got into a glossy magazine. It seemed like the thing to do, and I tried, but I could never get interested in this kind of free-lance writing.

If nothing seemed to be happening, it was because everything significant was supposed to be on hold pending resolution of my analysis. Getting up to 68th Street took a bite out of every weekday. Dr. Cederquist and I made little if any progress toward ordinary clear communication, much less resolution of my hang-ups, which were not hanging me up very seriously anymore. Presumably he deplored my gay sexuality, though I don't think he ever said so. Withholding comment was the cornerstone of Freudian technique, and Dr. Cederquist never said much of anything. Homosexuality was a designated mental disease, illegal in public and widely regarded as immoral. I liked it, though. The gay life took me out of myself, beyond the limitations of class and propriety into encounters with people I otherwise might never get to know—the same thing I had wanted from the army. I didn't see anything wrong with it; you could be a good or bad person regardless of whether you were straight or gay.

The burning issue was my writing, but talking about my indistinct ideas to Dr. Cederquist required translation into a different, flattening language. The only thing to say about writing was, do it; instead I was groping for words on a psychiatrist's couch. Analysis felt irrelevant to the rest of my life. I often lay there with nothing to say, feeling like a complete failure.

By early spring I had been going to Dr. Cederquist for six months, and my father thought that was enough. I was sick of it myself, frustrated, bored, ready to be done. Pressured by Helen, I persuaded Dad to keep paying until

May. After that, she offered to lend me the money to keep going. I declined and quit. Dr. Cederquist cost more than my whole income, and analysis was not doing me any palpable good.

A few days later Tony telephoned me at work. Helen had convinced him that it was crucial for me to continue my analysis, he said; therefore he, Tony, would like to pay for it. Money was not an issue, he was a movie star and could easily afford it, he said or I thought. I should think it over. He would call back the next day at the same time.

I accepted Tony's offer and resumed my five-day-a-week analysis. Dr. Cederquist moved into a handsome townhouse on East 94th Street, and there was a magnificent Steinway grand in the waiting room. I no longer had a piano, there were too many tight stairs to my present abode, and his piano begged to be played. When I asked if he could hear me through the double doors of his consulting room and whether it disturbed him, he said, "What comes to mind?" I started arriving early for my appointments, an improvement on habitual lateness, brought music, and played his piano.

In fall 1960 Brendan Behan's play *The Hostage* opened on Broadway in a gripping production directed by Joan Littlewood, originally at her working-class theatre in London. I went to see it with Helen and Tony. Afterwards they invited Alfred Lynch, the young English actor who played the title role, back to their house for grilled-cheese-and-bacon sandwiches. I offered Alfie a ride home on my Vespa, taking him instead for a dramatic spin around lower Manhattan and back to my apartment, where we lay side by side on my bed entranced, gazing into the hundreds of apartments in the huge building a block to the north. Finally one of us took the other's hand, we kissed, pressed together, made love, and plunged into a beautiful romance that flourished for a couple of months. It was thrilling to be close to someone I admired so much. Sweet and genuine, sane and generous, Alfie adopted me into his life and introduced me to the cast of his play, terrific actors with great esprit de corps, my first glimpse into the civilized English theatre world.

Alfie told me all along that he had a boyfriend in London, they had been together since they were schoolboys, he cared about him and did not intend to hurt him or leave him. Our affair would be brief. Still it was a shock when he ended it, his lover coming for Christmas. Telephoning him one last time, I broke down and cried in a Sixth Avenue phone booth. Donny Nardona had broken my heart. Alfie Lynch broke it a second time, and this time I had glimpsed what a mature, giving relationship might be. Impressed with my own misery, feeling that I was learning something that would be useful in my writing, I walked up the avenue, through Central Park in the dark, and east to my lonely bed.

Alfie Lynch

I TOOK PIANO LESSONS from Charles Turner, a composer who lived nearby, going over to his apartment several times a week to practice. A protégé and ex-boyfriend of Samuel Barber, Chuck was taken with my musicality, saying I brought a distinctive American touch to Ravel's *Pavane pour une Infante défunte*. Believing that I should get serious and be a pianist, he took me to play for Barber, then the head of Juilliard—who said I had no technique and it was too late to get one at twenty-five.

Chuck had a crush on me. He was not my boyish type, older and too fuzzy for my taste, which did not rule out a little cuddling, and we were good friends. He memorably took me to dinner with him at Frank O'Hara's apartment on East 8th Street and Avenue A, the first time I had been to that part of the city. Frank, a poet and a curator at the Museum of Modern Art, was a legendary charmer and irresistible talker, full of mischief and witty, provocative opinions about art, music, poetry, and life. Shocked that

I didn't know the Berg Violin Concerto, "one of the masterpieces of the twentieth century," he immediately played me a recording. Frank shared the apartment with a trim, blond, collegiate boy named Joe LeSueur; I was so taken with them that I stayed all night, sleeping with Joe. Frank and Joe were just friends by then, but Chuck was surely peeved.

A romantic fling grew into an extended friendship with Scott Burton, a bright, adorable Columbia undergraduate and budding critic. His artfully bare little apartment halfway between my house and Greenwich Village was convenient as I zipped back and forth to *The Voice* on my Vespa. Scott had recently had himself circumcised. I had never seen an uncircumcised penis so it was hard to understand what that was all about. He concurrently had some kind of relationship going with Jerome Robbins, the great director and choreographer, who arrived downstairs one day when I was there and had to be prevented from coming up. Scott took me to Robbins's house in the East 70s one afternoon when no one was home, and we got naked and rolled around together on the white carpet, his penis still too tender to do much with. What I liked about Scott was how smart he was. He was starting to write reviews for *Art News* and later became a significant post-conceptual artist.

Helen abruptly informed me that it was she, not Tony, who had been paying for my psychoanalysis for most of the past year, urging me to continue even so. Tony had been acting! Much as I resented these manipulations, I acceded to her conviction that I needed psychoanalysis and kept going to Dr. Cederquist. As far as I could tell, he was not helping me. According to Freudian theory, that was my own fault: we were working through my "resistance." Helen started pressing me to get the money from my father or find a job that paid better and start paying her back.

Eventually she cut me off, and I was glad to quit analysis, though I would miss Dr. Cederquist's piano. As a farewell gesture I wrote a short play I dedicated to him. My life was going well, and was that not the point of analysis? The play was an Oedipal joke, a frivolous skit about a mother and adult son in bed together, entitled *I Like It*.

MICHAEL SMITH

With Scott Burton on my 64th Street rooftop

The single time Helen and I made love—initiated by her on Tony's bed—she got pregnant, which may have been her intention. I didn't know about it until it was all over. She intended to have the child and raise it herself but regrettably miscarried. Then the issue of money for my analysis came between us, and that was pretty much the end of our friendship. I regret to say I never did pay her back.

7

The Village Voice GAVE ME MORE WORK copy-editing and proofreading, and I quit my job at PRAids. Friday afternoons and all day Mondays and Tuesdays I worked at a tiny desk in the corner of Jerry Tallmer's office on the second floor of *The Voice*'s little triangular building on Sheridan Square.

Late Tuesday afternoon I rode the Long Island Railroad out to the printing plant in Sayville with corrected proofs and final copy. The paper was set line by line by Linotype and composed on the stone according to paste-ups we supplied, a technology soon to be obsolete. Only when I had checked every correction and read through the entire paper in page proof could the forms go onto the big flatbed press. I embraced Jerry's high journalistic standards, striving to catch every typo and composition error and put out a perfect paper. We were only printing sixteen or twenty pages a week so it was not an impossible goal. I had to be stubborn with management to get the compositors to make the last trivial corrections. It would be after midnight by the time the press was rolling and I headed home, smelling of ink, damp paper, and molten lead.

As associate editor, Jerry was responsible for editing and laying out all of the editorial content except for the first four pages, which belonged to Dan Wolf. Passionate about theatre, Jerry gave it a huge amount of space in the paper, with emphasis on Off-Broadway and the nascent alternative theatre that he christened Off-Off-Broadway. Jerry founded *The Voice*'s Obie Awards for Off-Broadway theatre, and his reviews won him a George Jean Nathan Award.

Dan Wolf was a much-admired editor everyone was always trying to impress. Mostly he sat at his desk and listened to people talk, while Jerry and I did the editorial-side work of getting the paper out. The chemistry worked. Dan, a benevolent cynic, kept the paper from being seized by any one faction or co-opted by any ideology or single point of view. In the interest of good writing, he encouraged me to "rough up" my prose. *The Voice* attracted outstanding writers, giving them unusual freedom to write about their own concerns, and soon drew ahead of the dailies in registering the flavor of the changing times.

IN SUMMER 1960 Jerry took a break from his marriage, sublet an apartment from Garry Goodrow, an actor who was on tour in Europe with the Living Theatre, and had an affair with a hip chick who turned him on to marijuana.

Pot was a revelation. When I came to work the next day, he took me out for a walk and excitedly told me about it. Eager to share this amazing new experience, he invited me over later that evening for the express purpose of turning me on. He and his girlfriend sat me down on a mattress against the wall and plied me with marijuana cigarettes, coaching me to draw the smoke in deep and hold it. I complied, insisted nothing was happening, then realized the three of us were giggling with delight, and all kinds of new sensations were creeping through my body. Venturing out into the Village night, we headed toward Sheridan Square. As we walked along West 4th Street the familiar sidewalk, glittering in the streetlights, softly stopped moving, and everything in the densely busy world around me seemed to pause even as I kept gliding along, radiant with being, consciousness unfolding in a tangible matrix of timeless superreality. I had crossed over into the country of the high, and I never wanted to go back.

Jerry considered the Living Theatre to be the most important theatre in New York, a vital antidote to the commercialism of Broadway and the respectability of Off-Broadway, which was not doing anything new. In their artfully handmade theatre on the second floor of a former department store at 14th Street and Sixth Avenue, Judith Malina and Julian Beck and their collaborators produced plays by poets and modernist European masters. They had their first hit with Jack Gelber's *The Connection*, an expressionistic slice-of-life play about jazz musicians waiting for a fix. *The Connection* broke the silence about heroin, opening up a hidden world and blurring the distinction between art and reality.

Peter Hartman took me to Monday night poetry, dance, and music at the Living Theatre, my first glimpse of the avant garde in action—such poets as Frank O'Hara and Diane di Prima, dancers James Waring and Viola Farber, musicians Cecil Taylor, John Herbert McDowell, and Sandy Bull. I had met Peter in a bar, and we became friends by having sex and playing music for each other. A composer, slight, dark, tense, vivid, Peter took turns with me bashing through Beethoven sonatas on the big piano in his loft on 19th Street. He wanted to fuck me; I was tense but he was not very big and I sometimes managed to let him do it.

Peter asked me to play a duet he had composed to accompany a dance by Fred Herko, a handsome young experimental dancer, at a small theatre on West 42nd Street. Not all the music in Peter's score was written out; there might be a swooping line notated with the number of seconds one was asked to improvise, a range in which one could play any notes. Chance as an art strategy was new to me. I was alarmed by the freedom but did my best.

Peter Hartman

Unlike most people I knew, who were scraping along, living hand-to-mouth, Peter had family money, though it was never to be mentioned. In July he rented a house in Fire Island Pines and invited me to come out with him for the summer. It was a slow time at *The Voice*, a good time to take a break. I planned to stay a few weeks and work on my novel.

I was titillated by the licentious reputation of the Pines, where flocks of horny, near-naked young men notoriously cruised each other on the beach and boardwalk, picked each other up at bars and parties, and met for anonymous sex along the winding paths in the scrubby woods beyond the last houses. Once we were settled we had the best fuck yet.

That evening Peter invited a crowd of pretty people over to the house to drink and dance. I had never experienced such a hedonistic atmosphere, the night warm, Motown music pouring over us, colored light gleaming on moving bodies. I found myself dancing in the garden with a lissome lad, pressing my body to his, our cocks deliciously swelling in our shorts.

MICHAEL SMITH

Peter, coming upon me thus love-struck, was furious and hurt; I was taken aback, not having realized I was exclusively his. He abruptly shut off the music, turned up the lights, and told everybody to go home. The boy's friend reclaimed him. Peter shut himself in the bedroom, and I went walking barefoot on the boardwalk through the pines, giving myself to nature and the night, searching for my angel. The sky was bright when I came to the bay, and the boy was out there in it, water to his knees, his body waving above the surface, with his friend, wading away: the brimming sun just caught them. I departed on the afternoon ferry, a love casualty once again, tingling with immediacy.

PETER WROTE A FILM SCRIPT called *The Best Time*, fictionalizing his love affair with Diane di Prima, the poet, who lived with her young daughter, Jeannie, in a cold water flat on Houston Street. I was delighted when Peter asked me to direct and shoot it. The title suggests how we felt about our larger situation: that the culture was in decline, that the best times we were ever to have were now.

For the roles of Diane and himself, Peter recruited exotically beautiful Marian Zazeela and curly-headed Joseph Chaikin, who was playing the lead in Brecht's *Man Is Man* at the Living Theatre. I rented a camera, and we met in an empty apartment and did a good first day of shooting in the clear, hard Lower East Side light—slow, moody pans, meaningful pauses, tender close-ups. Greatly taken with Alain Resnais's enigmatic *Last Year at Marienbad*, I strove for a similar style, believing the slum could be as elegant as the palace. I shot 16 mm. with a Bolex; we would add sound later.

Joe failed to appear for the second day of shooting, having been arrested with Judith Malina and Julian Beck for protesting a civil defense drill, staying outside in City Hall Park with Dorothy Day and the Catholic Workers when the sirens went off.

That was the end of Peter's movie and the beginning of a warm, lifelong friendship with Joe Chaikin, a brother in art. Excited about theatre, ambitious to understand more and do more, Joe and I were drawn together by pure affinity, taking tangible pleasure in each other's company. We got together practically every day for the next few years to turn on, listen to music, and think together. Joe often came with me to see plays, and I spent many hours at the apartment on 12th Street he shared with Fred Katz, a sardonic social worker with two girlfriends. Joe was devoted to a powerful hypnotique called Doriden, a big pill he scored in quantity from a doctor brother-in-law and would sometimes share with me. He liked to take one early in the evening, not to sleep but to stay up and talk, the drug's dreamy mellow glow and delicious derangement loosening our mechanical habits of mind, opening channels of feeling and impulse we hadn't known existed. Half a Doriden was enough for me; I loved the feeling but still had to get home.

One night at Joe's we ran out of cigarette papers, and Judith Malina made do with a Tampax wrapper, rolling a huge joint that half a dozen of us passed around. Drugs were enjoyable and attractively transgressive, valued as a way to claim the autonomy of the body and bump us out of our ruts. I was amazed by the insights they enabled, unpredictable, anxious, exhilarating experiences that showed me unanticipated vistas beyond my conditioned barriers and limitations. Smoking pot and popping pills was risky but did us good, we believed, helping to energize the inner exploration needed for truthful art, as well as being viscerally pleasurable. Joe and I were hardly crazy or self-destructive: there was too much we wanted to do. We were both extremely busy and productive. I was somewhat neurotic and tormented, to be sure, but had a core of sanity, common sense, and balance I felt I could count on. Personally and as a writer, I was duty-bound to explore inner space and embraced the relatively class-free new art and drug bohemia, the antithesis of the respectable world I had grown up in. Being gay also helped to distance oneself from the constricting expectations of the toxic status quo. I felt myself to be opening up with the culture, writing out of an exemplary consciousness.

Judith Malina and Joe Chaikin in *Man Is Man* at the Living Theatre

JOE HAD BEEN POLITICIZED AGAINST HIS WILL by acting at the Living Theatre. He imagined doing a play there would be a stepping stone to a career in the commercial theatre. He hated acting in *The Connection*, which they toured in Europe. What did he have to do or want to have to do with these junkies and too-cool jazz musicians? He loved opera. He was a student of philosophy. But when he found himself talking directly to the audience in Brecht's *Man Is Man*, the next play Judith directed him in, he heard what Brecht was saying through him and who he was: Galy Gay, an innocent man transformed into a killing machine by a weakness for flattery. It was no longer possible to be innocent; we had to grow up. Brecht was tough, his plays more engaged with political reality than American theatre, which was not even trying to be real. Theatre is not required to be real or serious, but we were serious. We wanted something more from it than entertainment.

The Living Theatre had used the success of *The Connection* to finance a series of difficult plays by Pirandello, Brecht, William Carlos Williams, and Jackson MacLow, stark and fiercely experimental, part of a European tradition of poetic, political theatre otherwise unseen in America. Julian was an abstract expressionist painter; Judith had studied with Irwin Piscator, the German expressionist director; they carried forward a radical vision of theatre that had been cut short by Hitler and Stalin. They did not buy into the status quo but aimed to undermine it with "disturbing images."

Politically active in a mindlessly passive time, outspoken advocates for pacifist, nonviolent, anarchist revolution, Judith and Julian and their cohort demonstrated, brandished signs, spoke fiercely to the press, made flamboyant political gestures, and repeatedly went to jail for their beliefs. In the early sixties, ahead of their time, they sponsored a General Strike for Peace. Joe started an acting workshop at the Living Theatre, but the actors were more interested in radical politics and lifestyle. When his own acting teacher moved to Israel, her students asked to join Joe's workshop. He added some friends to the mix, found a loft to work in, and began meeting twice a week to experiment with new ideas of physical and vocal expression.

The new group called itself the Open Theatre. Besides actors and directors, there were a few critics: Gordon Rogoff, who had edited a progressive theatre magazine in England, Richard Gilman, theatre critic for the Catholic magazine *Commonweal*, and Arthur Sainer from *The Voice*. I was there as a would-be playwright, along with Megan Terry, Jean-Claude van Itallie, Irene Fornés, Sam Shepard, Sharon Thie, and Susan Yankowitz.

I brought in a one-act called *Refugees*, but nothing came of it. Joe worked less from texts than from fragmentary impulses he called "pebbles," from which the actors developed exercises and investigations. I shared the group's aim of beginning anew by pure experiment to reinvent theatre for our time, a new theatrical language that would match the higher frequencies at which our consciousness was expanding. Joe's way was not the way I wanted to work, though, and I dropped out of the Open Theatre after a few months.

Refugees, which has never been produced, is a two-character play about

Michael Smith

a man fleeing from a revolution gone bad. Crossing the desert he encounters a younger man who turns out to be his son and is eventually forced to kill his father. Realistic in a Beckettish style, it was not the sort of material Joe was interested in at that point. For me, it was another necessary Oedipal purging and step toward finding my voice.

8

PETER HARTMAN invited me to tea at his new apartment on Waverly Place and showed me a headshot of Paul Sand, a handsome actor with a slyly seductive look in his eyes. Peter thought Paul was hot and wanted to fix me up with him. Paul was acting in *From the Second City* on Broadway and outrageously charming in it. I went backstage afterwards on Peter's dare, we liked each other immediately, and Paul took me up to his hotel room, where we had a hot encounter in the shower.

Paul moved in with me on 64th Street: a live-in lover at last! It was what I had always wanted. We were both busy, caught up in our work,

Paul Sand

involved with other friends. It was sweet to have each other to come home to, fun to play at keeping house, terrifically exciting to kiss and make out. Our coupledom didn't have to be terribly serious. We were a critic and a star having a glamorous theatrical affair. Paul was imaginative, thoughtful, affectionate, romantic, sexy, and a marvelous actor.

Pleasant for one, my apartment was tight for two people as tall and vigorous as Paul and me, and an apartment tower rising right next door was about to block our bright east windows. I was already spending most of my time in Greenwich Village, working for *The Voice*, making friends downtown, and Second City was about to open a cabaret near Washington Square. So we decided to move to the Village.

For $150 a month Paul and I rented an apartment one flight up in a hidden rear building on West 3rd Street, a block below Washington Square. The passageway to our domain was a narrow hallway done up as a Rousseau jungle, with vividly painted walls and thick fake foliage overhead—decor courtesy of Tom O'Horgan, the eccentric harpist we sublet from, who would be the musician for Paul's cabaret. Tom lived in a loft in the front building and came through this little hallway to get to his toilet. Once inside there was a long living room with a bare brick wall and south windows into the quiet interior of the block. Sunlight poured into the bright bedroom onto a wall of books. I rented a piano. I could walk to *The Voice* in minutes.

Paul was fun and full of mischief, our sex life excitingly boys-together as we shared our twanging hard-ons on my big iron bed. One summer afternoon we had the windows wide open while I played Ravel's dreamy *Pavane* and Paul eagerly gobbled my cock. We were doubly swooning when a backyard neighbor's raucous voice broke the spell, yelling, "Quiet!!!"

We were right in the middle of the tourist Village. On weekend nights, the sidewalks outside our door were a maelstrom of youth avid for action. Coming home we threaded through a swarm of thrill-seeking Jersey teens and twenty-somethings outside the Cafe Bizarre just down the block. It was madness. But as soon as we went up the stairs, through the jungle, and into our hideaway, everything was calm.

I showed Paul my novel; he said he had not known I was so talented: he just thought I was cute. That encouraged me to finish it. Writing was more possible now that my love life was stabilized. I still wanted to direct plays and hoped that living with Paul would lead me deeper into the theatre.

MICHAEL SMITH

In early summer 1962, Jerry Tallmer abruptly announced that he was leaving *The Village Voice* for a job as second-string drama critic at the *New York Post*. Dan was shocked, hurt, and angry that Jerry had taken this decision without even talking it over with him; they had started the paper together, and it was just beginning to pay off. The move didn't make much sense to me either. At *The Voice*, with its small but influential readership, Jerry was a significant force for progressive theatre; and the senior drama critic of the *Post*, Richard Watts, was going strong. But Jerry was a family man. After seven lean years at *The Voice*, he wanted to be a pro and needed to earn a decent wage, and the *Post* was a major paper.

When I came in the next morning, Dan invited me to walk over to Washington Square, sat us down on a park bench, told me Jerry was leaving, and offered me his job as associate editor and chief drama critic. It was a big jump for someone my age. I stepped right up to the opportunity. I already was doing much of the work and picked up where Jerry had left off. I was now the lead critic and could review the plays that mattered.

My work load increased mightily six months later when the Newspaper Guild went out on strike, closing the seven New York dailies, leaving the *Voice* classifieds as the major outlet in Manhattan for apartment ads. We extended our distribution borough-wide, and within a few weeks circulation jumped from around 15,000 to more than 80,000. The size of the weekly issues grew from sixteen or twenty pages to sixty-four or seventy-two. Without immediately adding staff, apart from an assistant for me, we added writers, gave them more space, and somehow kept up. The newspaper strike went on for almost four months, and *The Voice* kept most of the gains after it ended, suddenly prosperous after years of barely surviving.

The paper hit the streets every Wednesday morning. I urged my regular writers to hand in their stories on Friday, but most of them wrote over the weekend. Monday and Tuesday were heavy work days as the typewritten copy came in to be cleaned up and shipped off to the printer. I reviewed two or three plays a week myself and recruited several other critics to send out as well, now that there was space for more reviews. I wrote my own reviews late Monday night. On Tuesday I edited the last stories, laid out the paper with Dan, and late in the afternoon headed off to the printing plant in Brooklyn, Long Island, or later Newark, where final proofreading and corrections went on deep into the night. Eventually I staggered home and had nothing much to do for a couple of days before it started again.

9

PLAYS HAD BEGUN POPPING UP in coffee houses, churches, art galleries, storefronts. Any room with seats and a few lights could be a theatre. Jerry had often sent me to review such shows, and I was delighted with some of what I saw—Tennessee Williams and Beckett one-acts, sprightly little musical revues within arm's reach.

Now that I was my own editor, with my pick of assignments, and I tried to see every show of any consequence even if I wasn't reviewing it, including much superlative artistry on Broadway. I loved any act of theatre, but as the sixties got going I found myself increasingly alienated from the bourgeois values of the mainstream audience. It was painful to be the only one not laughing at a Neil Simon comedy. Joe Chaikin scorned commercial, "consumer" theatre, and radical thinkers from Artaud to Jan Kott proposed a more authentic encounter between artist and spectator. With doubts about the established theatre and no way into it anyway, we embraced the emerging experimental, alternative approach. We wanted to be in the same room with the actors. We wanted theatre we could do ourselves, bold, engagé, hip to the experimental personal lives we were living and the burning issues of our time. I increasingly came to value the intimacy, immediacy, even the makeshift production values of the new little out-of-the-way theatres, where there was no money at stake and artists could afford to take chances.

The most active and persistent of the off-off-Broadway venues was the Caffè Cino, an Italian coffee house in a narrow storefront on obscure, block-long Cornelia Street, not far from *The Voice* in the Italian heart of the

A performance at the Caffè Cino

Village. Other coffee houses, concentrated a few blocks away on MacDougal and Bleecker Streets, hosted poets reading their work, sometimes with a jazz musician, although the city's licensing law forbade live entertainment without a liquor license. The Caffè Cino started out presenting art shows and occasional poetry readings, opened itself to actors and directors, and before long was offering a different one-act play every week. Some weeks Joe Cino, the ebullient proprietor, called me at *The Voice* and asked me to review the show—my policy was not to express an opinion unless asked. The plays were under an hour, with two performances a night, three on weekends. I could catch one after seeing an earlier show uptown.

On the Cino's tiny platform stage, Wilde, Williams, Gide, Anouilh, and Ionesco one-acts gave way to a new generation of writers trying out every style and subject they could imagine. Joe Cino provided a welcoming free space where visionaries and beginners were encouraged to follow their dreams. Numerous talented young playwrights, actors, and directors emerged once there was a place to show their work. The uptown press hardly noticed at first, but the raw earnestness of the bare-bones Cino shows, scraped together to express real life and make something new, called out to the person I was trying to become: a sensitized free spirit surfing the immediate present and writing up the future as it unfolded. Something was happening here, and I was perfectly placed to watch it be born.

Interspersed among the wide-eyed tourists at the Caffè Cino was a flamboyant in-group of regulars, giddy, campy, funny theatrical types inclining gay and flourishing a range of eccentric personalities. The Cino was not serious enough for Joe Chaikin, not professional enough for Paul, and I generally went there alone, drawn to the scene as well as the plays. My preppy style and critic identity felt awkward and alien there at first. I was welcome, but an outsider, and for months hardly dared talk to anyone. The Cino people were as strange to me as gypsies. I was too square to know what was going on.

I couldn't keep my eyes off the waiter. Small and quick, with dark eyes, Indian cheekbones, straight dark hair to his shoulders, he flaunted provocatively tight pants, soft boots with Cuban heels, a narrow change apron snug around his hips, and a sassy attitude. I had never seen anything as sexy as the way he sashayed through the crowded room, getting everybody served so the show could start. At quieter times he chatted with Joe Cino behind the coffee machine, cued up opera records, visited with customers. Then he often ran the lights.

The lighting for plays at the Cino was alternately credited to Jon Torrey and John Dodd, and at first I didn't know which was which. One winter night after the second show, Joe Cino asked if I would like to come home with him and "John." To my dismay the sexy one said good night and left, and I found myself walking east with roly-poly Joe Cino and lanky, saturnine Jon Torrey, his boyfriend, through a cold, crisp night to their loft on the Bowery. The floor in front of the space heater was strewn with muscle magazines, which I had hardly ever seen before, handsome fellows posing with little triangles of cloth on strings restraining their private parts. We took off our

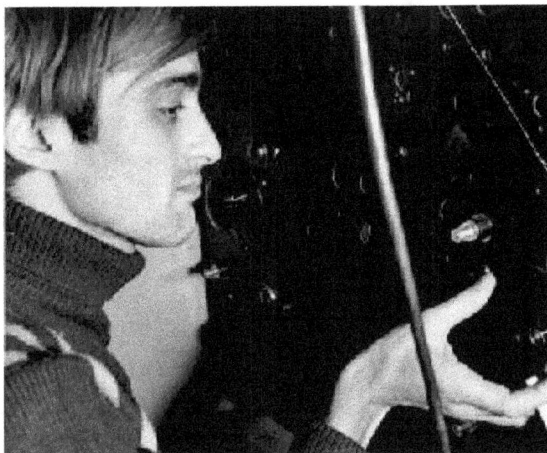

Johnny Dodd at the Caffè Cino lightboard

Joe Cino and Jon Torrey

clothes, got high, and made out on the rug, but there was no chemistry with either of them: I was more turned on by the magazines. John Dodd was the one I wanted and had been cruising, but I was still not sure he knew me.

JOE LeSueur, GUEST-EDITING *Kulchur*, a literary magazine, published my little play *I Like It*. I showed a copy to Joe Cino, and he gave me a date—a week beginning June 20, 1963—to put it on at the Caffè Cino. That was how it worked: he gave you a date. Roberta Sklar, one of the Open Theatre directors, directed; I was too busy, and it was taboo in those days for writers to direct their own plays. Paul was out of town. Denis Deegan helped me carry my own bed over to the Cino and played the young man. *I Like It* was not much of a play, not even sincere, but it would be a thrill to see my whimsical imaginings brought to life before actual audiences.

Paul had gone to Italy, hired

by Jerome Robbins to act in experimental plays at the Spoleto Festival. Paul proposed that he and Mildred Dunnock perform my little play at Spoleto. Robbins, who had just directed Arthur Kopit's first play off-Broadway and put him on the map, wrote me a note saying he liked *I Like It* and would try to do it. I took three weeks off from *The Voice* and followed Paul to Europe, my first trip abroad.

Before I left, John Dodd signaled that he was aware of me and not unfriendly, pressing his warm hands down on my hand one night as he served me coffee at a table in the Caffè Cino, leaning over my shoulder in the Bagel, a tiny restaurant on West 4th Street where I was eating dinner alone, setting a cherry-chocolate bonbon before me on the counter, saying, "Have a good trip." He was going to Paris, but there was no way for us to meet up. We barely knew each other.

I FLEW TO ROME, took a bus into the city, walked around stunned by the dense amalgam of old and new, drank definitive coffee at an outdoor cafe, gazing at a spectacular fountain as I fended off shoeshine and beggar boys. I got on the wrong train north, sat up on my suitcase most of the night in the corridor, and arrived at dawn in Florence. Checking my bag, I walked to the Piazza della Signoria, ogled Michelangelo's boldly naked David, sat outside at a deserted cafe watching the city come to life, enjoyed a coffee and pastry when the cafe opened, and headed back to the station.

Spoleto was an astonishingly picturesque Umbrian hill town full of palaces, theatres, dancers, musicians, and international cognoscenti. Paul had rented a room with one big bed from a friendly, accepting local family. I saw splendid performances, including an unforgettable *La Traviata* staged by the great Luchino Visconti. I was blown away by how beautiful everything was. We ate long lunches under arbors, the best food I had ever had. Visconti invited us to dinner in the country and amused the party with the Truth game, asking outrageous personal questions. *I Like It* did not fit into Robbins's schedule after all, but I adored Italy.

We went on to Paris, where our tiny hotel room looked out across the

Seine at Notre Dame. Tanks rumbling down the quai woke us on Bastille Day. In a tiny Left Bank theatre I saw *The Bald Soprano*, a key text in the emerging Absurdist theatre, and went off by myself to visit a young French actor I had met in New York. He took me to meet Nicolas Bataille, Ionesco's director, and eventually gave me a look at his forbiddingly large penis. I walked home along the Seine in a misty, melancholy dawn, wondering what point I was making with Paul and what was happening to our love affair.

PUTTING OUT THE PAPER was like opening a new show every week. Working at *The Village Voice* was a job I could care about, with real rewards, although I never made much money. It must have been hard work, but I had the limitless energy and stamina of youth and did it without measuring what it took. We had many terrific writers, among them Jonas Mekas and Andrew Sarris on film, Jill Johnston on dance, Leighton Kerner on music, and Nat Hentoff on jazz and politics. I ran whatever they gave me. That was *The Voice*'s policy: it was a writers' paper. I also copy-edited Dan's writers, Jane Kramer, David Gurin, Vivian Gornick, Sally Kempton, and many others, not that they needed much editing. It was a heady moment. Promoting itself as "the newspaper of the trend-makers," *The Voice* spoke for a scene bubbling with ferment and transformation.

In the late summer and fall I got out of the city on weekends by helping Diane Fisher, my assistant editor, build herself a summer house. Diane's design was simple but ingenious, a large, sturdy plywood box with built-in accommodations, shutters hingeing down and up to become a deck and sunshades. We built it in her friend's backyard in Saybrook, Long Island; when the house was finished, he would barge it across to Fire Island, where Diane had scoped out a site on unclaimed land (soon to be national seashore). I enjoyed the physicality of the work. Her ostensible boyfriend, an addict of some kind, was in West Virginia and never around. The potentiality of intimacy arose only once, taking her home from a play, when I kissed her on the steps outside her apartment, triggering a yielding softness so alluring it scared me. I thought I was gay!

10

PAUL AND I WERE MOVING in different circles and different directions. After the Second City cabaret closed, he no longer had work in New York; I was more plugged in than ever. He was suspicious of drugs and dubious about my new ideas. Paul and I had loved each other enthusiastically and well, but I was falling in love with Johnny Dodd, a wild boy, which made me gay in a way that paradoxically excluded Paul, who preferred straight men.

Johnny patiently courted me with occasional postcards mailed to me at *The Voice*, inscrutable messages fanning my curiosity about him. He was flirtatious with everyone at the Caffè Cino and treated me with amused irony, keeping his distance. Only after Paul decamped and I was free did Johnny take me up to his apartment down the block from the Cino and begin to let me in on his magic.

I had never been so intensely attracted to anyone. Johnny's every word and move was charged with mystery and meaning, his touch electric. He was nothing like anyone I had met before, untamed, waking wild desire in me, drawing me like a moth to flame, knowing I would be burned. Making love, we melted together. He was a champion pot-smoker, and cannabis indulgence intensified the experience as we lost ourselves in love and music. It was mild Mexican marijuana in those days so you could smoke a lot of it.

I was afraid of being arrested when Johnny and I went out to score but tried to be cool. We smoked mostly leaves and were forever cleaning grass, as we called it, shaking it in the top of a shoebox or heaping it on a record jacket, separating out the seeds and stems. Johnny taught me how to roll smooth, substantial joints using two Bambú papers stuck together. He was obviously dangerous, a sweetheart and also an intractable outlaw spirit with a devil in him. I kept efficiently getting out a paper every week even as I felt a sublime madness overtaking my personal life, confident that I could handle it.

Johnny was equally drawn to me, but it was hard to get used to his capricious behavior. So far I only knew the polite world. He was not polite but ruthless about his work and pleasures. His speech was not tempered or tethered to propriety, whether he was raving about opera singers, denouncing rude customers at the Cino, or contending with the directors of the plays he lit, who would later say he was the best light man they ever worked with—or completely impossible. He had no respect for rules, conventions, or received opinion, gave no quarter to insecurity and uptightness, hated the rich. He was a challenge to everything I knew.

Everybody around the Cino recognized his charisma. Johnny was gay in a way few others dared to be in that up-tight time—not effeminate but delighting in

Johnny on the fire escape at 5 Cornelia Street

mischief, openly sexy and provocative, not pretending to be straight like the rest of us. His long hair, his swagger, his tight pants projected a confident, defiant personhood that I envied and passionately desired.

Some nights he had something else to do and slipped away. Nothing was explained. Or there might be other people getting stoned in his living room, listening to opera and carrying on, when I longed to be quiet and have him to myself. It was a hard routine. He worked till after midnight, and later still on weekends. If I missed him at the Cino or wanted to see him at other times, I had to shout up at his fifth-floor windows to be let in. The buzzer was broken, and he had no phone. Many a time I stood across the narrow street crying, "Johnny! Johnny!" until, if I was lucky, he appeared at the top-floor window and threw down the key. I could never be sure he would respond even if he was there. When I couldn't find him I lost all confidence in our bond. Then he welcomed me in, passed me a joint, unleashed Maria Callas, hugged and kissed me, and it was utter bliss.

One of my duties at *The Voice* was running the annual Obie Awards for off-Broadway theatre. I invited Gordon Rogoff and Richard Gilman to judge them with me, and we extended them to include Off-Off-Broadway productions as well. *The Voice* threw a big awards party at the end of the season at the Village Gate, a nightclub on Bleecker Street, and everybody from the downtown theatre scene came.

Denis, who had been crashing with me on West 3rd Street since Paul left, departed for Paris. After that Johnny spent endless hours at my apartment making a collage on a long plywood panel framing three doors along one wall of the living room, carefully snipping George Washington faces out of cancelled five-cent first-class postage stamps with nail scissors and gluing them up in tightly spaced horizontal rows with Sobo glue. It made no sense to me—art, presumably—but I liked having him there. He needed an insane number of stamps; we ran ads in *The Voice* and people mailed them to him from all over the country. I helped him soak the stamps off the envelopes and dry them on blotting paper, wishing he would stop gluing up stamps and come to bed.

11

Summer arrived. Longing for fresh air, wide skies, long vistas, and a getaway with Johnny, I rented a house outside Taos, New Mexico, sight unseen—the rent was $25—and took a two-week vacation from *The Voice*. I bought a Plymouth two-door sedan for $75. Two friends came west with us. Søren Agenoux, a wispy blond writer who worked at Judson Church, had been putting out a witty zine he called *The Sinking Bear*. Kirby Doyle, a straight California poet friend of Diane di Prima's, had appeared at Judson in Freddy Herko's ballet *The Palace of the Dragon Prince*, which Johnny lit. Kirby and Søren, coming down from amphetamine, were not much fun in the back seat. We must have been a disreputable-looking carload. When I detoured into the Country Club District in Kansas City, wanting to show my friends the genteel environs of my long-gone childhood, a policeman pulled us over and suggested we head on out of town.

Søren Agenoux

Arriving at the house I had rented in Arroyo Seco, a few miles outside Taos, we swallowed psilocybin, the gentlest of the psychedelics but still intense, and went out into mighty nature, vast vistas of the Rio Grande valley opening to the west, peaks of the Sangre de Cristo serenely looming to the north and east. Friendly people in a handmade house up the road gave us water. I took shelter from a shower under a bridge and communed with the primeval slime, emerging to a rainbow.

Søren and Kirby left for the Coast by Greyhound the next day. I set up a table in the backyard and started writing a book. My mental processes had a whole new energy and scale, as if I had come out of a small, tidy room I had thought to be the world, where I specialized in clear, orderly thoughts, into the feast of a great chaos, blown away by the forgotten spaces of America,

and by Johnny, who gave me an unforgettable blow-job on the sofa on the back porch in the high mountain sunlight. He had just eaten a large number of tangerines from the tree in the yard, choked on my cock as I came, and the tangerines, still fresh, splashed across my body.

My inclination was to kick back in Arroyo Seco, work on my book, bliss out in the sun in the backyard of our empty house. Johnny wanted to explore the town, go see the Indians at the pueblo, take in a movie at the drive-in. The Indians made a powerful impression, allowing us to wander around and think what we liked. Later, Johnny tossed an empty Camels pack out the window of the car with our last two joints in it, and we spent a long time searching for it in the scrub under the eucalyptus trees along the Santa Fe road.

After Taos, Johnny wanted to go to California. I obligingly turned west, phoning Dan Wolf from a gas station to say I would be away another week. Diane would cover for me. We found Søren in Hollywood staying with Gerald Ayres, whom I had known at Yale: I published his poems in my magazine, *Voices*. Now a producer at Columbia Pictures, Gerry offered Johnny a part in a movie about Nazi concentration camps, based on his cheekbones and skinny frame. Johnny thought Gerry wanted to get into his pants and was more interested in his collection of Ray Johnson collages.

Søren came with us up the coast. I wanted to show them the scene in Santa Barbara, though my parents were in Europe. Dad would hear about my appearance at their beach house on Padaro Lane with two long-haired men in boots. We climbed over the garden wall to get into the house on San Ysidro Road, scaring their German housekeeper, Marthe—who rallied, cooked us dinner, and served us in the dining room.

The next day I took the coast highway north. Johnny, freaked out by the Big Sur cliffs, had to lie down in the back seat and not look. His love-hate relationship with the Catholic Church required us to stop at every major church. In Santa Cruz, as if I dared him to do something I would really hate, he stole one of the dressed-up dolls people pray to from a lighted glass case raised up on a plinth, little silver arms and legs pinned onto her elaborate

MICHAEL SMITH

embroidered dress as offerings by the afflicted. We got away without anyone seeing us, but then we had the beautiful doll with us in the car. My paranoia fanned by Søren with snorts of crystal amphetamine, imagining it might be a famous treasure, I monitored the radio for news that the theft had been discovered and we were pursued, taking back roads up the peninsula to San Francisco, wandering through forests along the crest of the mountains. The sun set into a blanket of fog so solid-looking I tried to walk on it.

At City Lights bookstore Ferlinghetti warned us that Kirby was trouble. Kirby appeared with his wife DeeDee and took us across the Golden Gate to get high at a house backed up on the woods in Mill Valley, where every room was filled with machine parts and disassembled mechanical devices, the owner calmly working under a bright magnifying light at a workbench. Kirby gave each of us a poke of amphetamine. I went into a state of ecstatic bliss; a deer came out of the woods and talked to Johnny. Later, DeeDee and Kirby went off on some caper to the city, taking Søren with them, and a gun, first leading Johnny and me to an empty house in another town, where we made love for hours before we sweetly slept. In the morning we barely knew where we were. Kirby phoned, having lost DeeDee and Søren in the action of the night. I knew Søren wanted to come with us, but we didn't know where he was and it was time to go. I didn't want to go back into San Francisco and get caught up in God knows what, I wanted to drive east. It would take Søren a year to get back to New York.

Johnny, realizing the holy doll was voodoo and not to be kept, handed it over to a Mafia connection of Joe Cino's, who said he would see to getting it back where it belonged.

12

ONCE JOHNNY FINISHED his wall of George Washingtons, I had to go over to his house to be with him. He liked to stay up all night and sleep until early afternoon. I often met him after he finished at the Caffè Cino, well after midnight, and went home with him to spend the night lounging around in his tiny rococo living room smoking pot, talking, listening to opera, making love, watching old movies on the *Late Late Show*, until the garbage trucks came around, their roars and crashes signaling bedtime at last. It was difficult to wake up in the afternoon and not have clean clothes.

I no longer wanted my own apartment or my own life. I was madly love-struck, transfixed by a sex-plus connection that promised to renovate my being—a dubious formulation, but there you are. I wanted to be with him all the time. So I sent back my rented piano, gave my apartment to a friend, and moved in with Johnny. He loved me too, I felt it, though it would not have been cool to say so. He gave me a key. He knew I would be trouble and thought I was worth it.

His tiny, shadowy fifth-floor apartment seemed like a palace with infinite space. The hall door was permanently shut: you had to duck in through a smaller door Johnny had crudely sawed out of it, with its own hinges and lock. The first room, originally the kitchen, was painted black, with nothing in it but a sink in the corner and a miniature bathtub behind a tapestry. The toilet was in the hall. Beyond the first room through a curtained doorway was a dark, narrow bedroom with a mattress on the floor, beyond that the small, square parlor, tattily resplendent with gold damask on the walls and a faux-baroque painted ceiling. The shutters were painted black and nailed shut, heavy velvet curtains hung in the doorways, and layers of figured carpet padded the floor. The furniture came from the street and the sets of Caffè Cino plays: a papal armchair in tattered petit point, a rhinestone cross with Christmas bulbs in the arms, a big dark green velvet sofa, an Egyptian throne. The tall shelves of LPs were heavy on opera.

I brought along a few prized books and personal things, my manuscripts, clothes, and left everything else behind—bed, toaster, books, sound system, furniture and lamps, tasteful modern dinnerware, all the comforts assembled for my formerly respectable bachelorhood. There was no kitchen at Johnny's; we ate most of our meals at Joe's Dinette, a family restaurant around the corner at West 4th and Jones Street, where we ran tabs. They squeezed orange juice fresh for me for breakfast any time of day.

MICHAEL SMITH

I arrived at Johnny's thinking I would change nothing, then went back for my mattress so we would have a more comfortable bed. My former apartment devolved into a drug bazaar famous for its lazy susan of pills and mounds of amphetamine crystal. Eventually everything disappeared. Johnny's stamp collage, long thought lost, reappeared decades later in the storerooms of the Andy Warhol Museum in Pittsburgh.

Lust was not enough to account for Johnny's effect on me. He was nothing like anyone else I knew. On his own since he was fourteen, he was tougher than he looked, with a fiercely independent sense of himself. My responses to the world were conditioned by my complacent bourgeois upbringing; he had turned his back on all that, making his way with nothing but his native charm, good looks, and intelligence. I was vulnerable to others' opinion, outwardly confident, secretly unsure of myself; he was wide open and better defended, with a wild energy and heedless hunger for thrills. He frightened and excited me, daring me to go beyond my habitual limits, take more chances, let go of my judgments and preconceptions, so many of them conventional and second-hand. I was older, almost twenty-nine; Johnny was twenty-three. I was "better educated" and should have known more; he had educated himself and had more self-confidence and bravado. I had more money and status, but he had more power. My good manners, convincing to others, carried no weight with him: he wanted me more elemental and unrestrained. Convinced that he held the key to a deeper way of being, I struggled to keep up with him and let go of my fear without actually being destroyed.

JOHNNY WAS FINDING HIS WAY into a real career as a lighting designer. He quit waiting tables at the Caffè Cino to light thr 1963-64 season of plays for the Playwrights Unit, a showcase for young writers that Edward Albee and his producer, Richard Barr, supported with a slice of the profits from *Who's Afraid of Virginia Woolf?* Johnny kept lighting select shows at the Cino and increasingly branched out to do lights for dance concerts and plays at beautiful, historic Judson Memorial Church on Washington Square,

Left, Diane di Prima with LeRoi Jones; right, Fred Herko

which had begun providing space for performing artists to show their work. Snobby Yalie light-guy that I was, I tended to patronize Johnny as a primitive, not realizing he had already apprenticed with Nikola Cernovich, the leading downtown lighting designer, who had worked with Merce Cunningham at Black Mountain College in the fifties.

Johnny was friends with a wing of the hip downtown post-beat avant garde who seemed privy to secrets of art I wanted to know. Diane di Prima, the poet and publisher, coedited an insider newsletter called *The Floating Bear* with the poet LeRoi Jones (later Amiri Baraka). Johnny had had some kind of love affair with Diane's best friend, Fred Herko, shortly before he took up with me. With balletic modern choreographer

John Herbert McDowell and James Waring

James Waring, composer John Herbert McDowell, and Diane's husband, Alan Marlowe (Freddy's former lover), Diane founded the New York Poets Theatre, producing a series of obscure verse plays in galleries and undiscovered theatres in Nick and Johnny's ineffable light.

Johnny's two dearest friends had been students at the Herron School of Art in Indianapolis when he was putting himself through high school across the street. Trim, bright, brittle Michael Wiley, a former dancer, was resident in Johnny's apartment on Cornelia Street when I moved in, and he stayed on for a couple of years. He generally stayed out till the bars closed, took the bedroom if Johnny and I were still up, or slept on the sofa in the living room if we had gone to bed, rising early to go to his job as a travel agent at Greyhound.

Ken Burgess, an artist who made posters and washed dishes for the Caffè Cino, had painted the crude, sincere sky of muscular baroque angels on Johnny's living room ceiling in trade for opera records. Johnny had made him add wisps of cloth veiling the hunky angels' loins, to my regret.

Kenny was an enthusiast of sex in subway men's rooms and other public places. Amazed to learn of this

Michael Wiley (years later)

Ken Burgess

flourishing clandestine sex-world, imagining a book about it, I taped several interviews with Kenny on the subject in his art-choked loft on the Bowery. The story turned out to be less titillating than I had hoped, endless blow-jobs in squalid conditions, but oddly charming thanks to Kenny's ineradicably innocent point of view.

Johnny brought home a large wooden desk he found on the street and put it in the living room so I would have a place to write, painting it silver, blue, and orange, nailing on Pepsi caps around the edge, gluing on shards of broken mirror as decoration. My big manual typewriter was magically hidden inside. I went back to work on the book I had started in Taos, using chance and collage to break open fiction, randomly filling a spiral notebook as if taking dictation—odd things people said, snatches of story, riffs on found texts, fragments of whatever I was reading, long lists of the names of the charismatic people I encountered in this character-rich moment of my life, dozens of people in the course of a day, at home, at *The Voice*, at gallery openings, at the Open Theatre, at the Cino, at Judson Church, people I signed petitions with or saw on the street or slept with or remembered from the past. How extraordinarily full my world had become! When I was not at work putting out the paper or out reviewing plays and running around, I sat up all night behind my desk in the living room getting high with Johnny and his friends, talking, writing, burning my brain, excitedly living the moment.

An invasion of impish artists from California intensified the drugginess. DeeDee Doyle had ditched Kirby, who was strung out on speed, and taken up with Bobby Driscoll, a former child movie star turned junkie. Ondine, a famously witty opera queen from Queens and key Warhol superstar, shot amphetamine in the toilet in the hall. Freddy was getting deeper into speed. Johnny always had marijuana and liked to turn people on so they dropped in day and night to get high with us. We tried whatever drugs came our way, LSD, mescaline (which was glorious), peyote, heroin (once was enough), cocaine (rarely seen), poppers, occasional opium, and who knows what other pills and powders, some of which made us delirious: Turn up the music! Fall on the floor!

Søren Agenoux, back from California, entertained me with snorts of amphetamine, which Johnny encouraged, saying it made me more interesting. Søren took to supplying me with little flat tinfoil packets of the glittering white powder; I usually had one in my shirt pocket. I learned to make lines of it on a mirror with a single-edge razor, stick a rolled-up ten-dollar bill into my nostril, and sniff it up, one nose and then the other, or slip away into the john and dip in a fingertip. I was tireless on speed. I could write, or more likely talk, through the music, all night long.

Charles Stanley

It was amazing to hear Ondine carry on about sopranos with Charles Stanley, a tall, bony all-purpose aesthete who worshipped Licia Albanese and sometimes went to her apartment for spaghetti. I hadn't yet learned to like opera, but Johnny and his friends were deep into it; there was nothing to do but give in, sopranos shrieking day and night.

Charles was Johnny's partner in mischief and my nemesis for a time, competing with me for Johnny's attention and sometimes winning, although it was clearly me Johnny loved. The two of them shared with Joe Cino a streak of anarchic wildness. Bob Heide said this trio looked like a pack of wild dogs as they came out of Johnny's front door dressed in black and hit the streets, looking for action. I struggled to defend my rationality and despised myself for being so square.

Johnny periodically grew tired of people dropping in at all hours to get high and tried to stem the flow. One night when Ondine yelled up from the street, Johnny chose not to respond. Ondine got upstairs somehow anyway, knocked and called our names from the hall for an hour, hearing us talking and listening to music in the inner room, scratched at the hall door with amphetamine relentlessness until he broke through and came in. Johnny was so annoyed that the next day he hammered large nails through the door, points out, to deter further intrusions.

13

Ondine could handle amphetamine, in fact thrived on it, but Freddy frightened and saddened his friends by losing control of the drug, giving himself over to it, turning into a ghost of his formerly juicy self, bent on self-destruction. He made no secret of his intentions, inviting everyone he knew to a suicide performance on a rooftop on the Lower East Side. No one came except Peter Hartman and Deborah Lee, who manned the downstairs door. Freddy only posed and pirouetted on the parapet.

Early on a Tuesday evening, October 27, 1964, a few days after I'd moved in with Johnny, I finished my work at the newspaper office and stopped by Cornelia Street to see him before heading off to the printing plant, now in Jersey City. Sitting on the stoop was Larry Ree, former carnival geek, future ballerina, who informed me that Freddy had jumped out the window of Johnny's apartment and was dead. I had pried open the shutters and opened the windows in the living room because it was Indian summer and the nights were hot. Freddy had visited Johnny that afternoon and taken a bath. Dancing naked around the living room, reportedly to Mozart's Great Mass in C Minor, he suddenly ran around the desk, climbed through the window onto the fire escape, and dove off. I saw his blood in the gutter. Diane di Prima did Bardo readings for Freddy in her house on Cooper Square. Johnny and I stopped by for a while. I had no idea what Freddy's death meant to Johnny. He never talked about his feelings, and I was trying hard to keep up.

To give us more privacy, I built Michael Wiley a loft bed in the first room, with a carpeted ladder and fake-fur curtains on a track, cozy and private like an upper bunk in a Pullman car. Michael could whisk tricks up into his bed and out the door without our even knowing they were there.

Johnny impulsively acquired a large green parrot. Søren, who was camping on our sofa, was with him when be bought it and went back to the pet store later and bought it a good-sized cage. Johnny kept the cage door open, and the bird more often perched on a lampshade. It was beautiful with its weird bird alertness. Periodically it started thinking about the jungle, chuckling softly to itself. The chuckling turned into gabbling, which turned into loud squawks, which escalated into jungle screams, at which point it took wing, careening around the apartment, tipping steeply through the narrow doorways. Gradually everything was chewed up and powdered with parrot poop.

The parrot flew out the window when the weather warmed up; Johnny went up on the roof, found it shivering on a tv antenna, and brought it back. I added screens. It lived with us for months, sometimes fun, often irritating, and then at one point it was gone. I got the impression that Johnny had accidentally killed it, or perhaps not accidentally, it was never said. There were some things about Johnny I didn't want to know.

The parrot episode had tragic consequences for Søren, who had bought the parrot cage with a forged check: the pet store owner tracked him down and had him arrested. He wrote me desperate letters from the Tombs. I hired a lawyer for him and tried to raise bail, but Søren had burned all the West Coast friends he referred me to, who thought it served him right and declined to help, and none of our New York cadre including me had money to spare. I despised myself for not saving my friend, although I couldn't think how to. It turned out he had violated probation on an earlier petit larceny charge. He wound up serving eight months in the prison on Riker's Island.

Joe Chaikin had taken up with Jean-Claude van Itallie, a Harvard-educated television writer and aspiring playwright, about the same time

I took up with Johnny. One day in March 1965 I ran into Jean-Claude and his oldest friend, Tania Leontov, pushing a baby carriage full of props and bedraggled costumes along the Christopher Street sidewalk. Jean-Claude's one-act play *War* had opened the night before at the Caffè Cino—I had been there to see it. Later fire broke out and destroyed the interior of the cafe. Jon Torrey had disappeared; it was rumored that he had set the fire in a fit of jealousy. Over the following weeks Joe Cino's friends and beneficiaries— the many people who wanted to do their plays at the Cino—rallied to the rescue, organizing several benefits to help him reopen.

As part of a Caffè Cino benefit at the Sullivan Street Playhouse, I made my New York directing debut with a goofy little romp by Gertrude Stein called *Three Sisters Who Are Not Sisters*. I did not exactly understand what Stein was getting at, but I liked and believed in her writing and followed her whimsical stage directions as well as I could. At the end of each scene, she wrote "Curtain," which posed a problem, as we were performing in the round, on the set of *The Fantasticks*, and there was no curtain. I asked an artist I will call Sarah Marx, a girlfriend of Joe Chaikin's roommate Fred Katz, to make a painting of a curtain and had Johnny and Charles walk it across the stage at the appropriate times. They had recently bleached their dark hair blonde and looked very strange. My parents happened to be in town and came to see this one-night show. It was the first time they laid eyes on my lover. I hardly imagined they would approve and felt too awkward to introduce them, much less invite them up.

Stein's ambiguity played well, and people liked my production, or said they did—I had to factor in the idea that they were flattering me because I was a "powerful" critic. After the one-night benefit, we moved the play to Judson Poets Theatre for a two-week run.

14

My aim in moving to New York had been to get into the theatre, become a director; instead I was gaining a reputation as a critic, my name

Diane Fisher, Deborah Lee, and Marva Abraham in *Three Sisters Who Are Not Sisters*

appearing on reviews every week in *The Voice*. I was useful as a critic, I thought cynically, so that was who people wanted me to be: media access. There were plenty of playwrights and directors, but I had, like it or not, the power of *The Village Voice*.

It was an exciting time. A new theatrical vision was emerging on the little downtown stages, and I had a role to play simply by paying attention. The modus operandi was that critics went to shows because they were given tickets by press agents; non-commercial theatres did not have press agents so the shows received little notice from the press. Many times my review was the only public notice a show would get. Some of the new playwrights were prolific. I tried to see every play they did.

A friend took me to see *Cowboys* and *The Rock Garden*, two one-act plays at Theatre Genesis, in a room upstairs from the parish hall at St. Mark's in-the-Bouwerie Episcopal Church. The plays, Sam Shepard's first, had been dismissed in the *Post* and the *Times*, and he was about ready to quit writing. My belated notice brought in audiences and put him and Theatre Genesis on the map. Sam quickly became one of the most active of the new writers. I loved his work and would be much influenced by it.

Nick Orzel, the lover of Dick Gilman's wife, Esther, asked me to help him edit an anthology of new American plays for Bobbs-Merrill, and I signed a contract for my first book. Our anthology introduced playwrights Jean-Claude van Itallie, Sam Shepard, Paul Foster, Lanford Wilson, Maria Irene Fornés, Megan Terry, and included two poets, Joel Oppenheimer and Frank O'Hara. I wrote an introduction identifying five key downtown theatres and groups and interviewed their leaders: Joe Cino; Ralph Cook of Theatre Genesis; Al Carmines, arts minister and composer-in-residence at Judson Church; Ellen Stewart of Cafe La Mama; and Joe Chaikin of the Open Theatre. *Eight Plays from Off-Off-Broadway* was the first book about Off-Off-Broadway and defined the field.

CHARLES HAD BEEN TO MOROCCO, and Johnny wanted to go too. By the end of the season I was worn out and ready for something else. After seeing four or five plays a week for months, my appetite for drama was failing, and the editing job at *The Voice* was ever more demanding, the weekly schedule relentless. I wanted to write other forms besides journalism, travel with Johnny, and make theatre myself, not just promote other people's work. When I asked Dan for two months off in the summer of 1965, he said it was unfair to keep giving Diane the job and taking it back, suggesting I let her have it. I agreed. I would continue as theatre critic and curator of the Obie Awards. Writing reviews was not much of a job, but I didn't want a job. Career and future meant nothing to me: the whole economy was on the brink of collapse and transformation, if we did not blow ourselves up first; and I needed very little money: our rent at 5 Cornelia Street was $63.50 a month, split three ways.

Uncle Al and Aunt Maxine came to Brooklyn to see Johnny and me off on a Yugoslavian freighter bound for Casablanca. I loved the idea of taking a boat across the Atlantic Ocean but the reality was boring. The other ten passengers avoided us, and the feeling was mutual, the food appalling. I tried to write but had nothing to write about except my own twisted thoughts and slippery emotions. The more I pestered Johnny for sex, the more he felt trapped. Somewhere in the middle of the ocean we took LSD, which at least was not boring. Sitting in the prow of the ship, I pondered the history of my family in relation to the westward expansion of the United States, an arc completed in my father's generation. He had reached the Pacific: the arrow had landed. It was clear but no comfort.

In Marrakesh we scored kif from the desk clerk at the hotel and found pipe sellers in the souk behind the square. It was fascinating but too hot so we fled up into the mountains, taking a series of buses over the Rif to the edge of the desert, attracting an eddy of curious boys wherever we stopped. In Tangier we moved into a tiny, elegant, modern hotel overlooking the beach, not sure what to do next. Joe and Jean-Claude turned up at another hotel; we rented a car together and drove out to Chaouen, a famously picturesque town in the mountains, where we watched women beat laundry on the rocks and young men chop up kif with black tobacco. Joe had a panic attack on the steep streets, had to inch his way down on his butt.

Imagining Morocco as a hotbed of homosexuality, I tormented Johnny with my horniness. I wanted him to pick up a boy we could share. He was offended and distant, only interested in finding hashish. We made a concerted effort with no success, winding up instead with majoun. There was confusion of terms and no such thing as information: people told us whatever they thought we wanted to hear.

Johnny wanted to go to Alexandria. I liked the idea, having read the

Alexandria Quartet, but there didn't seem to be any way to get there. Eventually we escaped to Italy on another Yugoslavian freighter. Disembarking in Naples and wandering around Pompeii in a funk, we arrived in Rome at midnight. A taxi driver took us from hotel to hotel, waking up a dozen desk clerks, eventually lodging us in a bedbug-infested dump with prostitutes and their johns coming and going on the stairs all night. My needy state of mind drove Johnny into defensive withdrawal. The vibes turned rancid; he declared he was going back to New York. Rising early, I left him asleep, went out and rented a Vespa, booked us a room at the Inghilterra, a beautiful hotel near the Spanish Steps, and bought us tickets to *Aida* at the Baths of Caracalla. That was more like it!

I GOT TO KNOW SAM SHEPARD, who lived next door to La Mama with Joyce Aaron, an Open Theatre actor. Knowing I wanted to direct, he gave me his new play, *Icarus's Mother,* to direct at the Caffè Cino. He had already cast it with five good actors from Joe's workshop, which was all right with me: I always hated casting, so crucial and so difficult to get right. I went into rehearsal, thrilled to be directing but seriously hampered by my lack of technique and experience working with real actors. Focusing on symbolism and meaning instead of the reality they had to play only confused them. As they struggled to bring Sam's play to life—he was there but not much help—I was preoccupied with solving the technical problems, which included sending smoke signals from a campfire in the confines of the Cino. I kept turning up the volume on the sonic booms or explosions at the end. John Coe, the actor who had to talk over this racket, practically lost his voice; I remember him squeezing his diaphragm with his arms to get more pressure. Josie Lemma, the Cino's landlady, whose bedroom was directly over the stage, banged on the floor with a broom handle and came down in her bathrobe to complain. Joe Cino told me, "Do what you have to do." I hung up a large borrowed painting of Icarus by Julian Beck for inspiration and had a breakthrough with the actors just in time for the opening: it was a picnic!

MICHAEL SMITH

Cynthia Harris, Jim Barbosa, Lee Worley, John Kramer, and John Coe in *Icarus's Mother*

IT WAS HARD TO CONCENTRATE in the living room at Johnny's: to write anything serious, I needed to be by myself. I had worked well late at night in my old office at *The Voice*, but I no longer had an office there. So I built a study for myself in the middle room, with a snugly curtained overhead bed for Johnny and me, up a little staircase in the corner. It was like adding another room.

There I finished the book I had started in Taos. A nameless man, having slit his wrists, lies on the floor in a brightly lit white kitchen surrounded by oranges and blood, remembering, hallucinating, slipping in and out of consciousness, waiting for the ambulance he may or may not have called. It was not real enough to be depressing, more an experiment in style. There were parallel texts on facing pages, the one on the left including long lists of names. It may not have been a novel but it was definitely a book. I called it *Near the End.* That was the way I felt—dire.

15

I HAD SPENT A LONG SUMMER WEEKEND with Joe Chaikin and other friends at Jean-Claude van Itallie's family's country house near Charlemont, Massachusetts, in the northern Berkshires. Jean-Claude was generous and welcoming, the vibes friendly and relaxing, the company lively. I loved the plain old farmhouse, the sweep of meadows and sky around it, and the down-to-earth, kitchen-centered life with friends. Serene timeless nature was a huge relief from the city. The New England forest felt like home.

I went to Charlemont again to spend Christmas 1965. Johnny, busy lighting a show, stayed home. My week there proved to be an

Jean-Claude van Itallie

enigmatically revelatory personal moment, a joyous ordeal of self-discovery, unexpected and fraught with elusive meanings.

Besides Jean-Claude and Joe, the party consisted of Joe's roommate, Fred Katz; Fred's girlfriend Sarah Marx and her four-year-old son, call him Stefan; Marianne de Pury, a Swiss composer who worked with the Open Theatre; and Jean-Claude's friend from high school Tania Leontov, all of us thrilled to be in "the country." The house, seldom visited since Jean-Claude's mother's death not long before, had no telephone and no electricity except a generator in a shed, used only for washing dishes after dinner. Joe, who never wanted be without music, had brought a battery-powered phonograph. The spring water supply was off for the winter so we couldn't use the toilet and went outside. A wood stove warmed the kitchen, and a coal furnace in the cellar sent waves of heat up through a register in the living room floor. Fred and I went down to the basement and shared a joint in front of the open furnace door, shoveling in the coal and keeping everybody warm.

I relished the quiet, emptiness, and disruption of all habits. For number two I waded up through the snow to the top of the meadow and into the edge of the woods. In the sharp air I was intensely receptive to all sensations, feeling radically exposed when I dropped my pants and sat over a log, as if my soul had been wearing armor in the city and I had taken it off.

Always up for experiment, Joe had the idea to take a break from words, to see what other kind of thinking and communication might occur if we stopped talking. Fred and I agreed to join him: not a word would pass our lips. It was amazing how not talking made us feel and how it changed our interactions with other people. Joe and Fred stuck it out for a few hours; I stayed silent for five days.

Not talking was heavenly, Zen enlightenment before I knew anything about Zen. Freed from the need to apologize, explain, or account for what I did, I could simply be and act. Unable to question or be questioned, I no longer questioned my self, which dissolved into the empty air.

Far from separating me from the others, not talking brought me a heightened sensitivity and intensified awareness of them. I could no longer argue, justify myself, or compete for attention. Another level of contact emerged. I spent hours with Fred, rambling in the snowy woods and fields as the light changed. Fred talked and did not mind my silence. Stefan thought it was funny. Others were sporadically unnerved, urging me to say what I was thinking, what was happening, what was the point. Missing the normal, chattering Michael, one after another of them tried to make me talk. Jean-Claude's father came for a couple of days with his mistress and her teenage son, who only spoke French. Jean-Claude said it would be rude to his father not to talk; but I was enjoying myself too intensely and only smiled, and his father was charmed. I did not utter a word the whole time he was there.

One evening Tania and I, drawn to each other, cuddled up together on the sofa in the living room, went to her room, and made love by candlelight, listening to Mozart. I had forgotten how natural and good it felt to fuck a woman. It was no obstacle that she was fat; I relished her abundance. We slept through the night together and did it again in the morning, interrupted by Joe banging on the door, demanding his phonograph.

The following night, I went back to my own room upstairs. I felt friendly toward Tania, I had liked sleeping with her, but I was not looking for a "relationship"—I had Johnny, one was enough. She demanded an explanation; I thought my actions were clearer than words. My refusal to talk bugged her so much that she decided to leave. She would hitch a ride with Fred, who was driving to the city to go back to work. Before they left I sat down at the typewriter in the living room and dashed off a column for *The Village Voice,* meditating on the pleasures of country living and how too bad it is that one has to be in the city to do theatre. Fred took the column in for me. Fred was simpatico. There was nothing to explain.

Jean-Claude organized an outing to Deerfield to see the second most beautiful view in the world, according to Henry Adams. Still not talking, I went along in one of the cars as far as the village of Charlemont. After a stop for coffee and goodies, I bailed out, smilingly waved goodbye, and walked back to the house alone, an hour up the snowy road climbing through ever-changing woods. How often was I ever alone? In the meadow across the road from Jean-Claude's house an apple tree stood by itself on a rocky knob; I thought of it as *the* apple tree. Sitting under it, alone in the snow, I swallowed a tab of LSD.

When the cold got to me, I let myself into the house, stoked the furnace, and lay shivering on the grate in the living room until I thought it was branding me. The house was full of light bouncing off the snow. In the upstairs hall I studied a local topographical map thumbtacked to the wall, which could have been a map of the world, seeing myself as a tour guide for my own consciousness, arranging experiences for myself, escorting myself to continuous performances of the theatre of life.

When the others returned they had no way of knowing that I was in a drastically altered state of mind, as I was still not talking. It sounds as though I was crazily isolated, but that was not how it was for me. I felt present with and for the others and present in myself, which was not always the case, tuned in to my comrades, seeing, feeling, embracing everything.

After dinner I went outside and looked up at the stars. Whenever I looked up in those days I expected to see missile trails slashing across the sky. I dreamed it, dreaded it, felt it coming, looked for it, waited for the silent flash of nuclear explosions over the horizon, the lurid light preceding the sound, the shock wave, ghastly death. In that moment I accepted whatever was to happen. "Kill me now," I said to the stars, accepting. But I loved to live.

Later that night Sarah came into my room and warm into my bed. Making love with her was uncomplicated, pleasurable, joyful. We both had other, primary attachments, but we liked each other. My liaison with Tania had been negotiated publicly in the living room; this was between the two of us. Sarah did not seem to mind that I said nary a word and went back before morning to sleep with her little boy.

I started talking again when we headed back to the city. It was tempting to stop talking forever and play out the rest of my life as a holy fool. It hurt to resume the habits I had so loved escaping for these precious days. Back in my ordinary state of mind I talked too much, said stupid things, argued, indulged my ego, reproached myself, everything I had feared. I had a full life in New York, including a passionate love life, and much that I wanted to do. I had glimpsed an alternative, and part of me wanted it more.

16

ONE NIGHT AT HIS APARTMENT on 12th Street Joe played me a recording of Inge Borkh singing *Salome*. My first long play, *The Next*

Thing, was inspired by the way Strauss raised the intensity of feeling to an ecstatic pitch and held it there, extended it, the power of emotion swelling, time stopped—like hovering at the brink of orgasm, delaying the release, stretching out the pleasure—something I was doing more these days as a side effect of sniffing amphetamine, which made me hornier than ever. Obsessed with masturbation, I could make it last for hours.

Johnny cared little what I did with other people, or so I thought, but he unaccountably minded my self-love and resented the pictures I liked to contemplate to turn myself on. John Button had given me a homemade book of artistic photographs of naked boys and young men, hard to find in those days, after I introduced him to Scott Burton, saying he no longer needed it. The uncircumcised youths in the photos must have been European. I studied them closely, trying to see through the surface into the breathing reality, feeling warmly toward the various boys in their frozen semitumescence.

If the essence of modernity is refinement of sensation, I thought, then what is more modern than to contemplate one's own sexual circuitry? Making love with another person is more fulfilling, with more dimensions, but the autonomous processes within each mind-body make each of us a self-contained world of sexual function as well. I loved my beautiful, endlessly interesting penis, warm, swelling, radiant with pleasure-waves, smooth and exquisitely responsive to the touch of my sensitive hands, themselves erogenous, standing up asking to be squeezed and stroked and fondled, looking at me with its little mouth.

Johnny feared images, destroying any pictures of himself he could get his scissors on. One night I came home to find he had thrown out my book of boys along with my album of memories—photographs of Denis, Donny, Frederick, Scott, Tony, Helen, Doon, Serena, Paul—seeing my past as a dilution of the present and rival for his favors. I took his aggression to be meant for my own good, but I had my own path to sainthood and wanted my books. Johnny gave in and led me across Sixth Avenue and a few doors up West 4th Street to a garbage can. My personal picture album was there, intact, but the arousingly naked boys were gone, never to be seen again.

MICHAEL SMITH

Ed Setrakian and Barbara Vann in *The Next Thing* at Cafe La Mama

JACQUES LEVY DIRECTED *The Next Thing* as part of an Open Theatre playwrights season at La Mama in spring 1966. The play is claustrophobic and surreal, depicting a grown-up son who shoots his wheelchair-bound mother and finds love with a girl who has spent years pretending she can't walk—a bitter little story, not intended to be realistic.

We rehearsed at Jacques's loft on Bleecker Street. One day I arrived early and found him unusually excited. In a burst of inspiration, he had cut up the script with scissors and scotch-taped it back together in a radically different configuration. Instead of three long, sustained scenes building to a dreadful ecstasy (like *Salome*), he had deconstructed the action into eleven shorter scenes jumping back and forth in time. After a spasm of reflexive defensiveness, I thought why not, it would probably make the play more interesting—and it did; I published *The Next Thing* in this form and can't imagine it working as well the way I originally wrote it.

Jangly harpsichord music by Robert Cosmos Savage started on the blackout that ended each scene and cut out when the lights came up on the next. Sarah Marx painted the set, big flats leaning slighting inward, in murky colors suggesting the airless, abstract apartment I imagined. I wanted Joe Chaikin to play the leading role, which would have raised it to another level; he hesitated but finally wouldn't do it—a great disappointment. Johnny designed the lights, then blew up at Jacques and Sarah at the dress rehearsal and walked out.

One night I dropped acid and walked across town to La Mama to have a look at what I had wrought. The performance had already started. Ellen Stewart, sitting on the stairs guarding the door, quietly let me in, and I stood at the back watching. To my astonishment I saw not actors on a set but actual human beings in a shadowy room at the other end of the loft, real, present, and astonishingly weird. I had to rush into the costume room to muffle my laughter, not to distract the audience.

17

IN RESPONSE TO THE COLUMN I wrote at Charlemont over Christmas, after days of not talking, I received a letter from Wolfgang Zuckermann, a maker of harpsichords in kit form with a workshop on Christopher Street, whom I had earlier interviewed for the paper. If I wanted a theatre in the country, Zuckermann wrote, he had one he would gladly sell to me. Buying a theatre was out of the question, I had no money, but desperate to get out of the city with Johnny, I called him anyway, and one weekend he drove me out to look at the place.

A stone gate and narrow drive off a wooded back road near Upper Black Eddy, Pennsylvania, two hours west of New York, led to a gravel parking lot, whence a broad footpath meandered through birches to a pretty little outdoor amphitheatre. Zuckermann had built it with a friend; they had put on a chamber music festival there for the previous three summers. It was called Sundance (this was long before the one in Utah). The small, covered stagehouse was designed for music, with burlap walls and the names of the great composers lettered in gold across the fascia. Chairs for the audience fanned out in tiers under the open sky. Farther up the drive was a cottage in a clearing, where we could live, a rambling red barn, a smaller house up the hill beyond, a tennis court, and down in the woods a

Wolfgang Zuckermann

big concrete swimming pool, with a screened-in summer house in the trees close by. Surrounded by wild state forest, it would be a romantic getaway.

Born in Berlin in 1922, Wolfgang had come to New York with his family as a teenager. He was a lively fellow, small, quick, idiosyncratic, a familiar figure in the Village, gaga over pretty young girls, who were often charmed by his funny ways. I liked him, and we agreed to produce a summer season together at Sundance, his previous partner having relocated to Paris. I would be paid a modest salary as resident manager. Wolfgang would book chamber music concerts on the Friday nights; for the Saturdays we organized a New American Arts series, bringing plays, dance concerts, poetry readings, and new music out from the city, with an evening of experimental films curated by Wolfgang. He agreed to hire Johnny to do the lights.

In the meantime, Wolfgang and I played chamber music once a week in his West Village mews house. He was an enthusiastic amateur cellist; joined by a violinist, we read through trios by Mozart, Haydn, Beethoven, and

Mendelssohn, all new to me. I loved playing music with other people and looked forward to playing tennis with Wolfgang in the summer.

MY PARENTS CAME TO NEW YORK on one of their periodic visits, and Johnny had encounters with each of them. Excited about Sundance, I borrowed Wolfgang's car to drive Johnny and my mother out to show it to them. I wanted Mother's approval of my choice of a mate. He was disarmed by her graciousness. Perched on the edge of the sofa in the dusty living room of the empty house, she even tried a few puffs of marijuana but didn't sit still long enough to get high on it: she preferred gin.

The next day, she was mean about Johnny. She did not mind that he was homosexual, she said, or that I was sleeping with a man, but she told me he was dirty. She said he could not speak properly, which was not true. She said he was a dope fiend and was turning me into a dope fiend. She said he was destroying my life. It was class warfare.

I was too upset to keep this to myself, and Johnny was shocked as if he had been slapped. He had thought he was okay, he said, a good, honest, straightforward, charming person who was a real catch. He had thought he could meet enough of the little bourgeois criteria to pass. She had wounded him. Never trust a Capricorn, he said, and he never did trust her after that, certain she would wait for years to have her revenge.

I put on a tie and went uptown to have dinner with them, and Dad invited me to join him for the next day's matinee of Verdi's *Don Carlo* at the Met. I had a *Voice* obligation and couldn't go. He gave me the extra ticket to sell. Pretending I had sold it, I gave it to Johnny: *Don Carlo* was one of his favorite operas. He slid into his seat next to my father just as the lights went down, then slipped away quickly at each intermission. They sat through the whole opera side by side without speaking. When King Philip ordered Rodrigo to be burned at the stake for helping the prince to free the people of Flanders, Johnny turned in his seat and glared at Dad, who in his view was oppressing us by being so bourgeois. He told me about it later. All the people on stage were saying, "Don't be so cruel, it's your own son, he's only

MICHAEL SMITH

being noble." Philip was saying, "Oh no, there are rules, you have to play by the rules." My father knew the opera well. Johnny hoped seeing *Don Carlo* would make him aware that if he did not watch out, he would turn into King Philip and do his son serious harm.

As Johnny took on more and more lighting work, the only way to be with him was to pitch in and help. I thought of it as joining him inside his obsession. He needed a helper, and I loved lighting; it was my art too, and I had the time. I frequently worked as Johnny's unpaid assistant, wielding my crescent wrench deftly as I hung and focused the heavy instruments, tying off the plugs as I ran the cable as I had learned to do at Yale, staying up all night in empty theatres, lending Johnny my analytic mind to figure out dimmer boards and plugging systems and how the show could be run, coming out into the morning dirty and exhausted. Sometimes I ran the performances myself as he went on to another project. In program listings I called myself Key Grip, because I believed he needed me. The designs were his, unrestrained by conventional technique and often very beautiful.

For a series of experimental musicals at Judson Church, Johnny made a breakthrough, envisioning light that breathed with the action. I ran the light board for many of these performances. "Never stop moving" was his instruction, and I danced my own invisible performance in the dark at the dimmer board in the balcony, moving the dozen long interlocking levers with hands, elbows, shoulders, hips, knees, feet, phrasing intensities and color harmonies in sync with the music, action, and flow of feeling on the stage, the light breathing with the performers; I was one of them, the hidden power supply, buoying the show along in a living fluid of glowing color. It was like jazz improvisation, the changes sometimes impulsive, with sharp rhythmic accents or comments, sometimes smooth, the picture always different from the instant before, colors dissolving, brightness melting into darkness or blossoming in the space like the coming of dawn or spring or love, ebbing and flowing with the rapture of the song.

We gave Johnny an Obie for lighting design that year. It was outrageous to honor my lover for work I had helped him with. On the other hand, it was not fair to deny him recognition because of our personal connection, or so I reasoned. His lighting was original, radical, unlike what anyone else was doing. With limited equipment on the makeshift downtown stages, he had been forced to devise a conceptual aesthetic, and the performative aspect of his vision was something new. Gordon and Richard agreed that he deserved an award; I was sure of my integrity and believed we should do as we liked. It is lastingly valuable to have an award, good for anyone's résumé and self-esteem. Johnny was embarrassed and managed to be out of town for the award ceremony. The inimitable dramatist H. M. Koutoukas accepted on his friend's behalf.

JOHNNY AND I MOVED TO SUNDANCE in early June to get ready for the season. I loved our intense, sexy isolation in the hot, buzzing clearing surrounded by wild forest. To transform the chamber music shell into a theatrical stage, I persuaded Wolfgang to buy bolts of cheap black velour to mask the burlap walls and create wings. He bought additional lights and hired an electrician to move the dimmers from backstage to a booth behind the audience so Johnny would have a view of the stage. I bought a Dodge convertible.

There was plenty that needed doing: grass to mow, the big swimming pool to be cleaned and filled, publicity for the coming season, endless handyman chores. Wolfgang came out on weekends with his collie, Toby, in his Triumph convertible and bustled about, sleeping in the house up the hill and playing tennis with me or a girlfriend. He bought a pony for his pony cart.

Sarah Marx came for two months, hired to sew the curtains for the stage, mind the phone, run the box office, and help with housekeeping. Some of the performers would stay over a night or two, and we all had to eat. Johnny was suspicious, but nothing was going on between us—although in fact I had slipped away and made love to Sarah at her apartment in the Village two or three times that spring. She set up her painting studio in the

MICHAEL SMITH

The pool at Sundance: Allen Ginsberg, center; Johnny Dodd next to him with me in the water, bearded, at his knee; Jerry Joyner next to me; Wolfgang Zuckermann behind Allen, Stefan Marx next to him; Søren Agenoux and his boyfriend Arnold Horton, top left; Ronnie Gilbert, an Open Theatre actor, and Paul Giovanni, front right.

barn, and Stefan went to a day camp down the road where the other kids were deaf. Johnny drove him there and back every day in Sarah's Peugeot, discussing philosophy.

We put up posters in nearby small towns and signs at crossroads pointing the way to the theatre. Sundance was not easy to find, but good art always draws an audience, if not always enough audience to make it pay.

The Friday night concerts leaned toward Renaissance and baroque music using the harpsichord: Wolfgang expensed the Sundance losses as promotion of his kit business. On successive Saturdays, the Open Theatre performed Megan Terry's protest musical *Viet Rock*; Judson Poets Theatre brought *Pomegranada*, an opera by Harry Koutoukas and Al Carmines, who also performed an evening of his theatre songs; La Mama Troupe premiered a new play by Ellen Stewart's protégé Paul Foster, directed by Tom O'Horgan. Allen Ginsberg and Peter Orlovsky came for the weekend to give a poetry reading. There were three different programs of modern dance and mind-blowing concerts by La Monte Young and Cecil Taylor. It was an amazing range of artists, all pushing boundaries. Many of them came early and stayed a few days. I encouraged one and all to swim naked in the pool, wanting everybody to be happy, including myself, and tried to take care of every little problem that arose.

The weather held all season. It was hot in the woods, but it never rained on a Friday or a Saturday night.

18

Bob Amussen, the editor in chief of Bobbs-Merrill, gave me a $3,000 advance to write a book about new theatre in Europe. That fall Johnny came with me to Berlin to see the Living Theatre's new collective creation, *Frankenstein*. The cool, cerebral, poetic Living Theatre we had known in New York had morphed into a roving anarchist community of upwards of thirty rampant non-violent revolutionaries, their example as potent as their work. At the Frei Volksbuhne, *Frankenstein* was extreme theatre—spectacle, agitprop, ceremony, vision quest—on a much larger scale than the 14th Street Living Theatre's dimensions had allowed. Julian Beck played Dr. Frankenstein, and the large international company were diligently demented and inspired. It was astonishing to see the stage transformed from the inside of the monster's head into three stories of prison cells set ablaze in a riot. I filed a qualified rave for *The Village Voice* and tried to get my thoughts in focus around the book I was supposed to be writing, interviewing actors, making notes, not at all clear what my subject should be. The Living naturally imagined a book about themselves.

Getting high was part of the Living Theatre trip. I had brought some Mexican marijuana from New York, which everyone enjoyed; after that there was only hashish. Running around in Berlin, I developed a painful racking cough from smoking and overexcitement; it felt like it was tearing my diaphragm. Opium, Judith Malina's "drug of choice," was smoother and soothing but hard to find. Taking whatever mind-inflaming potion came my way, I was seriously edgy, and Johnny was not much comfort. "Keep your anxiety to yourself," he said, "I have my own." And: "Write that book!" He was refused admission to the Berlin Opera because he didn't have a suit.

Berlin was haunted by decadence past, hostage to history present. I began writing a phantasmagoric, incantatory story about public toilets and a fetishist of shit (not my thing!), hallucinating myself a naked consciousness detached like a character of Mann or Kafka. I thought if only I could open myself wide enough, everything would be revealed. I may have been running a fever.

After a week of this, Johnny decided to go back to his own life, insisting I buy him a train ticket back to Luxembourg to catch the plane to New York, leaving me at the pension. Luke Theodore, a big, affectionate, hairy actor friend of ours, kissed me and wanted to make love. Johnny was gone; why not? But that was not what I wanted, I wanted Johnny, my heart was breaking. I rushed to the station, found Johnny on the train, persuaded him not to go, bought him a banker's suit to satisfy the operatic dress code, and he saw a production of *Der Freischütz* that had balls of fire flying across the stage. I still did not know how to enjoy opera, seeing it as old-fashioned, irrelevant, and boring. He

Luke Theodore

made it sound better than *Frankenstein*. To Johnny, the essence of music was performance, in the present; to me it was text, what the author and composer had written—historical; and history was over. I tried to absorb his continuing lessons.

Conscious of having a book to write, I continued to hang out with the Living, seeing most of their performances, pining slightly for a couple of the beautiful young men. Considering the Living Theatre's principled permissiveness, and my own, it is surprising that I never had sex with any of them.

Ekkehard Schall as Arturo Ui at the Berliner Ensemble

Johnny and I repeatedly braved the crossing into East Berlin to see the Berliner Ensemble. Conspicuously long-haired, Johnny was searched at the border; the joints were in my pocket. We introduced ourselves to Helene Weigel, Brecht's widow, but I was too awed and uninformed to converse. Amid the rubble of East Berlin her theatre was an unexpected jewel, with a large company of actors on salary, first-class scenery and costume shops, an orchestra, a big, well-run, splendidly equipped playhouse, and numerous support staff. The productions were exquisitely crafted: we saw *The Threepenny Opera, The Resistible Rise of Arturo Ui,* and Sean O'Casey's *Purple Dust.* It was ironic to find this level of support and respect for artists in Communist East Germany, while serious American theatre makers were scraping along, unregarded, scrounging for scenery, hanging our own lights and sweeping our own stages, with too little time to rehearse and no place to do it.

The other theatre I particularly wanted to see was Jerzy Grotowski's legendary Polish Lab Theatre, which had not yet come to America. So off we went into the dread red East, hindered but not stopped by visa hassles. Typically, I had made no advance arrangements. Soon after we arrived in Wroclaw, a man from the Culture Ministry turned up at our hotel to find out who we were and what we were doing there. He helpfully took us to the Writers Club, which was nicer than any club I could get into in America, and led us to Grotowski's theatre, where we bought tickets for *The Constant Prince*. Performed in a kind of rude operating theatre, starkly lit by two harsh movie lights in opposite corners, with a single raised row of spectators looking down on the action over the top of wooden walls, the work was fiercely disciplined and intensely affecting, although we could not understand a word of the text.

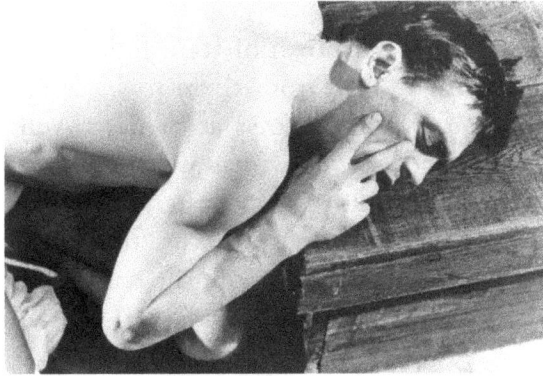

Ryszard Cieslak in *The Constant Prince* in Wroclaw, 1966

I went back to the theatre the next day, watched a rehearsal (entirely in Polish), and interviewed Grotowski's charismatic leading actor, Ryszard Cieslak, who was fluent in English, over lunch at the Theatre Club. Grotowski, inscrutable behind dark glasses, was too intimidating to approach.

We saw *Madama Butterfly* in Polish, took a train to Vienna, saw *Tristan und Isolde* at the State Opera and an operetta at the Volksoper, and rejoined the Living Theatre in Venice. Judith and Julian invited us to dinner at the pensione. We sat down, exchanged greetings, Judith said, "Tell us about Poland"—and I went faint, the world around me rapidly fading into a whitish red-rimmed haze. Unable to speak, I stumbled out into the lobby, fell onto a sofa, and passed out. Johnny was quickly at my side. I soon recovered but never had another chance to tell Judith and Julian about Grotowski.

In Venice I sat in on the Living Theatre's rehearsals for the Sophocles-Hölderlin-Brecht-Malina *Antigone*, with Judith as Antigone and Julian as Kreon, co-directing a laborious process of collective creation. I was fascinated by the play of ideas and personalities as the staging ever so slowly emerged. Judith invited me to join the company and travel with them as stage manager of this new production, and I wanted to do it. I was sick of New York, burned out on reviewing, frustrated with the progress of my non-career as a playwright and director. I said I would think about it and let them know in Holland in a couple of weeks.

As the Living Theatre toured on across the north of Italy, Johnny and I went to Rome to visit Peter Hartman, and on from there to Paris and London, where we saw Stravinsky's *The Rake's Progress* at Sadlers Wells, the first opera I truly enjoyed, and Chekhov's *Uncle Vanya* with Lawrence Olivier, Michael Redgrave, and Sybil Thorndike at Chichester, one of the greatest stage productions I have ever seen. We met up with the Living Theatre again in Amsterdam, but I had decided not to join the company. I wanted to be with Johnny, who was impatient to go home.

19

I EXPERIENCED all these places, people, and theatrical marvels through a shifting haze of anxiety and paranoia, artificially energized by "recreational" drugs, convinced that my turbid, often tormented personal state of mind was part and symptom of a more general agony and confusion gripping the entire culture—that if I wanted to be an artist and a serious person, I had an obligation to suffer through it, painful as it was, not merely have a good time. From poverty and injustice to politics to sexualities and the environment, a profound crisis was tearing the country and the world apart, the dominant paradigm crumbling under our feet in multiple dimensions. Artists in New York felt ourselves to be the central expressive organ of the culture. We marched for nuclear disarmament and peace in Vietnam, joining together as Angry Artists Against the War. We smoked pot, grew our hair, mocked sobriety, celebrated sex, advocating liberty and justice for all. Radically sensitized and opened up, we experienced politics within ourselves, our artistic expression a metaphor for everything else that was going on, our personal lives paying the necessary price.

With fellow *Village Voice* critics Ross Wetzsteon and Robert Pasolli

As a critic I declined to set myself up as a judge or consumer adviser but tried to be an exemplary sensibility reporting on my own experience. The theatre felt freshly relevant, original new playwrights appearing from all over—Beckett, Genet, and Ionesco from France, Osborne, Pinter, and N.F. Simpson from England, Edward Albee, Murray Mednick, Sam Shepard, Ronald Tavel, Rosalyn Drexler, Rochelle Owens, Robert Heide, Lanford Wilson, Megan Terry, Jean-Claude van Itallie, Bill Hoffman, Irene Fornés, and more emerging in the particular stratum of downtown theatre I was part of, with actors, directors, choreographers, and designers striving to seize the high ground and reinvent a theatre that spoke to the contemporary condition. However drugged and desperate I may have been privately, I wrote about their work seriously and lucidly every week in *The Voice*, playing critic with an existential edge, not standing back from the work and the people doing it but implicated in the thrust and quality or lack of quality of the work—doing it myself when I could. This led to a selectivity of enthusiasm based too much on personal affinity and my own ups and downs, try as I might to be open to everything. It couldn't be helped. Self-indulgence was part of the path: how else find one's truth?

The psychic discomfort that increasingly poisoned this exuberant artistic moment, the snake in the garden, was not just psychological or a consequence of one's own self-indulgence. We all felt it; it was what we were trying to make art about. Prizing civility and security, our parents' generation were overcommitted to costly illusions. Something else was called for.

For my circle, Freddy's suicide had been the first dire omen. The Living Theatre's departure left a gaping hole. I was tempted to join them in Europe, where theatre mattered, but they were living too much on the edge for me. I agreed with their revolutionary stance, but I wanted a personal life as well as a mission, love and home comforts as well as the naked blade of art and politics. History was grinding on. It was 1966, and the idealistic awakening of the early sixties, just now coming to wide notice, was already corrupted, co-opted, backed into a corner.

MY PRODUCTION of Søren Agenoux's surreal dramatization of Charles Dickens's *A Christmas Carol* that Christmas at the Caffè Cino would be a significant nexus and fiasco in several of the lives recorded here, peak creative collaboration and synergy of madness. Inspired by Scrooge McDuck, Søren's speed-driven play conflated backward and forward like the original story, the language delirious. Cardinal Spellman as Christmas Present took the truculent miser on a helicopter tour of Vietnam, obscurely identified as the Dismal Swamp. Ondine was an ideal Scrooge, crotchety and sarcastic, then radiantly sincere; Charles Stanley played Tiny Tim on his knees, with a child's crutch; Arnold Horton, Søren's sweet, handsome boyfriend, was Bob Cratchit to the life; Donald L. Brooks was spooky in winding cloths as Marley's ghost; Søren himself appeared in a frilly dress and mob cap as Mrs. Cratchit, awkward and ridiculous but oddly fetching. Jacque Lynn Colton from La Mama Troupe, inspired by European study, had a star turn as Christmas Past, wearing a crown of flaming candles. She was the token woman—otherwise it was gay boys together.

Joe Cino, unique among producers, never held you back, always encouraging you to go further. I took Søren to be writing at the edge of the unutterable, my sense that the text was barely coherent to be proof of its brilliance. It was a fantastic challenge to fit such a complicated multi-scene play into such a tiny space. Johnny's lights made it work. I was inspired—we all were.

When Ondine did not appear on opening night, there was no alternative but to go on as Scrooge myself, script in hand. Ondine showed up for the second show too deranged to go on, hid under the counter in the dressing room, and I had to do it again. After that the run went well.

Late one night we did a performance sans audience so Andy Warhol could film it. I was horrified when Billy Linich set up his own bright lights. Andy kept switching the camera off and on, fast-forwarding through the play—turning it into a Warhol.

Charles Stanley, Arnold Horton, and Ondine in Søren Agenoux's *Christmas Carol* at the Caffè Cino

Johnny was busy elsewhere after that, and it fell to me to design and run the lights for *A Funny Walk Home,* a painful play by Jeff Weiss that crystallized the dangerously unhinged spirit that was loose in the Caffè Cino. Jeff was rivetingly real as a deranged young man coming home from the asylum, where he was raped, I only now realize, and confronting his parents. At the climax, as it became clear that the next step was to murder them, Jeff stopped the performance and forced the audience to decide if he should go on. Would they be accomplices in the slaughter or let the parents off the hook? Usually, appallingly, the former. My lighting was pitiless, a row of white spotlights hitting the actors almost horizontally from one side; then ended, after the tragedy, with an ever-so-gentle fade-to-black on George Harris III, a radiant blond teenager playing the mad son's innocent younger brother.

20

JOE CINO HAD COME TO NEW YORK to be a dancer, but it was years since he had danced in front of an audience. Bravely, he signed on to do a piece in January at Judson Church, sharing a program with James Waring, Charles Stanley, and Deborah Lee, a dancer in Jimmy's company. Joe decided he would dance to Ravel's *Bolero*, music so corny as to seem boldly original. Johnny was to light it. We went to the church late one night so Joe could rehearse. It was unclear what if anything he had planned. We were speeding through our lives on a dangerous mix of chemical and cosmic energy, a transit of Jupiter making matters seriously worse.

We lit Joe with two white follow-spots, me manning one in the balcony, Johnny on the other behind the wide pivoting wings at one side of the broad performance space. *Bolero* builds for twenty minutes to a Dionysian ecstasy. Pinned in the lights like a fleeing prisoner, Joe danced to this mad music on sheer shattered nerve, spinning, writhing, running about the gaping space, wildly spinning the wing panels, which flashed almost unwatchably in the sharply angled light. I could not tell whether his dance was ineffably brilliant or completely empty, whether he had something in mind or was just riding the inspiration or lack of inspiration of the moment. The Living Theatre too sometimes achieved passages of what I called "highly charged nothing," transcending any conception of form or content.

JOE CINO'S HEART WAS BROKEN. Jon Torrey had been gone for almost a year; then we learned that he had been electrocuted on the job in an upstate factory. Joe had no private life anymore, no place of his own except the cafe, where he slept on the stage in a nest of rags, if he could sleep, the steel gate on the front door padlocked. He was a big-hearted man surrounded by people who loved him, but after the show everyone eventually went home, and Joe was alone with the jangle of accumulated stimulants.

One Tuesday night in March, returning to the Village from the printing plant in Newark at two in the morning, I called a number Johnny had given me. He was at a party at Ondine's friend Orione's apartment off Fifth Avenue in the 90s and invited me up. Orione was a high-class call girl and, on her own time, a witch. She, Ondine, Johnny, and Joe Cino had been tripping on acid. I was too far behind to take LSD at that point but caught up on snorts of speed. Inspired to write, I set about collaborating with Johnny and Ondine on a delirious little play about Richard Wagner and King Ludwig of Bavaria, high and happy with people I loved. Joe Cino, though, was miserable and desperate, feeling isolated and unlovely. One of the aims of tripping is catharsis and getting as far out as possible. I had come in for the second act and had no context to interpret his state; nor did I feel I was as close to Joe as the others were, though I probably was, except for Johnny. I tried to comfort him, talking to him for a long time, assuring him that we loved him. He decided to take a bath and wanted to be left alone. Fearing he would hurt himself in his despair, I removed the razor blades from the bathroom cabinet.

In the morning, feeling hollowed out, we shared a taxi to the Village, got out on the corner, and Joe headed off down Cornelia Street to crash in the cafe. He looked forlorn as he walked away up the narrow street, but I thought he had come through.

Joe was thirty-six. I was thirty-one. Johnny was twenty-five.

On the following Friday, March 31, 1967, the phone rang a little before six in the morning. I was still up, at my desk, Johnny asleep over my head. It was Joe Cino, asking for Johnny. Sounding dazed and far away, Joe said he was calling to say goodbye. When I asked him where he was, he put down the phone without answering. I roused Johnny and told him Joe had called sounding desperate. He said he was probably at the cafe, told me to take his keys, and went back to sleep.

Inside the cluttered cafe there was barely any light, only twinkling Christmas lights and a rosy glow in the back by the coffee machine. There I found Joe slumped on the floor in a mess of blood. He had been hacking at his arms with a kitchen knife, still had it in his hands. It was weirdly like the suicide I had imagined two years before in *Near the End*. Beyond speech, Joe saw me but paid no attention. As I stood there horrified, he tried to stab himself in the chest. The knife blade bent and wouldn't go in. Wild with frustration, he grabbed another knife and tried with that. He could hardly hold them, he was so bloody. I grabbed his arms and tried to take the knife. He was slippery with gore, the floor was slick, the knives were sharp, his will fierce.

I ran for help, across the street to Murray's, the Italian cheese store, where workers were getting ready for the day. I told them Joe Cino was in the cafe killing himself and begged them to come help me stop him. I must have looked like a madman. I ran up Bleecker Street toward Seventh Avenue, found a pay phone, started to call 911, and just then a patrol car came by. I ran back to the cafe leading the cops; then they took over and there was nothing more for me to do. Joe had lost so much blood that he was barely conscious. The ambulance came. The medic was not very excited. I thought Joe was probably dead. They only questioned me a little. They put Joe on a stretcher and took him away, and I went home to bed.

I had lost my scarf, one of those striped English public school scarves we used to wear in college, and I went back to the cafe later that day to look for it. Friends were coming in and cleaning up. My scarf had been cut in two; I found half of it, bloodied.

Joe was in St. Vincent's Hospital. More than a hundred people came to give blood for him. I heard he might live but probably not recover full use of his hands. I went by on Saturday and talked to Ellen Stewart and others who were keeping watch downstairs in the waiting room. Some people went up to visit him, but I could not bear to. He wanted to die, and I had only made it harder for him. The next day he did.

MICHAEL SMITH

21

JOE CINO'S DEATH was profoundly demoralizing. Johnny and I were too panicked or stunned to even talk about it. We kept going, tender with each other but conscious of the void beneath us. Joe Cino had been the benevolent godfather of our love affair as well as the whole alternative theatre enterprise.

In May, Johnny departed on a months-long tour of Europe as light man for a major dance show, Donald McKayle's *Black New World*. I felt abandoned, unable to accept that he had gone away—for reasons that had nothing to do with me. He hated leaving me. It was not personal, he was *working*.

Charles Stanley and other stalwarts hung in and kept the Caffè Cino going. I still had the date Joe Cino had given me to direct Søren's new play, *Donovan's Johnson,* and started rehearsing it just as Johnny left on tour. Ondine and Olimpio Vasconcelos, a demented Brazilian queen, played two wacky criminal types making their way back to the city after doing time at Sing Sing. Arnold Horton was a small-town kid who tried to help them. He actually came from Ossining so it was not entirely unreal.

Desperate for affirmation, I had a brief, speed-soaked fling with a pretty boy I met at Olimpio's orgy loft, playing Della Reese's "Love, Sweet Love" over and over again in the cafe until people begged me to stop. Then Johnny started writing me letters from the cities of Europe that made everything clear: he loved me, and he was doing the hardest work of his life.

Donovan's Johnson was a singular fiasco. Ondine, shooting speed in the dressing room, was glitteringly deranged. Olimpio was on Obetrol, his energy and timing coming and going in chemical waves, bursts of dazzling beauty, grace, and wit alternating with empty, dazed longueurs laid arbitrarily over Søren's barely intelligible script.

The dialogue for the middle scene, drawn from the stage directions to Verdi's *La Forza del Destino*, was a wholly abstract conversation during which the actors swept up and down the center aisle of the cafe with brooms, playing bowls with imaginary balls in blue-green and lavender moonlight to a soundtrack I taped myself, according to Søren's precise directions: the first minute of Beethoven's "Moonlight" Sonata, a stumble, a mistake, and beginning over, again and again. It was strangely beautiful.

The play concluded with the wordless presentation of a mysterious object meant to symbolize the electric chair (I think). It had to be non-literal but *something*. Søren borrowed a sculpture from an artist he knew, Paul Thek: a glass pyramid eighteen

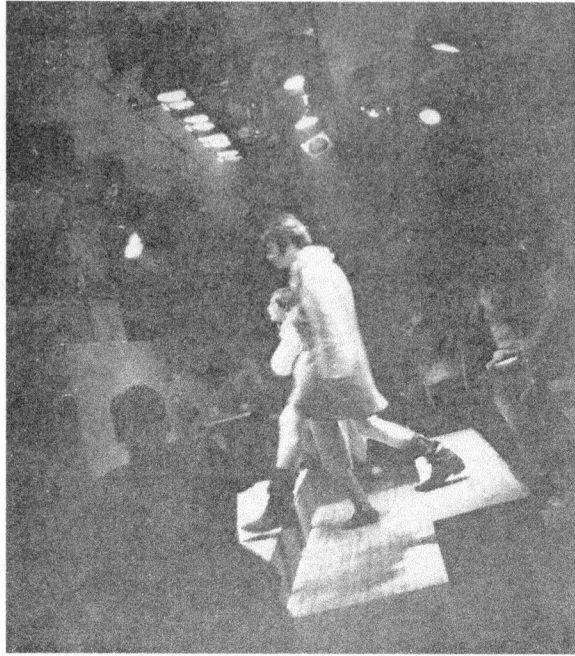

Olimpio Vasconcelos and Ondine in *Donovan's Johnson* at the Caddè Cino

inches high enclosing a day-glo red meat-like lump with wires rising out of it topped by tiny day-glo yellow disks. This inscrutably baleful object was brought out at the end of the final scene by a workman in a white jumpsuit who showed it to the audience very briefly before taking it away again, leaving everyone wondering, "What was *that?*"

We staggered through a week of performances, the dwindling audiences as disoriented as the actors. Arnold couldn't bear it and left town; Gerard Malanga stepped into his part. Søren was in despair, and the play was dying. After a stumbling second show on the first Sunday of the two-week run, Charles intervened to put the play out of its misery, appearing with a hammer just before the sculpture was whisked off and smashing it. That was the end of *Donovan's Johnson.*

MICHAEL SMITH

To fill the empty week, I helped pull together a variety show including *Vorspiel nach Marienstein*, the playlet I had written with Johnny and Ondine the night Joe Cino went crazy. It was ideally cast with Ondine as Wagner, Charles Stanley as Ludwig, and Deborah Lee as Wagner's Kundry, appearing at the climax of the simultaneous monologues, throwing herself around on the floor screaming as the lovers are engulfed in a tinsel waterfall made by Magie Dominic, declaring, "Kisses are the language of love!" In tandem with this tiny, goofy extravaganza, I directed Charles, who had his own ideas, in a revival of Harry Koutoukas's exquisite *With Creatures Make My Way*.

I POWERED THROUGH THE OBIES on automatic before gratefully withdrawing to Sundance for the summer. I brought out a young boyfriend to keep me company for the first couple of weeks pre-season. He taught me how to listen to rock and roll—Beatles, Mamas and Papas, Lovin' Spoonful—standing with me over the turntable, putting the needle back over and over until I could understand every word. I taught him to drive.

We had a shorter, less ambitious season than the year before but some great performances—Ravi Shankar and Alla Rakha, Terry Riley, and Ralph Kirkpatrick among others. Sam Shepard repeatedly came to see me in his Karmann Ghia. He was hanging out not far away with a group from Theatre Genesis who were working on a show that would become *The Hawk*. I was too lonely to write. Amphetamine was not helping anymore, only scattering my thoughts, making me grind my teeth and obsess about sex.

Every day I walked down the long driveway to the mailbox to look for a letter from Johnny, who told me to be careful and not fall for anybody else while he was away. One letter said straight out that I should quit taking speed; he was worried about me. If I did not immediately follow this good advice, at least his unusual directness got my attention. I still thought amphetamine would help me write the book I owed to Bobbs-Merrill. I had all summer to write but nothing I wanted to say.

Touring all over Europe with *Black New World*, Johnny learned to cope with a bigger, more professional, commercial theatrical context, but he never learned to like it. The producers wanted consistency, while he was looking for inspiration and surprising beauty at every performance. After a summer of zigzagging around the continent, they were a hit at the Edinburgh Festival and booked into a West End theatre in London. In Edinburgh Johnny ran into La Mama Troupe, who were going to London at the same time and needed a light man. Johnny signed on to do their shows as well.

He needed my help, so as soon as I wrapped up Sundance, I joined him in London. La Mama brought three fantastic plays, *Futz* by Rochelle Owens and *Melodrama Play* and *The Holy Ghostly* by Sam Shepard, brilliantly directed by Tom O'Horgan. Johnny and I set up the lights, and I ran them for him at the Mermaid Theatre while he ran *Black New World* and *The Emperor Jones* at the Strand, which I was never free to see. He was making good money, and we lived in a nice hotel in Bloomsbury, doing our respective performances for several weeks, our days free. We went to see a new band called Traffic and were blown away by Steve Winwood. I got sucked into a shell game in front of the W. H. Smith bookstore on Charing Cross Road and lost forty or fifty pounds in about five minutes.

I had not seen Tania Leontov for ages, though we had done a little transatlantic business in LSD—sheets of blotting paper ruled in squares, with a drop of acid in each square, which she mailed to me across the Atlantic. I met her at a Sloane Square pub and she told me about Buddhist meditation, the first I heard of it. Tania had been in Scotland studying with Chogyam Trungpa, an exiled Tibetan lama, and passed on the basic instructions: sit cross-legged, spine straight, eyes three-quarter closed, relax, and count your breaths up to ten, then begin again, round and round, keeping your attention on your breath. I tried it when I was by myself, and it was surprisingly difficult: thoughts kept bubbling up. I would count to seventeen or twenty-five before I noticed.

Johnny and I both were pursuing complicated lives, but it made everything better if we were together. If other people were content to live alone, good for them. I wanted to be with him. He wanted to be in New York.

22

BEING A CRITIC CAME TO ME NATURALLY, thoughts and the impulse to express them arising of their own accord in response to whatever I saw. Writing was never easy, but reviewing was the easiest kind of writing: if I paid attention, I always had something to say. I had the obligation of any journalist to write energetically and get the facts right, but my opinions were my own. In the spirit of the time, I wrote personally, passionately, denying that there could be objectivity in the realm of art. I was not a public official, not obliged to be impartial. I went everywhere to see plays, prided myself on liking all kinds of theatre, and presumed to feel existentially responsible for the life of what I saw, believing that the audience is always part of the show. Writing was a kind of performance, too, a second-hand art unto itself. If reviews were my principal literary form, I had to write well and keep them surprising. The source was sensibility; I had nothing else to go on. Finely tuned, I could see what was happening or not happening in the theatre in the living moment and enjoyed suggesting thoughts about it. No one has a better opportunity to indulge the love of art than a critic.

Brandeis University gave me an award for my criticism, and a professor at the University of Missouri edited a small book of my reviews, which he described as "sensitive and sensible," little knowing how deranged I was when I wrote them. I made it crazily hard for myself, tested the limits of my sanity, put off writing my column till the night before the morning it was due, hung out with Johnny and Charles, raving over the music, smoking pot and sniffing speed, or alone in my snug study teased my cock until midnight or three in the morning before I finally started writing—then at dawn, exhausted, walked my copy over to Sheridan Square and handed it to Dan Wolf, who came in early, before putting myself to bed.

As for the book I was supposed to be writing about new theatre in Europe, I was thinking instead that I should write about the new American theatre, the theatre I knew. The anguish of not actually writing this book went on too long, my enthusiasm no longer spontaneous and fresh.

Somehow the air had gone out of the whole situation. As a critic I felt isolated and empty. By the time of the Brandeis awards presentation, I was painfully alienated. The honors were bestowed at the Hotel Pierre with the dignity of a great benevolent institution. I had no truck with institutions, having dropped out of Yale without regret. The respectable world was largely indifferent to the people and work I cared about, and so be it. I never went uptown anymore if I could help it. I was not there as myself but the shell of myself, recognized as a critic but really something else, cultural subversive, would-be visionary artist, gay love-nut. The disjunctions were too weird. I was succeeding within a rational, self-congratulating status quo I believed to be false and pernicious. It was all a muddle in my mind that night, a mood disorder in eruption. When I went up to accept my award, all I managed to say was a terse, ungracious "Thank you," missing an opportunity to speak truth to power.

I had come alone and afterwards walked alone on the dark paths of Central Park farther uptown to a reception hosted by Lita Hornick, the art collector and publisher of *Kulchur*. There should have been pleasure in being praised and feted in the higher reaches of the art world, or at least some melancholy, narcissistic pleasure in feeling so alienated; I felt lost, numb, depressed, sorry for myself and no fun at all. Being a critic, I kept hearing myself think, was not what I had set out to do or wanted to do. I wanted to direct plays, work in the theatre myself, be a real writer. Joe Chaikin denounced critics wholesale, hurting my feelings, but deep down I agreed with him. My ego was continually stroked, seducing me into writing reviews, which were useful to others but not to me. I felt like a parasite on the body of art, settling for secondary expression.

I was still in this mood when Richard Barr and Clinton Wilder, the producers of *Who's Afraid of Virginia Woolf?*, took me to meet Michael Bessie at Atheneum, proposing that I write a book about Edward Albee. This was an invitation to step aboard the elevator to success, and after a few days' thought, I foolishly declined. I was too pure. I told myself Albee hadn't written enough to be a serious subject. I had reservations about his work and didn't want to be co-opted into overpraising it. I wasn't sure I liked Edward, although he had been generous to me—it was he who nominated me for the Brandeis award. I didn't want to think about him. I didn't want a career. I wanted to get high with Johnny and write the spontaneous unbounded image-thoughts burning in my mind. So I let the opportunity slip away.

Further fuel for my discontent arose from a peculiar weekend sponsored by the New York State Council for the Arts. I was recruited into it by Richard Schechner, the pioneering director of environmental theatre and NYU professor. With more than a dozen other theatrical types (not including Richard) I was driven to a former resort hotel in the Catskills, ostensibly to listen to a tape-recorded talk by Grotowski—which we never did hear. Instead we were subjected to a high-pressure encounter group under the guidance of Daytop, the drug rehabilitation organization. Held together in a room for many hours with a skilled, manipulative facilitator, we were guided through trust exercises and persuaded to confess feelings we normally suppressed. By the end each of us was systematically brought to tears, begging the others for acceptance. After a brief sleep break we did another several hours the next day. It was an unnerving experience to confront one's life situation like that, the flaw being that the program was designed for alcoholics and drug addicts, on the assumption that whatever they were doing was not working and needed to be radically dismantled. Amphetamine was the tip of the iceberg; my whole life was not working, and I went home profoundly unsettled. I tried to talk to Johnny about it, and he tried to understand. As he was central to my life, he was probably the problem, which he did not care to believe was real. He had problems of his own as he struggled to make a livelihood from light.

23

After Christmas, Wolfgang and I went out to Sundance and finished boarding up the front of the theatre against the winter. As he drove us back to the city in the early dark, I lit a joint and introduced the subject of the Caffè Cino, which was still going nine months after Joe's suicide. Charles Stanley had been running it with a cadre of true believers, and there had been some high times, including several spontaneous comic book productions, innovative pop theatre using comics as the script. Charles was buckling under the stress, hiding out in his apartment on East 2nd Street, not answering his phone, sneaking into the cafe to pay the bills at odd hours when no one else was there. Leaderless, the Caffè Cino was on the verge of collapse. I proposed to Wolfgang that we rescue it and run it together, as we had done so pleasurably at Sundance. He was up for it. The experience taught me not to make major decisions when I'm high.

We went directly to the cafe. Nothing had been changed since Joe's death. The stalwarts were still there—Magie Dominic, Kenny Burgess, Tommy Garland, Bob Patrick, Eric Krebs, Wally Androchuk. They kept things going, and plays were coming through, but everyone was exhausted and the room was depressingly grungy. The photos and posters on the walls were tattered and grimy. Cockroaches had taken over the cork wall in the kitchen. The sink leaked. The dimmers were giving out. Tables and chairs were collapsing. The coffee machine had broken down. Wolfgang agreed to put in some money, buy a new light board, and pitch in to clean the place up and help me put it back on its feet. I would handle booking plays. Charles was glad to let go, and Johnny came down with Denis Deegan's gold-sheathed sword to bless the transition.

We closed for a month for renovations, stripping everything off the walls and painting them white, more like a gallery than a theatre. I boxed up the memorabilia and gave it to the Library of Performing Arts at Lincoln Center. We had the coffee machine repaired, and Wolfgang built a new counter for it. We fixed the plumbing, repaired and repainted the tables, bought new chairs, replenished the china. I had a new dimmer board custom built to fit the space.

Not everyone was happy with the change of management. Joe Cino, a Sicilian from Buffalo, had the landlady and the invisible Italian powers of Cornelia Street on his side; Wolfgang and I, a Jew and a WASP, were not so welcome on the block. Caffè Cino regulars, who had been through heaven and hell with Joe and then Charles, saw me as press and did not know what to make of Wolfgang, an outsider with money, whose brisk, chilly Teutonic manner they misinterpreted, perhaps, as disdain. The walls layered with memories had become a sacred artifact, although in the glory days Joe Cino himself had changed the look of the place whenever he felt like it, often redecorating the whole room to suit the week's new show. People thought the magic had been taken away; I thought the magic was themselves, the artists, unless Joe Cino had been the magic, in which case it was hopeless. I wanted to run a cafe and put on shows, not maintain a memorial.

We reopened with a play Charles had booked, *Empire State* by Tom LaBar. The room looked too clean and new, but plays, players, and public passing through would soon take care of that.

A week into the run, two cops came in and saw a rather foul-mouthed play with a ten-year-old boy acting in it. Wolfgang happened to be there and was arrested. Apparently we could not have a child working in the absence of his parents, although the boy was accompanied every night by his aunt and everything was perfectly cool. Wolfgang spent the night in jail.

For Wolfgang this was too much like Nazi Germany, the police state showing him its power and his helplessness against it. In the confidence of his success and independence, he had believed that the United States was different, that he was safe now. But his father had prospered in Berlin, and look what happened there.

Wolfgang stayed away from the Caffè Cino after that, and I was busy elsewhere, helping Johnny with lighting setups and seeing three or four plays a week. I looked in most nights, talked to playwrights and directors about their projects, booked productions a couple of months ahead, and came to see the shows. At the end of each week I went over the accounts with Wolfgang, and he paid the bills. Business gradually picked up, enough money coming in to pay the staff and basic expenses. The actors passed the hat. It was a perfectly reasonable little business, and the shows were good.

Only now we had the attention of the police, who dropped in practically every night. I had heard tales of Joe Cino taking cops and inspectors into the back room and giving them money and/or blow-jobs but never quite believed it. Stung by his run-in with the law, Wolfgang was thinking about leaving the country.

The Cino was in a no-win situation: we had a restaurant license, but you needed a cabaret license to present live entertainment. The catch was that you could only get a cabaret license if you had a liquor license, which we could not get and did not want. There was no license for what we were doing—putting on plays informally in a coffeehouse—hence it was illegal. Cops started writing us summonses several times a week. Wolfgang hired a lawyer and we went to court; the $250 fines had to be paid.

We met with the deputy license commissioner. I went to see the capo of the block. I talked to the captain of the Sixth Precinct. What was going on? I blamed it on Ed Koch, then a city councilman, pandering to the Italian vote, although we were three blocks away from the tourist mayhem on MacDougal Street. To make things worse, we suffered a couple of robberies from the cash box, presumably by insiders. Wolfgang felt betrayed. I respected the outlaw mentality, but Wolfgang was a friend of mine, and I hated to see other friends rip him off. It is especially depressing to be robbed by someone you know.

We held out as long as we could. The last production was *Monuments* by Diane di Prima, eight abstract monologues for and about herself and her friends, mostly played by themselves, exquisitely directed by James Waring and Alan Marlowe. Two or three of the monologues were given at each performance, depending on who could be there. At last the Cino had a decent lighting setup; Johnny's light danced with the actors, adding theatrical magic.

I blamed myself when we closed the cafe. If I had made the kind of commitment to it that Joe Cino had, if I had been willing to give my whole life to it, I should have been able to keep it going. But I had other work, another identity and livelihood, I had my escape ready, and so I could let the Cino die. I came to feel that my function had been to finish it off, that it was not meant to continue after the death of Joe Cino, whose personal warmth

MICHAEL SMITH

and generosity had created and defined it. It had fallen to me to finish the ritual of Joe's death and deliver the news that the party, perhaps the age, was over.

24

AL CARMINES SET MY "*I Ching* poem (for Johnny)" to music, Remy Charlip choreographed a dance to it, and it was performed on a Judson dance concert. The *I Ching* was à la mode, and I had been casting oracles, trying to tap into knowledge of some deeper movement in my life, abandoning rational efforts to find meaning or make sense of things in favor of letting images resonate, avoiding interpretation, looking to chance for guidance. I had no sense of a god's immanence, of being the instrument of a higher intelligence; it seemed more likely that we humans *are* the high intelligence, one speck in the universe becoming conscious of itself, tiny but significant. An eastern fatalism had replaced the cause-and-effect Enlightenment model. Will was discredited. I wanted to go with the flow, not fight it and suffer.

Theatre Journal, Winter 1966 came out, very quietly, from the University of Missouri Press. I kept going to plays and writing about them for *The Voice*. I edited another anthology of new plays, for Dutton, and included my own play *The Next Thing*: if I did not promote myself, who would? But it was hard to care about any of it. I had seen too many plays. My life in art had turned into a habit, workable but unrewarding, like speed, which I had stopped enjoying. The scene itself, the intimate, radical theatre where I had felt so much at home, seemed increasingly polluted with crass opportunism, losing its spontaneity, dissipating its original sincerity. I was sick of being a theatre critic, convinced that "we are not likely in our lifetimes to see anything good," as I said in the introduction to my new anthology. Irene Fornés had nailed it in a song lyric: the moment had passed.

After we closed the Caffè Cino, I hated New York, longing for quiet, space, real time, nature, a different life. Everyone I knew was fixated on their latest project, especially Johnny, who was scrambling to make a living and often unavailable. Martin Luther King Jr. was assassinated, then Robert F. Kennedy. The whole country was going through a dark time.

Alan Marlowe departed for a Buddhist monastery in India, and Diane di Prima announced that she was moving her household to San Francisco to study with a Zen master. Lee Fitzgerald, one of her decorative hippie acolytes, urged me to join the exodus, seducing me to make his point. I didn't like the sex and was not interested in the long-haired boy. Even so I decided that I too would move to San Francisco once I finished the New York and Sundance seasons. I had to do something.

Kvetching to Jacques Levy about the book I still had not written for Bobbs-Merrill, I realized I already had the pieces of it: *Voice* columns about the Living Theatre and Grotowski, interviews with actors, letters from Europe to Joe Chaikin and others. Jacques said, "Take it all to your publisher, put it on his desk, and say, 'This is the book.'" I did just that. Bob Amussen read through it, asked me to put the texts in chronological order, and it was done. Johnny insisted I take out his name so I referred to him as "J." Our barely-hinted-at love drama was the most engaging part of the story. I titled the book *Theatre Trip*, dedicating it "To the Living, in Love."

I NEVER STOPPED LOVING JOHNNY, but we were not really getting along. He was preoccupied, working all the time. I was tired of helping him set up lights and hardly saw him otherwise. Horny from snorting amphetamine, I played with my cock for hours behind the curtains at my desk, the only space I had to call my own, and tensely tried to provoke him into sex play when he just wanted to relax and chill. He was adamant, I thought, and I was too yielding, giving up too much of myself, trapped in his tiny apartment, where every possibility of fun was shadowed by dead Joe Cino. I had no desire to break up; but I was not getting any satisfaction. We needed a drastic change to save our love. I needed a drastic change to save myself.

Other critics were panting for my post at *The Voice*, and after the Obies I bowed out, packed up everything I wanted to save, mailed a few boxes of

MICHAEL SMITH

papers and books to Santa Barbara to be stored at my parents' house, and left for Sundance, intending to relocate to San Francisco at the end of the season and start a new life, hoping Johnny would come with me.

Wolfgang had sold his house in the Village and his harpsichord business, put Sundance on the market, and was moving to England, having married in the spring and bought a manor house in North Devon. The previous summer, when Johnny was in Europe, I had done the lights for Sundance myself, and though Johnny was now available, Wolfgang could not be persuaded to hire him. He would stay in the city and try to find work.

George Harris, the teenage kid from *A Funny Walk Home*, kept me company in the country for the first couple of weeks. He was a playful, sex-positive, mischievous boy. We frolicked in the pool and took a shower together for so long that water flooded out onto the living room floor. When he was gone and I went into the city to see Johnny, I was taken aback to find George in our bed, wearing my bathrobe. It served me right.

I had a few other boyfriends off and on during my years with Johnny. I never loved any of them the way I loved him, but I enjoyed them and valued their easier friendship. Before the mass decadence of the seventies and the onset of AIDS in the eighties, being young and homosexual was romantic and fun. Gay boys were cute, and gay love was free. With a woman there was always a question whether the moment's intimacy promised something more lasting, unspoken at first but not for long, an inevitable issue of commitment and domestic contract. Boys, though, the young men I was attracted to, had their own lives, and I had mine. We could make love if we wanted to without its needing to have any meaning beyond the revelations of the moment, care about each other without having to take each other on.

The present moment, I believed, was all that existed. Polymorphous sexuality was implicit in my Dionysian dedication to the beautiful nonviolent revolution. My heartfelt desire was to broaden the flow of tenderness in the world and love as much as I could. Sex kept me young, kept my mind open, skin smooth, juices flowing, body legible. I was devoted to enlarging the sphere of freedom.

Johnny had taught me this attitude. At the start he had staked out an inviolable liberation for himself and flung it at me like a challenge, force-feeding me lessons in being cool. When he stayed away all night, it would have been too prying and square to ask where he'd been. He may have been doing a little hustling on the side. He let some random person give him a blow-job in the light booth at the Cino. He had a suburban girlfriend for a while. He let desultory three-way sex happen with an extra friend, Freddy one time, Ondine another. He did whatever the moment offered and left me to deal with any feelings I might be so uncool as to have about it. He was not going to stop being himself and doing what he liked just because we were in love and living together. I was not jealous so much as envious, titillated, curious.

But years had passed. When Johnny told me he was tormented with jealousy, it took me completely by surprise. I only made it with other people when he was out of town, or busy, preoccupied, unattainable. It took some of the pressure off him, and I liked my boyfriends. It turned out he hated my friendships when they crossed that line I had not known existed in as liberated a relationship as ours supposedly was. He said I was completely immoral. But Johnny always held my heart in his hands. How did my loving friendships threaten him? I thought possessiveness was over.

IN ITS FINAL SUMMER Sundance became a tiny music camp as well as a festival theatre. The great Catalán harpsichordist Fernando Valenti was in residence, shut up in the back bedroom with an air conditioner and his enormous John Challis harpsichord, guzzling Pepsis and practicing Scarlatti sonatas. Wolfgang remodeled the horse stalls in the barn into practice rooms, with little brass plaques naming them after historical harpsichord makers, and four of Valenti's teenage students came from Cleveland, staying in the house on the hill. The master gave me one revelatory lesson on a Bach Prelude and Fugue, and I played in a student recital.

One day a psychic summons drew me back to Cornelia Street. When I pulled up in my Thunderbird convertible (reupholstered as a present from my mother) Johnny was waiting for me on the stoop atypically dressed in white with a glamorous slouch hat, and I swept him away to the country. After the initial ecstasy, though, he was trapped again, torn away from his own life with nothing to do, while I was busy with other people, leaving him to his own devices in a situation where I had him at my mercy and ought to have protected him. He wanted to leave, I resisted, and we played out a familiar, agonizing scene, Johnny asking me to drive him to the bus and buy him a ticket home, me insisting, "I don't want you to go, I want you here with me, why should I help you go?"

In late August Johnny came west with me after all, giving his apartment to Michael Wiley's cousin Tommy Garland. Calm and unhurried, we steered well clear of Chicago and the tumultuous Democratic convention. In Kansas City we spent the night with my dear grandmother, now widowed, who served us her special iced tea and charmingly entertained us on her second-story screened-in porch. We slept together in my grandfather's bed. I believed in our love and was happy.

We drove on across Kansas and eastern Colorado to Denver, where Uncle Alfred and Aunt Maxine had opened a theatre called The Changing Scene. Driven out of New York when their loft was demolished for an office tower, Al and Max looked for a city that needed them and chose Denver, creating an intimate but workable theatre on the second floor of a narrow downtown building, with a large, bright dance studio and apartment upstairs, embarking on what would stretch into three heroic decades of presenting new, original work in all media. They had invited us to come put on a show.

To open our program, Johnny composed an original multimedia theatre piece, *Political Sonata Vision*, an ahead-of-its-time fusion of dance, music, lights, projections, and texts by Cummings, Aristotle, Hitler, and Thomas Paine. I directed *Dr. Kheal*, an antic monologue by Irene Fornés, with a good Denver actor, Bob Breuler; followed by Ronald Tavel's eccentric docudrama *The Life of Juanita Castro*, with Johnny gamely playing the title role and three bearded, cigar-puffing girls as Che, Fidel, and Raoul. Al and Maxine were delighted.

We played for two weekends, sleeping on the green room floor. When it was time to go, Johnny had me drive him to the Greyhound station and went back to New York. I had envisioned us venturing together into the unknown; he correctly saw other people at the end of this road, not the void but an existing scene I was aiming to join, if only to ease the transition, and nothing for him to do—no work. He was practical now and I was the radical, impulsive one. Sad but resigned, I drove west through the Rockies alone.

Johnny with Gay Boswell, Carol Book, and Anita Newman in *The Life of Juanita Castro*

25

For the next six months I lived in San Francisco with Diane di Prima and her four children in a pleasant four-story house two blocks from Haight Street. Diane, an energetic self-appointed spokesperson for women and the coming new age, was in the middle of writing her long series of poems called *Revolutionary Letters*. A young hippie girl lived in the attic with the children, Jeannie, Alex, Minnie, and baby Tara. Two young male Zen students were on the back porch. I shared a room with Lee Fitzgerald until he freaked out on acid, stopped talking, and moved out. Alan Marlowe,

MICHAEL SMITH

Diane's husband, came and went. A Digger family lived separately in the basement. Diane's house was a species of matriarchal commune, with cooperative sharing of chores. She paid the rent with advances doled out by Maurice Girodias of Olympia Press as she turned in chapters of the "pornographic" book she was writing, *Memoirs of a Beatnik*. She had us all on the macrobiotic diet, occasionally slipping away with me to North Beach for espresso and cannoli.

Every morning before dawn a group of us drove across town to the Zen Center to sit for forty minutes with Suzuki Roshi, Diane's teacher. Zen meditation—*zazen*—is just sitting, but it was hard! My knees hurt, my nose itched, my mind wandered, I fell asleep. The only thing to do was keep doing it as best I could: it was better than speed. One undeclared point of this whole move was to kick amphetamine.

Living on dwindling savings, I helped out as best I could, chiefly by driving people around in Diane and Alan's VW bus. My Thunderbird was a liability in this situation. I drove it to Bolinas one day and got a costly ticket because the hitchhiking kids I picked up were carrying a jug of wine. When the power steering went bad, I couldn't afford repairs and put a For Sale sign in the window. A couple of guys came to the house, I gave them the keys to check it out and never saw it again.

Diane had complicated relations with the local chapter of the Hell's Angels, who at one point stole our bus. At a party they dosed us with a drug called STP that gave us the horrors for days. We were off drugs, apart from ritual tripping once a month on the night of the full moon. We closed the house to outsiders, spent the day cleaning it from top to bottom, fasted, then gathered after the children were in bed to ingest psychedelics and stay up all night together, singing, drumming, talking, bonding. One or another of the children might join us for a while and absorb the elevated vibes.

I was pining for Johnny, living a monkish life and doing without sex, except for one time, ill-advisedly, with an otherwise forgotten friend at the bitter end of an extracurricular acid trip. We'd had a good time wandering around in Golden Gate Park, but the mood darkened as the afternoon wore on. Crossing a busy street coming out of the park, we saw a dog hit by a car, which was so cosmically depressing that we fell into bed when we got home to console ourselves. The result was herpes, which would plague me off and on for years.

There was indeed no room for Johnny in this situation, another dependent existence that would have made him feel trapped and desperate. I didn't see how we were going to get back together until Ellen Stewart brought him to the West Coast to play a bit part in the movie of *Futz*, Rochelle Owens's play about a man persecuted by his neighbors for loving a pig. I caught a ride to Los Angeles, met the La Mama actors' plane, and spent a few days with Johnny at the Montecito Hotel in Hollywood, where the company were waiting for Tom O'Horgan ro finish directing the L.A. production of *Hair*. Over a company dinner at a Polynesian restaurant, Ellen offered me a job stage-managing La Mama Troupe on tour in Europe in the spring, after the movie. Johnny would be going as the light man. I said I would do it.

BACK AT DIANE's, I continued soaking up Zen from Suzuki Roshi and set to work building myself a clavichord from one of Wolfgang Zuckermann's kits. I needed something to play; it would be small and very quiet. After a noisy blow-up with Diane, Alan had departed, and I moved into his big room at the front of the house. Sitting on my meditation pillow at a low table in the bay window overlooking the panhandle of Golden Gate Park, I laid out the parts, turning them in my hands, studied the instruction manual, and patiently made myself an instrument, careful in the rainy light, lonely but happy. I was writing another book, mapping our daily existence with oracles from the *I Ching*. The lives around me were tumultuous. I stayed calm, finished my clavichord, sat cross-legged on my cushion playing Bach.

My Zen practice climaxed with *sesshin*, an all-day round of sitting and walking meditation at the Zen Center. The next weekend a group of us drove to Tassajara, the Zen monastery in the mountains back of Big Sur, to hear Lama Govinda speak about Tibet. Oncoming flu made this trip hallucinatory and strangely ecstatic—the interminable twisty drive into the wilderness, arrival after dark, sleep in a bare, cold cabin, meditation before breakfast, Zen eating, more zazen, silence. I soaked in the deep tubs of hot spring water, steamed in the sauna, plunged for an instant into the icy stream.

Futz was finally shooting, near Stockton. When I was well again, I went there to visit Johnny, taking him a beautiful concho belt as a token of my love and esteem. La Mama Troupe were housed and fed in a comfortable motel and bused to the shooting location, which was remote, cheerless, and raw, the tempo excruciatingly slow for all but the key people. I watched them film Sally Kirkland riding naked on a gigantic pig.

Johnny came back to the city with me for the weekend to see the Living Theatre, which had returned from Europe for a tour of American universities. We spent a night at Diane's and went back to Berkeley the next day for lunch with Judith Malina, who was horrified by the violence around us. Students were fighting the police on Telegraph Avenue, hurling tear gas back and forth. The Living Theatre arrived with its vision of the beautiful nonviolent anarchist revolution, but the Berkeley hotheads didn't buy it. They wanted confrontation. So what if it cost some blood and property? Judith argued for peace. They refused to listen. She was simultaneously breaking up with her lover, Carl Einhorn, not a happy moment.

That night the Living Theatre faced an audience who wanted something else. At the start of *Mysteries and Smaller Pieces*, as actors sat cross-legged in meditation trying to levitate, someone in the audience lobbed a cherry bomb over their heads.

I heard about a house for rent dirt cheap near Marysville, north of Sacramento, and took Johnny up to look at it, a bare, airy house on a hilltop surrounded by olive groves, blissfully far from the anxious agitations of the city. I was greatly drawn to it. I imagined I could live by writing wherever we were. In fact I had no assignments and was rapidly running out of money, and the place held no attraction for Johnny.

I was stubbornly blind to the centrality of work and livelihood in his decisions. Insulated by prosperous parents in the background and a dubious sense of invincible entitlement, I had felt free to walk away from a perfectly good career as a theatre critic in New York. To me work was what you did to make sense of your life; for Johnny the issue was survival. He would not need money if he stuck with me, or so I imagined: I had chipped in when he was broke at times in the past. Now, though, I was not even supporting myself, and he was unwilling to be dependent on another of my protectors. I kept setting my love in competition with his work, making him choose. It was unkind and agonizing for us both.

Futz was in the can. My barely audible clavichord was playing, another unpublishable book draft was finished, and I was broke. Irving Rosenthal, a writer I admired, urged me to open a video center in San Francisco, an excellent idea, ahead of its time, but I felt no power to do anything there. Anyway, before long Ellen would be sending Johnny and me to Europe. After the tour ended we would go on to India to visit Deborah Lee and her husband Bob Lawlor at Auroville, an idealistic international community outside Pondicherry, then rejoin La Mama in Japan.

I embraced the Buddhist view, but that was enough Zen for now. I left my clavichord at Diane's, imagining I might come back.

26

THE RENT FOR THE APARTMENT at 5 Cornelia Street had risen to $87.50 a month, but life in the Village was still cheap. Johnny and I ate at Joe's Dinette for under $100 a week. I was glad we were back together though dismayed to be back in New York. I loved the human energy and the work I could do in the city, but I could hardly bear to live there between projects. Formative times in a Kansas farm town made me a country boy at heart. My hunger to be grounded would not go away.

The tour fell through. Johnny was busy with lighting jobs and took care of me too, setting me up to run his lights for a rock musical on Bleecker Street, *Earthlight*, which carried me for a couple of months. My book *Theatre Trip* came out, to a few positive reviews. Friendly introductions by Judith and Julian complained that I ignored the political content of the

Living Theatre's work, seeing only style and lifestyle. I believed that style is the power of art. My new anthology was published as well, but I was no longer writing for *The Village Voice*, no longer a critic.

Emanuel Peluso asked me to direct a Pinteresque play he had written about an amateur cellist and his wife, to be played by Lucy Silvay, and a mysterious black visitor. I had supported an Obie for Manny for an earlier play, and met Lucy at the Caffè Cino when she acted in Bob Heide's play *Moon*. Living together in Lucy's tiny apartment on Bethune Street in what was then the remote West Village, Manny and Lucy had become precious friends, their fantasy world of glittering acrylic and colorful scarves a refuge of warmth, good cheer, and good grass when Johnny was out of town or lost in his work.

Manny and I came up with his title, *Hurricane of the Eye*, in a taxi on the way to La Mama. I gave the play an immaculate production on an elegant Magrittean set painted by Jerry Joyner. Johnny and I invented a delicious conceptual lighting convention for this play that I called a "red-out," which

Rob Thirkield, Lucy Silvay, and Lamar Alford in *Hurricane of the Eye*

functioned exactly like a blackout, red light substituting for darkness before and between the scenes, bathing stage and audience alike.

JOHNNY DEPARTED for a gig at Tanglewood in Massachusetts lighting a music-theatre piece for Gunther Schuller. Trying to feel at home in the apartment without him, I decided to redecorate. It had always been too small for me, dark, airless, and constricting, once it stopped being infinite. I proposed that we move to Westbeth, a new artists' housing complex in the West Village, where we would have qualified for a sizable, subsidized live-work loft. It sounded ideal to me, but Johnny loved his apartment on Cornelia Street and never wanted to move. He said, "If you don't like it, change it." I took him at his word—threw away the tattered furniture in the living room, pulled up the worn-out carpets, sanded and varnished the floor, tore down the faded, fraying damask on the walls, and painted them white. The reed organ, never a satisfactory instrument, was long gone. The only thing I kept in the living room was the pretty glass chandelier and sconces Johnny had bought in Venice, paying for them with a forged check on my Chase account. I built low couches to fit below the mural of famous Indians Kenny Burgess had recently painted below the chair rail and made long, sheer white curtains to soften our view of the offices across the street.

Tanglewood kept coming up with more projects for Johnny, and he stayed away for weeks, sharing a dorm room with a trombonist, writing me funny letters about his adventures.

For want of other work, I gravitated back to *The Village Voice*, not writing for the paper but filling in for vacationing editors, first Diane Fisher, then Ross Wetzsteon, who shared my previous job. Ross's office looked out across Christopher Street onto the little triangular park at Sheridan Square. Against the railings opposite, pretty brown boy-girls posed and flirted with me through the open windows, showing me their fresh little breasts. The Stonewall bar was a few doors down the street, and gay liberation broke out right under my eyes. I edited the news story a young, straight reporter, Lucian Truscott III, wrote about the Stonewall riots, thoughtlessly letting

MICHAEL SMITH

him use a flippant phrase: "the forces of faggotry" (which would be widely quoted on the 50th anniversary of Stonewall in 2019). The newly empowered gays were outraged and picketed the office, marching, shouting, and waving angry signs outside our windows. It was scary. Dan and Ed held a meeting in their office with leaders of the demonstration and invited me to join in. The gay spokesperson complained that everybody at *The Voice* was straight, which was largely true. "I'm gay," I said. It may have been the first time I said it out loud, although my relationship with Johnny had always been out in the open. I apologized for the unfortunate phrase in the article, which I had thought was funny: faggots was what we affectionately called ourselves among ourselves. I hadn't realized it would be offensive.

27

JOHNNY'S PASSIONATE OUTRAGE on behalf of Native Americans led me to write my next long play, *Captain Jack's Revenge*, based on a famous episode in American history. In 1872-73 Kintpuash, a Modoc man known to his American friends in northern California as Captain Jack, led his people in the last of the Indian wars. Displaced from their land and driven to violence, fifty or so Modoc men and their families holed up in the rugged lava beds northeast of Mount Shasta and held off the U.S. Army for months. At the peace conference Jack pulled out a gun and killed the American general, Canby, for which he was tried and hanged. History was against them: they were doomed. This pitiful story seemed to embody an existential desperation I was feeling myself, equal parts political and personal. The Modoc War was well documented at the time; I found news reports, trial transcripts, and poignant photographs of the principals in the American history room at the 42nd Street Library. The Vietnam war was on everyone's mind, phony negotiations going on, and the story of Captain Jack seemed to me relevant in an appalling way. Looking at his picture, I felt an inexplicable affinity.

I had written two acts of *Captain Jack's Revenge* when Gregory Long, whom I knew as the boyfriend of Bob Pasolli, a *Voice* theatre critic, telephoned inviting me to go around the world on a two-month theatre study trip funded by the Rockefeller Foundation. Gregory had replaced the original traveler, who had bowed out for medical reasons. Now he had decided not to go. All the arrangements were in place: I would leave in ten days. I was sorry to leave Johnny, who was finally back, but I couldn't resist the opportunity.

I gave my play to the up-and-coming director Ellen Stewart had lined up to direct it at La Mama. Over lunch, he was excited about it, saying it was a "major" play, only it needed more work to realize its potential, the ending was not right. In fact it probably needed another act, which I already knew. I should not go around the world, he said, I should stay in New York and work on my play. No, I said, I would be back in two months, I would have the play finished by the middle of January, we could open at La Mama in March. I knew about deadlines—it was tight but doable.

INDIA WAS OVERWHELMING, not only the sights, sounds, smells, and scenes but also the quick, warm connections with people that kept happening, so different from New York, where everybody defended their boundaries. I traveled with a photographer, Charles Biasiny; I liked the way he stopped and smelled the flowers. We jumped around the country for an intense three weeks, flying or taking trains from one language and vibe to another every two or three days, guided to amazing events by local theatre enthusiasts, connected through the International Theatre Institute, frequently taken into their homes. We saw a one-man puppet show in an encampment of Rajasthani shepherds, a vast, spectacular *Ram-lila* across the Ganges from Varanasi, a Kathakali dance class before dawn in Kerala. Everywhere we met openness, generosity, and lively curiosity that melted my heart and refreshed my soul. By comparison with India, my own culture seemed poor in spirit, our interactions thin, dry, cold, our existence isolated and frustrating. I could only make it different by transforming my own life.

I took a day off to visit Deborah and Bob Lawlor in Auroville, on the southeast coast. Otherwise we worked relentlessly, witnessing one highly evolved theatre form after another, all of them incorporating live music.

I made tape-recordings and extensive notes as Charles took photographs. However we might feel about our own culture, we were inevitably its ambassadors, two tall Americans moving swiftly through dense fields of human energy, paying as needed to make things happen, recording sights and sounds for mysterious purposes of our own. Our presence changed the situation, which repeatedly turned festive, with ourselves as the guests of honor, garlands of flowers festooned around our necks. I was fascinated by all I witnessed, endless particularities like eddies in a rushing stream. After the first week I was scrambling to keep up, writing about what we had seen two or three stops back. Modern distortions everywhere racked the social fabric, tribes of puppeteers displaced by cinema and television, classic dance styles kept alive by anthropologists in academic festivals. It was heartbreaking to see the old societies losing their ancient riches.

We spent a second month hopping around Southeast Asia, giving Vietnam a wide miss. It was surreal and horrible to think of the war going on there. I loved Bali as much as India, but other places gave me the creeps. In Java we fell in with a "friend of the generals" who commissioned a weird field day on our behalf; one of the acts was rams charging each other and violently butting heads, musicians wailing along. In Taipei we saw Chinese opera elegantly performed with puppets, and the producers treated us to a feast of the best food I had ever tasted, with many whisky toasts to each other's well-being. By the time we reached Bangkok I was exhausted and lay beside the hotel pool reading Isadora Duncan.

Only years later did I learn that Johnny had turned down a tour with Alvin Ailey that fall to stay in New York with me.

Home again, I pushed through with a third act for *Captain Jack's Revenge*, my mind having worked it out in flashes and secret mullings, then found myself at odds with the director. He liked the psychological, tormented-couple part of my play and wanted to delete the historical, documentary play-within-the-play—virtually the whole second act. My central idea sprang from conflating Captain Jack with my own suprapersonal, quasimarital angst. I was trying to say something about the existential tension between singularity and relationship and intuited parallels between the Modocs' situation trapped in the lava beds and the Vietnam trap facing young American men. The connection was far-fetched, but the poetic of the play depended on it. Having allowed Jacques Levy to restructure *The Next Thing*, this time I wanted to realize the play I had imagined. So I let him quit and set about directing it myself.

In March 1970, as I was starting rehearsals, Johnny departed on a tour of colleges in the Middle West with Tom O'Horgan's New Troupe, leaving me running his lights at La Mama for *Cock-Strong, Son of Cock-Strong*, and *Heaven Grand in Amber Orbit*, three glitzy, campy, demented plays performed in repertory by John Vacarro's Play-house of the Ridiculous. I relished abetting John's wigged-out sense of camp and beauty and the strange sexy brilliance of his trashy art.

CAPTAIN JACK.

I certify that L. HELLER has this day taken the Photographs of the above Modoc Indian, prisoner under my charge.
Capt. C. B. THROCKMORTON, 4th U. S. Artillery, Officer of the Day.
I am cognizant of the above fact.   GEN. JEFF. C. DAVIS, U. S. A.

Directing a play at La Mama or the Caffè Cino meant doing everything needed to get it on. Far from producing, Ellen had not even read my play; much as I appreciated the freedom, I could have used some help. I cast Lucy Silvay and Ondine as Mary and Jack, the hip New York couple who morph into California Indians from a century earlier; John Vaccaro played a deluded preacher. Their acting was far from naturalistic. I was pursuing something other than the illusion of reality, more real than real, closer to dream, where feelings are recognizable, but heightened, obscure, even arbitrary associations tug the dreamer below the surfaces of life. Reality was not the point: the play concluded with Captain Jack being shot from behind the audience as he ascended the scaffold to be hanged, a theatrical moment so ambiguous that even I could not parse it. That weird feeling was Captain Jack's revenge.

I designed a stripped loft apartment with practical hanging lights, Mary sitting on the floor cutting out pictures from magazines amid a barrage of media: television, telephone, ringing doorbell, slide projections, home movies, sirens outside. Jack comes home from work, puts on a Beatles song ("While My Guitar Gently Weeps"), and they listen to it all the way through. Their younger friend William (named for one of the Modocs) is hiding out with them, on his way to Canada to evade the draft. The second act flashes back to northern California in 1873 where there is no light but fire, no technology but guns. Mary's father, an Army general, becomes Canby in the historical reenactment.

Captain Jack's Revenge was a *succès d'estime* at La Mama. Bill Hoffman, a fellow playwright and editor, called it "the first seventies play" and claimed it for his next anthology. Lucy, Ondine, and John were brilliant, to my mind, but Ellen had persuaded me to cast an unsuitable protégé of hers as the hippie boy. I thought I should recast that role, move the show to an off-Broadway theatre, and start having a real career—for which I needed a producer. It didn't occur to me produce it myself, and I wouldn't have known where to begin. My old friend Helen Merrill, now a high-flying agent for playwrights and directors, came to a performance and did not much care for my play, still angry, more interested in new, younger talents.

I somehow could not imagine myself successful. After years of immersion in the do-it-yourself bohemian counter-culture, I had internalized a self-defeatingly anti-professional stance, ostensibly preferring a clumsy, homemade quality to the skill and polish I could not afford, too alienated to think clearly and exploit my talent and intelligence. My whole persona was staked on rejection of the mainstream values that had given us racism, capitalist exploitation, nuclear stalemate, Vietnam, the Nixon government, and Kissinger's realpolitik, not to mention slick commercial entertainment. The "system" made me sick. I didn't want to be part of it—even as I suspected that attitude of being a cop-out, born of fear of testing myself in the greater world.

I had no idea whether my play really worked and no one to talk frankly to me about it. I was supposedly the expert. People thought I was self-sufficient, but no one is. Undoubtedly it could have been improved: rewriting always helps. Directing it myself deprived me of the objectivity and imagination of another eye and mind. I loved directing, but it was incredibly hard work and did nothing for my life. I did not even want to be in New York without Johnny. *Captain Jack* played out its run and that was it.

One consolation in this lonely time was a curly-haired boy named John Albano, a senior at Dalton, who acted in the Play-house of the Ridiculous shows and hung around La Mama during *Captain Jack*. I was delighted to have a groupie, a fan, a charming boyfriend. John led me on long walks through the city streets, his native habitat, pausing on stoops to rest and talk; his fresh enthusiasm cheered me no end. A few times he came home with me and cheerfully, affectionately fucked. Then Johnny came back and that had to stop.

28

IN MAY JOHNNY DEPARTED for the New Troupe's long-bruited European tour, which no longer had a place for me. Sick of New York, I took myself to England to stay with Wolfgang Zuckermann and his wife Lynn, dropping off a script of *Captain Jack's Revenge* at the stage door of the Royal Court Theatre as I passed through London. Parts of Stafford Barton, the forty-room North Devon manor house Wolfgang had bought, dated back to the fourteenth century. A wide lawn shaded by ancient trees led to pastures and moorland beyond. There was a decrepit tennis lawn, a once-famous stand of overgrown rhododendrons lining the long drive, a village at the bottom of the hill. Wolfgang practiced a medieval austerity; Lynn fancied herself pre-

Stafford Barton, Wolfgang Zuckermann's house in North Devon

Norman. I enjoyed living simply with them in this glorious setting, milking the goats, eating homegrown spinach and local bread and cheese.

May and June were high summer in England; dusk lingered for hours. Wolfgang kept busy, trotting through the house with boards, while Lynn floated around in velvet. I compiled a book of dreams, writing down my dreams first thing in the morning, sliding back to sleep to dream some more, napping after lunch to dream and write, waking from dreams in the night in my cell and snapping on the light to faithfully transcribe them. It was peaceful and calming. I dreamed of partings and departures.

In his workshop Wolfgang was making parts for a new Italian-style harpsichord kit. Trying out the prototype I stumbled upon a famous piece by François Couperin, "Les Baricades Mystérieuses," that made me want a harpsichord of my own. I played it over and over. Fernando Valenti came for a visit. Ed Brewer, director of music at Judson Church, arrived from Germany with the latest instrument made by Martin Skowroneck, reputedly the best harpsichord maker in the world, and gave a recital in the dining

Wolfgang's Italian harpsichord

hall with its ornate plaster ceiling for an audience from the local arts center.

I could have stayed at Stafford Barton indefinitely, writing, dreaming, living plainly, consuming almost no resources. There was plenty of room, and I felt at ease with Wolfgang and Lynn. But I did not want to give up on love and be alone; and really, nothing was happening. When the New Troupe finished its tour, I followed Johnny back to New York.

I WANTED TO BE WITH JOHNNY. I loved him as much as ever and felt indissolubly linked. But the city was horrible. With nothing to do, I hated being there. It was midsummer: I wanted to be in the country. So I went up to Charlemont to join the little community evolving out of Jean-Claude's house parties. He had produced three of his one-act plays off-Broadway under the title *America Hurrah*, which made him famous, and made enough money to buy the farm from his father. Joe Chaikin was there, and Sarah Marx, my old friends, with Stefan, now ten, friendly and self-contained, and Fred Katz. Other people I had known for years came and went. Joe and Sarah loved to cook. There would be ten or a dozen of us around the dinner table in a lovely atmosphere of mellow fellowship. We had endless discussions about how Jean-Claude should remodel his kitchen, though I liked it fine the way it was. He made me feel welcome. I bought myself an aging VW of a pleasing faded blue and settled down to stay a while.

Tania had come back from England to set up an American center for Chogyam Trungpa Rinpoche, whose followers had bought a farm in Vermont and named it Tail of the Tiger. Head lama of a major Tibetan monastery in his teens, Trungpa had fled when the Chinese invaded, studied at Oxford, taught in Scotland, and was now bringing Tibetan Buddhism to America. I went up with Jean-Claude to hear him speak. He had an extraordinary warmth and brightness, his presence unaccountably uplifting, and what he said made perfect sense, tantra another illuminating Buddhist vision of truth and liberation.

Idle, stretching out my latest book advance, writing desultorily, spending almost nothing thanks to Jean-Claude's generosity, I urged Johnny to join me—it was heavenly in the Berkshires. He had to work. Touring all spring, he had lost the momentum of doing one show after another, which was the only way he could make a living as a lighting designer, and the only way to get lighting gigs in the city was to be there. I wanted to be with him, but if I went back I would have to plug in again to a consuming energy that seemed to me destructive and evil.

Jean-Claude reflected that we are all alone, but I didn't accept that idea. I thought the loneliness of an empty bed too high a price to pay for the bliss of solitude and having my own way. Love is all-important; if you are lucky enough to have it you should make the most of it. Johnny felt the same. Yet we were apart.

29

PLANNING TO MAKE CHARLEMONT his principal residence and wanting friends around him, Jean-Claude proposed to Fred and Sarah and to me that we build ourselves houses on his land. We could choose sites anywhere on his several hundred acres that did not intrude on the sweep of meadows around his house and barn. After much pleasurable wandering through the dense, varied forest up the hill in back of his house, I zeroed in on a rock outcropping low on the flank of the mountain, well out of sight of the meadow. I could build on the solid rock, and my house would float in the second story of the forest. Jean-Claude said I could have the site for my lifetime but not pass it on—meaning to Johnny, presumably, as one had no thought of children. I did not care about or believe in ownership of land.

The forest felt weirdly empty, wanting the presence of a consciousness. I would make no mark except to let in more sunlight, open it up a little with the tenderest regard for each tree. I would build beautifully and lightly, create an ideal setting for the Buddhist life I wanted to live.

I had $1,500 to spend on a house, my father having cashed in a life insurance policy. Mary Lucas, visiting from the West Coast, suggested that her brother John, who had recently graduated from architecture school and built himself a cabin in Vermont, could help me design and start building my own. We found him at a lake in New Hampshire where he was spending Labor Day weekend with friends. A week later he arrived in his Buick, sleeping by choice in the hayloft in Jean-Claude's huge old barn. We set right to work, spending our days up at the site, clearing brush and studying the space and changing light, our evenings at John's drafting board in the workroom off Jean-Claude's kitchen as he drew what we talked about. A plan emerged for a house fanning out over the rock, big enough to hold a grand piano and a harpsichord, with a kitchen in the center, a writing studio above, a cantilevered sleeping nook, a Japanese alcove for washing. Norman Hicks, a friendly neighbor, would cut wood to order and haul it up to the site on a trailer behind his tractor. The overgrown lumber road was too rough for a car.

We started by building a woodshed to have a place to keep our tools. I was already reasonably handy, and John taught me a few carpentry tricks. I liked the rough, practical directness of this kind of work, so different from the elusive, ambiguous tasks of writing, directing, editing, what I did in the city. I loved being out in the woods all day. We had no electricity at the site and made every cut by hand.

My parents came east to visit Virginia, who lived over the mountains in Pownal, Vermont, and one day they hiked up the hill to see what John and I were up to. We were attempting to erect the frame of the woodshed that day and ridiculously inept, with nothing to lean the ladder on as I tried to nail the crossbeam to the posts standing on rocks. It was unpleasantly hot and buggy, too. They were not impressed.

By late November the woodshed was up and roofed, and we had finished the footings and deck for the central section of the house. It was getting too cold for comfort, darkness coming down early, flurries of snow hinting pointedly at winter. We stacked lumber on the deck, wrapped it in plastic, stowed our tools in the shed, and quit for the season. John departed for a paying job in Vermont.

I stayed on with Jean-Claude. He was busy writing, and I was trying

On Jean-Claude's porch

to make something of the book of dreams I had started in England. I had no regular income. The only way to get myself out of the hole I was in, I thought, was to write, but this book hardly seemed saleable. Dreams are not interesting to other people. Johnny and I were still "together": he came up to visit me, I went down to visit him. But I liked being in the country too much to go back. I envisioned myself living at Charlemont, going to the city only now and then, and traveling to do theatrical projects.

Johnny came up for Christmas. There were nineteen people in the house, all except the two of us Jewish, and suddenly that year it mattered: embracing one's Jewishness was the new coming out. A group of us walked down the snowy road to cut a Christmas tree, as we had done five years before. Jean-Claude, whose mother was Jewish, suddenly balked at celebrating the Christian holiday. Christmas trees are not Christian, I reminded him, they are Druid. I regarded myself as more Buddhist than Christian, but that was no reason not to celebrate Christmas. I cut a beautiful little spruce; Jean-Claude chose a bare deciduous sapling, like the tree in *Waiting for Godot*. We dragged them back and set them up side by side in the living room, mine decorated as prettily as I could manage, his its satiric shadow.

Jean-Claude was going to California for the month of January but said I was welcome to stay on in his house. I begged Johnny to stay with me. I wept. He went back to the city to work, suggesting we take a break for a few years.

Then I was alone. The snow was deep, the weather turning seriously cold. I loved the emptiness and quiet, the slowness of time, the blue of twilight, the stillness of the deer in the meadow. But I was too conscious of the elements trying to kill me, the new oil furnace laboring to keep me warm. And I was bored. I did not have the courage for long solitude, and I too needed to work. So I went back to New York.

30

JOE'S DINETTE HAD CLOSED. I preferred home cooking anyway now and set about building us a kitchen in the first room, ripping out Michael Wiley's loft, he being long gone to an apartment of his own, nailing down masonite over the battered, gappy floorboards, building plywood cupboards and counters along the wall. A plumber friend bridged the gas meter so we could have a stove; this was discovered the next time the meter man came around, and some outrageous deposit was demanded to turn on the gas. We could use propane. We already had a small refrigerator in the closet.

Meanwhile I was having a tiny flurry of success as a playwright. To my delighted amazement, the Royal Court Theatre in London picked up on *Captain Jack's Revenge* and produced it in their upstairs theatre. I didn't get to be there but conferred with the very simpatico director, Nicholas Wright, by telephone, and it got good reviews. It was also produced at the State University of New York at Oneonta; I went up to see it and talk to the kids. An opera version of *A Dog's Love*, an earlier play, was scheduled to open in May at La Mama.

Johnny designed the lighting for *Deafman Glance*, one of the great early works of Robert Wilson, in the opera house at the Brooklyn Academy of Music, a spectacle on a huge scale and a challenge in every way. I went along to a technical rehearsal, sat in the balcony looking down on him, and watched him being bullied by the stage manager all day as they worked on the cues. It drove me crazy. Tech rehearsals are excruciating unless you are part of the process.

I restrained myself until we were homeward bound on the subway, then said something like, "Why do you let this strong woman push you around?"

Johnny thought of explaining that it was the best way to get things done, but what he really thought was, "Why are you spoiling this for me? Why are you spoiling my little triumph?"

I had not actually spoiled it. Edith Oliver in *The New Yorker* called Johnny's work on *Deafman Glance* "the subtlest lighting I have ever seen." What he minded was that I *could* spoil it, and would. The tension between his work and my desire to get away from it all had been building for a very long time.

Johnny made up his mind then and there, he told me years later, that he had to stop sleeping with me and get away from me. "Love doesn't die," he said, "it has to be killed."

The atmosphere at home became extremely strange. Johnny turned me off, without rancor or sharpness but also without appeal. He did not throw me out. We did not argue or fight. He hardly spoke and stopped coming to bed with me and snuggling, much less making love. He brought home Bill Elliott, a young composer, and fucked him on the sofa in the living room. I did not take Bill seriously as a rival, figuring this was an ordeal I had to survive in order to win Johnny back. I could not believe he was actually rejecting me.

Then Johnny and Bill tore down the wall between the kitchen and the middle room, where I had my study under the loft bed. Johnny stopped talking or responding to me, and Bill was openly hostile. I sat cross-legged on the shiny new floor of the kitchen patiently sanding the cabinets I had built while Bill helped Johnny lug box after box of broken lath and rubble down to the street, destroying the home I was trying to improve. The ceiling sagged. I was afraid my bed would fall down. I had no quiet and privacy to write. It was untenable. When the dust settled, I gave the new kitchen shelves and counters three coats of varnish and moved out.

Sally Kempton, a writer I knew from *The Voice*, was going out of town and needed someone to feed her gerbils. Her apartment on West 11th Street was more to my taste: big rooms with polished parquet floors and sunny bay windows on a pretty tree-lined street, houseplants, a proper kitchen, bedrooms, a bath. I was sick of the cramped tub, pissy sink, smelly hall toilet, and general meanness of Johnny's disintegrating tenement pad.

THIS WAS AN IRONIC MOMENT to be doing *A Dog's Love*, a bittersweet fable about my original feelings for my wild young lover, written in the early summer of our affair. In Miami Beach, an opera producer and his wife both have sex with a beach boy, then reconcile and leave the boy alone with a wheelbarrowload of money. As a one-act play it was too insubstantial to be quite worth staging, the parable ambiguous, the subtext patronizing. It had occurred to me that the ecstasy I envisioned might be better realized by turning *A Dog's Love* into an opera. I had given the script to Al Carmines, who passed it on to John Herbert McDowell, who embraced the project, to my amazed delight.

John Herbert was one of the originals of the downtown scene, friend and collaborator of people I admired, composer of music for any number of far-out plays and dances at Judson Church, host of fun parties at his 14th Street loft. I had done the lighting at Judson for a notorious three-minute dance John Herbert choreographed for a hundred performers, who appeared in phalanxes all over the church marching and waving banners to the Righteous Brothers' "Unchained Melody."

Basing his harmony on seconds and fourths rather than thirds and fifths and using instruments in unconventional ways, John Herbert made *A Dog's Love*

Author at the harpsichord

Diane McAfee and Eddie Barton in *A Dog's Love*

into a delicious little chamber opera, with three singers accompanied by oboe, cello, and harpsichord. His score was gorgeous, with several grandly operatic little climaxes. It was a trip to hear my language set to music and sung, and I gladly wrote more words where the music needed them. In the final stages of composition, John Herbert indulged himself outrageously, wandering around his loft naked from the waist down, drinking whisky, chain-smoking cigarettes and coughing horribly. Trying to get the dear man to sit down and compose the final scene was agony. We had to postpone the opening for a week.

I played the harpsichord in the little pit band, happy to be playing the music although my world had fallen apart. John Herbert prevailed on me to let him direct, which allowed him to have his beloved, Eddie Barton, strip naked as the beach boy, displaying his taut body and large, hose-like cock in an extended gymnastic routine. My parents came and doubtless saw this as a provocation; in truth, much as I like male nudity, I was against it here, feeling it violated the delicate cartoon realism. Operas have set pieces: I didn't begrudge John Herbert his pleasure.

I had written *A Dog's Love* as a gift to Johnny, punctuating the action with sunrises and sunsets as a pretext for flamboyant lighting effects. He arranged for Beverly Emmons to design the lights, and she did a first-rate job.

31

THE SIXTIES WERE OVER, and I had lost my great love, after struggling for years to keep us together. To my mind love is the heart of a full and fulfilling life, but I had unrealistic expectations. Part of the problem was our being two men, both Alpha. Johnny was the more unyielding, but I had a demon in me too and eventually always did what I wanted. I could not be contented with our life together, and my thrashings were a terrible distraction. We both wanted to get on with our lives and work, both interfered with the other's ability to function. I kept trying to pull him away from New York, tormenting him with my unhappiness.

There was some sexual issue too, something I wanted from him that I couldn't get, although I didn't know what it was. I was less crazy now that I had stopped taking speed, less obsessed, but sex was still much on my mind.

Johnny and I had been together for almost nine years; it would take that long to get over him, if I ever did. But it was a relief to be done with the protracted agony of splitting up. I felt emotionally emptied out, with no place to live and no reason to stay in New York anymore. I seemed to be starting from zero.

Still half-heartedly trying to be gay, I stuck around until after the Obies in late May, although I had nothing to do with them anymore. This year the entertainment would include Lucy Silvay performing my sardonic monologue *Tony*, which she had done brilliantly, I thought, on the double

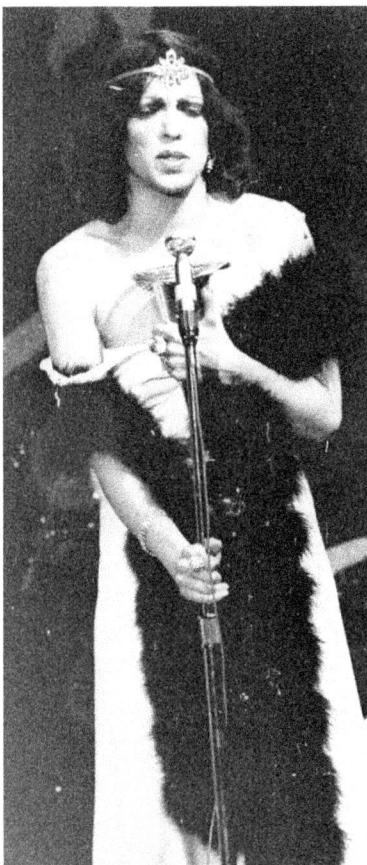
Lucy Silvay in *Tony*

bill with *A Dog's Love* at La Mama. On the morning of the Obies, Mary Lucas and her new husband Lee Myers blew in from the West Coast with a shopping bag full of Acapulco gold, the strongest marijuana I had yet encountered. Naturally I invited Manny and Lucy over to Sally's for a taste. The result was that Lucy got so stoned she had to be dragged off the stage in the middle of my play. Or perhaps the black comedy was truly offensive. *Tony* is a satirical acceptance speech in which the actor tells a weird story about his (in this case her) sexual passion for a woman with one leg. I was through with being a critic and sour about the whole business of awards, making a joke of them in appallingly bad taste. That was how burned-out I felt about the theatre scene. I was not present for this fiasco. I couldn't face my peers. I would only bring them down.

The gerbils died. Sally came home, it was summer, and I went up to Charlemont, where people I knew and liked were coming and going in Jean-Claude's numerous bedrooms, which he had decorated with gingham curtains, antique lamps, and beautiful quilts. He gave me the new back room, paneled in weathered barn siding, with windows looking down the meadow toward the road up to my unbuilt house.

His other guests were vacationing, but I had nothing to vacation from. Needing to take some kind of action, I applied for a Guggenheim fellowship and wrote letters to the Rockefeller Foundation and similar long shots. There was some pressure to produce articles or a book about my journey through

Asia. I tried to imagine another book like *Theatre Trip*. But the experience had lacked a personal dimension; there was no inner story I wanted to tell, and I thought it would be presumptuous to write about theatre forms I had barely glimpsed and knew nothing about. I turned over my field recordings to accompany an exhibition of Charles Biasiny's photographs at the Lincoln Center Library and left it at that.

I needed to write, but what? I didn't want to be depressing, even if I was depressed.

I USED TO WANT TO THINK. Now all I want to do is love," said Dick Giannone, a new friend of Jean-Claude's. I lay naked in the sunlight on the lawn stringing pale blue beads so tiny they were almost invisible. Joe was cooking. Other people, tripping, romped and laughed in the meadows. I felt the same way as Dick, but what was I supposed to do about it? I got a sunburn on my hip from lying there so long.

Dick, a Fordham professor and Willa Cather expert, was a fellow member of a gay consciousness-raising group Jean-Claude and I had independently joined the previous winter, having seen the notice on the bulletin board at the gay firehouse in the Village. Half a dozen of us had been meeting regularly all spring in the city to talk about our gayness. They had come to Charlemont for a country meeting and joint acid trip.

The struggle to define a gay identity made less and less sense to me. I liked being homosexual well enough, but having lost Johnny, I was not sure I wanted to start something with another man. He was my man. Anyway, I was not entirely gay, not the way the other guys were. I had affection to give and a great desire for intimacy with somebody I could love, and I was starting to think I wanted it to be a woman. My eyes kept being drawn to sexy guys, and I was turned on by images of male arousal—still am—but truth to tell, I was more sexually comfortable with a woman. I resisted the word bisexual, thinking it was normal to be open to anybody, only slowly realizing this is not true for everyone. I evidently had a choice, and there was much to recommend the female. It was funny to join a gay group and

MICHAEL SMITH

discover I was not gay. These people were not going to understand my situation. I didn't belong in their group.

My best hope for clarity and inspiration was to stop swirling in Jean-Claude's vortex, spend more time alone, and write every day. I was too broke to go on with my house-building project just now. So I fixed up my woodshed, building a high work counter across one end, under the big window, and a wide sleeping platform, bought a foam mattress, mosquito netting, and a Coleman stove, and moved up the hill. The shed made a fine retreat cabin in warm weather. Jean-Claude had given me a sliding door he no longer needed. I could write at the counter next to the open door or sitting naked in the sunlight on my porch, vibrating in the solitude of woods that seemed to be my own. I had no electricity or running water; I carried jugs of water up the hill and lit candles after dark. I made myself coffee and simple food and relished the natural flow of unclocked time.

U<small>NCLE</small> A<small>L</small> <small>WROTE FROM</small> D<small>ENVER</small> offering me $300 to come do a play at the Changing Scene. I wrote a transformation play about a family whose son has been killed in Vietnam and called it, punningly, *Peas*. Jean-Claude gave me a one-act to go with it. I envisioned staying in Denver for months, directing a whole season of plays. I brought along the score of *A Dog's Love*, I wanted to stage a production of Bill Hoffman's beautiful play *XXXXX*, which I had seen at La Mama, and I had several fanciful scripts by Harry Koutoukas. Years of writing of my own were gestating in my head.

Maybe I would find a lover in Denver. Maybe a woman. The women I knew in New York were too strong, moving too fast, too caught up in their own affairs to have attention for me, too plugged in to the city.

As I was preparing to head west in my VW, Alan Marlowe, back from India, appeared at Jean-Claude's house looking for a ride to Boulder. He had seen Johnny, who didn't want to see me, so we skipped New York. It was pleasant to travel with Alan, his ordinarily hyper energy mellowed by months of meditation at a monastery in the Himalayas. He cooked brown rice and veggies and we slept on the ground by the side of the road, whizzing up into the Rockies to hear Chogyam Trungpa talk. I left Alan there and presented myself at the Changing Scene.

32

AL AND MAXINE HAD ORGANIZED A PICNIC in the mountains for the cast of Al's latest show, a multimedia dance-poetry piece I had seen the night I arrived, which included lyrical film of Al's young troupe dancing naked in a mountain meadow. I felt like a different person in the West, breathing in new possibilities with the chi-charged air. After lunch I headed off by myself for a walk, and a pretty girl named Michele Hawley came running after me. In the finale of the performance the night before, when the cast invited members of the audience up on stage to dance, she had chosen me. We found our way to a precipitous canyon view, scarcely talking, sat on a rock, watched a hawk circling below us. Walking back she held my hand.

Michele offered me a ride back to the city in her truck and let me drive it. After dropping off a load of picnic equipment at the theatre, we stood in the bright mercury vapor street light on Champa Street leaning against my Volkswagen's round fender kissing and pressing our bodies together. I felt alive for the first time in months. We were both turned on and wanted to make love, but she was having her period; we would have to wait a few days.

Young and innocent though she seemed, Michele had been out in the world on hippie adventures for a couple of years before moving back into her parents' house. Her mother, three sisters, and two teenage brothers were all involved with the Changing Scene, taking dance classes with Al and Maxine and appearing in plays. Al had recruited her sister Tina to play the flute in *Peas*. Her father, a prosperous pathologist and a Catholic convert, had strict house rules: Michele at twenty-four was not allowed to stay out all night. That didn't stop us. She started coming over to my rented room at dawn, exuberantly sexy and accepting like one of the women waiting for Muslim men in Paradise. I had forgotten the luxurious, natural pleasure of making love with a woman. Sex with another man always seemed to be a

MICHAEL SMITH

Michele

problem. Two dicks don't fit together very well, and anal fucking invited pain and the body's resistance. Penetration felt good to Michele, it went in easily, all pleasure, and she he was all for it. There was nothing to think about. I could let myself go, follow the instinctual urge. It was utterly wonderful. Sleeping with a woman I felt reborn as a capable man.

Peas IS A PARABLE about a "typical" American family in a time of ambiguous war, when everyone is freaking out and emotions can only be expressed obliquely. The mother and daughter shell peas, the father talks to his pickup truck (which dryly replies), and the soldier son comes home in a coffin, his spirit rising from it as a wisp of smoke. Russ Stevenson, an artist friend of Al's, built the witty front half of a truck coming through the side wall of the theatre onto the stage. The acting was stylized and suggestively unnatural, lending *Peas* a dreamy, mournful, ceremonial quality, with flute and guitar music accompanying it from the side of the stage, as in India.

Jean-Claude's short play *Eat Cake*, which I directed on the same program, depicted a lonely housewife manipulated into grossly stuffing herself with cake in a big, messy orgy of eating, cake all over the floor: an image of rape, which was not really to my taste but worked.

Directing plays and making love with Michele cheered me up no end! I imagined myself settling down in Denver, renting a house with Michele and Tina, who also wanted to get away from her parents, and doing more plays at the Changing Scene. Audiences were sparse, though; there was no way the theatre could support me. Al found a little more money from the Colorado Council and asked me to stay a little longer, do another play, and look after the theatre while he and Max took a vacation. After that I would think of something else.

Pat Madsen and Melanie Kern in *Peas*

One night Michele and I went to see Nicholas Roeg's film *Performance*. I came out feeling jazzed up, seduced by the movie, a sophisticated connoisseur of decadence. Michele thought it was ugly, and suddenly a chasm opened up between us. Our boy-girl romance had been thrilling, a revelation, but how could I be myself with someone who would not acknowledge a more complex, ambiguous level of being? I was trapping myself in a straight, limited, provincial, middle-class, totally alien scene. Michele had no resistance against this kind of thinking, which only confirmed her self-doubts; but she could not give up her revulsion for this sick movie.

The next day I was supposed to make a deposit on a house, but I no longer had the necessary confidence. Michele withdrew to the mountains, and we found ourselves sadly estranged.

By then I had begun rehearsals for *XXXXX*. The title was a problem. The Changing Scene was upstairs from one of the first X-rated movie theatres in Denver (you could hear gasps and moans coming up through the floor in quiet moments), and *XXXXX* inevitably suggested more of the same. The play in fact opened with a naked man having a conversation with his penis. Far from salacious, though, it was actually a poetic riff on the birth of Jesus. I presented it under the title *Jesus Play*.

As usual I made some groovy new friends in Denver, adding them in with actors from *Peas*. The Changing Scene was designed to be flexible; they helped me rearrange the risers and seats to create a wide, shallow stage with the audience along one long side. Al and Max were away, and I had the place to myself. I rehearsed blond, long-haired Burt Kruse in his nude monologue in front of the dance studio

Dennis Stull (above) and Burt Kruse in *Jesus Play*

mirrors, just the two of us, and was proud of myself for keeping hands off, lovely as he was. By the week before we opened, I remembered what fun it is to have a theatre.

Returning in time for opening night, Al and Max admired my work, and I was pleased with it myself. The ideas were provocative, the colors and people glowing. I did everything the author asked for: specified iterations of the chorale from Bach's St. Matthew Passion and Buffy Sainte-Marie singing "Before It's Time for You to Go." The result was a gorgeous, abstract, Expressionist theatre of sound, sight, and movement, taking the audience into its spell and drawing them through its mysterious ritual.

Hearing that we had a naked man on stage, two cops from the vice squad showed up. Al stalled them in the lobby until Burt had his pants back on.

Michele stage-managed for me, but our love affair had not recovered, and with Al and Max back, the theatre was not mine after all. I was reduced to what would fit into my Volkswagen.

A letter from John Albano reminded me that I still had some fragments of a life in New York. I would go on to Santa Barbara for my thirty-sixth birthday, visit my parents, spend a few days in San Francisco, then see. I left *Jesus Play* running and said I'd come back soon.

33

BOB AMUSSEN, MY PUBLISHER and a member of the vestry at St. Mark's Church, had been serving as president of the Theatre Genesis board, otherwise all playwrights. A few months earlier, Bob had come to see me in the light booth at La Mama, told me he was dropping out, moving to Seattle, and asked me to takes his place. I had worked with Steve Facey, the church administrator, to put together a grant proposal to the National Endowment for the Arts but didn't really believe it would happen and had almost forgotten it by now.

Arriving in Santa Barbara, I found a letter from Murray Mednick, a leading playwright at Theatre Genesis and fellow board member, telling me the season was funded and I could have the second production. That got my attention. I immediately set to work writing a play about a crotchety, dreamy old man who lives alone in a New England farmhouse much like Jean-Claude's, naming him Boppo in honor of my grandfather, although he was nothing like him. Two city couples, one gay, one straight with a young daughter, come for a visit and stay through the winter, the serenity roiled by something savage beneath the surface. I tentatively called it *Carnage*.

After two weeks with my parents, I had an act written and headed out. In San Francisco. Mary and Lee had moved to a loft upstairs from the North Beach theatre where the Cockettes, a gay theatrical troupe, had been doing wildly popular midnight drag shows. George Harris III, calling himself Hibiscus, was one of the leading lights. He wanted to keep the shows free, others wanted to cash in on their popularity, and the dispute was tearing the company apart. I had barely missed the chance to see them. On a date with Hibiscus I watched him hold court in a gay bar on Market Street, looking and acting quite a bit like Mae West. I was not gay enough to be amused, but afterwards he was a boy again, and we went back to his attic and made love.

With Mary Lucas, her ex-husband J. P. Jones and his new wife, and Lee Myers in their North Beach loft

Snorts of cocaine improved the following day. I worked on my second act in the morning. Cocaine made me take my clothes off; in a smiling picture with Mary and her former and present husbands, I am the one who is naked. That afternoon I saw my first gay sex film, *Seven in a Barn*. The sex looked too much like working to make each other come, but seeing the guys visibly turned on turned me on, which always feels good. I saw no good reason to resist my weakness for pornography, increadingly available and ever easier to indulge.

Mary and Lee fixed me up with a companion for the drive east, a cute Puerto Rican boy named Peter who had recently joined the *Nam myoho ringe kyo* religion: chant *Nam myoho ringe kyo* enough and you can have whatever you want. I went to his initiation. We stopped for an afternoon in Denver, where I enjoyed a blast of love from Al and Max and my *Jesus Play* friends and an hour of friendly, tender kisses and hugs in the green room with Michele, which blew my mind.

I imagined doing sex with Peter in motel rooms all the way across the continent; it never happened. After Chicago we drove straight through. A hitchhiker advised me: "Don't stay too long in New York City, it will drive you crazy, just do your play and split." In western New Jersey it was a beautiful morning. As we neared the city, a dusky murk appeared behind the Palisades. By the time we reached the George Washington Bridge the sun was gone, Manhattan submerged in a blob of dirty air. Midtown poked up into it darkly; Wall Street and the World Trade Center were completely obscured. The city looked deadly, frightening, hellish. My instinct was to drop Peter off at the bus depot and turn north, cut and run to Charlemont, where the air was clear. I couldn't do it. I had come too far. There was no such easy way out.

WITH NO LODGINGS OF MY OWN in the city, I was taken in by my brother Lewis, who was working for the Book of the Month Club, living between wives in bachelor splendor in an Upper East Side high-rise. He was friendly and welcoming, though having me on his living room sofa living out of a suitcase was hardly ideal for either of us.

My new magic-realist play was suddenly finished. The younger gay guy transforms himself into a beautiful woman before our eyes and with his lover plays a scene from *The Cherry Orchard*. The first act, in late autumn, fades into a long winter night; the second act is morning in spring, and everyone is much older as they leave to go back to the city. The little girl has turned into a baby bear, then a big bear, finally emerging from the fur as a fairytale prince who stays on in the country with the gaily dreaming grandfather. I retitled it *Country Music* and set to work producing it at Theatre Genesis.

I was aching for love, painfully conscious of my lack of an actual life. My morale was saved when I came home after a grueling day to find on my pillow another letter from John Albano that had followed me from Denver. I got in touch and asked him to play the bear-prince: poor John had to lie there sweating in a bear costume for most of the second act, then step out of it for about a minute at the very end, radiant, and deliver the final speech. He was a loving boy, and occasionally sleeping with him made me feel much better. In New York I was apparently still gay.

I directed *Country Music*, designing and hanging the lights myself when Johnny declined. Light is a key structural element

Nevele Adams and Charles Stanley in *Country Music* at Theatre Genesis

in modern theatre—part of the direction, to my mind—and I lit all the plays I directed after this. Scott Burton stage-managed. Scott, who was starting to make installation and performance art of his own, understood the importance of getting all the details right, but he was critical of my

bastard style. I wanted to blend realism and formalism, pictorial literalism and musical patterning, using character and emotion to draw the audience in, refined form to reward them aesthetically. I wanted to make something as beautiful as Robert Wilson's spectacles with narrative too.

I was doing my best work so far, but directing was lonely, obsessive, inevitably an ego trip; that it was my own play doubled the discomfort as well as the creative pleasure. The set designer, Jerry Marcel, built a virtual replica of Jean-Claude's original kitchen at Charlemont, and we transformed Theatre Genesis into a little piece of the country, with a sloping, grass-covered platform for the audience to sit on and a painted horizon all around. I did everything I wanted to do and loved the way it came out.

Lacking any other idea how to support myself, I reinserted myself into *The Village Voice* as a critic, making a deal with Dan Wolf to have first choice of plays to review and slightly more money than my colleagues—that is, to be *The Voice*'s senior critic again, resuming my "Theatre Journal" after a three-year hiatus. Dan and Ed had sold the paper, but Dan was still the editor. *The Voice* now had several good theatre critics, notably Michael Feingold, who were probably not glad to see me back. The big change was that theatre no longer had priority in the paper, having lost ground to dance, rock and roll, television, and movies. I finished editing a new anthology for Bobbs-Merrill, *More Plays from Off-Off-Broadway*, relieved to be somebody again.

I was wearing out my welcome at Lewis's but ambivalent about getting an apartment and recommitting to the city. When Charles Stanley invited me to move into the vacant room in his fifth-floor apartment on East 2nd Street, it seemed like the perfect temporary solution. The room was big enough, with a wide view over rooftops to the west. Over Christmas I scraped and painted, bought a mattress from Macy's and a desk from Ondine's friend Dorothy Podber, who lived downstairs. It was a great improvement to have a room of my own. Charles was friendly and fun to live with.

Country Music was a grand success, audiences jamming the tiny theatre. Many people came on to me. I rejected all of them except John Albano. If I imagined this to be a serious relationship, though, that fantasy blew up on

New Year's Eve, when I went along to a party and met John's "sisters." The next party would be Asian queens, he said, and I went home alone, shocked awake to our age difference. He was twenty. I was practically middle-aged—and not really gay. The next morning I was as unhappy as if a major love affair had ended, wallowing in the "empty life" thought form. But it had not ended: we went on as before, moments full of sweet, steady love. I wanted a woman.

Michael Feingold criticized *Country Music* in *The Voice* for not measuring up to Chekhov but raved about my production. Irene Fornés said she hoped it would change the whole course of theatre. I was invited to bring it to the Belgrade Festival the following September and imagined pulling a company together and touring with a couple of other Theatre Genesis plays. Henry Pillsbury, a classmate from Hotchkiss, came to see me, saying he had $200,000 to spend on starting a theatre and could raise a million. Did I have any ideas? I tried to think.

Bummed out by slum living in wintry New York, I went to the Virgin Islands to warm up and find some perspective. High on acid at a budget campground on St. John, I realized I was the only person there alone. Coincidentally, my father and sister were vacationing on nearby Tortola. I had not been invited but took a ferry over anyway and checked into a cheap hotel not far from their fancy resort, joining them for dinners and outings, taking Bicky out for an exhilarating sail. The balminess of the Caribbean was divine. I wrote a letter to Michele, just to say hello.

In the spring Nevele Adams, who had played opposite Charles in *Country Music*, died of leukemia. It was hard to imagine reviving the play without him, and I let the possibility of a tour slip away. Henry Pillsbury went to Paris and took over the American Center, commissioning a building from Frank Gehry. I was again turned down for a Guggenheim. I did the lights for Jean-Claude's play *King of the United States* at Westbeth. New York had me again.

The other Obie judges made me leave the room while they discussed *Country Music* and awarded me an Obie for direction. They also voted one for the set designer, which I inadvertently screwed up by talking too frankly after the meeting to Arthur Sainer, a fellow critic, Obie judge, and playwright. I had mapped out the set for *Country Music* in my notebook when I first started writing the play, myself had the idea for turning the whole theatre into an environment, forced Jerry to rebuild the wall flats a foot lower to make it feel more like a low-ceilinged New England farmhouse. Arthur took this the wrong way, polled the other judges, and they withdrew Jerry's award.

34

A MONTH SPENT TEACHING an artistic-enrichment workshop for high school teachers in Dalton, Georgia, bogus as it was, clarified my mind about the ongoing necessity of earning money in order to pursue my aims. Like it or not, I would have to settle down and work. Needing a place of my own, I rented a pleasant-enough apartment on 5th Street east of the Bowery, a scuzzy neighborhood but close to the theatres I was involved with. I looked forward to writing and playing my clavichord in the sunny back room, La Mama visible a block away across the low roof of another theatre. I reassured *The Voice* that I would resume my column in the fall, agreed to teach a graduate course in playwriting at Hunter College, made moves toward directing a play at Theatre Genesis, and split for Charlemont. It was already August, the time for building slipping away.

I had come to my senses about living in the northern woods and decided to build a smaller house, at least for now, on the platform John Lucas and I had erected two years before—a cabin, not a substantial year-round residence. I had been studying where to put windows, low for the forest views, high for the moonlight. John came for a design session. I ordered more lumber from Norman Hicks, the farmer down the road.

Theo Ehrhardt, a young friend I had met at a theatre festival at Brown University the previous spring, came up to help me build. He had just graduated from Rutgers and was strong and energetic. We built an outhouse

The house Theo Ehrhardt and I built for me in Jean-Claude's woods

with a view into the woods and rapidly framed the house, one wall after another, then the roof. I slept in the woodshed, occasionally with Theo. The summer days and nights were heavenly, Theo fun and full of light, the work satisfyingly concrete. We nailed up board-and-batten siding and tar-papered the roof. Windows arrived, we installed a wood stove, and the house was enclosed and habitable.

My cabin was fanciful and beautiful. I was deeply pleased by the expression of the framing, the dynamic asymmetry of the space it enclosed, the complex dance of natural light, the strongly peaceful vibes and proportions. John Lucas came to see it and declared me to be the architect. Like a play, like any creation, the house had emerged from a spirit energy deeper than emotion, thought, or quotidian instrumentalities. My underlying energy was positive. When I am true to myself, I am joyful.

THEO AND HIS DOG STAYED ON in the cabin, and I plunged back into the city to teach playwriting at Hunter College, write reviews, and direct *Bigfoot*, a major play by Ronald Tavel. It was pleasant not to be so broke. This was the first time I'd had an apartment of my own since before Paul. I had abandoned my own style when I moved in with Johnny, and for most of a decade subordinated my tastes and desires to his. Now I hired painters to refresh my walls instead of doing it all myself and started reassembling a domestic equipage. I liked the old-fashioned black-and-white tile in the bathroom and kitchen and the shiny parquet floors. I was lonely but glad to have my own address, however déclassé..

Scott Burton and I went together to the gay baths. He seemed surprised that I still looked good with my clothes off. I picked up a guy in the steam room and brought him back to my new navy-blue bedroom, in the morning remembering how little I was interested in one-night stands.

One weekend my sister Bicky came from Washington, and I drove her up to Charlemont to see my house. Theo was away, and we had a heavenly couple of days, played recorder duets, and drew closer than ever. Lolling around on the bed with her I was so turned on I would have gladly fucked if she had not had the sense to stop. It reminded me how much I wanted a woman, which in the context of my gay city life kept fading away.

35

RON TAVEL WAS THE FIRST GAY PLAYWRIGHT, apart from Irene and myself, to be produced at Theatre Genesis, a notably straight, even macho scene until I came into the picture. *Bigfoot* was an ambitious, scenically spectacular play, much too big for the space and too demanding for our budget. Ron and I searched for a better situation but found no alternative to squeezing it into Theatre Genesis and making the best of it. The sheer density of the text was fabulous. I didn't entirely understand the plot or the significance of Jacob and Esau as stand-ins for Ron and his brother Harvey; but I loved the play's theatricality and its complicated set and characters—

Bigfoot: top left, Nancy McCormick, Scott Gordon, Walter Hadler; top right, Bigfoot family; left, Nancy McCormick and Amlin Gray; bottom, Ben Kushner and Billy Natbony with Harvey Tavel

the forest of redwoods, the monastery schoolroom, the beautiful lighting girl, the yetis in their fur, played by the tallest twosome I could find, with two pre-teen boys as their furry offspring, Harvey Tavel as himself, the stairway to heaven. It was really something!

Thanksgiving was funny that year. Lewis, who was dating a cousin of ours, Betsy Flower, treated me to a lavish early dinner at the Four Seasons and came downtown to see *Bigfoot*, which seemed wordy and interminable after all that food. After the show the whole cast came to my apartment bringing all the components and we had another complete Thanksgiving dinner, this one homemade, which suited me better than uptown luxe. I love actors.

Bigfoot had brought together a richly varied and talented group who had worked incredibly hard, giving themselves to Ronnie's vision body and soul. The process was consuming. I was beyond exhausted. Ron, possessed by his work, had forceful ideas about what he wanted that inspired me to go to any lengths to make them come true.

Directing *Bigfoot* was a huge challenge, artistically satisfying and thrilling in every way. I hated teaching at Hunter, though. The only question for my students was whether they had the mojo to actually write plays and somehow get them on, and most of them obviously didn't. How much did I want it myself, I wondered, if it did not bring me love and a full life? I gave my best student a slot at Theatre Genesis to do his play but otherwise felt I had little to offer, depressed by the chilly classroom.

MANNY AND LUCY HAD A BABY and urged me to join them in Park Slope, an up-and-coming neighborhood in Brooklyn. They took me to see a pretty floor-through apartment on a street lined with mature trees and handsome turn-of-the-century houses, half a block from Prospect Park. Being mugged in front of my building on East 5th Street made up my mind for me. I crossed the street without paying attention one night into the path of a man who accosted me practically on my doorstep, demanding my money. Saying, absurdly, "Cool it, man," I pushed him aside and fled down to the corner of Second Avenue, where stores were open and lights were bright. After I calmed down I realized he had poked me in the stomach with a knife, barely piercing the skin.

So I moved again. I thought it would help my state of mind to get farther away from the "scene," such as it was, cut back to seeing two plays a week, stay home more, write for myself, and build myself a harpsichord. Fred had brought my clavichord from San Francisco, but it was too quiet. I was tired of whispering. I wanted to play "Les Baricades Mystérieuses" on an instrument people could hear. Wolfgang urged me to build one of the new Flemish-style kits being produced by David Way, his successor in the American kit business, saying they were better than the Italian-style kits he was making in England. I loved the harpsichord I played at Stafford Barton and wanted one like it, and he eventually shipped me a kit. Theo helped me collect it from the dock in Bayonne.

Building a harpsichord in my sunny living room was peaceful, meditative, useful, an excuse to stay home and calm down, happily engaged. "Kit" sounds like something

Harpsichord under constructionin my living room

you snap together; in reality I was actually building an instrument. The wood parts had been cut for me, the hardware provided. The work of gluing it all together neatly and making it play was complex and exacting.

My highest pleasure in these lonely days was playing music with Ken Wollitz, a dear man and superior recorder player who had a small German spinet harpsichord in his walk-up off the Bowery. All that year I went there every week to make music with him. Ken, an original member of the New York Pro Musica, played the recorder with the sweetest, most beautiful singing tone I ever heard. His understanding of the music was peerless, his playing full of expression. I was flattered that he believed in my musicality and liked to play with me.

I contributed a skit and a couple of monologues to Johnny Dodd's second original show, *City of Light*, a collage of projections, music, and wacked-out performance that played for two weeks in January 1973 at La Mama. Charles Stanley and Lucy Silvay rendered my texts with a rare madness amid the aural and visual overload. Ken and I played Bach as a prelude to the show each night; Johnny told me years later that he hated it, it was the wrong kind of energy, and I could see his point. His handsome new lighting assistant and boyfriend, Russell Krum, invited me to come home with them and shoot up speed, if I understood correctly; I regretfully declined.

Bill Moor and Ben Masters in *Tango Palace*

In January 1973 I directed Irene Fornés's play *Tango Palace* at Theatre Genesis on a double bill with Murray Mednick's production of *Blue Bitch* by Sam Shepard, who had moved to England and gone into greyhound racing. Irene's play chronicles a warped, destructive power relationship between a beautiful young man and an evil clown of ambiguous gender. I had read *Tango Palace* years before and loved its sublime weirdness. It quickly emerged that Irene was prepared to do everything herself, not about to yield to my ideas; I backed off and we co-directed, and the results were good if not exactly mine. We must have auditioned fifty young actors to find Ben Masters, who was perfect. I had someone in mind for the clown who was truly between sexes, neither one nor the other but something else entirely. Irene insisted on casting Bill Moor, a skilled actor who was unmistakably queeny. He was very good, certainly, but I thought there was more to it than this arch gay pas de deux. I may be wrong. Irene subsequently directed all her own plays and became a superlative director and theatrical auteur.

I missed love-making. Physical intimacy is a matchless restorative, and I felt the need. Anybody will do, in a way, but how do you make it happen with satisfying regularity unless you have an equally desirous mate and can get along with each other's personalities and lives? I had lost my faith in gay romance and my curiosity about gay sex, but that was all I knew how to do.

MICHAEL SMITH

I went on a few dates with interesting women and failed to break the ice, or they had someone else or another agenda.

My downstairs neighbor engaged me as a sex object while her husband was in California, which was okay with me: I liked sex on principle, whether I liked it or not, and always did like it on some level. She was fun, if tense, and I would have loved to get involved with someone; but she was married, for one thing, and really not my speed.

Her husband reappeared and invited himself up to Charlemont to see my cabin. It turned out he wanted to have sex with me too, supposedly never having done it with a man. I satisfied his curiosity as well as I could, although I didn't particularly want to. He did not feel bad afterwards, he reported, he felt good, but it meant nothing to me. When they split up soon after that, I felt I had been used.

Manny and Lucy moved to the Chelsea Hotel, and I was alone in Brooklyn. I needed to be by myself for some hours every day to get any writing done, but all the time was too much. I could barely remember what it was like to make love with a person I loved and was actually attracted to. I longed for someone to come home to and stay home with, someone to love me, someone to love. This idea would not go away, relaxing as it was to have freedom and a space of my own. I am incurably romantic. Horniness I could handle on my own, but the desire for affirmation by the touch and closeness of an intimate beloved was not appeased.

I strung my harpsichord, a daunting task, then set the instrument low to the floor on milk crates, sitting cross-legged on my zafu in front of it to finish the slow, repetitious fiddly-work of making it play, one note at a time, which demanded a degree of patient attention I had not exercised since my bead-stringing, clavichord-building Zen days in the Haight. Charles Stanley came over to oil and wax the case, rubbing it for hours, reminding me of Johnny and his wall of stamps.

Ken Wollitz and I inaugurated my instrument with a Sunday afternoon concert in an upper West Side church, performing recorder-harpsichord sonatas by Telemann, Bach, Handel, and Frederick the Great. I was no match for Ken's virtuosity and scholarship, but we loved playing together and declared our love openly in the music.

36

My life was much improved, but I longed to escape from the city and my city self. When the season ended I decamped for Charlemont with a sigh of relief, taking my harpsichord with me. My cabin was cluttered with Theo's winter furnishings. Wanting it bare and serene, I set about making it my own, stripping out shelves he had put up, stashing his stuff under the bed in the woodshed, building myself a writing table and bench where I could sit cross-legged beneath the high trapezoidal window to work and play with words. I hid shelves for food and kitchen stuff behind a half-wall matched to the length of my harpsichord, built shelves for my few clothes and books and my music and tuning tools, hung a Mexican string hammock diagonally across the middle of the room. Jean-Claude gave me a pair of rocking chairs. I made a cushion for my writing bench.

On the way back from a run into the city, my VW's engine blew up in the hills on the Taconic Parkway: high on pot, I had fogotten to shift and was going too fast downhill, I think. Jean-Claude drove down to rescue me and the psilocybin mushrooms I was bringing him in a cooler. Then I had no car.

Murray Mednick won a Guggenheim and bought himself a Citroen DS. He and his lady, Kathleen Cramer, visited me for the weekend and reintroduced the possibility of having ideas. I was badly out of practice. Drinking bourbon and grilling steaks on an outdoor fire, we elaborated a comprehensive historical hypothesis to account for the terrible underlying discomfort we all kept feeling even when everything was going well. Murray described traces of ancient knowledge in Yucatan, Peru, pre-Druid England, Egypt, China, Tibet, a lost geometrical-crystalline science of electromagnetic energy. One has to believe there was once another race on this planet, probably giants from a larger world. Some of their works are still faintly visible. Another reality lies behind the one we experience. We are mysteriously exiled from paradise, where we belong. We have been abandoned in the dark. An atavistic awareness that what we experience is not all there is nags at our minds. The giants, angels, gods departed, suggesting they will one day return; now even stories about them have lost their force. We are overwhelmed by alienating technology and trivia. They are gone and who are we? The highest creatures of a lowly world? A genetic experiment? A mix of gods and higher apes? Perhaps some of them chose to stay and assumed the form of earthlings.

I HAD ANOTHER MUSICAL PARTNER in New York, Frank Lilly, a geneticist at Albert Einstein University and sometime stage manager for Judson Dance Theatre. Frank and I shared a sensibility we expressed most exquisitely by playing French piano duets, a delicious repertoire we explored on many a high night side by side at his Steinway. Frank came to my cabin with his teenage boyfriend, now more an adopted son. I wound up canoodling with the boy in the bed while Frank slept or pretended to sleep in the hammock, not minding or at least pretending not to mind. The next day he drove us to Bar Harbor, Maine, where he had a scientific conference and the use of a "cottage," one of the huge wooden houses of the original summer settlement, now stranded amid tourists and commerce.

After two or three days and a memorable hike on Cadillac Mountain, I boarded a bus to Nova Scotia to visit Sam Shepard and his wife, O-Lan, who had been living in London. Sensibly terrified by the proliferation of nuclear weapons and the dull-witted intransigence of national systems, it made sense to us to stay away from the obvious targets. Cities would not sustain us after calamity. Sam typically had gone farther and faster than anyone else, buying a farmhouse on the Bay of Fundy, where he and O-Lan were painting the bedrooms different bright colors "like a cheap Mexican whorehouse." Murray and Kathleen were there ahead of me, along with

Sam Shepard

O-Lan's beautiful mother, Scarlett, and her young husband, John Dark. I stayed for a couple of weeks, playing poker and badminton, practicing archery, exploring, walking on the beach, reading, writing, talking, working on the house, enjoying the sweet natural life of artists between gigs and hard work. I liked being with straight men and women for a change. In the context of family and coupledom, I was painfully conscious of my singularity, no one to snuggle with at night, tired of being alone. I had a good time with Jesse, Sam and O-Lan's little boy, who was five or six. I hardly ever saw children, having spent all my time with gay men while my generation started families.

Sam and I both were more centered and together than the last time we had talked, when he had phoned me at Johnny's from the Chelsea Hotel. He had temporarily ditched O-Lan and Jesse and taken up with Patti Smith, who was turning him on to poetry, Rimbaud, cocaine, probably, and high literary romance. He invited me to come over and dig the scene, or perhaps he was crying out for help; I failed to rise to the occasion, too crazy myself at that moment, my great love and the very walls crashing down around me, too unhappy to want a good time.

What had taken Sam and O-Lan to England, I learned, was Scarlett's discovery of a system of thought I had never even heard of, the then-secret teachings of G. I. Gurdjieff. The whole family had been doing "the work" under one of the leading Gurdjieff teachers. Sam told me about it as a friend because it was important (much the way Jerry Tallmer had turned me on to

MICHAEL SMITH

pot a decade earlier), putting into my hands his annotated, underlined copy of the Gurdjieff source-book, *In Search of the Miraculous* by P. D. Ouspensky.

The ideas were a shock. Ouspensky's "G." told people they were asleep. You're not even people, you are machines, he said, trampling their self-esteem. And it's true! Just try to stay awake and continuously aware of yourself for more than a couple of minutes without drifting off into mechanicalness. We don't even notice. We have three brains, he said, intellectual, emotional, and physical, and often address issues with the wrong brain. Emotion and the body are not susceptible to reason. (Sex is a separate, fourth brain.) G., according to Ouspensky, had synthesized a technology of self-development based on an alternative chemistry that made it remotely possible, with work, for an enlightened few to wake up, become human, and develop souls. Such ideas were entirely new to me. I was ready, not to join any group or school but to feast on the thought itself. I had been asleep, acting on automatic, no wonder I felt so aimless and confused. To make any kind of positive move, I needed to wake up and be a person—possibly someday, with effort and work, myself.

I went back to my cabin with my own copy of *In Search of the Miraculous* and assessed my situation. Not having a car helped me stay in one place and think. I needed to be where I was before I could go somewhere else. I was not who I had thought I was for the past ten years, but who was I? I couldn't look to Johnny or any other man for identity or how to live.

I wanted a family of my own. I had vaguely reverted to being gay in New York, but I had no enthusiasm for it, no appetite for another serious relationship with a man. It was time for real change.

37

Al urged me to come to Denver and do another play at The Changing Scene so I resurrected the little family from *Peas* and began writing a sequel of sorts, looking forward to having the same actors continue their roles. Working out the plot was a way of deciding whether or not to pick up with

Michele and bring her back to New York with me, if she was still free. We had not been in touch for nearly two years.

I no longer had a car, but Theo was moving to Boulder just then and gave me a ride. Theo s a gentle, kind soul, lovely to be with.

Al and Maxine departed for California in their Studebaker the day after I arrived in Denver, leaving me their apartment and theatre. The moment I was alone, I telephoned Michele and said, "This is Michael Smith. Do you remember me?" She came right over, and we eagerly made love, good as new. My life was no longer empty but full of romantic and artistic possibility.

I set right to work putting together my play, *Double Solitaire*, which was slow going. The unpaid actors had jobs and families so rehearsals were limited to a few hours in the evening and weekends. I had only written one act of the play; the second half would be variations on it improvised by the cast. It was depressing and alarming when inspiration failed and energy flagged, but we had a date with an audience and had to give them a show. More often, these rehearsals were truly creative. My Denver actors would do the most far-out things I could think of—slow motion, distorted speech, abstract movement, contradictory characters, multiple realities, dance. I felt lucky to have them. The downside of doing these plays at the Changing Scene was that nobody in New York saw them: they could do nothing for my reputation or career. They were my invisible masterpieces.

MICHELE WAS TWENTY-SIX but seemed younger. I was thirty-seven and felt like a teenager, doing things I had never managed to do when I actually was a teenager, exploring how a man's and a woman's bodies and hearts fit together, giving in to mutual pleasure and satisfied desire. I felt rejuvenated, repositioned to do essential growing up, ready to take on the man half of the man-woman duality, which is inherently rewarding. It was deeply invigorating to exercise my potency; we had fun and great romantic sex.

The eldest of six children, Michele was still living at home and locked in a power struggle with her father, who had forced her to sell her beloved truck because she couldn't afford to replace the king pins. Her mother was an artist and free spirit. Michele, who had a special talent for drawing and painting, was newly enrolled in commercial art school, learning a marketable skill, still trying to escape from her family.

Hesitant to disrupt the life Michele was struggling to pull together, I did not immediately ask her to come back to New York with me. I was not entirely sure she was the one for me, remembering how our communion had crumbled after a too-hip movie two years before. Making love with Michele was far more satisfying than it ever had been with a man, but if it turned

Double Solitaire

out we could not build on it to make a harmonious, mutually creative life together, I might be doing her serious harm. There was no ready-made role for her in my New York life, nothing to take the place of her lively family and friends in Denver.

I was sick of New York but didn't know where else to go. I had a comfortable, affordable apartment in Brooklyn, and *The Village Voice* was ready to go on paying me $125 a week to write my theatre column, from which other possibilities arose. I could get $800 for writing and directing another play at Theatre Genesis. The amounts were pitiful, but I needed to make a living and had no idea how else to do it.

Thanks to the imagination of the actors, *Double Solitaire* blossomed into a fanciful, entertaining play about two young couples switching partners, with an anything-goes looseness of style expressive of the ethos of its time—back to nature, free love, comic detachment, ironic self-awareness, idealism and paranoia, fantasy and reality blurring together. There was room in the second half for a spontaneous dance to the accompaniment of spoons by a pretty girl with pretty breasts visible through her clear vinyl dress. Set in Denver and a cabin in the mountains, the plot concluded with one of the pairs of lovers departing for New York.

The play had spoken. There was no sense in not taking Michele away with me, struggling on alone when it felt so good to be together. Living with this woman promised to be a radical change and renew my whole feeling for the situation; I would be stronger with an ally and a dependent, more able to move ahead. I was not helplessly in love with Michele the way I had been with Johnny—still was, really; but I certainly loved her, tenderly and passionately, loved making love with her, found her fascinating and mysterious, and she was crazy about me, a semi-mythical artist from semi-mythical New York, thrilled at the prospect of living there. Al and Max always talked about how great New York was and never stopped missing it; Michele had only been there once, with a busload of hippies.

Dr. Hawley refused to see me, but Michele's mother had me to lunch at their art-filled modern house in Cherry Creek. If we wanted to live together, in her opinion we should get married; but we hardly knew each other, and neither of us was ready for that. I was not declaring any intentions though I certainly hoped our relationship would work out and lead to happiness and fullness of life. I said as much to Ann Hawley, who in effect gave us permission and her blessing, only asking me to cherish her precious Michele. That seemed like a very good idea. I resolved to do it.

Early Music

1973–1986

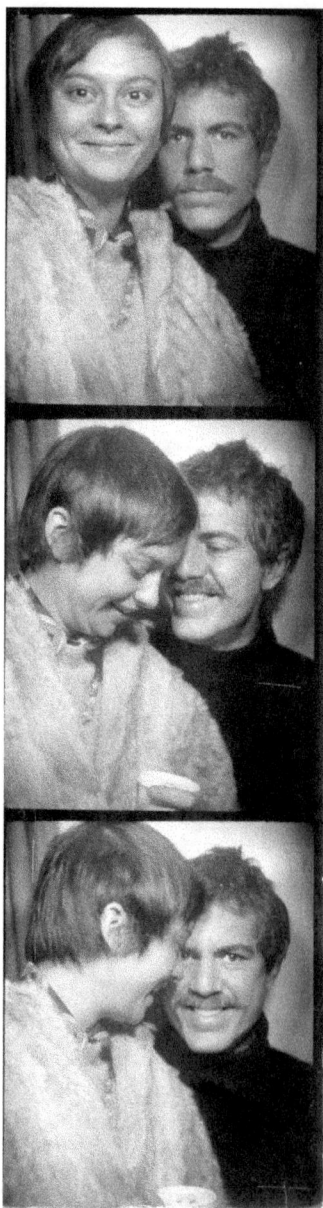

MICHAEL SMITH

1

MICHELE AND I FLEW INTO NEWARK and rode the airport bus across the industrial marshes, Manhattan's massed towers radiant in the setting sun. Our first stop was my brother Lewis's East Side apartment. My parents were in New York on their way to or from Europe, and I wanted them to meet Michele. She was intimidated, thinking of my family as sophisticates and herself as a simple girl from the hinterland—or so I imagined. Lewis had dinner catered by a gourmet chef, and my parents were on their best behavior. It was more like a romantic movie about New York than reality. It was a great relief to get home to Brooklyn and be on our own.

I couldn't wait to get out of the city. Barely had we touched down in Park Slope before I borrowed a station wagon and whisked us away to Charlemont to retrieve my harpsichord. The autumn color was at its height, and I was overjoyed to share my beautiful cabin in the woods with a lover. Like a wood sprite or naiad, Michele seemed one with the creatures and earth rhythms. She painted watercolors of flowers and made tiny kites of leaves, twigs, and bits of thread, not caring that they didn't fly—how different we were! Making love, we played with the fantasy that she was the earth and I was the sun, or the sky, or an eagle, or one of those visitors from a higher civilization—or she imagined herself a virginal schoolgirl, I an avuncular professor: "Just put it in a little way." It was terrifically exciting.

I returned to *The Voice* for the beginning of the theatre season, only to find that the founders were losing control of the paper and the vibe was no longer so easy-going, new editors intruding. Writers were organizing to press management for more money and more control, resentful that Dan and Ed were walking away rich while we were still working for peanuts. I decided not to join this movement, feeling in my heart that the paper was doing me a favor by letting me write for it.

We had a party before Christmas so Michele could meet my gay friends. We decided to serve cookies and cider, enacting innocence for an audience of cynics. Michele found a cookie cookbook and made a dozen varieties. Cider was a taste of the northern woods. Several of my downtown theatre friends came out on the subway—Harry Koutoukas, Ondine, Charles Stanley, Bob Heide and John Gilman, John Vaccaro, John Albano, Johnny briefly. Ken Wollitz brought his recorder; we played Telemann and Bach.

For the February slot at Theatre Genesis I started writing a play set in a theatre lighting booth that was also the cockpit of the comet Kouhoutek, which was actually a spaceship. It was too fantastic, with nowhere to go. I abandoned it and instead wrote a play about Frederick the Great. Ken had told me the story when we played Frederick's music. The mortal conflict between the prince and his father, leading to his assumption of his royal role, could apply to any son and father; it could have been my father's imaginary tyranny, the poignancy of his waning strength, the power of succession I felt more acutely now that I was joined with a woman.

I called the play *Prussian Suite* and directed it myself, which earned me a second share of the Theatre Genesis booty. (We had a grant from the Ford Foundation.) Imagining music throughout, I enlisted John Smead, a talented guitarist from Chicago, to compose a score for guitar, harpsichord, and tamboura drone, which Michele would play, although she would have preferred to act. He came to Brooklyn to rehearse and taught me to improvise to his changes. The beautiful plucking mix was augmented by recorders, a tubular chime, the thunk of a hatchet chopped into a stump. I designed and built an elegant platform stage backed with a gleaming black and gold cloth I had brought back from Bali, bared the windows of the black-box theatre to the city night, and lit the play with candles. Ondine played Frederick's father, the king; Charles Stanley and Jimmy Camicia, a glitter-drag star, took turns as the prince and his friend Captain Katte, whom the king orders executed before his son's eyes to teach him a lesson; Walter Hadler's wife Georgia Lee played Frederick's sister, Wilhelmina. Each scene except the first and last was played twice, as in a classical suite. In thrall to conceptualism, I tried to meld psychological narrative with abstract formality in a type of performance art.

Prussian Suite: front, Michele Hawley, Ondine, Jimmy Camicia; rear, John Smead, Charles Stnley, the author, and Georgia Lee

Ondine was over amphetamine but drinking and erratic. Jimmy felt lost without makeup and glitter (gradually adding it as the run went on, and getting very good). Charles was doing two other shows at the same time and overindulged the poetic tone, crooning my lyrical lines. Michele was dismayed by the maelstrom of male egos. Still, the play was admired by a few choice people. I again imagined pulling together a company, doing another play at Theatre Genesis in May, then taking my own little repertory on the road, which was the only way to make any money from this kind of theatre.

Everybody hoped I would make it happen, but nobody helped, and sadly I lacked the confidence, chutzpah, and practical experience to do it on my own.

I TOOK ON ANOTHER temporary teaching gig that winter, at Bard College, then found I had no idea what to teach. The sophisticated students were already getting Stanislavsky, Open Theatre, improv, scene study, modern dance, and mime. Sick of criticism and lacking any shtick of my own, all I could think of was to put on a show. I imagined a collectively composed pageant called *The Seven Sisters*, with each of the major oil companies embodied as a character; alas, the kids were too busy with classes and other commitments, and my play was not on the schedule. It was too depressing to tear myself away from Michele's warm arms every week, ride the train up the Hudson, and spend the night alone in a chilly dorm room, racking my brain for some way to save face with the students, whom I tried to like but resented for setting me up to fail them. When it got too painful, I bailed. Larry Sacharow, the chair of the department, would take over my class.

Dan Wolf hired me to trouble-shoot the copy flow for several messy weeks in early 1974 as *The Voice* set up its own composing room, using the new, clumsy, transitional technology of film typesetting and pasteup. Michele felt abandoned when I left for work, making emotional scenes just as I was trying to get myself out the door. I felt for her isolation, but I had to make a living. It would take me years to grasp the female rhythm: these storms were often though not always related to her monthly cycle.

I had not been prepared for how much attention she needed from me. Johnny had been self-sufficient and increasingly preoccupied with work, often so busy that I hardly saw him. Michele had nothing to do. As a result it was virtually impossible to get any time to myself, which I needed in order to write, as part of our livelihood and to sustain my inner balance.

We had some difficulty too with verbal communication. Michele was not especially quick-witted or articulate, and I was sometimes impatient. I proposed that one day a week we not speak; there were other ways to communicate. We couldn't argue if we didn't talk. We kept up this practice for months. To better synchronize our vibrations, I taught her a humming exercise I had learned from Manny and Lucy, who got it from Arica. Sitting facing each other on the floor, we hummed for some minutes in resonant unison on three pitches in sequence: low for the belly and sex, middle for the heart, high for the head. We did this every day, and it helped.

Michele took a painting class at the nearby Brooklyn Museum Art School. One snowy winter night she brought me a kitten inside her coat, a bold, sweet gift. I didn't know I wanted a pet, but the black and white kitten was tiny and appealing, sliding around on the polished floor. I accepted him as part of the dream of domestic felicity and named him Cat in honor of the character in *Prussian Suite*.

Flying out of LaGuardia on my way to Iowa City to admire another experimental theatre troupe, I thought of Michele below me in Brooklyn. What would happen to her if the plane crashed? This was not cherishing, to leave her stranded. We had already speculated about getting married and having a child, and when I got back, we decided to do it. In our own minds we married each other the day we went to Cartier, bought matching wedding rings, and slipped them onto each other's fingers on the Fifth Avenue sidewalk. Both of us were hippies with no regard for convention, theoretically, but our children would be better off with married parents and their father's name, and we wanted to make our parents happy.

Ann and Bob Hawley invited us to have the wedding at their house in Denver, which they were about to sell: they were moving to Taos. I could do another play at The Changing Scene just before the wedding, which would keep us afloat for the early part of the summer. Then we would have to think of something else. Neither of us considered whether we could afford to get married. I needed to make a living anyway. Having a wife to support would improve my motivation.

Tired of the technical limitations and tacky taste of downtown theatre, I told Audrey Berman, the new *Voice* theatre editor, that I wanted to concentrate on Broadway when I came back in the fall, secretly thinking

I might not return at all. Manny and Lucy were having another baby and would sublet my apartment in Brooklyn. I spent my last afternoon in the city visiting Johnny on Cornelia Street. His advice was to take more chances with my life. If getting married was not taking a chance, what would have been?

Michele in the mountains

MICHELE STOPPED OFF to visit her parents in Minneapolis, where her father was studying cardiology, then joined me in Denver, and one ecstatic afternoon we started a baby in the sunlight on Al and Max's glowing oriental rug. (We had their apartment and theatre to ourselves while they took a vacation.) This is the highest sex gets, when the eternal, oceanic desire of the sperm to reach the egg, and the egg to attract the sperm, is not resisted but joined by loving wills.

We went up into the mountains for a few days, staying in a friend's cabin beside a beaver pond. While Michele fished and painted, I brought my new play to a happy end. Michele was adorable and sexy, and we were deliciously harmonious. This was the kind of living on the earth I wanted.

The trip of the play took over, one decision after another and hours of meticulous practice gradually adding up. *A Wedding Party*, a comedy, picks up the characters from *Peas* and *Double Solitaire*, adds some new ones, and marries them all off, completing a Denver trilogy. I wrote Michele a goofy

Rehearsing *A Wedding Party* at the Changing Scene: Rita Williams, Bill Dohme, Dennis Stull, me, Nancy Mangus, Jane Larew, Michele, and John Simcox

part as a sweet, randy old lady who marries a demented preacher, and my favorite Denver actors continued to develop their existing characters. The set was elaborate—a glade of trees on uneven ground, bushes and rocks that moved on their own, a trio of musicians perched in the trees playing recorders and twittering like birds.

I felt liberated from New York and all it represented, not judging anything I had done before, only letting it drop away. A general happiness underlay everything I did, although Michele's emotional volatility was not easy to negotiate. Al and Max came back, we had to move, and the water bed in our temporary quarters made her queasy. A few days before the wedding she freaked out completely, called it off, packed her suitcase, and made me drive her back to her parents' house in spite of my insisting I didn't want to, although I was sick of her at that moment. We drove across the city in a caul of misery. I stopped the car within sight of the house and talked her down, and we ecstatically kissed and made up. I blamed it on the hormonal changes of early pregnancy and normal pre-wedding panic.

At our wedding, attended by Theo Ehrhardt and Michele's sister Sandé (hidden)

We picked out a colorful African shirt and homespun cotton pants for me to be married in; Michele would wear her sister Sandé's hand-painted wedding dress. I bought her a yellow French bicycle called Mirage as a wedding present (later stolen from her parents' garage); she gave me a blond guitar. I played tennis with her father and won. Mother and Dad flew in from Santa Barbara, Lewis from New York, Bicky from Ithaca, Grammie, Aunt Ginny, Uncle Mark, and my godmother Lucy Hall from Kansas City. Jean-Claude came over from Boulder, where he was studying Buddhism with Chogyam Trungpa. Jim Scarritt, my friend from infancy, a political science professor at the University of Colorado, brought his wife Prudence and their three young daughters.

We said our vows barefoot on the grass in Michele's parents' yard, in view of the Front Range. Theo was my best man, radiant in tight white pants and a red kimono open to the waist. Michele's Uncle Bill, a former Episcopal priest, officiated in a gold brocade poncho that looked like a bedspread. Michele's sister Tina composed a flute and recorder duet for the occasion and played it with her boyfriend on the roof. Her teenage brothers wore zoot suits. In the center of the circle with Michele, I felt loved and buoyant, giving myself to her, taking her into my life, our commitment powerfully witnessed by sky, earth, and our families and friends.

MICHELE'S MOTHER GAVE US HER MUSTANG as a wedding present, and after a week's honeymoon at Eaton's Ranch in Wyoming, thanks to (and with) my parents, we drove west to the Pacific and down the coast to Santa Barbara, pausing in Bolinas to visit Diane di Prima, who had a new baby. Our plan was to live in Santa Barbara so our children would have grandparents in their lives and we would be there for my parents when they needed us. Michele's brothers and sisters were moving to New Mexico with her parents; mine were alone on the West Coast.

I had no idea how to make a living in Santa Barbara. The $500 Lewis had given me as a wedding present was rapidly running out. Mother and Dad had moved to a smaller house in the Montecito hills and had no room for us. Cat had fleas, which attacked Michele in a cheap State Street motel: I found her on the floor of the shower weeping.

Mother came up with a place for us to live, house-sitting at first, feeding a flock of murderous finches, and then, thanks to her friend Almira Struthers, rent-free indefinitely in the chauffeur's quarters above the garage on a seldom-visited Montecito estate. I strummed my guitar, learning the few chords Sam had written down for me, serenaded Michele with simple songs, and began writing a long poem about our idyllic new married life and coming baby. Michele found a job tooling leather in a factory in Carpinteria, which solved the immediate problem but obviously couldn't go on.

"What do you want to do?" filled me with anxiety; I could hardly bear to think about it. I wanted to write. I wanted to see my plays performed, and live on royalties. I wanted to direct. I had paid my dues; why wasn't I in the club?

I still had a job and apartment in New York, and Michele would have been glad to go back, but that life was over. I wanted to go forward, get away from the city, do something entirely different. I applied for various jobs in Santa Barbara but nothing clicked. My mother loved having us there, but my father had no idea of my competence and capabilities: instead of helping me find good work, he had me gardening for an elderly friend.

Michele and I talked and talked. I had loved building my clavichord and harpsichord from Wolfgang's kits. He might know of a harpsichord job. I wrote to him in England asking, hoping straightforward practical work would help me with my writing, not dissipate my imaginative juice like the kind of scattered intellectual work I had been doing in New York. That letter set wheels in motion. Wolfgang went to Charlemont looking for me and telephoned from Jean-Claude's house. The most interesting possibility, he said, would be to work for David J. Way, who had bought Wolfgang's harpsichord kit business and was moving it from Greenwich Village to Stonington, Connecticut. I went to the library and looked up Stonington in an atlas, surprised to find it at the far eastern end of the Connecticut coast, halfway to Boston. Aside from its proximity to the Submarine Base in Groton, a prime target for Soviet missiles, it looked like a fine place to live and raise our child. Wolfgang recommended me to David, and after a little back and forth, David offered me a job at $150 a week. It was factory work, he emphasized. Making harpsichords was like making nuts and bolts, he said, a business and a factory like any other, which I assumed could not be entirely true.

On my thirty-ninth birthday my parents took Michele and me to a farewell dinner at their new country club, Birnam Wood, the last word in luxury and a disconcerting contrast to my bohemian past, penurious present, and workingman future. Dad seemed half glad to see us go. Mother, who had done everything in her power to help us stay, was broken-hearted.

We packed our thrift-shop household into a U-Haul trailer and headed east, the trailer nearly ripping off the Mustang's bumper. In Denver we had a stronger hitch welded to the frame and traded up to a bigger trailer to carry our wedding presents and the rest of Michele's worldly goods. We stopped in Kansas City for Grammie's ninetieth birthday party at my cousin Ann's house and in Ithaca for Bicky's wedding to Steven Caldwell, a sociology professor at Cornell. My father rode with us from there to Stonington, sharing the back seat of the Mustang with Cat. We checked into a waterside inn, and I presented myself to David Way.

2

MY NEW EMPLOYER was a big, ruggedly handsome man in his fifties, with a mane of thick blond hair. He and his younger wife, Katherine, were restoring an old house in the

Washing dishes after Bicky's wedding

center of the village. When I appeared that first afternoon, he gave me tea by the fireside and rather dramatically asked Katherine if she was willing to have me working in her house. She could hardly not agree. Then he took me out and walked me proudly through the quiet village streets, colorful foliage glowing in the late October sunlight, showing me historic houses elegantly restored, immaculate gardens, views of the water opening in all directions. I told him I could do anything, but that I needed to learn how to work. I would start the next morning at nine.

Michele and my father applied themselves to finding us a place to live, and after a few days we moved into a second-floor winter rental on the other side of the tracks, an easy walk from David's house. Dad departed, and we settled in.

Ironically, Wolfgang's book *The Modern Harpsichord* made the original Zuckermann kit harpsichord impossible. Early music was newly popular in the early 1960s, and harpsichords were hard to find. Wolfgang made his name with a simplified, easy-to-build plywood instrument that worked pretty well. Wood parts for the kits were cut and drop-shipped by a display shop in Philadelphia. Keyboards came from a keyboard factory. The "action parts"—pins, strings, jacks, felts—and hardware were packed and shipped from a loft in Greenwich Village. With the craze for do-it-yourself, the Zuckermann harpsichord was wildly popular—thousands were made. But it was too crude and musically limited, Wolfgang saw, compared to the historic harpsichords and fine modern copies he learned about in his research. He was done anyway. After the debacle of the Caffè Cino and Nixon's election as president, he wanted to leave the country. So he had sold Zuckermann Harpsichords to David Way, the art-book printer and enthusiastic kit-builder who had commissioned and published his book.

David, realizing that the same production scheme could be used to make parts for an authentically classical instrument, set about improving the product. A small harpsichord in the Flemish style had soon replaced Wolfgang's slab-sided instrument as the basic kit. By the time I arrived, he had also brought out a kit for a French double, a larger harpsichord with two linked keyboards, the final, noble form the instrument achieved before it was supplanted by the piano.

DAVID WAS TEMPORARILY OPERATING Zuckermann Harpsichords out of his half-restored house. The future dining room was the office. The future parlor, stripped and unpainted, was the cramped, cluttered workshop, jammed with harpsichords in various stages of completion. David was a man with a mission, constantly refining the designs. For each new run of kits, the factory in Philadelphia sent him a sample set of parts to build into an instrument, checking that they were correctly made and devising building methods amateurs could learn, described in an eighty-page construction manual.

MICHAEL SMITH

Restringing an early Zuckermann harpsichord

He started me off painting the basswood case of the prototype of Flemish V, showing me how to brush on the paint, then sand it smooth and paint it again. I must have put five coats on that first instrument in a lurid yellow-green. He made me teach myself to tune.

David was a madman. I heard him on the telephone in the adjacent office while I worked, pacing around, raging and bellowing at the factory management in Philadelphia, demanding remakes of unsatisfactory parts, fighting about prices and schedule, or hashing out problems transatlantically with Rolf Drescher, his agent in Berlin. We were shipping harpsichord kits to Europe by the container-load, large sums of money changing hands, meanwhile falling behind on shipping kits to American customers, whose money David was using while they waited: he did not have to pay for the kits until they left the factory.

Now and then he took time to talk to me and began to open up this arcane new field of endeavor, showing me how to listen to a single note, separating the sound into its components: the quill, the plucking point, the material and tension of the string, the resonance of the soundboard and case, the attack and decay, the overtones that made the music live. Warned by Wolfgang that the work would be exacting, I had said that was what I wanted. There is no secret to harpsichord design, David liked to say: it is just a matter of getting everything right.

I embraced my new life, trudging off across the tracks to work in the morning, coming home for lunch and after work to wife, cat, and incipient child. Sex was sumptuous. Making love to Michele, I gave my spirit energy to the coming baby. Our friend Tom Hahn took pictures of us naked, awed by the miraculous process.

I relished our being pregnant, taking Michele to the doctor, sharing Lamaze classes, planning the birth and thinking about every little thing. How to pay for the baby was solved when Frank Lilly commissioned a harpsichord; I ordered up a kit and set about building it in the living room after work. Michele was to paint arabesques and flowers on the soundboard, the traditional decoration, and it was a race to get it done before the baby came. She was more and more uncomfortable with the enormous heavy moving form pressing out inside her skin and weighing her down. I ecstatically gave myself to the process, writing about it in my growing poem in moments stolen from the flow.

Relishing our pregnancy

Winter hit hard. I woke in the night and wondered what we were doing in this remote coastal village, wandering through the apartment bundled in a blanket, heard sirens in the distance and looked out for missile streaks coming down the sky. The sub base was just over the horizon; we were well

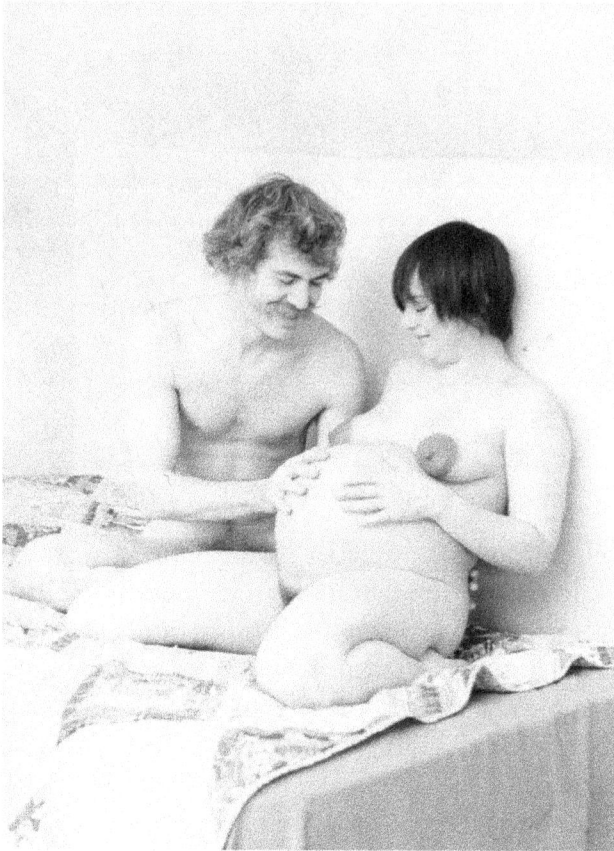

within the zone of devastation.

By early Junuary Frank's harpsichord case was together and the soundboard was in. Michele sprawled beside it on the floor, adding birds and insects to the traditional flowers, bringing summer into the room. Once that was finished, she could have the baby. She was more than ready, the last weeks slow and hard to bear.

WHEN HER CONTRACTIONS STARTED, we drove to the hospital in New London and checked her in; then hours went by and nothing happened. I read to her from a book about Harry Truman, watching the winter day go by outside the window. The nurses gave her drugs to push things ahead, although the doctor had previously agreed not to resort to drugs. Despite all-night efforts, the process stalled. In the morning we were sent back home.

Michele was miserable, exhausted, comfortable only when buoyed by warm water in the bathtub, depressed and desperate. Two days later the contractions began again, we went back to the hospital, and in a rush of effort, blood, and joy, a boy emerged into the light, opening his eyes and looking around even before he was all the way out. We named him Julian— Julian Bach Smith, in honor of Julian Beck and my favorite composer.

Snow started falling as I drove my loved ones home, and a delicious peace enfolded us. Julian was a full-force person from the first, Buddha manifest in our midst for our enlightenment and blessing. Seeing him suckle at Michele's breast melted my heart: I marveled at her abundance, and she gave me sips of breast milk too, so nourishing and protective. I felt radiant with the joy of fatherhood, transformed and more of a person than I had ever been before. Michele, fearful that Cat would be jealous, protected Julian from him; he understood, came close, and purred.

Stonington in winter was quiet, reserved, austere. Then as spring arrived the town was suddenly pretty beyond belief, bursting with daffodils, tulips, and blossoming trees. The summer people reclaimed our apartment, and we moved to the second floor of a big, decrepit wooden house at the top of the town. Finding gleaming maple under the ugly linoleum in the kitchen, we set about refinishing floors and painting the rooms in different lyrical colors. I rototilled a patch of lawn so Michele could put in a vegetable garden. We planted an apple tree.

Michele's mother had come from New Mexico when the baby was born, excited and admiring. Now my parents appeared, having rented a house for two weeks in June on nearby Mason's Island, entertaining us on evenings and weekends. Mother was precious with the baby. Dad got down on the rug with Julian and taught him to crawl.

With Julian, newborn

D AVID BOUGHT a long-empty factory building beside the railroad tracks for the harpsichord shop. Katherine could hardly wait to get the business out of their house, and David had been getting weird about it. "My wife cleans the bathroom," he said to me one day, "and I don't want her wiping up your piss sprinkles. Didn't anyone ever teach you how to take a leak in a private bathroom? You don't stand up. Where do you think the drops go when you shake it? This isn't a subway crapper where there's piss all over the floor. The floor is clean. You go down on one knee and hang it in over the side of the bowl. It's the most basic good manners. I can't believe you would stand up and piss in my wife's bathroom." Was this some bizarre gap in my social education? If I had not seen a smudge

Grandchild: with Ann Hawley in Stonington; with Mother and Dad in Mystic

on the wall where David's other knee rubbed when he knelt to pee, I would have thought he was messing with my head.

David put me to work clearing debris and sweeping out the huge empty factory. Over the next few months he added half a dozen workers and created a serious harpsichord workshop. Within a couple of years we would be making the parts for the kits ourselves, crafting keyboards from raw lumber, producing kits in a variety of historical designs, building not just prototypes but, increasingly, fine custom instruments for professional musicians. David's harpsichord-making mentor, William Hyman, had died with a backlog of thirty orders for French doubles. Determined to establish himself as a first-class harpsichord maker, David persuaded Hyman's customers to let him build the instruments his master had not had time to make, though their deposits were small and the agreed price impossibly low. Hyman's former apprentice, John Bennett, came to work in David's shop, and the next winter they produced the first of the "Hymans," a French Double luxuriantly rich and smooth in sound and action.

David and I both knew I lacked the "golden hands" of a real wood-worker,

but there were plenty of other things for me to do; I would have been bored with everyday shop work anyhow. Each new instrument required "playing in" before its quality could be assessed and final adjustments made, and playing harpsichords for a few hours every day became a legitimate part of my job. David couldn't play himself, but he had a deep understanding of the instrument and the repertoire. He showed me the kinds of attack and touch it takes to make the instrument sing and the secrets of ornamentation that bring the great French literature to life. I am stalled forever at what you might call B-level amateur, but with so much playing of Bach, Scarlatti, Rameau, and Couperin, I improved, enjoying it more and more. I started making a new instrument of my own, working after hours in the shop, using kit parts for the case and crafting my own keyboard and soundboard, patiently coached by John Bennett, a gentle, generous man highly skilled with tools.

MICHAEL SMITH

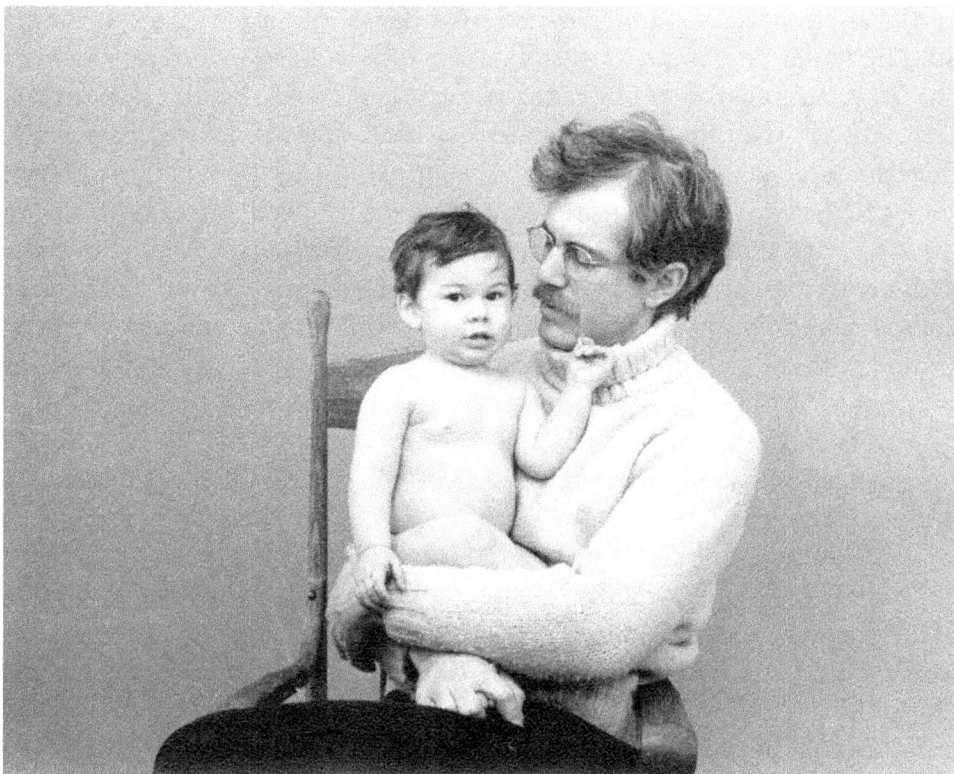

Father and son

3

IT WAS A SHOCK when I received a $10,000 award in playwriting from the Rockefeller Foundation, ironic now that I had given up on my theatre life. I was still a writer, of course, and kept trying to write, despite the interruptions of marriage, several moves, a drastic change of employment, and a baby. My long poem *American Baby* was finished. The Rockefeller grant focused my mind: I would write another play. I rented a writing room on the floor below us and started. It was lonely down there in the cold after work, my little family warm and longing for me upstairs by the stove. But all through the winter I plugged away.

What emerged was *Cowgirl Ecstasy*, a play about a rock band breaking up. The leader only wants to play Bach, and Bach harpsichord music is the only music in the play as he gradually turns into Bach, the ultimate family-man artist. Frank Lilly had urged me to write a play about environmentally caused cancer and the malignant transformation; in a subplot, a groupie comes to the band's hotel room with her father, who is dying of cancer from working with polyvinyl chloride and tells us all about it. Meanwhile the Feds are trying to bust the band for drugs. An FBI man, played by a lifesize doll, is comically depantsed. A documentary filmmaker follows the band around with a video camera, his close-up images appearing on a monitor at the side of the stage. At the end they are all magically transported to a tropical island with palm trees.

The play was imaginative, but what was it about? Giving up on show business? Destroying the theatre?

Uncle Al had nominated me for the Rockefeller grant. Michele said that obliged me to do my play at the Changing Scene, which would get a portion of my grant to produce it, although a theatre in New York, maybe the Public, would have been more likely to lead somewhere, if they would have me. David did not believe I was a real writer but agreed to give me seven weeks' leave to go to Denver and put it on.

As the time approached, however, he needed me. He had sold the loft building in the city where the musical parts had been warehoused and packed, and truckloads of instruments, wire, and machinery were arriving in Stonington. Steel shelving had to be erected, construction manuals produced for two new kits, keyboards and action parts packed in-house, all of this to be organized if not done more or less single-handedly by me. So I postponed the play.

I FELT ROBBED OF MY OWN FEELINGS when Michele developed a crush on Johnny Dodd. I had never made any secret of my feelings for my longtime lover, who was often in my dreams, and visited him whenever harpsichord business took me into the city. Michele thought I wanted to get back together with him and imagined the three of us living together, making love three ways, going somewhere new and making a life together, starting a theatre. Fantasy was part of her fey charm.

Johnny came to Stonington to help christen Julian. Friends joined us, the wind rising as the little party streamed down toward the harbor, Michele in an Indian shirt and Chinese hat carrying a bouquet of purloined lilacs and narcissus. Johnny climbed down the rocks in the wind and came up with a handful of water to anoint our little boy. Johnny daubed rose oil on his hands and belly, and flowers were flung into the sea.

That night Michele wanted to include Johnny in our lovemaking. I demurred but she persisted. Naked with an erection, I went to the guest room at the far corner of the house, where Johnny was awake and reading, and invited him to join us in our bed. He politely declined.

Michele decided she was in love with Johnny and forced me to listen to her talk about it, complaining that her women friends would not take her seriously. This is a small town, they told her, you can't be so free. She wanted to go to the city and seduce him. Ridiculously, my cock tingled at the very thought. I had nothing against it if she could handle it: I loved them both and thought they should do what made them happy. Thinking about Johnny turned her on; the whole atmosphere was sexualized.

She phoned and invited herself down for a visit, and he agreed to receive her. I was glad to stay home with Julian, now weaned. She took the train to the city in a fetching thrift shop dress that molded her curves, thin again and looking terrific. After hours of intense, thrilling conversation, she reported, Johnny left her alone in his apartment all evening, came back for a moment, then went out again and stayed elsewhere, leaving her alone all night. She came home humiliated.

I HAD RESCHEDULED THE DENVER GIG for midsummer and written most of the second act of *Cowgirl Ecstasy*. When David realized I was about to leave, he noticed me again and turned on the charm. There was no end of work to be done, and if I went away David would have nobody to dump it on. But what was I supposed to be scrambling for? I was a writer, whatever David thought, not a real harpsichord maker. David said it was a very inconvenient time for me to be going away. No worse now than later, I thought; but his will prevailed, and I postponed the play again. The business was in some jeopardy, it seemed, and I wanted to do what I could to help him get it moving again. Al and Max said they could adapt.

Michele eventually let go of the Johnny fantasy and came back to me, thanking me for humoring her. She called me her Kansas City honey, her flower of Missouri, and gave me all her love again. Nearing climax she became the huge golden squashblossom in the garden, she was my golden squashblossom in the sunlight, I was fucking the golden squashblossom that was her cunt, I cast no shadow, I was the bee fucking the flower. Such confidence and comfort there was in being a successful lover!

IN THE FALL OF 1976 I finally went to Denver to do my play. Flush with Rockefeller funds, I gazed at the Rockies from the terrace of a sleek apartment Al had rented for me in a newly built high-rise near the theatre. It was a shock to be alone: exciting at first, X-rated media proliferating, then empty as I finished my play and pulled together a production, sick with a cold. Al lined up publicity for me. The interview in the *Rocky Mountain News* was headlined "Job Pattern Can Wreck Life, Says Playwright."

Michele arrived with Julian in time for my birthday. I bought her diamond ear-studs at a pawn shop with one of the $100 bills Al was doling out from the Rockefeller grant. Michele's father, retrained as a G.P. and cardiologist, had set up his new practice in Taos, and she took Julian to New Mexico on the overnight bus. After ten more days of strenuous rehearsals, I gave the cast a few days off and joined them.

The Taos valley was luminous in the fall, the aspens flashing gold. Michele's family were warm and welcoming. The great mountains, sky, and distances depressurized my mind, opening up an ease I had forgotten. My roots, after all, were halfway west, on the borderline: my parents had pointed me east, but I always sensed another, more spacious sense of possibilities in the West, felt myself pulled both ways, east to money, power, peers, but inwardly, secretly, romantically west.

We drove out to the Valdez rim, where I had stayed the first time I came to this magical place, with Johnny. On the way back to town I said, "Maybe we should move to Taos." The thought brought Michele to tears—me too.

Michele and Julian came back to Denver with me for the last week of rehearsals and the opening of *Cowgirl Ecstasy*. Julian spent a few days with other little kids at a day-care center so Michele could pitch in to finish the big pink satin FBI man doll, sewing the cock and balls.

Once the play opened, it was time to go back to Stonington,

Michele and Julian in Taos

but we were short the airfare: Al and Max had gone momentarily broke without paying me the last $500 of the Rockefeller money, and we had spent the rest. I called Lewis and asked for a loan; he surprised me by saying no, suggesting I should ask Dad. Among WASPs, needing help from one's family in adulthood is reprehensible, and I did not want my father to know that Al had lost control of the situation. Michele urged me to tell Al the debt was forgiven. But that made no sense: we needed it as much as they did. It was a classic semicomical theatrical situation, "stranded on the road."

Finally Bicky said she could spare $200, and that was enough to get us home.

4

DAVID WAS A HARPSICHORD GENIUS but a very difficult boss. An egotistical bully who puffed himself up by humiliating his employees, he made it impossible to take any initiative in his shop. Everything hung on David's calculating and capricious decisions, sometimes dragged out for months. He was supporting me and my little family, and I was grateful for that, at the cost of submission. He was utterly dismissive of my writing. It was difficult to maintain my self-respect and not get depressed. Michele was dead-set against my continuing to work for him. In moments of confidence, so was I. But I had to work. *Cowgirl Ecstasy* had been a "success," but the money was gone, leaving us poorer than we were before I got the grant. I read scripts for a grants panel in New York, but I was not likely to win one.

I was up and down about my job, often down, bored, frustrated, wild to quit and leave, which Michele encouraged; then the desperation passed, and I was happy in Stonington, loving the music, the subtle, temperamental instruments we were making, and my beautiful child and wife. I loved my little family so much I wanted us to have another child, and within a month after her IUD came out, Michele was pregnant again.

We were barely getting by and living in limbo, poised between our actual life in Stonington and another life yet to be imagined. Secretly, theoretically, we were thinking about moving to Taos. Michele wanted to be near her family, and I already had a mystical relationship with the place. The editor of the *Taos News* thought there would probably be a job for me there or at *The New Mexican* in Santa Fe. I was simultaneously in correspondence with a Mrs. Willis Shackelford about the possibility of living and working on her organic farm outside Chestertown, Maryland, having responded to her ad in a health food catalogue. I studied maps and imagined the soft, long-farmed landscape of the eastern shore of Chesapeake Bay. I loved the idea of

MICHAEL SMITH

learning to grow food, so basic and real. The farm would be a wonderful place for children to grow up; this was my chance to be that person. I did not know how I would take to the hard work, only that what I was doing now was too easy.

Other ideas were floating around as well. Our closest friends in Stonington were Dan and Melisande Potter, delightful, endlessly creative fellow artists and free spirits with two young daughters, Gisele and Chloe. Michele performed with their

The Mystic Paper Beasts

fantastically costumed family theatre company, the Mystic Paper Beasts. There was the fantasy of sharing a rented farm in North Stonington with the Potters, possibly a European tour. A fire at St. Mark's in-the-Bouwerie had wiped out Theatre Genesis, at least for now; my New York theatre, which I had abandoned, no longer existed. I had vague ideas of starting a theatre at the Westerly Arts Center, five miles east in Rhode Island. A New York production of *Cowgirl Ecstasy* was starting to cook, thanks to Irene Fornés, Murray Mednick and their playwrights' collective, New York Theatre Strategy.

Or we could move to Albuquerque or Santa Fe, live communally with Michele's sister Sandé, husband J.D. Browning, and their two little boys, I could partner with J.D. in a harpsichord- and kayak-making business. Clear thinking would have shown we needed startup capital. I had never heard of making a business plan.

I reached an impasse of unhappiness with David, seeing him as a monster crushing everyone in his path. I was unable to transform the situation because he had all the power. I asked for a raise but he put me off. The farm was not going to happen: Mrs. Shackelford needed someone with farming experience. I tried to get a job as a carpenter, but real carpenters were being laid off.

It was hardly the right time to quit my job and go, with no money saved up and a play about to open in New York; but I could not stand it another minute, and Michele, increasingly pregnant, was chafing to be gone.

J.D. telephoned on Ash Wednesday, and I said we would come.

"When?"

"Soon."

One harpsichord commission would pay for the move.

So I quit, ostensibly to become David's agent in the Southwest. He gave me a champagne send-off in the workshop, I wished them well, and we packed up the apartment in an orgy of friendship. At the last minute Michele decided against throwing in our lot with Sandé and J.D. in Santa Fe. Her father found us a house to rent in Taos. He would pay for movers. The furniture went, we said our goodbyes, and as we drove out North Main Street in the Mustang, Michele and I told each other we hoped we never set foot in Stonington again.

Once more we were moving across the country in the middle of a pregnancy. My feelings for Michele were extra tender, Cat was resigned to his box, and Julian was alert to everything. We had to hurry to be there for the moving van. We were eager to arrive.

5

THE HOUSE MICHELE'S FATHER found for us to rent on Lower Ranchitos

Road had been crudely built by a tough old lady, who bulldozed out a site below the road at the foot of the mesa, spiked together a house out of railroad ties, sheathed it with tar paper and off-cuts from a lumber mill, and lived in it with dogs. It didn't look like much, but it had enough room for our little family, and it was cheap. You entered upstairs into a pleasant big room with windows on all four sides. Downstairs, the kitchen was dark, with ugly brown vinyl paneling on the walls keeping out the wind, and the bathroom was disgusting. We bought a beautiful Glenwood wood-gas stove for heat as well as cooking, and a smaller wood stove for upstairs. A flimsy shed could be my workshop in warm weather. The bare dirt side yard was littered with dog shit and bones; Michele envisioned a lawn where Julian and the baby could play.

The house was built into the hillside, with two large ponds out front, enlivened by a flock of large white geese, and a glorious view. Across the ponds to the east lay the vega, a patchwork of fields, green and fresh with the coming of spring, a scattering of small adobe houses, and across the valley the majestic Sangre de Cristo range, Taos Mountain radiating a powerful magic from its secret Indian fastness and mystic vibrational core.

We dug up the dog yard and seeded a lawn, and I set to work paneling the downstairs with fresh pine boards, making a room for Julian with built-in bed and shelves. Then, ten days after we arrived, I had to tear myself away, take the bus to Albuquerque, and fly to New York for *Cowgirl Ecstasy*. Irene had found a grant to bring me to the last week of rehearsals and the opening. Our house was barely functional; Michele and Julian went to stay with her parents on the other side of town while I was away.

Quite apart from my strong desire not to leave my little family, this trip was a misery. Theo Barnes, the director, whom I had chosen myself, had transformed my play into a rock musical, casting it with musicians instead of actors, turning the long speeches into lyrics for rock songs, pushing the foreground action upstage. The songs lengthened the play so he had restructured it into three acts, with two intermissions, which the wispy plot couldn't support. The live video element, which had energized the show in

Denver, had degenerated into an actor walking around with a prop Bolex pretending to film. Arriving too late to restore my play's integrity, I struggled to master my dismay, stay open-minded, and help make it work, though it was obviously hopeless. Johnny came with me to the opening and left after the first act. It was my own fault, letting myself get distracted by "life" and allowing this to happen to my beautiful play. I was sick about it.

It was a huge relief to get back to Taos. The grass in our yard, unwatered, had sprouted and died; we seeded it again and this time mulched. Michele prevailed on me to build raised beds for vegetables on the flat between the house and ponds, rototilling the scraped-down subsoil and feeding it many wheelbarrow loads of dried manure from the neighbors' chickens. I finished the downstairs carpentry and improved the bathroom, replacing the funky shower with a tub, which Michele preferred. The grass came up, the garden grew, and by summer our new life was amazingly beautiful. Rain showers every afternoon were followed by brilliant rainbows arching across the sky above the gleaming golden valley.

I learned only after we had moved to Taos that it was the third poorest county in the nation. Tough luck. On the other hand, it was okay there to be poor, which had been embarrassing in Stonington. I signed up for unemployment, which brought in a little eastern money after the six weeks wait. I was required to apply for two jobs a week, although I did not actually want a job that would take me away from family and typewriter every day. What job in Taos was I fit for anyway? I was a theatre critic, harpsichord maker, playwright. There was no demand for such talents.

Sandé and J.D. moved back to Colorado; I would have to do the harpsichord business on my own. I placed ads in Santa Fe and Albuquerque where the musically inclined might see them. It was hard to do any writing with Michele resisting my need for solitude. She could not be persuaded to stay downstairs with Julian while I worked upstairs, or vice versa, to leave me alone for a couple of hours a day, which was all I needed. I had no writing room and less time for it than ever. It was maddening.

Nothing was too pressing, though. I needed this time out to work on the house and garden, stay home with my darling child and ballooning wife, recover from two years as David's dogsbody, and figure out what to do next. Improving our little homestead was more useful and satisfying than looking for a job or worrying about money. Out back, beyond the lawn, my pot plants grew taller than my head.

In the fall I imposed myself on the weekly *Taos News* as arts editor, which was not much of a job but gave me entrée into everything I was interested in. For $25 a week, I produced the arts page that led the second section, writing features and news about the local art scene, reviews of exhibitions, plays, and concerts, shooting and printing my own photographs using the newspaper's camera and darkroom, and laying out the page. Taos is a historic art colony, it was a nice little paper, and I enjoyed the work. Between that and unemployment, somehow we scraped along.

Toward the end of her pregnancy Michele started feeling overwhelmed. Diane di Prima came through just then to give a reading and saved her with a dose of Rescue Remedy and her powerful mother vibe. Michele and I had tried and failed to pull together a home birth for Julian in Connecticut. Here, where there was more freedom, a midwife, Tish, befriended us and took on helping Michele through the birth of our second child.

Judging that Julian was too young to go through the birth with us, Michele sent him off with her mother when her contractions started at noon on Halloween. They went on all afternoon, the hours charged with flavor like an acid trip, the two of us riding the energy of the coming event. Darkness brought Tish, followed by Michele's doctor father with a tank of oxygen and her sister Sylvie, now a respiration therapist. We ensconced Michele on the couch upstairs, and everything went fine until the baby started to emerge, a loop of umbilical cord coming along with the baby's head. Tish conjured a rush of energy. And then Alfred was out among us, crumpled up and blue at first but wide awake once Sylvie had cleared his passages so he could breathe. Michele was exalted and exhausted, having given her all. This new boy baby was infinitely precious to us. We named him for my Uncle Alfred,

Alfred joins the family

who had brought us together, whom we both loved, with Miche's mother's maiden name, St. John, for a middle.

I had built him a sturdy wooden cradle that hung from the rafters beside our bed. The weather was getting cold, the nights were longer, and Julian's room downstairs seemed far away. I gave Julian extra love and attention now that a baby brother had usurped his place, hanging out with him at bedtime, reading to him, playing with him, or just lying with him and snuggling. I wanted to give my children more physical affection than I remembered getting from my father, leave them in no doubt that closeness is precious and good and how totally I treasured them. I stayed with my sweet little boy until he went to sleep, often falling asleep myself for a while before going back up to Michele and baby Alfred.

I arranged a gig for the Mystic Paper Beasts at the Taos Community Auditorium, and the Potters, Dan, Melisande, Gisele, and Chloe, came in December, driving across the country in a rickety pickup with their costumes and props, staying with us through Christmas while they gave workshops and performances in spite of Melisande's walking pneumonia. Performing for an audience of rapt kids, wearing roller skates under a ten-foot-tall bird costume, Dan was blinded by my side lights, rolled off the stage, and fell into the orchestra pit. Chloe, in the audience, shrieked: "Daddy!" The big bird struggled back onto the stage and fell off again, this time breaking an arm. He clambered back onstage and did a bird duet with Melisande, fainting with pain, after which Michele's father arrived and took him to the hospital. Melisande played the second half of the show without him. Then she collapsed. Still it was lovely to have our dear friends come so far and expand our life.

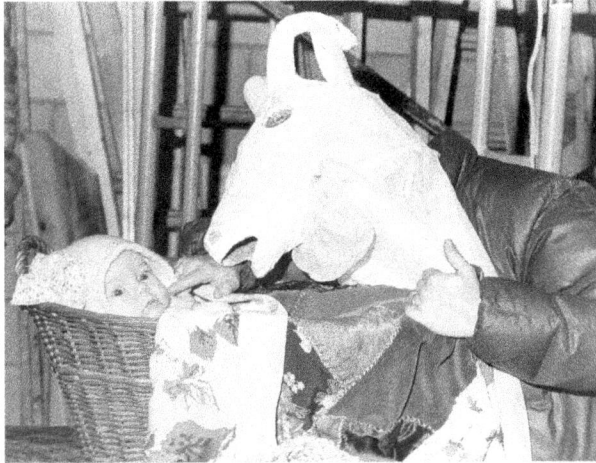

Alfred backstage with Beast

6

THERE WAS an unexpectedly lively theatre scene in Taos, considering the limited size of the theatre-going population. I plunged in. Liking a play put on by the Taos Theatre Company, I called up the actor-manager, Bill Bolender, who came right over and agreed that we should work together. He wanted to do Beckett's *Krapp's Last Tape*, a solo, and Albee's *The Zoo Story* with his partner Steve Parks. This was a classic off-Broadway double bill, and I was eager to direct it. Bill Whaley, the owner of the

Bill Bolender in *Krapp's Last Tape*

movie theatre on Taos Plaza, agreed to let us have the theatre after the early evening movie on five nights in early February, and the show went well. The Beckett is sublimely touching, and Bolender made the most of it. He and Steve did a fine job with the Albee.

After that Bill Whaley offered me $500 to direct *West Side Story* at the Taos Community Auditorium. Bill produced, putting together a solid team to back up the cast of forty: two choreographers, one for each gang, an excellent musical director, and a scrappy pit band. I had a great time

Rehearsing the dance at the gym in *West Side Story*

directing and lighting the show, in spite of the severe limitations of the situation. *West Side Story* was a huge success, mixing up the town's Anglos and Spanish on stage and in the audience, making everybody delirious with joy. John Nichols gave it a rave review in the *Taos News*.

I could have done anything I wanted after *West Side Story*, but Michele asked me not to direct another play for a while, which left her too much alone with the children. Besides, we had an order for a harpsichord, which would keep me busy for some time. A couple from Albuquerque saw my ad, came up to see us, admired my pink harpsichord, Honey, and ordered one like it in navy blue. I agreed to make it for $3,000, a ridiculously low price for a harpsichord but a big amount to the little Smith family. Half in advance more than paid for a set of parts from David; balance on delivery.

Alfred was the sunniest baby ever, and Julian was more interesting all the time. We had no money, but our life in Lower Ranchitos was idyllic as spring came around and the garden went in. Michele taught me how to bake bread; I made seven loaves at a time, trading bread to a neighbor for goat milk, loving my country life.

My town life, though, drove me nuts. I had a job as technical director at the Community Auditorium that was alternately grueling and dull. The editor of the *Taos News* hassled me to write about the schlock tourist galleries as well as fine art. How was I to make a living?

Julian

MURRAY AND IRENE were starting a playwrights festival near Los Angeles and invited me to come out in July to teach and do a play. I took a month off from the newspaper and the auditorium, then at the last minute could not bear to trade beautiful Taos and my rapidly changing loved ones for solitude and egoistic art struggle in the hot, smoggy San Bernardino Valley. I telephoned the day before I was expected to arrive and bowed out, abject about letting my friends down but ecstatically happy to be staying home.

And I did have to finish the harpsichord. I begged another $1,000 advance from the customers to keep us going and pretended I had gone away as planned. I didn't show my face in town, and Michele told anyone who called that I was in California and would not be back for a month.

THIS WAS THE BEST TIME YET, staying home, working on the harpsichord, looking after the children, making love with Michele, starting to write a play inspired by Ashley Montagu's book *The Elephant Man*, although it seemed an unlikely subject for a play. The miraculous summer days unfolded, crowned with a rainbow every afternoon.

I was not a real harpsichord maker, but I was careful, patient, and precise, and with Michele's decoration the instrument turned out a beauty, the dark blue case banded in gold leaf, the keyboard well gilded, with a Latin motto boldly lettered on, a French-style reverse keyboard in ebony and bone, and an elegant, witty French soundboard painting by Michele in gouache. Once I had it working I played and played on it, reading through Bach partitas and preludes and fugues, only stopping to refine the action. It was a noble instrument with a vivid presence, its sound rich and warming up.

The customers rushed us to finish: they were moving to Sardinia. On the last day of July we delivered the harpsichord to their half-packed-up house in Albuquerque. They were undecided whether to go to Italy, back to California, or stay put. We hated leaving our exquisite, rather fragile instrument in this disintegrating situation. But we needed the money, and the buyers professed themselves thrilled. Within weeks, I heard, they resold the harpsichord for a $3,000 profit. It went on to an active concert career in Southern California: I kept hearing about it for years.

"Back from California," I intensely wanted not to go into town to work at the newspaper and the auditorium. In the galleries the artists were starting to come around a second time; it ws hard to get it up anymore for the paper. Nobody appreciated my fine writing, and I was a flunky at the auditorium, trapped apart from my darlings several evenings a week, the last one out to switch off the lights. *The Elephant Man* was announced in New York in someone else's version.

High up on the mountain twenty miles north of Taos was the Lama Foundation, a legendary hippie outpost where diverse spiritual teachers had been coming since the sixties and a dozen families lived communally on the land in homemade houses. Taos was a spirit center, one of the power sites of geomancy; Michele and I had been doing Sufi dancing, an ecstatic, fun form of worship and communion invented by Sufi Sam, a Jewish holy man from northern California, one of the main teachers at Lama.

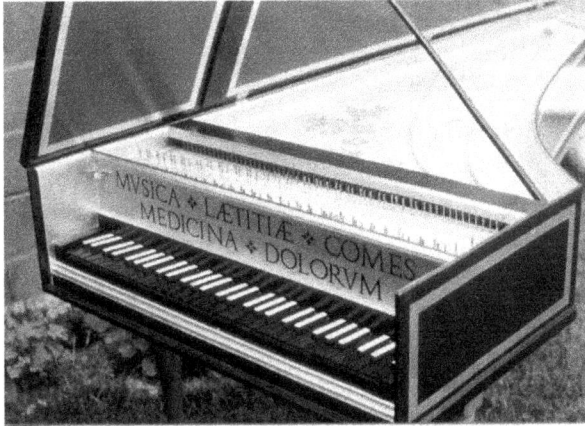
The harpsichord we made in Taos

We went up with the boys for a Sunday open house and danced in the dome looking out over infinite space. I liked it so much that I wanted to join the community and move up there for the winter. We were not making it on our own, and the idea of joining my energy to others' had a powerful appeal. We might have been accepted, but Michele was fearful of being so far from town and her doctor father and of losing our autonomy in a group of strangers. I was willing to take that chance to get beyond ourselves but not confident enough in my impulse to impose it on Michele.

I was keenly interested in the idealistic aspects of my life, preponderant in this little-children moment, and tried not to worry about money too much of the time. Clearly I had to do more, not less. To survive as an artist in Taos you had to work several jobs and as a result came to your art tired.

Fortunately, the tired brain softens up and lets things arise that a more alert consciousness might brush aside.

I did a grueling nine-hour setup at the auditorium, following somebody else's design for work I had not chosen. Writing for the *Taos News* had a certain spurious glamour, but the two-bit salary showed what it was worth. After I paid the October rent, we were down to $20, credit stretched tight, bills due, no more money coming for two weeks, and then not much.

7

I STUMBLED UPON A PLAY that fascinated me, Calderón's *La Vida Es Sueño*, a Spanish classic, and started writing a new English version. Sigismundo, the hero, would be a great role for Bill Bolender, who said the Taos Theatre Company would produce it. Lacking Spanish, I worked from two standard translations, turning to the original and a dictionary when in doubt about what was meant, feeling an intuitive affinity with this great seventeenth-century dramatist, grasping his thought from moment to moment and sensing what it demanded in the way of language. It was exhilarating to write poetry on a grand philosophical scale, a welcome release to write melodrama. I compressed the play to about half the number of lines for the late twentieth century's speeded-up attention.

Larry Bell, one of the art superstars of Taos, told me some of the same things Michele had been saying: that I was passively waiting, that each artist is responsible for his own work, that if you go after it and take action, action follows. I pushed on with *Life Is Dream* and sent letters flying out, wondering if I actually wanted re-entry to the world I had struggled to escape. I passed my forty-third birthday in doubt and confusion.

Michele took an aikido workshop. A flutist, a recorder player, and a violinist came to the house singly and in pairs and played Bach with me and my harpsichord. Michele weaned Alfred, and we moved him downstairs with Julian so we had a room to ourselves again. I did odd jobs to keep us going. As I painted the outside walls of a gallery near the plaza, Indians and passing hippies called up to me on the ladder, "Don't work too hard"—the Taos mantra. I was not working hard enough!

Marianne de Pury, a Swiss composer I knew from Charlemont, was running a theatre in Santa Fe. She brought her children up to visit and meet mine, and we talked about starting a theatre together in San Antonio or Austin. Michele too was almost prepared to give up on Taos. The reality of how beautiful it was and how fucked up other places were would not disappear; but I could not throw my life away grubbing along, I had to do better and get on with my work: I had a spiritual message to deliver through the medium of theatre *and* a family to support. I had fantasies of selling my *Life Is Dream* translation to Minneapolis. I had fantasies of directing a play on Broadway. It was time for fantasies.

Marianne de Pury in our backyard with her children, Julian and Sophie

Wolfgang wrote from France proposing that we team up to open a theatre café, perhaps in Boston. We both liked the idea of a place where civilized people could gather and actors and musicians could perform. The Caffè Cino modeled a way to put on plays relatively free of money hassle. I imagined an elegant Viennese café, with a little alcove stage set into one wall with a harpsichord where I could play chamber music in addition to doing plays. Michele was all for it.

Dan and Melisande Potter were also pulling us back east, urging us to come along on a summer tour in Europe with the Mystic Paper Beasts. *Life Is Dream* was scheduled for production in Taos in early February; then like it or not we would go, somewhere.

The Mustang was giving out. I wrote to my father feeling him out about a loan to help us buy a new car. He wrote back strongly advising me to get a full-time job and stick with it; the alternative, he said, was grim. What job?! I helped Bill Bolender build a dome house in Talpa, a nearby adobe village. He could only pay me $3 an hour, ridiculously little even then, but when the weather was good, it was the pleasantest of jobs. His wife, Dorothy, made us grilled cheese sandwiches with mayonnaise for lunch. Bill was a rough, poetic, warm guy with a mean wit. I enjoyed him, liked working with him, and it was mutual. If they could keep the Taos Theatre Company going, he said I could direct all their plays.

It helped when Peter Hartman commissioned me to make him a clavichord. After Rome, Peter lived on a farm in Wales for several years and was now in San Francisco, where he had opened a free-music gallery. He sent a deposit, and I ordered a kit from Stonington.

As my translation of *Life Is Dream* approached its conclusion in the great reconciliation scene between father and son, when the savage prince forgives the king and achieves nobility (cf. my *Prussian Suite*), I needed extraordinary forbearance from my little family. Without a vibe-space clear of emotional static I was helpless. Writing made me hypersensitive to the people around me, who could easily overwhelm my own subtle, inward good sense. I had to fight them to finish my play.

I lit *Fiddler on the Roof* at the auditorium. Bill and Dorothy's dome rose day by day on the foundation we had poured. Bill rented a scaffold, and it was a rush when we wrestled the frame together at the top. We moved on to piecing together oversize plywood triangles with fiberglass—nasty work— and nailing them on to close it in. We had a first rehearsal of *Life Is Dream*. My work was good and I loved the play. But getting it on would not help our pressing lack of money.

Michele made wonderful dolls with papier-maché heads and cloth bodies and sent them to the Potters for Christmas. They invited us to live with them in Stonington, make that a base, go with them to perform in Avignon in June, maybe settle in France for a couple of years.

AFTER NEW YEAR'S, disaster struck. I had parked our faithful Mustang on the county road above the house because the driveway was impossibly deep in mud, and one night somebody smashed in the rear window. In the morning the car would not start. We were stuck, with no way to get to town, no way to afford a new battery and rear window.

The day after that, the car was gone. By chance Bill Bolender saw the people towing it away and got their license number, which I gave to the sheriff, who nabbed three teenagers and recovered the car. I went to see it in Levi Cohn's junkyard. The kids had taken out the engine and transmission, removed a door, a fender, and a bumper, wrecked the grille, tried to take out the windshield. Relieved of all that weight, the car stood high on its tires, looking ready to go; but I knew it was finished. I went home and listened to the Verdi *Requiem*.

The court offered me a deal: the boys' parents would pay me $800 if I agreed not to press charges and they could keep the remains of the car. It felt like a rip-off, but I didn't want anybody to go to jail, and the money would get us through another month. Michele's mother came to our rescue, lending us her Dodge Ram. But the situation had to change.

Peter's clavichord kit arrived without its drawing, which entailed another call to Stonington. The resident harpsichordist had quit, driven over the edge by David: there was no one to play the instruments. It sounded as though they needed me, and they were so friendly that I almost wanted to go back. It was certainly dismal in Taos, getting up to a freezing cold house and clumping around in the mud nailing up plywood panels on Bill's dome. Michele said my work for Bill was noblesse oblige we could ill afford; but Bill needed me: I would have helped him for nothing, and I didn't have any other job. It was pitiful that we were all so broke.

SLOWLY *Life Is Dream* TOOK SHAPE. Bill played the prince imprisoned by his father in an isolated tower; Michele was Rosaura, wandering into Poland disguised as a man; her father, Dr. Hawley, appeared as the misguided, ultimately contrite king; Jonathan Gordon, a serious theatre guy hiding out in Taos as a carpenter, played Rosaura's comic sidekick, Honker in my version, with other stellar personalities in the other roles. I had decided when I was thirty-five that I was a professional and would no longer do theatre work for free; Bill would pay me $200 for the months of writing and rehearsals. When I lost control of the production, I started to seriously wonder what was the point.

My idea had been to abstract and energize the play by compressing it into an unnaturally small space close to the audience. This was hard to conceptualize in the wide, rigid community auditorium—I imagined building a small, canted wooden stage projected out over the orchestra pit—or putting the audience on the stage with the play. Bill talked Larry Bell into designing a set for us, a coup. I went over to his hacienda to discuss it, and he gave me a snort of cocaine. Larry proposed to make the set out of big sheets of heavy paper coated with molecules of metal in the high-tech vacuum chamber he used to make his high-priced reflective art-glass sculpture. He wanted to see what it would look like. The paper could be stapled up on walls and parapets, like a "castle." Lumber and plywood was bought and a crew started building ramps and platforms. So much for my vision.

Bill's wife Dorothy, grumpily doing the costumes, did not even try to give me what I wanted. I imagined Velázquez, the men wide at the top and narrow below, the women small at the top with huge wide skirts. Dorothy said I was being frivolous and trying to ruin the Taos Theatre Company; I saw myself about to settle for capes, tights, and finery recycled from other plays. Instead of the deconstructed tragedy I had in mind, we would have a historical pageant. Bill was playing his own interpretation of Segismundo, not mine, turning him into Richard III, with a hump, an exaggerated limp, and a fang custom-made by a friendly dentist.

Could my depression have been viral? Viruses were taking over the planet: mankind was finished. But how sweet it was to sit by the stove burning incense from Nepal and listening to Beethoven quartets, Michele painting by lamplight, both boys sweetly asleep! It was the usual problem playwrights face of losing their vision in a series of compromises. I was

MICHAEL SMITH

Michele's costume sketches for
Life Is Dream

spoiled by Theatre Genesis, which was run by playwrights; this was an actors' theatre, run by Bill and Steve.

Word came from Stonington that Alice Potter, Dan's mother, did not want a commune in her house: we could only stay with the Potters for a couple of weeks. Did they need us for the Beasts? Were they taking us to Europe? Would David have me back again? I felt like a blob of jelly. I did not even want to go to Europe with the Potters. Michele loved me and would have given anything to see me happy; she pined for adventures I had already had.

I needed a whole new relation to my life: repetition of forms was not likely to take me there, even the café theatre with Wolfgang. I needed outward stability and a chance to open myself to inward currents and accumulations. What hurt me most in the present situation was how little good I was for my darling Julian, how little I was able to give him now when he was completely open and receptive. Julian knew how tenderly I loved him, but I was not much fun. It worried him to see me worried.

WHEN I CALLED DAVID and proposed that I come back to work for him, he said he would stew about it for a few days, then wrote saying he would welcome me only if I committed myself to the work: he did not want to be a short-term convenience for us while I waited to see if Wolfgang's café would happen and looked for theatre jobs. I had lost all faith in my theatre work anyway. How was I to reactivate a career that never had amounted to anything or offered me a credible livelihood? It was even less likely to happen now. Wolfgang's idea was based on nostalgia for something that had often been desperate and lame at the time. How long did I have to go on with the same old ideas about myself?

Peter Hartman came from San Francisco to make incidental music for *Life Is Dream*, and at his urging I turned on the gas wall furnace we had so far disdained. Suddenly, after months of shivering and struggling with wet wood, we were warm. Peter composed a score for trumpets, timpani, and tenor and set to work recording the cues; it lifted my spirits to have his high-quality work as part of my play. Michele, insecure about her performance, required constant propping up. She got into one fight after another with Dorothy and Gwen, the other actress in the cast. She wouldn't let up even at home, trying to get me to take her side. Without a break from the play my energy was exhausted. Wonderful as she was, the emotional price was too high: I swore I would never direct her in another play.

Peter showed me the right way to throw coins for the *I Ching*, which rewarded me with The Gentle changing to Pushing Upward: "The beginning has not been good, but the moment has been reached when a new direction can be taken. Change and improvement are called for. Such steps must be undertaken with steadfastness, that is, with a firm and correct attitude of mind; then they will succeed, and remorse will disappear." I called David and said I would stay this time, and he sounded happy to have me coming back. He said he would pay me more than before, enough for us to live on decently, and spoke of helping us to buy a house. I said we would come in the middle of March.

Peter had never expected to make it to 1979, he said. Nor had I expected to survive the sixties, not that I saw myself as an individual casualty: I had expected general catastrophe to destroy all the forms. Yet here I was, everything more real than ever, despite years of Buddha. In the family phase

Julian in Taos

of my life cycle I was obliged to give the world existence for my children by taking my place in it. Julian kept asking, "Is this a dream?" The thought was a poetic conceit, a way of opening the mind. He knew what was real.

I made beautiful lights for my play, amber and lavender in the mountains, pink and green at court. Everybody got happy as we came up on opening night except Bill and Dorothy, who said the show was destroying their company and their marriage. It was not my fault: it's a great play, but I did not make the misguided decision to produce it in Taos. How lame is it to put on a Spanish classic in a Spanish-speaking town in English translation?

Sixty people came to the opening, and the play had some glorious moments. The second night it was exquisite for an audience of five adults and one child. Dorothy suffered running the lights and made too many mistakes so I took over and watched from the wings. The performances were erratic; it was hard for the actors to concentrate in front of so many empty seats. Bill garbled the words and thought of his opening speech. Michele had to deliver a ten-minute monologue while Bill lay on a rock with his back to the audience and made faces at her. He was only fooling, but it drove her nuts.

I had a wretched cold. Dr. Hawley gave me an EKG and detected a heart murmur; I decided it was just stress. I stole a few hours to finish painting the upstairs of our house, even though we were moving out; friends were moving in, and I wanted it to be nice for them. I sold my Italian harpsichord for $600, half in cash, though it did not work very well: I didn't have time or heart to fix it. With $300 more from my father, who approved of my going back to David, we had just enough for the trip. I rented a twenty-foot truck, and friends came to help us load. I loved my Taos friends.

Michele wanted to fly east with the boys but we couldn't afford it so we all went together in the cab of the truck. Cat's box took up the right front floor, padded on top so Michele and the boys could spread out, to some extent. Driving over Raton Pass out of New Mexico, I immediately felt better. We spent the first night in Colorado. The second day we drove across Kansas, made it to Emporia after dark, and the next day stopped to see Grammie in Kansas City, wanting her to meet Alfred, her youngest great-grandson. She was in her nineties, living in a nursing home, weaker and almost completely deaf, but cheerful and loving as ever. Aunt Viv treated us to lunch in a private room. It was precious to us all to see my dear aunt and grandmother again.

"Julian has gone to sleep," said Alfred in a motel in Allentown, the first whole thought he was heard to speak. The truck was too crowded, the motels too little respite, but I treasured our closeness.

8

STONINGTON WAS THE SAME. Dan and Melisande received us with exquisite grace in their familiar house down by the point, and the same friends gathered to welcome us who had watched us drive away two years before. Alfred was new. Otherwise no time had passed and nothing had happened. After sunset I walked alone to the lighthouse lawn and anointed myself with the sea. The town and its setting were even prettier than I remembered.

We unloaded our battered possessions into a horse shed at Alice Potter's farm in Old Mystic so I could turn in the truck. Dan and Melisande moved up to the new tower room in their expanded, idiosyncratically elegant house and gave the four of us their small, low front bedroom. The old house was light and pretty the way Dan had opened it up, but there was little privacy. I had a reverse altitude attack, barely able to breathe at sea level, chilly whenever I sat still—tension releasing after months of pressure. Alfred had a screaming fit at bedtime. Julian was thrilled to be with other children but aggressively competed with Chloe, talked of being bigger, shooting, killing, ideas he had learned from the babysitters' tv while Michele and I were doing the play. The mommies took sides with their children, mad at each other. Obviously we could not stay long.

David was in Europe, and nobody at the shop had any idea what I should do. John Bennett's hugely pregnant wife Alice was doing my job, sitting at my desk, using my typewriter. Michele looked for a place for us to live within walking distance of the shop so we could manage without a car. She wanted us to buy a house on the other side of the tracks for $55,000; I had $61 to my name, and my father declined to loan me the $10,000 down payment, saying I would not be able to afford the mortgage payments. Loving and loved, lucky in so many ways, I could not understand why we were sinking. Our situation, apparently so unnecessary, seemed to express a larger reality. Millions sink.

Mother arranged for us to crash at a friend's spacious, comfortable house on Main Street, which gave us a week's respite. After days of confusion and struggle, Michele found us a big, romantic, cheap apartment on the third, top floor of an old building on Water Street, in the middle of the village. It had many rooms, beautiful light, and a narrow stair up to a cupola looking out in all directions. We painted the rooms bright colors. A pair of cardinals sang in the treetop outside the kitchen window. Stonington was picture-perfect as the fruit trees came into blossom.

David returned, and I was relieved and happy to be back at work. The alternatives faded away. Scouting in Boston for a location for our café theatre, Wolfgang had quickly been discouraged by the urban decay and economic hurdles; he was fixing up a house in Virginia instead. Michele and the boys could not get along with the Potters well enough for us to think of traveling with them in Europe, for which there was no money anyway. So I accepted the resumption of this reality absolutely, intending to live with working, give it my whole five days for years to come. David said, "This is your life!"

The atmosphere at the shop was upbeat. David said, "How do you like

Alfred in the cupola

working for the greatest harpsichord maker of the twentieth century?" He promised me plenty of assignments—construction manuals to write, catalogues to produce, a mail-order sheet music business to set up, a possible magazine, with the primary task of "killing off" Frank Hubbard, the only other maker of harpsichord kits. Once I had glued together the new clavichord, David handed me the instructions for an Olivetti text-editing machine he had installed in the corner of his office and told me to teach myself to use it.

Two of Michele's sisters drove east for a visit. Sylvie decided to stay for the summer to study dance at Connecticut College. I hoped her wry wary presence might take some of the pressure off me—make Michele feel less abandoned when I went to work, less dependent when I came home. It helped that Sylvie had a car. We drove Sandé to the airbus in New Haven, and I took Michele to see egg tempera paintings at the Yale Art Museum, which inspired her to start painting every day. She was excited and said she was becoming a real artist. I hoped it was true. Raising a family was not the whole story. We were both artists; our work was our only hope.

T HE HARPSICHORD JOB did not pay quite well enough to answer our needs, nor could it begin to satisfy my ambitions. My writing held no promise of immediate return, but I had nothing else. I set up an office in the cupola and got up early every morning to write for an hour before giving myself to the day, chipping away at a memoir of my long-gone life in New York, trying to make sense of what I had done and experienced. Parts of the past held an undiminished power. Rereading old letters from Johnny, I almost wished I was still gay, missing the fantasy, frivolity, craziness, and good times, longing for him in the worst way, although I was far happier with Michele, our love-making profoundly satisfying. Looking back was painful and dangerous; I needed to integrate what had gone before with what was happening now in order to move ahead.

We settled down in Stonington again but my feelings were all stirred up, happiness shadowed again by fear of the bombs in the bellies of the nuclear subs lurking up the river in nearby Groton, the frailty of our good fortune, my sons growing up to no innocence, my own energy waning, mind unclear, body creaky, achy, stiff. Michele was strangely distracted, falling apart with the children, wearing out early, plagued with headaches and other pains. I was alarmed by the distance between us: I had to say things two or three times before she heard me, and she entirely missed my subtle choice of words. Attempts to express her own thoughts came to a halt in mid-sentence: "I mean . . . you know . . ."

It turned out she had a uterine infection. The gynecologist popped out her IUD and she immediately felt better, in a rush like an orgasm, she said. He put her on ampicillin and proposed to put in another IUD the first day of her period after next. For now our lovemaking would not be quite so free.

I went to New York for a weekend hoping to freshen my perspective, scope out work alternatives, jazz myself up to write another play, and exorcise my fantasy desire by confrontation with its object. Johnny took me seriously when I said I needed to do something more interesting with my life. We went out to dinner, and afterwards, back at his shattered apartment on Cornelia Street, where he had torn down another wall, I had a nervous breakdown or overdose of cannabis or both—felt myself on the brink of falling apart completely.

When the fumes cleared I had an idea: to write a tv series based on the Caffè Cino. The charismatic Joe Cino character would be the star of the matrix, pulling the handles on the espresso machine and making everything happen, with a lovable crew of sidekicks based on the oddball regulars— Kenny Burgess washing dishes, Johnny the waiter and light man, Charles Stanley the doorman-host, Harry Koutoukas the eccentric dramatist—and a fresh band of theatrical types coming through doing a different play every week. Ten years after Stonewall, it was time for a gay show on tv. In the good old days at the Cino we made no particular fuss about being preponderantly gay men, although we flourished it freely. That was the way to play it.

Johnny recommended a return to New York, where the money, people, and action were, and when I got home I made some calls. Ellen Stewart said I could direct a play at La Mama, but if I needed to make a living I should go uptown. John Albano said if I wrote a play he would direct it at Theater for the New City. I could not imagine a way to support my little family in the city—and hadn't I left on purpose? So the escape fantasy faded. I would go on working for David, loving the music, and sell *Joe's Cafe* to the networks. I wrote a hilarious opening scene for the pilot and put out feelers to agents and producers.

9

I came home for lunch, and Michele and I made love in our newly painted bedroom, consulting my notebook to see if I could come inside her, better for both of us than pulling out. Her period was due in three or four days; we were relaxed and happy, loving and natural. After a weekend at Charlemont, though, her period had not come and she felt unwell, and eventually we confronted the dismaying reality that she was pregnant. She hated having an abortion but did not want to have another child, which would increase the pressures we were barely managing to cope with already, broke, carless, inadequately housed (no yard), only raggedly getting along with each other and our own demons. How sweet it was, though—another baby—it was hard not to give in to the sweetness!

Michele, who did not believe in the unconscious, had made three appointments for a new IUD, broken them all, and left the record-keeping on her menstrual cycle to me. How pleasurably the procreative impulse moved in me, how powerful was the urge to put my semen where it could find the egg: I must have fudged the numbers. I took her to Planned Parenthood in Norwalk to drop off urine for the pregnancy test. Later in the day she was so upset that she called me home from work. I found her kneeling in front of the stove, her head in the oven. "Cut it out, Michele," I said, turning off the gas.

I made an appointment with Marianna Wilcox, the village's Reichian therapist, and poured out my woe. She did not see how my feelings could be preempted by Michele's. I should open the door and go right in. I took her advice and concentrated on opening my heart, reaching back to our original love and bringing it into the present. I was not a glamorous New York director anymore, and she had never been a simple Colorado girl. Our relation was deeper than that. She was the earth and I was the sky. She was the mother, and even if I had failed in Taos and mislaid my confidence and sense of natural authority, I was the father. We would have to be strong; there was no alternative.

It was hard waiting for the abortion, Michele's body going into the changes of early pregnancy. It helped when friends loaned us a tiny television set, which we had so far lived without. Julian and Alfred were delighted to watch cartoons in the morning and *Sesame Street* in the early evening, just when Michele wore out and it was time to think about dinner.

I was dreaming up a play set in Taos, about Bill Bolender, Steve Parks, and myself, workmen artists, and our women. I sent *A Wedding Party* to John Albano. I wrote a love poem to Michele. She said writing was my other wife and she would not share me without a struggle. David contemptuously dismissed my literary yearnings. Wolfgang, on one of his consulting visits, said in passing, "I forgot that you're a writer."

My parents came to visit the day after the abortion on their way back from Europe. In our ritual talk, my father said I should make a commitment to David and the harpsichord business and stick to it and everything would work out. He said not to expect much satisfaction from work. "Everything is black and white when you're young," he said. "When you get older, you learn to love gray." I could hardly bear his condescension. He said that he himself had wanted to paint—implying that my writing was a comparable hobby, though in fact he never did paint. Not to let myself be a term in his discourse, I wanted to tell him to fuck off, that age did not excuse him. But that would have been disrespectful. I would swallow my anger and love him too.

It was a revelation when Marianna said I did not have to choose between job and writing: I could do both. Bob Dylan agreed: "You can have your cake and eat it too." I discontinued our weekly therapy sessions, which I could ill afford, and plunged into writing a play about Santa Claus, which I called *Lieb und Arbeit or The Last Red Wagon*, imagining Santa, his wife Lotte, elves and elfim (elf children) named Elmo, Marfa, Fufo, Djidjo, Tono, Roni, Coli … A money-maker for sure, if I ever finished it.

John Albano wrote to say he loved *A Wedding Party* and would do a production at Theater for the New City, which had moved into the former Gate Theatre on Second Avenue. I had the sweetest of birthdays, my forty-fourth. I sent out scripts to agents and producers and applied for grants to the National Endowment for the Arts and the Guggenheim Foundation, asking for time to write plays and see them through to production.

Julian was more and more interesting, bursting with insights and imagination. He told me that fairies come from outer space. First they fly around us and kiss us, because they love us. Then they turn into bunny rabbits, which grow up into big rabbits. The rabbits turn into worms, which crawl into worm skins they find. The worms grow big and round and come out of the worm skins as fairies again. Fairies don't die, he said. They can make people not-old or take them away to the place of not-dying.

On Alfred's second birthday Michele dressed him as a bear for the Stonington Halloween parade. I carried him on my shoulders, and he won a competition as the cutest. He hated being cute. The prize was a whole box of Hershey bars.

Life settled into a routine, just as I had planned. The boys and I got up at first light. I shaved, made myself a cup of Nescafé, and went up into the cupola while they watched cartoons, rolled myself a joint, tuned in classical music on the radio, and sat at my desk, writing. At eight I came down for breakfast. The Headstart bus came at eight-thirty; I tried to get down to the street early with Julian so we would have a little time to play. Work. Home to lunch, possibly a lie-down with Michele. Home at six. Dinner. Putting the children to bed took till nine; Michele and I were in bed by ten or ten-thirty. She had taken up belly-dancing with two of her lady friends. I was thrilled by her curvy body, lithe waist reappearing.

I was turned down for the grants and did not even get nibbles from agents and producers.

Julian wrote a book with my help called *The Paper Boy*, which Michele set about illustrating, a potential talent of hers I hoped to activate. We had another idea for a story about a man who was really a lion. The idea was, as the animal population shrinks and humans multiply, what happens about spirits? Must new humans do without souls? Do the extra animal spirits "disappear"? Or do many, or most, humans have animal spirits? Are they animals in human form, not actually human beings at all? There may be three types of humans: real humans, spiritless humans, and humans who are really animals. I myself am a horse.

Sylvie stayed on into the fall, studying dance at Connecticut College. She begrudged us her Rabbit, and we wearied of her studiously neutral presence. In moments of madness Michele threatened to take the children and go back to New Mexico, complaining that I was David's "slave"—hardly a useful way to think about it!

Delivering Peter's clavichord at long last, I proposed to collaborate with him on an opera about Milarepa, the Tibetan holy man. Peter loved the clavichord, a sorry little instrument, in my opinion. He was interested in the Milarepa project—I should write the libretto.

Sylvie flew home to New Mexico in time for Christmas and decided to stay there. We were glad to have the house to ourselves, and the car, temporarily. Hideous scenes between the sisters had left Michele strafed and unwell, confirming Gurdjieff's alternative chemistry, which explains how subtle substances essential to development are destroyed by the expression of negative emotion and wrong work of centers. Julian, more enlightened than his parents, said grace at breakfast on Christmas Day: "Thank you for the lords and the gods, and thank you for all the people below us. Amen."

J.D. came from New Mexico to retrieve Sylvie's Rabbit. We bought a thrift-shop washer and dryer: trips to the laundromat had been the main reason we needed a car.

The five-year crisis of our marriage climaxed in a horrendous scene. I spoke sharply about something, and Michele gave way to fury, insulted me, said she hated me, getting dressed in the middle of the night intending to take the grocery money and leave. Julian, sick all weekend, had thrown up on his bed, and I was sleeping with him in Sylvie's room, driven out of the marriage bed. Michele and I talked in the kitchen. She had no place to go and no way to support herself, and her helplessness enraged her. I would not give in and tell her it was all right to go away.

Having a family was a radical adventure, and working a steady job was an education: this was the life I needed in order to become a whole person and have something to write about. My artist friends in New York, living alone, or alone with a child, were equally frustrated in their work: it was harder and harder to put on a show. I did lights for the Mystic Paper Beasts in the big theatre at Connecticut College and played harpsichord in a shop concert with Ed Kottick, a musicologist and skilled recorder player from the University of Iowa.

Michele painting a soundboard

MICHELE WAS A GIFTED PAINTER, and David needed traditional painted decoration for the soundboards of his finished harpsichords. She had painted a few soundboards already; now she began to take it seriously. I took her to museums in New York, New Haven, and Boston to look at historical examples. She went to Boston for classes with Sheridan Germann, the reigning queen of harpsichord decoration. Before long she was painting meticulous traditional borders and exuberant flowers on soundboard after soundboard, working in the studio we set up for her at home, going on from the early Flemish styles in egg tempera to the later, looser French style in gouache. She was remarkably good at it, producing a convincing simulacrum of period style and sensibility, investing each instrument with personality and dancing immediacy. I loved her work, and the dollars she brought in made a big difference, some weeks more than doubling our income.

I gave her a pogo stick for her thirty-third birthday.

10

A YOUNG GERMAN CABINETMAKER, Hinrich Müller, came to work for David. Hinrich had little English and seldom spoke, seemingly dour, but there was a twinkle in his eye, and he was a fine oboe player. His wife, Laurel, a big, intelligent, loud, warm-hearted girl from Los Angeles, talked all the time and played the flute. They invited a group of us over for *tafelmusik*. I set a spinet harpsichord close beside my seat at the table, and we played trio sonatas before, during, and after a good meal.

Square as they were, we introduced the Müllers to the Potters and started including them in social events. Michele invited them to dinner, and before long they were folded into our life. There was talk of possibly sharing a house. I found them boring and did not understand why we were getting so tight with them until I realized that Michele and Hinrich were having an affair, for which she wanted my blessing. I tried to withhold it, finding the situation annoying and dangerous. She insisted this was what she needed, claiming she was too unhappy to go on without it. I believed her and even helped them engineer an hour or two alone together in the afternoon by hanging out with Laurel, who asked the most tactless questions: did I feel humiliated? would things ever be the same?

I declined to buy into Michele's fantasy of a "relationship" with the Müllers and tried not to get sucked into the whirlpool of sex, delaying it as long as I could. But she needed me to sleep with Laurel, and the inescapable group hugs were inescapably steamy. Finally, on the Fourth of July, once the children were asleep, I went along to bed with the three of them and fucked Laurel while Hinrich fucked Michele alongside. Fucking was fun enough; but when they wanted to sleep all four in the one bed, I opted for the couch and let them toss and turn without me.

They were there for dinner every night and sat around talking after I put the boys to bed. When I could stand it no longer, I said it was my bedtime and slipped away, leaving them to sort out the rest of the night. Sometimes they let me go; sometimes Laurel pursued me. I tried to go with the flow, but one night I snapped at her when she trapped me in the hall, hugging and kissing me on the way to the bathroom, Michele and Hinrich necking on the sofa in the pink living room in the dark. I was sorry Laurel's feelings were hurt, but it was a ridiculous situation. I wanted to be Michele's only husband, not one of two. Michele kept telling me how wonderful Hinrich was, but he hardly said boo to me.

Even so, I gradually started to like them, and it all made more sense to

MICHAEL SMITH

Country dancing with Laurel and Hinrich Müller

me when it emerged that they wanted me to make Laurel pregnant. They wanted a child, and Hinrich had an undescended testicle or something, no viable sperm. I could do that. Even when Michele panicked, I came to favor our moving in together. Sharing a house would solve several of our problems. I wished my own little family was more self-sufficient, but evidently we were not; the boys needed a yard, and love-drama aside, joining up with the Müllers seemed like a creative, practical move. They were good-hearted people. Michele and Laurel set about finding us a house to rent.

WE STILL DIDN'T HAVE A CAR and hadn't been to Charlemont since we moved back from New Mexico. Borrowing Laurel and Hinrich's Datsun one August weekend, Michele and I drove up with the boys. Bicky drove over from Ithaca with her son, Ben, and cousin John came up by bus from New York. Being in the woods with people from my original life, I felt like myself again.

I had vacation time coming, and after another week at work, I went back to the cabin for a week by myself. The Müllers had taken over my study and only laughed when I objected. Writing was relegated to the cupola, which was unbearably hot this time of year, my real work unreal to everyone but me. I was sorry to ditch Michele and the boys, but I needed some time to myself before our communal life began.

Getting there without a car was complicated. Well before I tramped up the familiar path through the woods to my house on the rock, lugging clothes, writing paper, water, and food supplies, I had lost track of why I was coming away. Once I was on my spot, though, all confusion dropped away, and the natural blessedness of living took me in its arms.

The cabin was completely disconnected from the human world. Having no electricity released me from the sixty-cycle electromagnetic hum we are inexorably bathed in throughout our ordinary lives. I could feel the difference. Gradually natural rhythms reemerged, no longer synced to the electric grid, overpowered and preempted by technology. I listened to the the silence. In the empty breathing woods I satisfied a powerful urge to strip away persona and everything else, down to the essential thinking animal, bare my body and soul to the world as it is—or was. I imagined myself a Native American, a caveman.

I went down the hill to Jean-Claude's to check in and stayed for dinner. Fred had married Debbie, a nutritionist, and they were living in the house he had started building with Sarah, commuting every week to the city, where they kept an apartment on Greenwich Avenue with side-by-side consulting rooms. Ed Field, the poet, was staying in the old schoolhouse on Jean-Claude's property with his lover, Neal. Shami Chaikin, Joe's sister, was visiting with her lover, Karen Ludwig. A boy named Raoul, an ex-student of Jean-Claude's at Princeton, was piercingly beautiful in the light at the end of the table.

Did my ineradicable bisexuality have anything to do with the problematic quality of my life with Michele? I had not made love with anyone else, apart from Laurel, since before we were married—hadn't wanted to. I loved Michele and our sex life together. So what if I visualized cock when I wanted to come? Fantasies are good!

I brought along pornographic magazines as masturbation prompts for my time alone. I knew myself: if I did not somehow have an orgasm practically every day, I would hardly be able to think about anything else. Sam Shepard, exemplar of masculinity, once told me he had to come before he could write. This inner wave action did not let up when the lover was inaccessible or uninterested. Best give in and do it. Even when my sex life with Michele was going strong, I liked to keep in touch, literally, with myself.

I spent most of the first day at my cabin playing with my cock. Needing a ceremonial moment of no work, I cut a sliver off a Snoopy and ingested a tiny dose of LSD. It was a beautiful twinkling day. Naked, I admired my cock and balls from various angles in my shaving mirror, observed my arousal, took my time squeezing and rubbing my radiantly sensitive dick, oiled it up and nearly climaxed; stopped, put clothes on, did something else for a while; then came back to absorbing self-sexuality as the sun swung through the hours. Wasn't this the "Roman aberration" Gurdjieff denounces in *Beelzebub's Tales to His Grandson*, which I had been reading that very morning? But I was starting to feel happy. There's nothing like extended masturbation to take the mind off everything else. Hours with the beloved are even better, but when do you both get the time?

I had brought along a short novel I'd written, *High Points of Youth*, about myself and my friends in our thirties. How long it had taken to grow up! I threw in as much accumulated life-material as I had, trying to straighten out the painful passages and find my story, spanning the dozen years from before I met Johnny Dodd until after we split up, hoping for closure.

Needing someone to read it, I took the manuscript to Ed Field, whom I respected as a poet but hardly knew. I felt considerable trepidation, hesitating outside the schoolhouse door, two typewriters going strong within. I pricked up my courage and knocked.

"Is it long?" Ed wanted to know.

"No, it's short," I said. "It's not hard to read." He said he would read it aloud to Neal.

With that out of my hands, I made a list of the writing projects I had in mind: *Heavy Pockets*, a "thriller comedy" set in Taos, for the Changing Scene; *Lieb und Arbeit*, my play about Santa Claus; *I Never*, a collection of stories; a play about centaurs, requested by Ellen Stewart for La Mama; *You Can Be You If I Can Be Me—Otherwise Trouble*, a novel about marriage that I had abandoned in the press of events; *Joe's Café*, the television series; the Milarepa libretto I had promised to Peter; and a movie about a high-speed cross-country car race, based on an article in a police magazine. That was years of writing; better get started.

I plunged into the play, *Heavy Pockets*. A first act came out fully formed, as if I had been thinking about it. Writing every day, happy in my hermitage, I relaxed, calmed myself, and my mind cleared. I went down the hill a couple of times and ate and talked too much; Jean-Claude, Fred, and Debbie were on an extreme raw diet, looking gaunt and sinewy. Shami made an alternate dinner of chicken and potato salad. I ate both. Robbie Anton, a delicate, brilliant, sexy young puppeteer, looked at me desirously, I imagined. I vaguely hoped he would venture up the hill to my cabin, sorry he didn't.

I had come to the forest frightened by the onrushing calamity of nations, the papers full of fresh talk of "limited" nuclear war. I was still frightened but in midweek realized I did not expect it to happen that day, which made a difference, although something in me never relaxed because of this fear. I was philosophical about my own death and suffering, but the thought of not being able to save my loved ones was unbearable.

Ed Field brought back my manuscript, saying it was a treat and he and Neal had enjoyed it. He said the beginning was confusing and I should make the characters clearer when they first appear, good advice that I appreciated. Of course, he added, they knew who everybody was and loved it as gossip. I needed to have someone read it who did not know the people.

11

Michele and Laurel found us a beautiful house with a big yard in Mystic, five miles from the shop in Stonington, and we rented it for a year for $500 a month. Our half was $50 more than we had been paying for our apartment on Water Street in Stonington, and it was well worth it. Half of the double living room would be Michele's studio. I claimed a small side room for my study. Upstairs were three bedrooms, the boys in the middle, the two couples at the ends.

I would have liked to cut back my hours at the harpsichord shop, keep just enough of the job to anchor my home base, and make my way back onto the public stage; but Michele and I, still without a car, needed more money, not less, and the only immediate way to get it was to insist on it and commit myself to working harder for David. He promoted a young draftsman past me to head the production shop: he and two others were making $395 a week, versus my $290. Michele made it an issue of pride and manliness: "Think how valuable you are!" David had been making me feel useless and inept.

To get a raise, I had to provoke the full bellowing-bull treatment from David, his four-year-old daughter Jessica looking on amazed. I felt touched and tender toward him even as he was screaming at me. He was the most interesting person around, and it was hard to get his attention. Jumping into the abyss, I demanded that he let me graduate from the underling-on-trial role, make me one of the "seniors," and pay me as much as the others; otherwise I would look for another job, although it was hard to imagine what other job I could get. The storm passed, and David staged a formal meeting of the senior staff. "Let right be done!" he said to me before he went in; it was quite comical. Afterward he reported that they all resisted but gave

The house in Mystic that we shared with the Müllers

in because they did not want to lose me. It was a relief to be transformed overnight from a failure to a success at my harpsichord career.

Now is the time to escape, I thought, having "proved I could do it."

Bicky hosted Dad's entire family in Ithaca to celebrate his eightieth birthday—his two sets of two children, their three current spouses, and his six grandchildren, half of them Mother's as well. We had a hike in a gorge, a picnic in the park by the lake, and a formal dinner for the grown-ups on Bicky and Steve's front porch. Dad was graduately going blind, but he was happy with us all around him and rose to the occasion with a graceful speech.

John Albano was stalled with *A Wedding Party*. A phone call from me got the attention of Crystal Field and George Bartenieff, old friends who ran the Theater for the New City. Crystal read the script and called to say she loved it, they would do it right away.

I went into the city for auditions, thrilled to be in a theatre, walk on the stage, watch actors read my lines and impersonate my characters. The play was wonderful! The little scenes were subtle, funny, beautiful, full of surprises, easily actable, hardly a word out of place. Afterwards, though, at Phebe's, the theatre bar at East 4th and Bowery, my attention wandered. Whole stretches of conversation got away: I might as well have been a

Picnic in Ithaca for my father's 80th birthday: front row, Shannon, Dad, Julian, Mother, Lewis holding Patience, Ben and Katherine in front of him; back row, me, Michele, Virginia, Bicky, Lewis's wife Alice, and Steve holding Alfred.

dead playwright. What did it mean that my real life was elsewhere? Kenny Burgess walked past outside, an intimate of earlier years whose loft was a few doors down—I let him pass. The scrappy East Village theatre world, my home turf a few years ago, was a poignant fantasy I less than half believed in, a hardscrabble reality I didn't really want to be part of anymore.

The home circle cranked up for my forty-fifth birthday, and I was not really present there either. Michele stayed home with Hinrich, and Laurel came with me to New Haven to hear Valenti play a recital at Yale, the best harpsichord playing I ever heard, grave and splendid. Access to the well-equipped shop and lumber supply at Zuckermann Harpsichords was a valuable side benefit of our jobs. John Bennett helped me make a Shaker table for our big new dining room, where we had dinner together every night. I took the whole gang to Charlemont in the autumn glory, wanting to be there with Julian and Alfred, and led a Columbus Day walk to the top of the mountain. Alfred was young for such a long, hard trek, but he made it.

In our communal house in Mystic, the four adults took turns cooking, each of us producing dinner every fourth night. After dinner, Laurel on flute and Hinrich on oboe joined me in Telemann and Quantz trio sonatas while Michele drew or painted.

Michele suffered periodic storms of insecurity that sometimes disrupted our coziness. One otherwise mellow evening she got so desperate that she jumped up, grabbed a screwdriver, and violently gouged the egg-tempera self-portrait she had been working on for a week. Her need for praise and reassurance had involved us all in the painting's success. We were horrified. I was frightened by her ferocity, as if she was attacking me.

Poor Michele! I could not help her, and I wished she would leave me out of it while she worked through her anxieties about making art. I wanted to revise my novel, to write the next scene of *Heavy Pockets*, to get on to Milarepa. But when I looked at her beautiful portrait of Julian that was hanging over my desk, I had to go out and hug and kiss her, apologize for the egoism of getting my feelings hurt and losing my sense of proportion, tell her I loved her, that I understood how hard it was and believed in her

Michele and boys in the side yard

with my whole being, how wonderful and precious she was, how blessed I was to be able to love her.

A WEEK BEFORE THE OPENING OF *A Wedding Party*, I went into the city and watched five hours of rehearsal. The play was good, whimsical and funny, with a clean energy that made me happy. John Albano directing and the cast and crew charmingly devoting themselves to bringing my fanciful characters and tale to life—what a gift!

I missed the opening but took Julian with me to see a performance a week later. Crystal was sublime as Sarah, the earth mother. In her dressing room afterwards, she showed me the technique she used for beading her eyelashes, melting black wax over a flame; I felt the presence of Duse and Bernhardt. Wonderful as it was, my play was lost in the shuffle at TNC. John Vacarro and his Play-house of the Ridiculous were doing one of their mad camp spectacles earlier in the evening in the bigger theatre upstairs, and a British drag troupe, Bloolips, did a late show on the *Wedding Party* set, both of them attracting young crowds avid for transgressive thrills. In this context, a pastoral-lyrical play like mine did not make much of an impression.

Eczema on my finger spread to my hands and forearms, a clear sign of stress. The dermatologist's prescription was to finish my book. I had been pushing on with *Heavy Pockets*, inserting speeches, expanding scenes, but had not started the second act. I put the play aside and turned back to my novella, *High Points of Youth*, straightening out the opening sequence and clarifying the characters as they enter. I was not worried about inspiration: the most uninspired drudgery often produces excellent writing. It was only a matter of time, and my position was that I have plenty.

My parents invited us to join them in Acapulco for a week that February. I did not really want to go. These artificial interludes of luxury underlined the poverty of our normal existence, and being with my parents was hard work, especially with Michele in the picture. Still, I wanted to broaden the boys' experience and give them time with their grandparents, and I was always glad to get out of the United States.

We stayed in a high-rise condo by the beach. Dad, who was afflicted with macular degeneration, could no longer see well enough to read and sat on the balcony doing nothing. Alfred practically drowned in the swimming pool, noticed at the last minute as he was going down for the third time. Michele kept worrying that he would fall off the balcony, although I repeatedly showed her that his head was too big to fit through the railing. Mother was cheerful and fun, wanting everybody to behave themselves and have a good time, and we did. Michele and I got away once to the market and lunch in the real town.

The beach out front was steep, swimming not advised. Dad loved swimming in the ocean more than anything and was not to be stopped. Michele and I went in with him, the waves big and thrilling. I came ashore, pulling myself in on a rope against the tug of the undertow, outran the next crasher, turned and saw Michele and my eighty-year-old father thrown down and rolled. After the third huge wave took my father under, three strapping guys in little black trunks materialized, plucked him from the surf, ran him up the beach, and set him on the sand. Michele came out buzzing with adrenalin, her suit full of sand, the crotch hanging down to her knees. They were badly shaken.

　　　　　　　　　　　　　　　　　　　　MICHAEL SMITH

The next day we flew home to cold, wet, Puritan New England. While we were on the plane, Dad, who always believed in doing what you are afraid of, challenged his fear by going in again. Again the lifeguard angels saved his life, but this time something was broken in his upper spine.

I only learned this a week later when Mother telephoned from Santa Barbara. Dad had been paralyzed, and there was very little medical care in Acapulco. The nearest hospital was in Mexico City, a four-hour drive over the mountains. Mother ran out of cash and had to borrow money to keep them going. After a few days a medivac plane came from Houston and flew them home. Dad was in the hospital, in a neck brace, in pain, unable to do anything for himself. I offered to come out. Mother said not to: I would just be one more thing to manage.

12

I finished *Heavy Pockets* but had to put off Xeroxing scripts because I had spent all our money on a dog Michele fell in love with in a pet shop window, a toy fox terrier she named Dandelion. My theatre dreams would not die. Bill Bolender might do the play in Taos. The Stonington Players could and would do a lot worse than an original play by Michael Smith, but I couldn't get them even to read it. Melisande and I imagined turning an old brick powerhouse on the road to Noank into a theatre, coffee house, and tea garden; I could do it there.

In my morning hour I read and wrote about Milarepa, the eighth-century Tibetan holy man, soaking up his extreme example—he lived in a cave for a decade, eating nothing but nettles and turning green. I made his life into a theatrical spectacle that would require the Metropolitan Opera house for a proper staging. I was sick of writing little plays, scaled to Off-Off-Broadway and the Changing Scene.

I went to Santa Barbara to see my father as soon as he was home from rehab. He had recovered the use of his hands and arms, but his legs were weak and pained him. A nurse was sleeping in the living room. Mother was exhausted.

While in California I prospected for a job. Laurel's brother Bim was the programmer for the Light Palette, the gold standard of computer dimmer boards, and he suggested there might be a job for me at Strand-Century Lighting, who needed someone to write a better user manual for it. I drove down to Carson, in the industrial wasteland southwest of Los Angeles, to meet Bim's boss, who it turned out knew Murray Mednick and Theatre Genesis. I did not mention this to my parents: the illusion of stability was all I had to offer my father, nor did I want to give Mother false hopes.

Michele and I had talked about living closer to my parents when they needed help, and the time had come. A small orchard out back of their house included a second lot, with access to another street around the corner. My father could profitably finance a house for us, I could get a job in Santa Barbara, they could see their grandchildren grow up, and we could put the family back together on a mutually nurturing basis. But it was too late for that. It was impossible to go on living where they were, miles from shopping. Even before his injury, Dad could no longer see well enough to drive. They were moving into the Casa Dorinda, a Montecito life-care community, and would not need us.

I VISITED JOHNNY whenever I was in the city on harpsichord business, still hungering for some secret knowledge I could get nowhere else, feeling there was a "real me" that only awoke when I was with him. He now cut me off with a sharply worded postcard saying he needed all his energy for survival, telling me bluntly not to call or write to him anymore: "Stay away." In truth Johnny was a distraction I could hardly afford any more than he could afford me. Break, heart, I told myself, as if it was not already broken, and let him go.

At David's behest I learned to use a primitive computer typesetter, coached by two applications guys from Mergenthaler Linotype. I built a prototype of David's latest kit, an English bentside spinet, and wrote the manual for it. I set up a mail-order music business and printed up a catalog. I organized concerts for David every few months, either at the shop amid the power tools and lumber or in the Unitarian Church in town. His customers included many sensational musicians—Trevor Pinnock, Lionel Party, Malcolm Bilson, Pamela Cook, Peter Sykes, Martin Pearlman, Lola Odiaga—who came to pick up their instruments and played recitals for us. The whole enterprise was about music and devoted to the most elevated pleasure. Early music was a culture unto itself just then in vogue.

Frank Hubbard, our chief competitor, had died. In May 1981, at the Boston Early Music Festival and Exhibition, David took the high road as the world's biggest maker of authentic harpsichords. In addition to the booth in the exhibition hall, he rented a large, elegant room on the first floor of the New England Conservatory to display our wares. We trucked up eleven finished instruments and two partly completed kits. John and I stayed in Boston all week to man the exhibits and keep the instruments tuned. We slept in a dormitory, and I had a funny, friendly one-night affair with a young would-be piano-maker from Wisconsin, curiously turned on by his clean white socks.

It was a welcome break from our Mystic household. Life with two wives was sticky, Laurel jealous of Hinrich making love to Michele, Michele constantly mad at Laurel, supposedly about the housework, the men forced to take sides with their own wives. It was hard to keep my balance. I tried letting out my anger, blowing up a few times, denouncing Michele and storming out, but that didn't get me anywhere. She was struggling with everyone and overwhelmed.

In June I persuaded Michele to go Charlemont by herself to calm down, paint all day if she liked, and be happy. I would have loved a week to myself just then in the cabin in the woods. She went by bus, taking Dandy with her in a basket on her arm, and Father's Day and the Summer Solstice went smoother without her. My twelve-year-old niece Shannon, Bicky's sweet, self-possessed young daughter, came to visit, and we joined the Potters' parade down the length of Stonington, Alfred on my shoulders in a vast, ballooning cape and monster mask, Julian as a darting, prancing fish. After the parade the village gathered on the lighthouse lawn to watch the

Potters' exquisite family circus. At the end of the week I took the boys to Charlemont to enjoy a naturistic interlude and fetch Mommy home. She had been miserable, she said, frightened to be alone in the woods in the dark, rain all day blurring her watercolors, which were pretty anyway.

Michele somehow imagined the Müllers would be gone when she got back: Laurel was pregnant, and they were talking about a house of their own. She brought me some positive energy too, eagerly joining me in meditation practice, having received direct transmission from Jean-Claude in the high meadow.

We went into the city to see Irene's inspired staging of *La Vida Es Sueño* in a small theatre on 42nd Street, essentially the very production I had wanted to do in Taos, which the actors could not and in Bill Bolender's case would not do. It made me think I had missed the boat and should give up the dream of doing theatre.

On the way home, as these thoughts were preying on my mind, Michele nagged me relentlessly about the Fourth of July picnic we were having the following day. I had every intention of pitching in—she knew I would— we were good at giving parties. Her bitter, groundless reproaches were unbearable as I drove through night rain and nerve-wracking traffic up the Hutchinson River Parkway. I begged her to stop, then was rude, finally in despair said, "How are we going to get out of this?"

"Out of what?"

"This horrible travesty of a marriage."

She suggested I go away, then said she would go to Taos to her mother. Regretting that I had lost control of myself, I kissed her on the bridge over the Housatonic River—we kissed whenever we crossed a river—and said we should forget it, and she quieted down and went to sleep while I drove us home. We worked all the next day on our party, which was a huge success.

13

Our year in Mystic was up. Laurel and Hinrich rented a house of their own in Stonington, affairs over, mission accomplished. Michele found a house for us in Westerly, Rhode Island, a quiet, attractive town on the Pawcatuck River five miles the other side of Stonington. It had been used as a doctor's office and private hospital and not lived in for decades. Though dingy inside and long unloved, it was exactly what we needed, with plenty of room, a comfortable, old-fashioned generosity of scale, and rich potential for good vibrations. The rent was $350 a month, which I could afford, barely. The landlord agreed to buy us paint for the interior walls; we could deduct material costs for

23 Cross Street, Weserly

other improvements from the rent. We asked for first refusal if they ever decided to sell.

Michele was happier once we were on our own, and we set to work to revive the beauty of the house. Dennis and Megan Pinette, artist friends from Stonington, had already moved to Westerly. The Potters and Pinettes helped us pull up thousands of tacks that held down layers of linoleum on the beautiful oak floors in the principal rooms. Hinrich helped me put in a new plywood subfloor in the kitchen and pantry, which I tiled in big black and red squares. A baby grand piano I acquired for $300 graced the living room; there was room in the dining room for my long pink harpsichord. I found a good recipe for granola in *Diet for a Small Planet*. I went halves with Dennis on a canoe for the Pawcatuck River. The three couples, Potters, Pinettes, and Smiths, united as the Westerly Arts Club, posing naked for each other and painting together.

We had a car now, a rusty Toyota I had bought for $200. Most days I left it for Michele and rode to work with Stephanie Blanchette, the new office manager I had found for

In the office with Stephanie Blanchette

David, who lived a couple of blocks away. David came back from Europe beaming and relaxed and gave everyone raises retroactive to July. Julian started first grade.

When Laurel went into labor, Michele called a babysitter for the boys and we rushed over to Stonington to be in on the big event. The Müllers had planned a home birth, and the midwife was already there, the house cozy, everything prepared. Laurel's contractions rolled along, the baby was doing fine. I brought my dorje to attract the higher energies. Laurel's brothers phoned. Michele breathed with her, Hinrich pressed on her back, the midwife listened to the baby's heart with a stethoscope.

Around midnight, the cervical dilation stalled, the baby not managing to duck its head, tuck in its chin, and move on down the birth canal. I knelt on the bed on all fours and Laurel lay back across me, searching for a position that would ease the birth. When her blood pressure shot up, the midwife decided more expertise was needed, so we jumped into the car, and I drove them on empty roads through the cold October night to the hospital in Westerly, where only Laurel and Hinrich were admitted, the midwife shunned and shut out with Michele and me in the waiting room. At five in the morning word came down that a girl was born. They were overjoyed. They named her Louisa.

I bought a new car, a green Buick station wagon only seven years old, and allowed the Toyota to finish disintegrating. The Buick cheered us up: with what we regarded as practicality came comfort, and the new house suited us perfectly. Michele and I found ourselves back in harmony, our love strong and sweet.

THE HIGH DOLLAR had killed the European market for our harpsichord kits, which had been half our volume. It was no longer profitable to export them, so David off-loaded the European business onto his French partner, Marc Ducornet. My duties at the harpsichord shop were increasingly nebulous. The business seemed to be running down: the most exciting prospect was picking up the pieces after some kind of collapse.

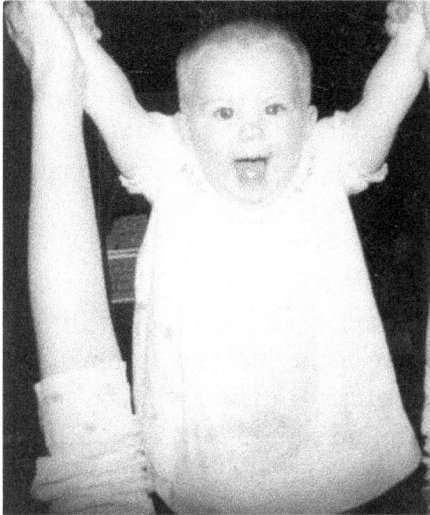

Louisa Müller

I followed up on my interview with Strand-Century in Los Angeles, who offered me a job as a technical writer. I asked for $30,000 plus moving expenses. How was I to decide if I should actually do it? Michele said it was all right with her, I should do what would make me happy. The *I Ching* gave me Dissolution changing to Inner Truth, which suggested we should go. The *I Ching* often recommends doing what you already thought you wanted to do.

I went to an electrical convention in New York to meet my future boss for final negotiations only to realize with a sinking feeling that this was not bringing me any closer to the life I imagined for us. With more money but also more expenses, we would be no better off in L.A. Michele would be torn out of her life, stranded among strangers in a depressing suburb, her career as a harpsichord painter at an end; and I would be no closer to doing theatre. I would have another little-gray-man job, writing promotional copy for transformers. I called it off; we would stay where we were.

Michele and I played the King and Queen in *A Celebration of Twelfth Night*, a splendid annual Christmas production by Westerly's excellent Community Chorus. Parading in grandly robed and crowned, we presided from thrones, Julian dancing and frolicking with the children, Alfred enchanting as a magical child carrying a magic ship. Thus we were symbolically accepted into the Westerly community. My courage revived.

ANY POSSIBILITY of making theatre in Westerly seemed to revolve around a person I will call James Swift, a tall, beautiful young man who had staged a Molière play on a barge in the river the previous summer. We invited him over for dinner to talk about a summer theatre project. James was more interested in talking about sex. I found him highly attractive but he focused his charm on Michele, feeling her up under the table right before her husband's eyes. Afterwards she was aflutter and asked me if I minded if she had an affair with him. I did, but I didn't want to rein her in, I wanted her to be happy and make her own choices. She urged me to have an affair of my own. Theoretically I would have been glad to.

Heavy Pockets was finished. I decided to start rehearsing even though I did not have a theatre and assembled a cast of friends, with Dennis Pinette as the heavy and James Swift as a tragic buffoon. My idea was to practice for a few weeks and then give script-in-hand performances in the dining room, with the audience in the living room, if we did not find a better place to do it. Julian was unhappy at being left out so I added a tiny part for him.

Heavy Pockets is a mocking portrait of three couples, including ourselves, and the incestuous small-town theatre scene in Taos. The murder-mystery plot does not quite pay off: I waffled over who had committed the murder, if indeed there was one; I could never believe any of my characters would actually kill someone, any more than I would. Otherwise the ambiguities were deliberate. In life I often did not know what even my closest familiars were talking about. My own attempts at communication were fragmentary revelations into which I deliberately inserted personal allusions, looking for the flash of recognition, hoping to elevate the moment onto a more aesthetic,

Rehearsing curtain call for *Heavy Pockets* in the Living Room Theatre

soulful plane. I never had enough data to know what else was crowding in on my encounters, barely an inkling of what was on other people's minds as they flew past. Nor did they know me better.

Fifty-five people saw the two performances. Everyone liked my play; some said they loved it. Michele was miffed at not being in it but came through in the crunch, painting scenery, providing friendly soup for the actors during rehearsal, and shoring up my confidence. We had parties after each night's performance with bountiful food and drink. *Heavy Pockets* was my breakthrough play, rich, complex, entertaining enough for Broadway or the West End. So far, nonetheless, that has been the only production.

MY PARENTS were there for Halloween and Alfred's birthday. Michele made wonderful masks and Mother took the boys out trick-or-treating after the birthday party. He was four.

Julian bravely went off to school every day, having honorably given himself to the idea of second grade, but he was visibly unhappy with himself and reported to be inattentive. No wonder. The material he brought home was impossibly dumb and boring. His mind could not move so slowly. We needed to get him out of there,

Halloween 1981: Mother with Alfred and Julian

not watch him fail. Michele found a Waldorf school not too far away to which we switched him on his seventh birthday, February 10. We would pay for it somehow. He had a wonderful teacher and came home singing, full of poetry and love, happier right away.

Funny the seesaw of marriage—Michele felt better; I felt worse. She had me cut her hair off short and looked great; I was suddenly old. She was painting beautifully but working so hard, one harpsichord after another, not to mention spending afternoon hours with James, that I was left to deal with the housework, laundry, and boys by myself. I didn't mind, but it was a bit much.

Irene Fornés hired me to come to New York to visit her playwriting workshop—part of a plot to get me to come back, she said. How was I to reconcile my imaginary world of writing and theatre and my actual world of job, wife, and children? Over a Peruvian lunch she conjured up a playwriting workshop for "masters," mentioning herself, me, Ken Bernard, Jean-Claude, and Murray Mednick. We agreed we should be working commercially; it was wrong to be keeping back our gifts.

Fun chez Dan and Melisande

The Potters threw a sex-reversed tea party. Michele went as a French sailor, I (conceptually) as my own mother, with my long hair in ponytails on either side of my head.

Word reached me that Hibiscus, the glitter-drag star I had known as George Harris, had died of a peculiar form of pneumonia, a new illness that had something to do with gay sex, which was flourishing on the West Village waterfront like exotic tribal rites. Frank Lilly raved about the new, nasty-sounding cellar sex clubs; I was titillated, envious, the way I always felt about other people's promiscuity, but not even slightly tempted to participate. I had lost all interest in being gay, much as I missed the social whirl and fun. I was lucky: my timing saved my life.

14

I HAD GRADUALLY become a specialist in fortepianos, which David had added to our line of harpsichord and clavichord kits and finished instruments. The piano of Mozart and Haydn's time, simpler and more lightly built, with a crisper, more transparent sound, is better suited to their music than the modern grand. In the spring I pushed hard to get two fortepianos ready for Malcolm Bilson, the Cornell professor and leading advocate of the historical Viennese piano. Malcolm talked only to David, who was trying various approaches to get the pianos to sound better; I was his hands and did the best I could.

Under David's direction, I put in several weeks redoing the action of Malcolm's personal piano, a copy by Philip Belt of an instrument made in Vienna in 1790, which Malcolm was using to record the Mozart piano concertos. When David went to Europe, Malcolm showed up in his van and took his piano away—then was desperately unhappy with what I had done to it. I had to drive to Ithaca and fetch it back, seven hours each way. Exhausted, I took to my bed, feeling awful, not so much sick as crazy. The next day I ran out of the shop in midafternoon like one possessed. I never wanted to be a piano technician!

The weekend after Memorial Day, while Michele stayed home painting a harpsichord soundboard for the rent money, I took Julian and Alfred and another little boy up to the cabin at Charlemont. After not writing for months, I had finished a story, "Lying with Blandine," about my randy downstairs neighbors in Brooklyn, and begun a fairytale play, *Turnip Family Secrets*, which had already given me some laughs and moments of happiness. It rained all weekend; we mostly had to stay inside. I relaxed and delighted in the boys, playing games, reading to them, going for walks in the wet, cooking with them. Reading *The Unbearable Lightness of Being* in the woods in the rain with the boys asleep was intense: how come the experience of the political victim and exile felt so familiar?! As we drove home, all the rivers in Connecticut were flooding. In Westerly the backs of several buildings on Main Street had collapsed into the Pawcatuck River.

We celebrated the summer solstice with a Father's Day cookout, the all-American dad presiding at the crumbling stone barbecue Michele had discovered under the backyard shrubbery, Julian making the fire and cooking the hamburgers. What with her diet and the second day of her period, she was "crazy," but the scene was "perfect."

By Bastille Day I had finished *Turnip Family Secrets*, a dark parable about a son saving his parents from evil, and started thinking about music for the fifteen songs. I had no way to put it on, except possibly in the Living Room Theatre.

MICHAEL SMITH

I HAD TAKEN THE BACK BEDROOM as my study but lost it when a German exchange student came to live with us for the following school year. The attic would be quieter anyway. I built a low bookcase under the sloping ceiling and worked at a low desk, seated on my meditation pillow on the floor, level with the low windows. I got up every morning ahead of everybody else to have an hour of writing time, and usually wrote.

Klaus Hensel, a sweet, self-possessed, pale sixteen-year-old from Frankfurt, was a bastard, he told us directly, the product of his mother's affair with a married man. He had never had a father, and I undertook to play this part in the lightest way, loving, supportive, friendly, and permissive. It was a wonderful change for Klaus, his mother having raised him strictly. He was a good kid and fit right in, kicking a soccer ball around in the back yard with Julian and Alfred, building a snow fort with them in the winter.

With Klaus in the backyard

After writing a few trial reviews of the local symphony orchestra, I was taken on as the regular music critic for *The Day*, a first-rate newspaper in nearby New London, wanting the money, pitiful as it was, and an audience to write for. It was challenging to try to put the ineffable sensations of music into words, convey the nobility and brilliance of performance, the profundity and sensuous joy of bathing in sublime vibrations, buoyed by elegant form. I averaged two reviews a week: work all day, often, home for dinner, drive to the concert, back to the newspaper office in downtown New London, write my review into the computer—I had a little more than an hour—then half an hour home. If Michele didn't want to go with me, I took Julian or Alfred, wanting them to know music, buying us doughnuts on the way back to the paper, where the boy would fall asleep on the floor while I wrote.

At the harpsichord shop I took charge of the shipping and parts department, managing an inventory of pins, wire, screws, felts, hinges, and every other little special thing needed by our own shop and do-it-yourself early-instrument builders all over "the world," as David liked to say. We were making our own keyboards now. I was responsible for packing action parts for our kits, getting everything into the box and the box out the door to the customer.

Domestic tranquility continued to elude us. Michele told me she was leaving, threatened to throw herself into the river, and not only when she was having her period. Required to take her seriously, I felt compassion but not much sympathy. I resented being blamed and jerked around. She said we should go to gay bars and I should sleep with boys. I could not avert some ridiculously rancorous conversations. She disdained my philosophy of cool, apparently preferring agonizing melodrama.

I loved Michele, and between these outbreaks of bitterness, I enjoyed her unique qualities and was overjoyed to have the family I wanted. Her problem was me, she said. If I had a problem, it was not her, it was myself, my artistic career warped and derailed by some astigmatic inner force, apparently, some psychological failure to connect, center, and engage the will, some feeble diffidence left over from early conditioning I should have long ago outgrown. I had tried to get at it through therapy, through metaphor, through action and drastic change, but I was still stuck, barely making a living and not doing my own work, at least not getting it out into the world. Given my multiple advantages, it seemed to me a special failure of my own.

I made scripts of *Turnip Family Secrets*, took one copy to Dennis and another to James, and skipped with joy in the street walking home. I started building an elaborate balsa-wood model of the complicated set, imagining it might be done with puppets. James called to say the play was brilliant, he loved it.

I had been keeping a journal for years. Not for the first time, Michele poisoned it for me by delving into it and using my earnest, unguarded groping to fuel her distress and blame. I wrote for myself, trying to understand the play of feelings between us and get a fix on what was happening. We went to a marriage counselor, but it seemed stupid to spend $45 we needed for bills to complain about each other to a stranger. After a few days the crisis passed anyway, and we loved each other again.

15

PASCALE CHEMINÉE, a dark, thin, boyish woman in her thirties who worked for Marc Ducornet in the Paris harpsichord shop, came to Stonington to learn to build a fortepiano action. I was working on an instrument that belonged to Cornell and tried having her releather the hammers with no success. She hardly spoke any English. Unable to muster my French, I wound up doing the work myself and letting her watch.

I invited Pascale to our house for Thanksgiving, which was also Klaus's birthday. It was a sizable gathering. I also invited a young German harpsichord maker who was visiting the shop. Bicky and Ben came from Ithaca, our cousins Mary and John Lucas from New York, there were four Potters, two Pinettes, plus Maribel and Nanette Belt. Maribel was a singer and musicologist I got together with once a week to revel in classical song.

With Mary Lucas on the back porch

The next day I took Mary with me to Charlemont for the weekend. She was at loose ends. I proposed that she move to Westerly and we start a theatre in an empty church overlooking the park in the center of town. She could have a studio to make quilts. We could open a theatre café and gallery downstairs and produce plays in the sanctuary. She was more interested in talking about how she had been shafted by her parents, her father having promised to buy her a house in Mendocino, supposedly, and then reneged, which seemed to me a fruitless, tiresome subject. Better we should do something ourselves than be mad at our parents.

By the time I got home again, Michele had embarked on a "passionate friendship," as she described it, with Pascale, who was camping out in an empty house David owned across the river in Pawcatuck, bicycling back and forth to Stonington to work. It was immediately apparent that this was different from Michele's affairs with men: she was really smitten. As usual, she asked me if I minded. Did I? She was happy—they both were. Could I mind that?

How ironic that Michele had fallen for a woman! Now she had taken away my homosexuality! It was a surprise that she wanted to be a lesbian. We had discussed the possibility along with everything else but it had never seemed to be an issue.

I was drawn to Pascale's seriousness and turned on by her unusual combination of womanly softness and boyish hardness. She said she loved me too. She told me she had once lived with a man for six months but he had just forced himself on her. She said I was the first man she had ever had feelings for.

Michele wanted the three of us to live together and all be lovers. I had nothing against a three-way love affair in principle, but it seemed like a recipe for disaster. We were not that cool. Michele herself would certainly not be able to handle it. Anyway I wanted one love, not a co-lovership, one woman, not two. I thought I had made that clear.

I was too worn down to be able to rise above jealousy and resentment.

Being strapped for money all the time was hard to bear, and Michele in her rapture was doing nothing to help, the flow of soundboards having waned. I did not even mention the $400 we needed for Julian's school. Occasionally sleeping with someone was not so serious, but she had fallen in love. All seemed lost.

Nobody around us realized what was going on, even David, who thought he knew everything. The neighbors in Pawcatuck called the police one night when Michele was there with Pascale, thinking the house was vacant, and David made crude remarks about Pascale's being with a man.

Pascale left for Taos to spend Christmas with an aunt who lived there. I told Michele I had to stop my complicity in her love affairs. I was not priggish, indeed I believed in free love and polymorphous sensuality and wished I could encourage her friendship with this interesting woman, but under the circumstances it could only be destructive. Her response was the litany of how I "beat" on her psychically and how unhappy she had been. I tried to stay positive and loving, but I was so sick of all this that for a moment I really did not want to be married to her anymore.

"Forgive me," I said. "Come back to me."

When we managed to make love, it gave me a sense of accomplishment as well as exquisite pleasure. I kept gnawing on the question of will: do I do things, or do they just happen? What is self-manifestation, what is mechanical repetition, what is deliberate, what is conscious, what in all this was aim-directed, what is true interaction, true collaboration, true emotion, vs. cultural or psychological reaction? Who is doing it? Michele wept, saying she had ruined everything, taking a perverse pleasure in her own destructiveness. We both had to watch out for that.

Pascale went back to France. In the aftermath Michele was preoccupied, studying French and planning a trip to Paris, which her father agreed to pay for out of his family education fund. I had already been trying to arrange such a trip as part of a campaign to expose Michele to antique harpsichords, for the betterment of her soundboard painting; now that she had a lover there, my feelings changed. She maintained that working for David was killing me, that I was rigid with misery, insisting that she was true to me even if she was running off to Pascale in Paris for a bit. Maybe she was right, my sense of betrayal a pose, an excuse to blame my discontents on her.

She was sweet to me even as she pursued her course toward other arms. She had me give her a sexy boy haircut, bought clothes for Paris, dieted for Pascale. She gave me $100 of the $900 her father sent her so I could pay the phone bill. Making an effort, I assured her that we would be all right and glad to see her when she came home.

The boys and I drove her to the airbus in New Haven. Hinrich had made her a handsome wooden carrying case for her paints. She looked elegantly bohemian. Then I was in bed with the flu for days, so dizzy I could not stand up, vision swimming, throwing up. Klaus was a light, pleasant presence, enlivened at the moment by a girlfriend, and took up the slack with Julian and Alfred.

Michele's absence was a relief, and once I had recovered, I set about taking advantage of my unaccustomed autonomy, doing some of the things I had been putting off. First I cut my hair, which hung well below my shoulders. Michele said it was beautiful, and I loved it myself when it was clean and shiny, sparkling silver and brown with hints of gold, soft, flowing, blowing in the wind. More often it looked like a witch wig, gray and stiff, which I tamed by tying it up in a ponytail; but that defeated the purpose, to feel liberated and sensuous, untied, free. Cutting my hair made me feel younger and renewed. I laughed my head off reading Joe Orton's farcical play *What the Butler Saw*, thinking "my kind of guy."

I found messes everywhere around the house and cleaned them up, rearranged furniture, set up the boys with a bunk bed and a mattress on the floor to bounce on, put away the stuffed animals they no longer cared about. They were glad to have me to themselves, everything easier without Michele making scenes.

I felt unusually free and less homosexual, not more, not interested in boy porn or even masturbation, certainly not sex or entanglement with

MICHAEL SMITH

anyone else. Running out of pot, I did not replenish my stash. I had to get the boys up in the morning for school and lost my writing time. A few times I managed to write at night after they were in bed; but there was no other time for housework, making their lunches, folding the laundry. I did not miss Michele a bit. The urge to write came back: I got up earlier and resumed work on a book I was starting, a novel in letters, about some of the tragic current events that pass for politics and history. I had an idea for a kidnapping plot, to turn it into an adventure.

I sent her a poem Julian brought home from school:

Do not fret get
wet you will and
dry by cry

Michele came home after a few weeks, and I was glad. I had loved the boys well and made the house more beautiful, she had had a valuable, relaxing, strengthening time in Paris; it was possible that much had been gained. She had painted a soundboard for Marc Ducornet and brought back $500, which solved the immediate crisis. Once she decorated a couple of instruments David had waiting for her, we would be solvent again.

16

TREVOR PINNOCK FELL IN LOVE with one of David's French Doubles and stayed up all night playing it in the paint room. The instrument, with a beautiful soundboard painting by Michele in classical French style, had been made for Chechi Mendez Hodes, a rich New York amateur. Chechi wouldn't give it up but let Trevor borrow it for a recital at the Metropolitan Museum, where he publicly praised David as the best of modern makers. David promised to make him one just like it, and this new instrument was almost done; Michele plunged into painting the soundboard.

In addition to intricate blue arabesque borders and large, formal bouquets, classic French soundboards feature a symbolic landscape of a broken tree with a goldfinch perched on it or, occasionally, a seascape with a sailing ship.

The latter is what Michele, fresh from the Paris museums, chose to do for Trevor, painting a three-masted ship under full sail heading toward a city on the far horizon, its misty towers subtly but startlingly suggesting the World Trade Center in New York. I called it the "New World" soundboard.

David hated Michele's painting and said it "turned Trevor's stomach." There was talk of sanding it off. The real problem was that the instrument lacked the magic oomph of Chechi's harpsichord, which Trevor needed for his high-powered performances in major halls. Chechi saved the situation by offering to trade: she and her husband had bought new Italian furniture for their East Side townhouse, which the color of the new instrument would complement; and they preferred the Louis XV stand with its graceful cabriole legs. I drove the "New World" to the city, humped it in its quilted canvas cover up the steep, narrow, curving staircase, and retrieved the first one, on which Trevor happily gave a recital at the church in Stonington, the most exciting playing I had heard since Kirkpatrick and Valenti.

As the days grew longer, I planted flowers around the house and built box beds in the side yard for Michele's new herb and salad garden, both of us making an effort to pull things together. When Stephanie, who had been running the office, left to have a baby, most of her responsibilities fell on me: there was "only me and you," as David put it, to run the business. I made him a cash sheet every day, wrote invoices, paid bills, processed orders, kept the books, and managed the overseas shipments and accounts—enough office work so I could hardly squeeze in any of my own work as fortepiano tech. By the end of the day my eyes were stinging, brain aching.

I took Dennis Pinette with me for a weekend getaway in my cabin, where we talked late about our boyhoods and got playfully sexual together in the dark in a boyish way, which was surprising, as I assumed he was straight. Dennis said it was his first outside sex encounter in nine years of marriage. Neither of us wanted it to be anything but friendly and "experimental." I bonded with him because he was a real artist: we shared feelings about being artists and men.

MICHELE STAYED HOME TO PAINT while I took Julian and Alfred to Santa Barbara to visit my parents, who had moved into a two-bedroom unit at the Casa Dorinda, a genteel retirement community on a former estate in Montecito. Dad had not fully recovered from the injury in Acapulco. His legs were weak and he was much slowed down. He exercised diligently, shuffling back and forth on the patio on his walker. Most of the time he was in his chair in his room.

With Poppy and Granny in Santa Barbara

Meals were delivered, and he emerged to have dinner in the living room. Mother went her own way the rest of the time. Dad could no longer see to read or write except in big letters with a marker—I missed his swift, graceful handwriting. He was getting books on tape from the Braille Institute, currently reading *The Golden Bowl* by Henry James. I could relate to that.

The boys and I had a roomy cottage at the Miramar, a pleasantly old-fashioned resort hotel with two swimming pools and its own stretch of beach. Mother had anticipated our arrival with flowers on the table and a pitcher of fresh orange juice in the refrigerator. The ocean was seldom very warm in Santa Barbara, but Julian was crazy about the pool and played wildly in the water; Alfred stayed close to the steps, wearing inflated yellow plastic "muscles" on his upper arms. We drove around in Dad's aging Cadillac, which he could no longer drive, went on hikes into the mountains, shopping, to the movies. Mother engaged a babysitter and took me to master classes at the Music Academy of the West and concerts at the Lobero Theatre, among them a piano recital by Jerome Lowenthal, her best friend on the faculty.

A few mornings Mother entertained Julian and Alfred while I took Dad swimming at a friend's house in a gated golf course community, where the million-dollar houses were like mausoleums, nobody in sight except the occasional Mexican gardener. Dad's friend, invisible or absent, kept the pool heated to ninety-five degrees for his comfort. He was pitiably weak, a big skeleton and a skin, barely able to walk, balancing with a cane. After our swim we went back to the Casa and made ourselves lunch, and Dad reminisced about his youth. He judged that I had improved in the past couple of years. I was glad he thought so. I was certainly trying.

17

PASCALE CAME AGAIN for the month of August, sleeping in the front room in the attic, riding to work with me and working on pianos. Michele spent one night with her, one night with me, and said she was the happiest she had ever been. I was glad to have her when I had her and happy that she was happy, though not particularly happy about the situation myself.

The year before, Pascale had given me a copy of *Agatha*, a play by her literary hero, Marguerite Duras. Fascinated by its obsessive immobility, its image of the fixed shape certain emotional encounters assume in one's inner life, I had read it by drafting an English translation, intuiting my way through Duras's adamantine French. Pascale's English had improved, and she worked through the translation with me, insisting on strict fidelity. She had edited dictionaries. We shared a deep relationship with words.

I was undoubtedly somewhat changed. The veil of pot and long hair was torn away, for one thing. Whether this did any good I could not say. Pot had been a consolation. The new clarity was pleasant, but I was still lost and still broke.

Even John Bennett, the steadiest of men, was distressed by the state of the harpsichord business and David's intransigence. We expected to come to work one morning and find that the bank had padlocked the building.

MICHAEL SMITH

David was spending half his time in Paris trying to sell the business to Marc; when he was away it was easier to concentrate and get work done. John and I thought we could do a better job of running the business by ourselves. Then David came back, and poof went our fantasy of control. Pascale said Marc might not be any better as a boss; anyway

John Bennett voicing a French double

it was unimaginable that David would get out of the way barring accident, major illness, or death. I lay awake in the night worrying about how to pay the business's bills.

Family aspects of the summer were delightful: we attended Friends meeting on Sundays at the beautiful old meeting house around the corner, hosted picnics, houseguests, parties in our lush backyard, the boys an endless joy. At Dan Potter's birthday bacchanal on the beach at Weekapaug, I drummed on an ice chest for a ring of friends dancing around a bonfire, sparks flying up into the black sky. Melisande had made cone-shaped party hats that everybody wore a different way. She put them on as pointy breasts. I wore two sticking out from the sides of my head. Julian had them around his hips, one in front and another in back, like a satyr's tail and phallus. Melisande bared her breasts, and she and Julian, age seven, danced lasciviously around the fire. It was truly Dionysian.

Michele was back in our bed because Pascale would not make love with her in our house. Michele, who had set the whole thing up, claimed I had tried to seduce Pascale. I might have liked to, but Pascale and I confined ourselves to refined literary collaboration, tacitly exploring the same intensity of forbidden longing as the incestuous brother and sister in *Agatha*, sublimating it into art. Michele struggled on, making beautiful soup, painting beautiful soundboards; but I did not feel I could trust her anymore, which hurt us both. I was afraid we were way beyond some awful break and there was no possibility of connection because something essential had broken. We had forgotten it was broken and went on without mending it, pretending everything was all right.

David, squeezed for money, was driving everybody crazy. I was doing the office work and wished he would let me manage the kit business that was giving him so much trouble. With John running the shop, David could back off and be resident genius, designer, master builder, and organ builder, his latest passion. I proposed this to him in the car on the way back from a Boston Early Music Festival board meeting. The next morning he talked it over with Marc, who was there from Paris to discuss recapitalization. Marc and his wife, Suzanne, came to dinner at our house, entirely friendly, and we tried to see how to seize the moment. John was bitter, and more than one person in the shop was on the verge of quitting. Everybody wanted David off their backs.

Wolfgang, who still had a financial interest in the business, came up from Virginia and talked for hours with David and Marc. David summoned the whole crew to the shop on Marc's last night, and Wolfgang made a brilliant speech, telling us that nothing was about to change, the company was profitable, the cash problem was only the result of a $600,000 inventory take-back, whatever that meant, David was difficult to work for but some kind of a genius, only the strong could take it, we were all part of a great success that David was creating. If I held on, Wolfgang told me privately, I would indeed come to be running things in a few years' time.

A T TIMES I WAS ALMOST HAPPY in the aura of David's power, struggling along from one detail to the next; but I saw this pleasure as part of a sick pattern of serving powerful people and letting love turn into a dependency destructive of my own will. I loved David, and abetting him at its best was gloriously creative; but he was a brutal megalomaniac, and a whole other spirit dance of ideas and imagination was dying in me while I drudged away at David's goals. I might succeed fairly well in the harpsichord business, but it was not my game.

If nothing was to change in Stonington, I would have to jump ship. Michele suggested I go to France and work for Marc, who had bought forty fortepiano kits that somebody had to build. Marc's associate Jean Bascou, in Provence, could make cases, I could make actions, and Michele could study harpsichord decoration in Paris, close to Pascale. Moving would surely be good for Julian and Alfred; we had no love for the culture they were growing up in. Westerly was a nice town, but the major employer in the area was Electric Boat in Groton, which built nuclear submarines, and the sub base up the river, which poisoned the vibe. I wanted to write and needed more peace of mind. Might I find it in France?

I took a week off in the fall and went up to my cabin by myself, leaving the car for Michele. It was raining when I arrived into the quiet and solitude. As always, arriving and departing, I bowed to my Buddha and invoked the Triple Refuge: taking refuge in Buddha, Dharma, and Sangha, the timeless brotherhood of Buddhists everywhere. Feeling numb in my skin inside my clothes, I stripped naked and lay on the wet leaves to reconnect to the earth, literally reground myself. Crouching, I struck myself all over lightly with a stick, threw wet colored autumn leaves on my naked body and thrashed myself with a wet leafy branch, which began to wake up my skin and put me in contact with the here and now. Inside, I dried off, put on soft clothes, put my things away, lit candles, and felt panicky in the face of a whole week by myself, my first break in more than a year.

Being alone all day proved heavenly, the night too empty. As the sun slipped behind the mountain and darkness slowly approached, I found myself peering down through the trees, hoping to see someone coming up the path to see me, love me, turn me on.

I chugged along with a play loosely inspired by Joe and Jean-Claude's relationship when we were younger and a story Jean-Claude had told me about himself. I called it *Half Life*, from the Platonic idea that each of us is half a person longing to find our other half. Writing it seemed pointless with no way to see it onto the stage, but it was my whole excuse for being. After a few days I walked into town for supplies. As I started the long trek back up into the hills, hoping to hitch a ride, along came Jean-Claude in his big blue Mercedes roadster with its VAJRA license plate. He was meeting a bus, it was late, and while we waited he filled me in on the complications, difficulties, overfullness of his life. His eyes were big, round, and blue as he told me all about it, attractively thrilled with himself. My concerns seemed stodgy and boring by comparison; but I gained new impetus for my play and an idea for the ending.

My writing table

I finished the play on Friday, rebuilt the front porch on Saturday, and came home to Westerly refreshed in my love for Michele. I read her my play the next night. It was good, strong work, more emotionally direct than anything I had written before. I set about making copies and sending them out into the world. Joe Chaikin, whom I had not seen in too long, called to say he was thinking of me and loved me.

THE BOYS AND I put up a beautiful Christmas tree, and fifty people came to our Christmas party. The day after Christmas we went into the city. I bought Michele a camera she wanted, an Olympus M-1. We took Alfred to see Alfred Brooks and Julian to see Julian Beck.

Al and Max were having their annual New York cocktail party. I gave them a script of *Half Life* and renewed some old acquaintances.

The Living Theatre, back from Europe, were rehearsing in a frigid loft on lower Second Avenue, preparing to present a repertory of four plays at the Joyce Theatre. I gave Judith a copy of *American Baby*. She gave me her *Poems of a Wandering Jewess*. I sat beside her and then beside Julian, getting high with each of them in turn, watching them rehearse Julian's play *The Archaeology of Sleep*. Not having smoked pot in some time, I got quite confused: Judith's lover, Hanon Reznikov, was especially welcoming, as if we were old friends, although I was not sure we had met before.

When the Living Theatre opened its season in New York, the anti-hippie backlash came down on them hard. Eighties people, primed to trash the sixties, scapegoated the Living for daring to offer nakedly beautiful visions and idealistic politics in an increasingly cynical marketplace. During one of their trademark incursions into the audience, Julian sat in the lap of Frank Rich, the critic of the *New York Times*, who was not amused. His review described the international cast as "a scraggly collection of indistinguishable riffraff."

I went into the city to see their plays and loved them. No one else was doing Expressionist theatre in America. The Living Theatre's uniqueness and integrity deserved respect whether or not you personally liked the work. The meanness of their critical reception should have made them a cause célèbre, as they had been in previous decades; but nothing was a cause célèbre in the eighties, everything was product. I wrote a big story about them in *The Day*, but that was no help. As a result of the bad reviews, they closed early in New York, their tour of colleges was cancelled, and the cast dispersed, many of them back to Europe. It emerged that Julian had stomach cancer and would not be able to travel.

I wrote about movies, plays, operas, and art exhibitions for *The Day* in addition to concerts, some of my reviews perfect little gems. I reviewed an admirable festival of American music in Waterford run by William Billings's

Judith Malina and Julian Beck in Hanon Reznikov's *The Yellow Methuselah*

granddaughter. I wrote about the art faculty at Connecticut College and drove to Providence, Hartford, and New Haven to review plays at first-class theatres. Writing reviews demanded a disciplined openness and warmth of judgment that helped me keep my balance in spite of everything falling apart at home and work. I prided myself on an underlying sanity not affected by the madness around me and felt an obligation to respond generously, genuinely, fully to artists' work, no matter my mood, energy level, or other worries, and to take pleasure in the process. I was not much of a Buddhist, but I liked being able to turn my emotions off or set them aside as merely personal. There was a lot more to reality than my frustrations.

I wrote down dreams in a notebook Pascale had given me and chided myself for not starting another heavy-duty writing project. There seemed to be no point in writing another play with no possibility of putting it on. I was already ahead, with three plays written but unstaged.

18

MICHELE LEFT FOR PARIS AGAIN at the end of April. Seeing her off in New Haven, Julian cried, Alfred acted cool, and I felt nothing, knowing the shell around my dismay was brittle. David was due back from another trip to Europe, during which John and I had worn ourselves out trying to get caught up; two more weeks and we would have had things running smoothly. If David picked on me, I was not sure I could take it.

Julian and Alfred were a constant source of sanity and good times, but we had to be careful, all of us shaken by Michele's desertion. When Julian came down with chicken pox, my first reaction was to call her in Paris and say we need you, come home; but there was no answer chez Pascale, and I could handle it. I was getting along better without her, the boys in good spirits too. I did variations on taking Julian to work with me and putting him to bed there; staying home with him; and leaving him tucked up on the sofa for a few hours by himself. I loved taking care of him. Alfred had croup but did not actually get sick. I loved them purely and completely. They were open, receptive, loving in response, the atmosphere delicious.

I threw a farewell picnic for Dennis and Megan Pinette, who were moving to Maine. Westerly would make less sense without them. On Memorial Day weekend I took the boys to Charlemont for a rendezvous with Bicky, Ben, John, and Mary, and we had a great time, cooking outside, hiking up the mountain, playing Kick the Can and Flashlight in the forest.

The night before Michele was due home, I stayed up late cleaning the house; then she called at six in the morning to say she had mistaken the day and was coming a day later. The return of petty irritation was a bad sign.

People kept telling me how good I was to take care of the boys while Michele went off to Paris, not that I had any choice. Pamela Cook, the harpsichordist, said I was wonderful to "let her go." Little did they know. Melisande said I was amazing. Mother Hawley opined that love blossoms when you get old together. Hold on, she told me, otherwise when I was old I would have nothing; like most advice, this reflected her own choices.

Bicky and Mary thought it was great that Michele had an opportunity to be a sex-role-free person. I agreed that parenting and housekeeping were as much mine to enjoy and drudge at as hers. One friend assured me it was worthwhile to be generous, that it would all come back to me, but I doubted it. She didn't want a man, she wanted a woman now, apparently. I no longer minded her going away, I minded her coming back.

JOHN BENNETT was relaxed and happy after a week off for home carpentry and dreaded going back to work, where instead of doing anything productive we were rearranging the offices. David had borrowed another $20,000 from the Washington Trust and immediately disbursed it for current expenses. We could be bankrupt by July. John would lose his calling as a harpsichord maker, and I would have to put myself in some other trap.

At the end of June our Westerly landlady, whose father had died and left her the house, dropped a bomb. Her daughter was getting married and buying it. A lawyer advised me that the daughter was probably getting the house at a bargain price. As we had first refusal, we could buy it ourselves for the same price. He would take the case if we were willing to fight for it. We certainly did not want to move. Any other house would cost more and not suit us as well. But the doctor's family had a right to the house. It would be too rotten to wrench it away from them by legal trickery. I was simply not litigious. Anyway we had no money and were in no position to buy a house no matter how cheap it was.

Michele had a new circle of lesbian friends and was "on a roll," she said, volunteering with two women who had a fabric design studio in New London. As always I wanted to encourage her work, but it cost money for her to drive back and forth and go out to lunch with her new friends. She had fallen out with David and was no longer painting harpsichords. I barely had the will to keep my nose to the often painful grindstone, and now we had to move, which is never cheap.

It made me crazy that all this was being taken from us—the house, the pleasant neighborhood with kids for the boys to play with, the perfect backyard, Michele's thriving garden. She would have to find us another house, as she had done so successfully in the past. However, she did not make any move to do it. Maybe we were breaking up.

Work was coming apart too. There was so little business that my office assistant could handle it. I could not bring myself to start another fortepiano action, not believing I would see it through. A Belt-Walter piano from the University of Michigan sat unloved, untuned in David's half-finished office, and he would not let me work on it. Nor would he fire me. I had a claim on the business, he said, because I had been there so long. I could stretch it out indefinitely.

I proposed that Michele take the boys to New Mexico for the summer, break the inertia, detach from this spiritually dead corner of New England. I would break free and follow, or do something else and see them later. I envisioned roving for a while, lining up a few directing gigs, getting a play on in New York. Or I could go west myself, and they could follow me, or not. Or I would keep the boys, and she could work things out for herself. She said she was not my jailer, I should go ahead and go if that was what I wanted, and she would manage. I knew she was counting on my support, and the last thing I wanted was to lose my children. I was sick of her being so little help and hated myself for not being satisfied with her as she was. I was sick of hating myself.

Was everything okay at home but fucked up at work? Or was everything fucked up at home but okay at work? Or was everything fucked up? Or was everything groovy? That was my basic position. I must have been appreciating it on some level, as Johnny used to say. Still, I had completely stopped writing, the only thing that could save me in the end.

I had an idea: to rent the two units on Main Street that Dennis and Megan Pinette had recently vacated, a small duplex apartment and a loft workshop in adjacent nineteenth-century buildings owned by our friendly neighbor George Utter, the publisher of the *Westerly Sun*. We could set up a textile business in the loft to exploit Michele's talent and eagerness to work and a shop where I could work on fortepianos and harpsichords on my own time. I had abundant contacts from my years with David. Dennis had nicely redone the apartment, which was humbler than our house on Cross Street but had enough rooms. The apartment and loft together would be cheaper than a conventional house, and we would have a workplace. I could do tasks for David by the day as needed, set type for him, let the harpsichord and piano work be just one of several income streams, write more for *The Day*, fill up the studio with plants, do plays.

Michele counter-proposed that we move to Las Vegas, New Mexico, a backwater town east of Santa Fe where her sisters Sandé and Sylvia were living. It sounded too nowhere to me, but a letter from Sylvie made me want to go there for the quiet and simplicity. Sylvie had become a weaver, with her own clothing and fabric business, and Michele could work with her. She had a baby and a house they could share.

Sylvie had ideas for jobs for me too, and I fired off letters to the addresses she provided. But after trying on the new New Mexico idea for a few days, I remembered that we had already done that, and it didn't work, and decided to hang in for now with David; otherwise we would immediately be broke. Once we had moved to the Pinette place, she could take the boys to New Mexico, visit her parents, and see how it felt with Sylvie, with whom she'd had trouble getting along. A powerful thunderstorm in the night turned me on but frightened Michele.

Meanwhile I had to drive a vanload of instruments to Ithaca for a week-long fortepiano workshop at Cornell. I would stay with Bicky, tune everybody's pianos, and sit in on Malcolm Bilson's master classes like one of the students. Malcolm was a brilliant teacher, and I looked forward to it. Michele was miserable with a lingering low-level flu, but Julian and Alfred were enjoying their summer freedom, having fun with the neighborhood kids. I promised to take them to Charlemont when I got back.

By the time I got home George had rented the Pinettes' workshop to someone else, and Michele had decided to move to Las Vegas with Julian and Alfred. She could feel it on my skin, she said, that I felt better right away, and I did not deny it, although I felt terrible about letting her down and horrified at losing the boys. I wanted to leave it between us that I would come at Christmas with all our stuff, after a few months of working hard and saving money. But she said not.

"Is she leaving you?" George Utter asked. That did seem to be the story. When I told Julian and Alfred that I would come later, Julian treated it as something of a joke. Alfred was especially loving when I bought him a few last things he wanted. We tried to think Las Vegas would be better for them, Michele working at home, grandparents, aunts, uncles, cousins close at hand, no parental disharmony staring them in the face. I agreed to pay their first month's rent and send $100 a week.

Then suddenly they were gone, after the obligatory farewell scene in the Boston airport, Julian weeping and wailing dramatically, pitifully clinging to me, Michele wanly tragic, me keeping a tight rein on my anger, guilt, self-pity, loss, and hurt, trying to stay positive, Alfred acting as if it was just another fun trip.

George Utter rented me the Pinettes' apartment for $200 a month. It had good vibes, too—better than the house on Cross Street, which was always a little cold and creepy, like the owners. George was a gentleman and friend in need.

I had three days to get out of the big house. Kind friends pitched in to help me move. I barely escaped being crushed as we bullied my piano up the narrow, steep front stairs of my new apartment. Michele had left everything she wanted piled on the enclosed front porch; I was to arrange a mover and pay for it with money her father had sent. Instead I trucked it all over to the shop in Stonington, clumsily, laboriously, fanatically packed it into three of the huge cardboard boxes we used to ship harpsichords, and sent it to her by motor freight, which was cheaper but far more trouble, unnecessary, masochistic, stupid. I sent Dr. Hawley back his money, furious that he had enabled her departure, though I suppose any good father would. I was too freaked out to be rational, primarily over losing my precious closeness with my two beloved sons.

19

My new apartment was upstairs from a comatose antique shop in a rackety old building in the oldest part of Westerly, across Route 1 from the river, next to the newspaper parking lot. Dennis had refinished the floors, put in a new bathroom, patched the tin ceilings, and painted the walls white. I had my piano and harpsichord,

86 Main Street, Westerly

Cat, and Jim the canary to keep me company. There was plenty of room. It was even rather pretty, if markedly less bourgeois.

I was shattered, but over Labor Day at Charlemont my nights were alive with intense, amazing dreams, reminding me how full of energy and fantasy my mind really was. I was on my own again. Something would emerge.

I demoted myself from running David's office to regular shop work and finished a fortepiano action; David said it was my best yet. My father asked me where I would be in ten years unless I was running the business. Ten years? I couldn't even begin to think that far ahead.

I came home from a movie to find Dan and Melisande Potter sitting in the dark on my back porch, back from Europe. I threw a party for my musical friend Maribel Belt, who was moving away, and invited the whole shop. I knocked out countless reviews for *The Day*, sometimes stopping on the way home late at the drive-in movie near the sub base in Groton, which showed pornographic movies on a giant screen, nothing more relaxing. At James Swift's wedding I felt like half of Michael and Michele.

On my forty-ninth birthday I visited Joe Chaikin in his ninth-floor apartment in Westbeth overlooking the Hudson River. It was the first time

I had seen Joe since he had suffered a stroke during heart surgery. He was suffering from aphasia and his speech was fragmentary. We had a funny conversation about philosophy and sex.

My mother went to Kansas City for Grammie's hundredth birthday.

I constantly refreshed my good intentions at the harpsichord works, but it made no difference. Paul McNulty, a serious young piano-maker, came to work for David. He would be far better at it than I was, and after that I was obviously superfluous. I would finish typesetting the new catalog and hang in until spring, when Marc wanted me to come work for him in Paris.

I FLEW TO NEW MEXICO FOR THANKSGIVING and was charmed by the funky, down-to-earth simplicity of my loved ones' life in the "other" Las Vegas, where low-consumption poverty seemed appropriate, though the down-at-heels town was sans culture aside from the dollar movie. To my infinite relief, my intimacy with Julian and Alfred was perfectly intact. Losing that had been my worst fear and grief. Reassured, I tried to accept the breakup of my marriage with equanimity in spite of Miche's tears.

I flew on to Santa Barbara, in sync with Bicky, for our parents' fiftieth wedding anniversary. Dad was gracious and gallant, in spite of pain and limited mobility. Mother was privately bitter. "Fifty miserable years," she muttered. It was not actually the case. I was appalled.

I was determined not to abandon my children the way my father had abandoned Lewis and Virginia, who never forgave him. I wanted Julian and Alfred and I wanted them to know it, wanted them with me, wanted to be with them for my own sake as much as theirs, loved them without limit.

I took a week off from work to stage-manage *A Celebration of Twelfth Night* at the Westerly Center for the Arts and immediately after that began evening rehearsals for *A Shot in the Dark*, a comical play I was hired to direct for a community theatre group at the library in Kingston, Rhode Island. Casting was mainly a matter of finding people willing to show up. I was nervous at first, not having directed in years. The actors did what I suggested without resistance. I started feeling confident and enjoying myself. Never one to be conventional, I turned the space around, disdaining the usual box set on the stuffy stage, instead using the architecture of the room.

Magie Dominic, an acquaintance from Caffè Cino days, called me looking for material for an exhibition about Joe Cino at the Lincoln Center library, which sent me back to old letters and papers. I went into the city to see her, and we talked about opening a new Caffè Cino—why not? People start businesses all the time. I visited Julian Beck and Judith Malina in their apartment on West End Avenue. Julian was being treated for cancer and terribly unwell. Judith in beautiful silks lit and passed joint after skinny joint.

Michele came to Westerly for a couple of nights on her way back from Paris and felt wonderful in my arms. She was offered more work in Paris, painting soundboards for Marc I encouraged her to go again in June, perhaps live there for a year with the children. I was about to go there myself, to work in Marc's shop, like a movie star being lent out to a different studio. We should all live in Paris—*pourquoi pas?*

20

MY TWO MONTHS working for Marc Ducornet in France were glorious, over too soon. Pascale was extraordinarily kind to me, meeting me at Orly when I arrived, showing me the city she loved, arranging for me to stay in top-foor maid's rooms first with her sister in the 13th Arrondissement, then with her brother in the Sixth. Her family all spoke English pretty well. My French was hopeless, and she kindly translated for me at work. We spent many evenings together, unmistakably fond of each other. She took me to meet her family in a fine old house in the country near Poitiers— deep France. She was a vivid personality, bright and alive, fascinated with language, relatable like few people I've known. One night as she saw me to my sixth-story door, an unmistakable erotic tension arose, surely mutual, and we might well have fucked. Sadly, I thought better of it in consideration of Michele's feelings, not that she considered mine; I've always been sorry.

Instead of pursuing love with Pascale, I found my way to Rue Saint

David Way and Marc Ducornet at Musicora, an exposition at the Grand Palais

Denis, a walking street close to the Pompidou Center lined with neon sex emporia that featured cozy private screening rooms where you could take your time watching any sex film you liked—much nicer than the cramped, grotty viewing booths of American porn shops. Opting for boys with boys, I quite enjoyed it, discovering a flavor of pleasure that I hadn't realized I liked so much.

I worked a regular week in Marc's mellow, well-organized factory in Vincennes, a close-in suburb. Twice he sent me on overnight trips out of Paris to repair pianos, and I spent a week working with his colleague Jean Bascou at his charming extended family's house in a village in Provence. I went up into the Jura with Marc and Jean to buy high-altitude tone-wood for soundboards. I had a wonderful time altogether, finished two piano actions, and came back with forty short poems, which I subsequently published as *A Sojourn in Paris*, hand-sewn and glued, covered in Arches paper, in an edition of fifty, giving them away to friends.

I MISSED JULIAN AND ALFRED and wanted them with me for the summer. When their school year ended, I flew to New Mexico and took them to California with me on the train. We spent a day at Disneyland and visited Manny Peluso and Lucy Silvay and their kids in San Diego, where they had set up a cushy suburban life. After several days with my parents in Santa Barbara, we celebrated Fourth of July in San Francisco with Mary Lucas, who had a quilt-making studio on the edge of Chinatown. Heading east, we visited Bicky and her family in Ithaca, and finally came home to Westerly. I had fixed up rooms for them upstairs, and the apartment was pleasant, its semi-enclosed back porch like an outdoor living room, with a big string hammock in which Julian did tricks.

The library and park were a block away, but I had to go back to work, and it was hard for the boys when they were left alone. In August Pascale sent over her amiable teenage nephew Jacques. Expecting a vacation, he found himself a reluctant au pair, responsible for two kids ten and seven, stranded in the middle of Westerly. Embarrassed to be taking advantage of him but lacking an alternative, I organized weekend excursions to New York, Charlemont, and Boston. At the end of the summer Alfred went back to Michele in Las Vegas. Julian stayed with me in Westerly for fourth grade.

JULIAN BECK DIED IN SEPTEMBER. The next day was Joe Chaikin's fiftieth birthday, and Jean-Claude was throwing a party for him at his loft on Jane Street. Julian came with me into the city for the party and the wake.

A huge crowd came to celebrate Joe, who was much loved. It was exhilarating to be among theatre people again. I stood close behind Joe as a friend sang him exquisite songs from Schubert's "Winterreise." After the music a handsome young man introduced himself: it was Stefan Marx, whom I had last seen when he was ten, living in a tent beside Fred and

Julian and Alfred at ease on the back porch

Sarah's schoolbus in the woods at Charlemont, now a graduate student in art at SUNY Purchase. Behind him was his elegant artist mother, her steel and silver curls jumping and shining, smiling at me warmly. Sarah and I had been good friends until she broke up with Fred, which left her too enraged to come to Charlemont anymore. I was delighted to see her again.

Johnny Dodd was there too, sleek and well-groomed in a blazer and flannels, with a young lighting designer, Anne Militello, in tow. Johnny had completed his five-year plan, he said, and could afford to be friendly again. When we had had enough of the party, he took us out for dinner at the Paris Commune on Abingdon Square.

We went up to the Becks' apartment on West End Avenue to join in mourning Julian. Judith's grief was theatrical in the deepest, best sense, passionate and dignified, intensely expressive. She and Julian Beck had been partners for forty years not just personally but as artists and public figures, anti-war protestors, leaders of the avant garde, visionaries of the great nonviolent anarchist-pacifist revolution. The Living Theatre had drawn thousands of people into its vortex and energized them once and forever with its beautiful dream. I sat with Judith on a bed in an inner room, nothing to give her but myself, and took away a sense of life powerfully flowing. Julian had lived to the end with great conviction, performing a Beckett monologue at La Mama when he was so weak he had to be tied to a post. That force continued now in the survivors.

Jerry Tallmer was there too, and Erica Munk, our successor as theatre editor of *The Village Voice*, who got so stoned she momentarily passed out, standing wedged behind a dresser in the corner.

Late that night, driving back to Westerly through the dark, my own Julian sleeping in the back of the speeding car, I was exhilarated, feeling my world opening up to me again.

It was fun living with ten-year-old Julian. The supermarket was across the street. I got a kick out of making dinners for us and generally keeping life going. He did not do particularly well in fourth grade but had developed

Julian at his computer

an interest in computers. The father of two boys he knew from school set him up with a simple Radio Shack computer. I bought a small tv to serve him as a monitor and let me watch tennis.

We rode out Hurricane Gloria together in our creaky wooden house. When the wind dropped we walked over to the park, where some of the biggest trees were down. I had been unwell for days and barely made it back to the house before I collapsed mentally and physically—headache, dizziness, sickened when I moved around. Was I so seriously demoralized? Was it barometric? Was it bad dope, those shreds of forgotten pot I had unearthed and immediately smoked? I wanted to be among the well and successful, not part of the general sickness and decline. Whatever the matter was, I could not cope with it and took to my bed. The electricity was off but the phone still worked, and Hinrich came over to fix dinner with Julian. I got up for a while and had a good time with them. It was days before I felt all better.

21

THE PREVIOUS AUGUST, at a fogged-out meteor-shower-watching party on the Stonington breakwater, I had met a drama professor from Connecticut College and boldly proposed that the college hire me to direct a play. To my surprise, she said yes, it was possible. Sam Shepard was the obvious playwright. I was interested in seeing what I could do with *The Tooth of Crime*, but the women students objected that the cast was mostly men, and Sam's agent denied the rights. Instead I would do *Curse of the Starving Class*, which I liked better anyway.

The moment I started working on the play, I felt vitally engaged, restored to myself. The morning after the first rehearsal I phoned John Bennett to tell him I was quitting at last. John said he understood and God bless. I drove to Stonington for an hour's good talk with David, who had already carried me longer than he could afford. And that was that. I called Johnny to share the good news. He said I should avoid thinking about what was next: if I held off, something interesting would develop. He advised me not to worry about money; and a few days later, David handed me a check for almost $5,000, closing out the company's pension fund, more money than I had ever had in my decade as a wage slave. I would be okay for a few months.

My production of *Curse of the Starving Class* at Connecticut College: above, Jaime Arze and Pamela Eliason; below, George Pratt and lamb

At Conn College the crew and budget gave me everything I wanted, and I loved my young actors. The play was a hoot, with a naked boy and a live

lamb on stage and any number of arresting images. Johnny came up to see it with Michael Warren Powell, the two of them welcome as knowledgeable eyes. Inexplicably, though, my fine production received a savage review in the college newspaper, the writer singling out my direction for opprobrium. As a critic I knew how hard it is to tell the director's work from that of the actors. Reference to dimmer problems that were fixed after dress rehearsal revealed that the critic was not even describing a public performance. Someone at the college had it in for me; I never did find out who or why.

I SPENT TWO DAYS IN NEW MEXICO on the way to Santa Barbara for Christmas, liking Michele's plain life and interesting women friends in Las Vegas. I borrowed her motorcycle and took Alfred for a long, leisurely ride around the quiet town.

The next day the Hawley family gathered at Michele's parents' big house in Taos to decorate the Christmas tree. Their wild family parties had always been a little much for me. I kept putting ornaments on the tree even after everybody else drank too much and wandered off. I was leaving Julian there and taking Alfred with me to visit his Granny and Poppy. Michele, who was about to depart for France again, made a huge unnecessary fuss about arrangements to switch boys on my way back from California. I lost my temper. Still boiling as I drove the four of us to her brother Robert's house to sleep, I furiously berated her in the car, telling Julian, wailing in the back seat, to shut up.

I should have controlled myself. I did not want to go back to being too controlled, but it was a waste of subtle chemicals to indulge the expression of negative emotions: I knew better. I had upset the children, tormented Michele when she was already freaked out, made myself hoarse, realized again how little I wanted to have these scenes with her. This was the real end of our marriage.

I was hollowed out by the time Alfred and I reached Santa Barbara, emotionally exhausted and inexorably coming down with a cold. Bicky, Steve, and Ben had already arrived. Mother had us staying at her friend Medora Bass's house, an exquisite Spanish villa and gardens built in 1925 and impeccably maintained in its original state. It was dreamy to be there, though in my weakened state the grandeur of our surroundings made me painfully conscious of my own relentless penury, failure as a husband, and shrunken horizons. I struggled to keep up with Bicky and Steve's spending in the frenzied countdown to Christmas, not wanting Alfred to feel short-changed.

Something was terribly wrong. Living in luxury, surrounded by beauty, I felt weirdly cut off from other people, who seemed weirdly cut off from each other, going through the motions of a perfect life while seething with inexpressible rages and yearnings, the whole thing somehow a mistake. There were multiple reasons for this distressing sensation: a) the poisonous commercialization and militarization of American culture; b) my personal failure, emotionally, artistically, economically; c) my parents' deteriorating marriage; d) political despair; e) a virus—try as I might, I was not at all well.

Bringing up the subject of AIDS at Christmas dinner in the Spanish mansion was probably not polite, but several people I knew had died of the new disease, and I was desperate for some sliver of reality to be acknowledged, some wisp of communication to occur; otherwise the idyllic scene we were playing out was too false to bear. My father had dressed beautifully for the occasion and was charming at dinner, which Bicky managed. It was like dining in a medieval room at the Metropolitan Museum, with a big painting on the wall of St. Lawrence being grilled over burning coals. No one wanted to hear about AIDS. Later in my room Alfred sweetly read me "The Night Before Christmas." These moments with Alfred made it all worthwhile. He loved Santa Barbara.

Too CHARGED WITH RESTLESS ENERGY to stay put at my desk in Westerly, I took Julian into the city, looking to renew my friendship with Sarah Marx. Instead we spent the weekend with Johnny, who was prickly with Julian, threatening violence, his opinions so intense I could only submit, feeling querulous and ill-defined. He took us out to dinner, gave me the keys to his apartment, and went elsewhere for the night. On Sunday morning he met us at the Metropolitan Museum, looked at a few pictures, spoke sharply to Julian, and stalked off without a word. Whatever we had between us was strictly one-on-one.

Two weeks later Julian and I went into the city again, and Cousin John entertained Julian while I took Sarah to a brilliant, overlong play by Ron Tavel at Theater for the New City and spent the night in her airy loft in Westbeth. I had a very nice time. Sarah had wonderful taste, we saw eye to eye on many subjects, and talk poured out. She showed me beautiful paintings she had painstakingly produced in her austere studio. Fred was long gone, and Stefan had grown up and moved away. She did not like living alone either, she said. I loved being a man with a woman and wanted to make love; but we held back, cautiously, and slept apart, restlessly. I was still shaken by the breakup with Michele. She was still mad at Fred.

22

HANON INVITED ME to a meeting about how to get the Living Theatre moving again now that Julian Beck was gone. In Europe their commitment to political theatre was respected, and they had a following. In New York they were viewed as embarrassing throwbacks to the sixties. Even so, Judith was determined to stay in New York, where they were needed. There was no politics in America anymore, just money. The theatre was not speaking out about peace, justice, disarmament, philosophical anarchy, and non-violent revolution, nor staging plays by poets. Judith wanted a space in New York to do plays and focus the community that needed the Living Theatre to speak for it. This was the world I cared about. Larry Loonin, a director friend who was also there, said I should realize who I was, well known and a good critic, that I could get a job teaching criticism and playwriting at a good university like so many of our generation. But somehow I never did.

I felt a great attraction to Ilion Troya, Julian's Brazilian lover, recalling Ilion's beauty and gaiety the night after Julian died, which brought light into that dark time. My head was spinning as I drove home through the night.

My attraction to theatre had always been partly sexual; this intoxicating gust of sweetness and desire was part of that. Maybe I really was gay! Maybe I had been straight long enough. I could change all my formulations about myself, which were mostly secret anyway.

This fantasy dissolved into nothing when I came down from the pot I had smoked with Judith. I didn't even know Ilion, who was about to get married. My interest in being gay was sporadic at best. A sweet letter from Sarah perked up my heart. And I was getting to know a couple of other very interesting women closer to home.

A CALL CAME FROM SANTA BARBARA. Dad, so weak he could not walk to the bathroom, had been moved to the Casa Dorinda's medical center, the thing he dreaded most. Mother speculated that he might never come back to the apartment. On the phone, Dad asked for news. Well, Julian had a paper route. I was not even looking for a job, if that was what he meant. I had taken pains to answer his letter urging me to go back to work for David, trying to be realistic, but he was too drugged and weak for serious talk.

Julian was frustrated by my unwillingness—inability, actually—to play Dungeons and Dragons with him. I saw a notice on the library bulletin board looking for players, brought him the telephone number, and eventually he called. The couple who had put up the notice were in their early twenties. Julian, eleven, said he was not prejudiced. They began picking him up on Saturday mornings and playing until late at night, sometimes clear through the weekend. The main guy had no front teeth, which made a strange impression. Julian liked and enjoyed them.

I repainted the apartment in softer colors. I played tennis once a week with a threesome of crafty septagenarians. I kept revising my short novel. I could almost imagine being happy again, but a crazy restlessness made it hard to settle down.

I had left Jim the canary at a pet shop while I was working in France, hoping he would find a mate, but he didn't, and when I brought him back home, he had forgotten how to sing. Jim had brought endless delight into our lives in earlier times warbling along with Maria Callas. Cat almost got him when I was cleaning his cage. Now I forgot all about him, he ran out of water, and one day I found him dead. You can imagine how bad I felt.

I went to New York for the weekend to see Sarah, and this time we did make love, the first time either of us had fucked in months. "Crossing a chasm," she called it. She was "wary," she said—at one point, "scared." I was glad to be sexual again. Sex was friendly and natural, no big deal necessarily, just a whole other level of contact. Joe Chaikin came down from the ninth floor for breakfast. The spring day was beautiful. I drove uptown to a Living Theatre meeting, then drove Judith and her children, Garrick and Isha, across town to the 92nd Street Y, where Judith narrated the Brecht-Weill *Mahagonny Songspiel*, and three hours back to Westerly. When Julian came home from his Dungeons and Dragons game, I was back at my desk.

Johnny asked me to man one of five follow-spots for a memorial service at Judson Church for Eddie Barton, a dancer who had died of AIDS. I had slept with Eddie once in his apartment on the lower East Side and remembered his warm smell and kinky body hair. Performing my monologue *Tony* at an actors' convention, Eddie had been dragged off the stage in the middle, like Lucy Silvay at the Obies.

Memorial services were turning into the artistic highlights of the period. Remy Charlip and Aileen Passloff danced. Deborah Lee (now Lawlor), back from Tasmania, recreated Wallace Stevens's *Carlos Among the Candles*, which she had performed at the Caffè Cino in 1965. New York was humming, the mood turned around from the dark days when I had left, a decade earlier.

I was running around like crazy for *The Day*, writing previews, interviews, reviews, all kinds of views. I talked to the managing editor about more of a job there. I drove to Hartford to work on Lola Odiaga's piano all one day for $100. Fighting the flu, a fever blister coming, I felt awful in the car; but when I pulled off the road and climbed into the woods to pee, the sun was so warm and the air so soft that I danced for joy. It was April first: for dinner I served Julian boiled string with ketchup. Later I finished retyping *High*

Points of Youth. It was only 124 pages, a novella at best, cleaving too closely to actual events to be real fiction. It seemed to me tight and cleanly told, an interesting story. I hoped it might find readers.

Leaving Julian with Laurel and Hinrich, I flew to Denver for a conference on theatre criticism, where I made the opening remarks, not too badly, then joined a discussion with the principal Denver critics, surprised to be in a situation where my experience meant something. Al and Maxine were kind and generous to me, as always, and Denver felt like New York in the sixties, talented people working hard for no money, making art for the love of it. I saw four plays in two days, preferring the poor, rough, intimate theatres to the big, sleek, new Denver Center for the Performing Arts, where I watched a few minutes of Chekhov in Jean-Claude's new translation. In the discussion after a fine show that had been panned by the critics, I did most of the talking.

When I got home, Sarah had written saying she wanted to see me, proposing dates. She would be spending April and May painting at Yaddo, the artists' colony, and wondered if we might be together somewhere in the country in July and August. Now that Sarah and I had broken the ice, it seemed inevitable that we would keep getting together, but I was not ready to make further plans. Julian would finish fourth grade in June. That was as far ahead as I could see.

If I hadn't slept with Sarah, I was well on my way to getting together with Carolyn Knox, a smart, beautiful, friendly widow who lived in Westerly, a witty poet, who made me quiches and took me to Boston to meet her mother. But I did.

23

JUDITH TELEPHONED with the idea that the City of New York might provide the Living Theatre with a building. I had an in at City Hall via my old *Village Voice* connections and nothing to lose by asking. David Gurin, now Assistant Commissioner of Transportation, advised me to call Dan

Wolf, now a close adviser to Mayor Edward I. Koch.

Dan was glad to hear from me. He could not help Judith, he said, forget it. But did I need a job? Realizing in that moment that this would change everything, I said yes, as a matter of fact I did. Dan said he would look into it and get back to me.

A few days later he called and put me on the phone with Bill Rauch (rhymes with 'how'), a protégé of his and a big success as the Mayor's press secretary. Bill tentatively offered me a job as one of his five assistants. It paid $40,000 a year, more than I had ever made before. "I'm blown away," I said to myself aloud after hanging up. "I'm blown to bits!"

I had a history with Ed Koch, whom I knew in the early sixties as *The Village Voice*'s attorney. Ed had represented me personally in a claim against a landlord and recovered several hundred dollars, of which he kept forty percent. Later, he had done nothing to save the Caffè Cino when he was on the City Council, sacrificing it, in my view, to his political ambition. I was trying to keep the Cino open and took it quite personally. But that was a long time ago.

Sarah came to Westerly for the weekend and hit it off with Julian, who was an interesting and friendly boy. We went to Hartford so I could review a play, and that night the fucking was splendid, freer and wilder than before. On Sunday I took her to New Haven to see paintings by Constable at the Center for British Art. She was a terrific person to look at art with, knowledgeable, passionate, articulate. I saw her off on the train to New York and drove home to Westerly to be with Julian and finish reading Koch's book, *Mayor* (written by Bill Rauch). When Julian asked me where Sarah had slept, I said, "With me."

On Monday morning I drove into the city to formally interview for the job, slow in traffic as I moved toward the center of money, hot in my only suit. Over lunch with Dan, Bill asked me if I was tough enough. Not really knowing what he meant, I said what I had to say, to wit, that I could be, and I was accepted on Dan's say-so, touched and grateful that he had confidence in me. After lunch we went back to City Hall, where Ed—the Mayor—took me inside his office for a moment and welcomed me. He was much larger than I remembered. Dan had a desk right outside his door.

Julian had been worried about my not having a job. He knew I was running out of money, that something had to happen. This was dramatic, and just in time. I still had to complete the changes set in motion when Michele broke up our marriage, do something with my freedom. This would get me moving. Reestablished in the city, I could work my way back into the theatre.

THE END OF APRIL was an awkward moment to be leaving Westerly. Julian's school ran on into June. He was already barely making it, needing more paternal attention, not less. But I had to start right away at City Hall, I was told, or forget it. My idea was to leave Julian with Laurel and Hinrich, who were practically family and would be glad to have him, but he begged me not to. Louisa, now four and a half, had bugged him incessantly the last time he stayed with them. I asked Caroline Knox if she would take him in for the last five weeks of fourth grade. She agreed, reluctantly. Julian would drop by the apartment after school to feed Cat and have a snack, and Hinrich would water the plants. I would spend weekends with Julian in Westerly or in the city. When school let out, he would go to New Mexico and Michele would have her turn.

Regulations at my new job gave me ninety days to find an apartment in the city. I asked Sarah if I could rent her loft in Westbeth for the two months she would be at Yaddo, but she already had a renter. Frank Lilly kindly cleared out a back bedroom for me in his apartment at 104th and Central Park West and made me welcome.

Julian was understandably depressed, left to slog through school and his paper route with no parental support. I was extremely sorry to end our sweet year together prematurely but excited about my new job, reading the *New York Times* with renewed interest. Maybe I was overdramatizing, but moving back to the city felt like coming home after twelve years in exile.

Return to New York

1986–1992

Photo op with Mayor Koch in Central Park, me at left, Dan Wolf at right.
(The Mayor was privately horrified.)

MICHAEL SMITH

New York City Hall

1

Behind the tall arched windows to the left of the Doric portico of City Hall was the Mayor's Press Office, a big, high-ceilinged room just inside the inner police perimeter, close to the center of power. Bill Rauch, the press secretary, presided at a central desk surrounded by five assistants, whose job was to field questions from reporters, manage and monitor press conferences, produce press releases, write statements and newspaper columns for the Mayor, coordinate information on policy with the various commissioners and agencies, above all get the Mayor on the news and in the headlines every day. Whenever he appeared in public, one of the press secretaries was close at hand, tape-recording every word he said so reporters could not misquote him. Ed Koch was a flamboyant personality with a flair for controversy.

Unbeknownst to me, scandals had begun to tarnish Koch's good repute in the months since his landslide reelection to a third term, and smart, ambitious reporters were aggressively digging for more. I was inexcusably innocent, whisked overnight from my quiet, solitary, early-music life in Westerly into a maelstrom of conflicting ambitions, some of the people dangerous, coming at me at any moment, crowding the halls, jamming our press conferences in

Dan Wolf (left), Bill Rauch (center), and the Mayor's Press Office staff

the Blue Room next door. It was a stately but unpredictable form of theatre. I was on duty daily from nine to five, at my desk or out and about with the Mayor, and on call one night a week plus one day every other weekend. Wherever I was, when my beeper went off, I immediately phoned the police desk at City Hall to learn which reporter was asking a question or where I was to rush to meet the Mayor. I was expected to wear a suit and tie. I needed a whole new wardrobe.

I was assigned liaison with the Departments of Housing, Parks, Cultural Affairs, and several others, each with its press officers and commissioners revolving around the Mayoral sun. It was full speed ahead from day one. On my first morning the Mayor announced a $4.2-billion affordable housing plan. My second day brought a mini-scandal involving Victor Botnick, a mayoral protégé who ran the Health and Hospitals Corporation and had

MICHAEL SMITH

taken too many trips to California at HHC expense. I watched Koch field questions in his office with Bobby Wagner and a Deputy Mayor at his side, bemused Dan Wolf watching quietly from the back.

That afternoon Bill had me sit in on an interview with Herb Rickman, a gay special assistant to the Mayor, by Marcia Kramer of the *Daily News*, a blonde bombshell with spike heels, scarlet claws, and a terrible cold. It seemed that Bess Myerson, the Commissioner of Cultural Affairs, had given a plum job to the daughter of the judge who was ruling on her lover's alimony. Myerson, a former Miss America, had been close to the Mayor during his first reelection campaign, helping to counter rumors that he was a closet homosexual. Rickman, a friend of the judge, denied everything, invoking his and the judge's sterling liberal credentials. Squirming in her tight skirt, wheezing and blowing her nose, Kramer protested that she hated this assignment, it was not the kind of journalism she wanted to do, he could not imagine how truly sympathetic

Playing my part

she was. Rickman suggested that her editor was a homophobe.

A few days after that I accompanied the Mayor to the funeral of a Brooklyn priest who had been murdered in his car in the middle of the night by a black youth he had apparently picked up for sex. The church solidified behind the priest, and the Mayor, a friend and ally of Cardinal O'Connor, added his presence and credibility, sitting in the front row beside the displayed body. The pews were filled with priests in robes. The bishop spoke of the dead priest's good works, acceptance of authority, and unblemished reputation, and the cardinal backed him up.

Crack was hitting the city; the Mayor proposed the death penalty for wholesalers of cocaine and heroin. I thought a better solution to the whole drug disaster was decriminalization. Marijuana is a harmless weed that should be grown at will and freely sold; addictive drugs could be managed through clinics. The law-enforcement approach creates the crime. I said something about this to Bill, and he gave me a little education: "It's not about crack, it's about headlines. He can't really do anything about crack, but he can avoid having people say he isn't doing anything about it." One of the cops in the front seat (joking) favored cutting off the hands of drug offenders. "Or their pricks," said the other.

Following Gurdjieff, I had small regard for the controversies of the moment. For better or worse, I had never been politically active or tuned in, although I had joined marches and art actions against the war in Vietnam. Party politics was never going to satisfy my pacifist-anarchist, anti-authoritarian, utopian ideals. I accompanied the Mayor to kick off Armed Forces Day on an aircraft carrier at a Hudson River pier. In the car, as cops were clearing a path for us through the anti-war demonstrators, he turned to me and said, "Whatever your personal opinion may be, just remember, we're on the side of the police."

After a while Bill told me to stop asking about everything and start using my own judgment, but I would never have any judgment about this game. Putting on a play was far more serious. The government would happen with or without me. Unless I wrote a play and put it in front of an audience, it would never exist, the world would not have it. What I cared about was art, I kept thinking, not politics. My politics is that only this moment is real, and people matter one by one.

Running around with the Mayor was fun, though. In contrast with David Way, Ed Koch was quick and decisive, with a forward-moving energy. It was exciting to speed through the city in the back seat of his Lincoln Town Car, two cops up front. When we were running late, the backup car took the lead and we pushed through the traffic with lights and sirens. On the way

The exuberant Mayor Koch: "How am I doing?"

from one "location" to the next, the Mayor talked on the phone, conferred with some adviser he had brought along, listened to music (*Phantom of the Opera*), chatted with Dan, or took a nap. Then we arrived and he snapped into focus, hit the event running, and galvanized the crowd with his celebrity charisma, shining his bigger-than-life personality on them like a floodlight. We walked into, say, a crowded ballroom at the Waldorf Astoria, the band struck up "New York, New York," and he strode up the aisle raising his arms high, crying, "It's me!" It was a rush like musical comedy.

To the farther reaches of the city, Coney Island, Yankee Stadium, or Staten Island, we traveled by police helicopter, taking off the from the World Trade Center heliport, scudding low over our impossibly dense and complicated domain. As we returned, spiraling in for a landing beside the towers of lower Manhattan, the concentration of power was tangible, inescapable, as if nothing else really counted.

Julian came to the city on the weekend I was on call. I went to Westerly the next, so tired I fell asleep on my bed still dressed. On Saturday night we played in the park—shook cherry petals onto each other off the trees, threw the frisbee in the dark, wrestled on the dewy grass. Sunday we went to the beach with Caroline Knox. Going back to the city seemed natural, though I was lonely at Frank Lilly's. He expected me to pick up Puerto Rican guys on the street and bring them home for sex. That was what he did.

Gradually the idea dawned that I should move in with Sarah Marx in Westbeth when she came back from Yaddo. The room at Frank's was temporary by design. It seemed senseless to set up my own apartment, then have "dates" with Sarah, have to go "out," probably sleep at her place anyway. She was the only one of the women I had been courting that I had slept with, and it made all the difference. I wrote her a letter and proposed it.

Victor Botnick had a physical altercation with the head of the doctors' union. A reporter from WCBS phoned the press office asking about Victor's age, title, salary, and educational background. Bill got Victor on another line and passed on his answers to me, and I passed them on to the reporter. We stuck at the education question. Bill talked to Victor a while, then said, "Tell them he's a college graduate." It subsequently emerged that Victor never had quite graduated from college. The Mayor "punished" him for the lie with six weeks of community service, but the flap continued even after Victor resigned. There were quasi-obits in the tabloids. Somebody on the news said they had "torn off the Mayor's arm." The President of the City Council and the Majority Leader were heard discussing whether the Mayor would resign. The Mayor said he wanted to die in office. It was truly theatre of the ridiculous, though the principals seemed entirely sincere.

I took Julian to Charlemont for Memorial Day weekend, the cabin just as we had left it in the fall. And then school was over. I went back for one final weekend and found Julian waiting for me in the apartment. He had comforted himself with food and put on weight. I was glad this awkward transition was over. After I put him on the plane to Albuquerque, though, to go back to Michele, I felt terrible, my little family lost.

MICHAEL SMITH

2

SARAH LET ME WAIT TEN DAYS and then said yes to my proposal to move in with her. I was excited—goodbye loneliness and solitary horniness—thank heavens! I had been explicit in my letter that I was not proposing any permanent commitment, but there was no telling what would happen.

My idea was to slip into Sarah's life without disturbing anything, leave my household stuff in storage in Connecticut for some future moment when I would need it for a place of my own, keep everything of hers the way it was. She seized the occasion of my arrival to pull the place to bits.

I had always wanted to live in Westbeth. I remembered looking at the bulky block of buildings beside the river with Johnny from three blocks away, standing across West Street from an early incarnation of Theater for the New City. The former Bell Telephone Labs were being converted into subsidized live-work apartments reserved for artists; I had written letters for several people attesting to their credibility. Johnny and I could easily have qualified. I suggested we move there, where we would have much more space. I loved the idea of living in a building full of artists; Johnny said it sounded like a nightmare.

The architect of Westbeth, Richard Meier, had ingeniously connected the several buildings of the old industrial complex, dividing up the huge, high-ceilinged floors into variously sized units, each with a small kitchen and bath, which artist-tenants could adapt to their own purposes. Sarah had moved into hers with Fred Katz, who had built walls to section off a bedroom for Stefan and a corner painting studio for Sarah with a raised sleeping platform for the two of them; later, living alone, Sarah had moved into the bedroom. Her studio was sacred, but the rest of the space was up for grabs. She decided I too must have a room of my own and talked me into taking the bedroom for my study, with a couch in it for visiting children. We would sleep at the other end of the big living space, where we had a grand view of lower Manhattan and the southern sky through a wall of windows, the World Trade Center towers shimmering like visitors from outer space.

We tried out the new location of the bed by making love in the afternoon, which was richly satisfying for us both. "What a gorgeous cock," she said afterwards. On the subway that night after a movie a young woman told us we looked young except for our gray hair and asked how old we were. "About fifty," I told her. She could see that we were in love. Indeed we felt that a blessing had come into our lives.

WHILE THE MAYOR's OFFICE was staging the splashy centennial of the Statue of Liberty, I was reading Julian Beck's last book, *Theandric*, which Judith and Ilion were preparing for publication. From Julian's point of view, I was working for Mammon, preserving the general enslavement he called Stupidity. Sarah's love of fireworks left no room for detachment. We watched them bursting over the Statue of Liberty from a ferryboat reserved for the Mayor's Office at the foot of Manhattan, pressing together on the end of the deck over the black water writhing with reflections.

Sarah helped me empty the apartment in Westerly and fill up a storage locker in Old Lyme. The few things I wanted in the city made a small truckload—my baby grand piano, the elegant, simple bed Hinrich had made for Michele and me, the four early American chairs we had bought with my Rockefeller grant, perfect for Sarah's round oak table, my files and some working papers. I left my harpsichord with John Bennett for repair.

Alfred came east for a ten-day visit, great at eight. On the night of his arrival Sarah served him squid; he coolly asked for a second helping.

She went to Vermont to visit a painter friend while I went to Charlemont with Alfred, who had not been sure he would see me this summer or ever come to the cabin again. As I sat at my little built-in table writing, Alfred came in the door and said, "Dad, I love you." I liked life better with him than without him and resolved to figure out a way for him to come live with me. Maybe Julian too, but not this year. It would not be possible to move a son or sons in with Sarah. Ultimately I knew they needed me, and I needed them.

Her warm, lively, literate, engaged circle of artist friends were suspicious of me at first, then liked me. I liked them, too, enjoying their individuality,

With Cat at Westbeth

cosmopolitan intelligence, and creative energy, although I often felt misapprehended. My job with the Mayor was so vivid, somehow, that they couldn't help thinking that was who I was. Sarah was an artist who supported herself by teaching; I was seen as a slightly off-beat bureaucratic functionary, working for the enemy. I could play the piano for them, that was something, but I couldn't be an artist myself.

Sarah was not easy to get along with, her intractable rage at Fred hardly an aberration in an otherwise gentle soul. When they had built a house together on Jean-Claude's land in the Berkshires, with a painting studio for her, she paid for the site with a painting. Then Fred took up with another woman, and the house was no longer hers. There were dark clouds in her mind—her mother's death, the Holocaust, the general indifference to her art. Both our fathers were small merchants, as it happened, but otherwise our backgrounds were more different than alike. Her family were poor orthodox Polish Jews, and she had lost most of her relatives to Hitler; mine were well-to-do American WASPs. We had radically different outlooks and expectations.

Sarah was afraid that if she loved me she would scare me away. I wanted to love and be loved, but I was barely recovered from eleven years with Michele, and seven years with Johnny before that, wary of another commitment. Nonetheless, my love-making made her happy, and it was tremendously satisfying to me.

Our cats fought. Shadow, a retiring creature getting on in years, kept Cat under the couch in my study. Horrible hissings, scrabblings, and screams ensued when he tried to escape. Shadow won these exchanges, but the effort made her sick; finally she went to live with Stefan in his squat on Second Avenue. So Cat won that battle of the sexes.

IT WAS PLEASANT AND CONVENIENT to have a car in the city, but finding a parking space late at night was agony,. My little Toyota was repeatedly broken into, window smashed. I thought of giving it to Michele, who needed a vehicle. Sarah wanted to take it to Northampton in the spring, when she would start teaching at Smith College. She said Michele's needs were not my problem anymore, that I was being paternalistic and disempowering. When Michele asked me to send her money to pay a debt and her college tuition, it was as if she was my child, not my peer coequally capable and responsible. I sent her an extra $100 and hired a lawyer to work out a separation agreement, enabling her to receive college loans and aid and relieving me of responsibility for her debts. I was not looking to be divorced. I had no desire to marry Sarah but wished I could sign her onto my city health insurance.

I took an evening off from Sarah every week or two and spent it with Johnny, who was invariably welcoming when I phoned. I took the subway to West 4th Street after work, climbed the familiar stairs to his apartment on Cornelia Street, we'd smoke grass and listen to opera, talk dish and philosophy, eventually go out for dinner, and afterwards he walked me home. Johnny paid for dinner; I accepted gratefully. After struggling for years as a lighting designer, working his butt off in the downtown theatre, doing a few industrials, touring with the New York Dolls, barely making enough money to live on, he had set up a profitable marijuana business to support his art habit. He had plenty of money now—and gave me little bags of pot whenever I ran low. I had never stopped wanting to be close to him. I could barely keep my hands off him, but he ruled out getting physical.

The Living Theatre reasserted its existence with an exhibition of Julian Beck paintings at Cooper Union and a benefit performance, the *Retrospectacle*, consisting of excerpts from Living Theatre

Johnny in the 1980s

productions through the years, most with the original cast. Johnny had his own lighting company now and provided the lights. I joined the all-star team running six follow-spots, linked to him by headsets.

The next day I moderated a symposium on the Living Theatre with Jack Gelber and Karen Malpede, playwrights, Bill Coco, dramaturg, and Richard Schechner, director, theoretician, professor at NYU. I opened in a laid-back

personal mode. The Living Theatre was unique and precious. Judith and Julian were my only teachers and did my politics for me. The attraction was partly erotic but I had never slept with anybody in the Living Theatre. I spoke of affinity and Judith's special clarity. I said the eager, serious audience for the *Retrospectacle* reawakened hope for the theatre and by extension the community of peaceniks, radical intellectuals, artist-hipsters, potheads, and other out-there types there present. Judith wanted to know what the Living Theatre should do next.

IF WHAT WE WERE SAYING at City Hall had any reality, I had timed both my exit from the city and my return about right, leaving New York at the start of a deep slump, returning when the effect of Koch's giveaway to developers and Wall Street was starting to be felt. New buildings were going up all over the city, and the devolution of the economy from manufacturing to finance was making New York rich again. We routinely referred to it as the world capital of communications, finance, art, culture, fashion, and ideas.

With Reagan in Washington, though, the streets were a different story. On the way home from a drop-in with the Mayor, I found a grimy, ravaged young man lying crookedly on the floor blocking the only toll gate onto the subway platform underneath the World Trade Center. Another man started back the other way. "Here it is, we can just step over him," I said to myself breezily. "I'll just step over you," I said to the man on the floor, who smelled revolting. Stepping over him, I fed my token into the slot and went through, sat down on a bench in the clean new station, put in my ear plugs, and read the *Times* book review until my clean new train came along.

My parents invited me and the boys to Santa Barbara for Christmas. I had been living with Sarah for a couple of months and was happy with our love affair, but it didn't occur to me to insert her into this family occasion, already as much as I could handle. She followed on her own, however, not letting me say no, arriving on Christmas night, nicely finessing the Christian moment. Good with other people, she was tense and touchy with me. We had a furious argument outside a restaurant on the pier, screaming at each

MICHAEL SMITH

Julian and Alfred in Santa Barbara

other in front of the boys. It was too much like fights with Michele and gave me black thoughts about myself. Sarah turned grim, setting her mouth in a thin, sour line.

Later that night she wondered aloud whether she was "making a family" with us. I thought not. The boys were in New Mexico with Michele, that was the family, with me as the absent father. In New York I was just me.

I drove Sarah to Northampton to start her new job teaching art at Smith College for the spring semester and took the train back to the city, leaving her my car. She only had classes on Monday and Tuesday, and most weeks would come home from Wednesday night till Sunday afternoon.

Denis Deegan called, out of the blue, and we met for lunch near City Hall. I had not seen Denis for fifteen years, since the time he showed up at Johnny's and sought to reclaim a few prized items I had been keeping for him. This made Johnny so mad that he threw most of them out the fifth-floor window into the street. Denis, whose directing career in New York had come to nought, had been living in Paris, married for a time to a Swedish model, with whom he had a son a little older than Julian. He had worked as a model himself, at one time "the most beautiful boy in Paris," later as a garden designer. I was glad to see him, despite his tiresome braggadocio. If he had so many rich friends in France who adored him, what was he doing in New York trying to impress me with the Latin names of plants?

It took several lunches for me to realize that Denis was broke and needed a job. I put him in touch with my contacts at the Parks Department and edited some of the pretentious bullshit out of his resume. He came over for dinner when Sarah was away teaching and stayed the night on the sofa in my study. Through the fog of name-dropping, it emerged that he was homeless and relying on the kindness of friends, of whom I was probably the oldest. So he moved in for the several days each week that Sarah was not there. He brought me flowers, cooked dinner, made me a martini when I came home from work. Much as I appreciated my dear friend's entertaining ways, I can't handle martinis, and I wanted time to myself. After a few weeks Sarah chased him off. The Parks Department hired him as a gardener, and he moved in with a lady friend uptown.

Julian was apparently okay in New Mexico. Alfred said the other kids were mean and, as if idly, wondered what the schools were like in New York. He was nine, and the Village had a particularly good elementary school, P.S. 41. When I talked about it to Michele, she said both boys should come; they needed more stimulation and challenge than they were getting in Las Vegas, and she wanted to go back to school and get a master's. Sarah was willing. Although I thought two boys would be too much for us, she felt that the brothers should not be separated. I could give them my study and move my desk up onto the loft in her studio. We each needed solitude for our work: I promised not to look while she painted if she would not talk while I wrote.

O N HER SPRING BREAK Sarah and I went to Madrid to see the Velázquez paintings in the Prado, and Goya, driving a rented car to Avila and

Toledo and south through magnificent landscapes to Granada. I loved Spain but hated the grisly Christian art we encountered everywhere. Sarah sought out abandoned synagogues, Spain still haunted by its missing Jews and Moors.

From Malaga she flew to Boston and went straight back to Smith, while I flew home to New York. I liked having the place in Westbeth to myself when she was away. Exhausted from work, I could knock off and not do anything. Or I could entertain friends she disdained, homosexual potheads whose company I enjoyed, go to shows she would not like without leaving her behind, get high without provoking her disapproval. Then she came home for a few days, and I was not alone and unloved after all.

The back and forth to Northampton made it impossible for her to focus on painting, which drove her nuts. She was too tired to make love when she got home, then preoccupied with leaving. She was jealous of my friendship with Johnny. She told me I could still get together with Caroline Knox. She told me she did not want to be nice, fun, good. Her "darkness" was precious, vital to her identity. I too embrace the complexity of existence, indulge some murky predilections, and realize our civilization is going downhill fast—but temperamentally I am on the side of light. Evil can take care of itself; I would rather harmonize and look to the good. Her mood did not improve. At the end of a year together we had polarized into heavy and light, dark and light—which she spelled "lite," with a sarcastic edge—and Jew and Christian, although I regarded myself as a Sufi Buddhist.

The public middle schools were problematic, so I was grateful when my father agreed to pay for Julian to go to a private school for seventh grade. He came in April for a test and interview at the Village Community School. You hardly noticed his weird-looking Mohawk because his personality and presence were so sparkly and solid. He liked VCS and was immediately accepted. We had fun exploring the city.

Sarah kept saying she wanted my children without reservation, although her friends told her she would never paint again. Willy-nilly, they were coming as soon as school let out. I built a partition to give us some privacy in our bed; built a half-wall to screen the loft in Sarah's studio and set up my desk and files, cozy, glowing, focused; brought the boys' beds, desks, and bureaus from storage in Connecticut. My porn magazines had to go lest Julian and Alfred come upon them and be freaked out; I threw them down the incinerator rather sadly, porn still somewhat hard to get. In Sarah's opinion, masturbation was what inclined me to be homosexual in the first place. It still turned me on to look at pictures of turned-on guys; but making love with her was far more satisfying.

KOCH WAS REELING from a series of press attacks on Bess Myerson, who eventually resigned as Commissioner of Cultural Affairs. Bill Rauch had departed in a moment of calm. Morale in the Press Office was shattered. The Mayor's appetite for press was his Achilles heel, and his new press secretary, George Arzt, himself a member of the press, instinctively fed it. I got a kick out of marching through the Village with the Mayor in the Gay Pride parade. The gay activists were furious with the his inaction on AIDS and gay rights; we were surrounded by police but close to the people.

I finished *100,000 Songs*, my opera libretto about Milarepa, and Sarah encouraged me to pull together a reading before we left for the summer. I gathered a fine, wild cast of actors. Sadly, Ondine was laid up with a hurt leg, on his way to becoming a cirrhosis invalid. They all loved the play, which took four hours to read through. There were many great scenes, but it was obvious that the songs in which Milarepa presented his teachings were much too long. I needed to cut the text by half before I could send it to Peter.

3

DETERMINED TO GET OUT OF THE CITY in the summer and paint in the country, Sarah rented a house in West Nyack for the months of July and August, to be paid for by subletting the loft in Westbeth. I could commute to the city by train. Julian and Alfred, ages twelve and nine, would go to day camp, and she could paint all day. They arrived full of life and love and ready to have fun, and we immediately moved to the country. "Uncle" John Lucas

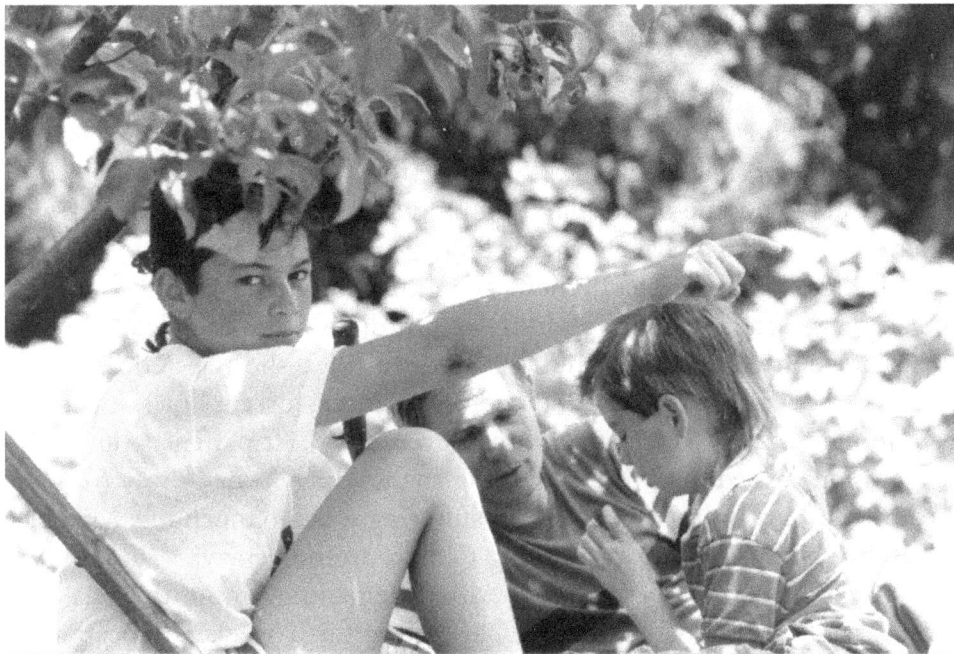

Julian and Alfred with John Lucas in West Nyack, July 4, 1987

came from the city to visit for the Fourth of July, bringing fireworks he had bought on the street in Chinatown. I was so happy that I got up early and wrote a poem called "Hooray for Everything!"

Weekdays after breakfast Sarah and the boys drove me to the train, which carried me like a corpuscle to the World Trade Center, where a river of workers flowed up ten parallel escalators from under the Hudson into the insatiable city. Meanwhile the bus to day camp collected Julian and Alfred at eight-thirty, leaving Sarah to herself, and brought them back at four. They all met my train, and we might have time for badminton before dinner, darkness, and bedtime.

I hated commuting, and Sarah felt overwhelmed by three Smith males, bullied by the boys when they came home from camp, jealous of my attention when we were together. She wanted more of me, and so did they, but there was no more.

She took to pulling me out onto the lawn under the great trees at midnight, not for love but to recite her woes where the boys would not have to hear, ragged with bitterness and fury. She did not want to be pleasant and fun, she said, she was evil and full of darkness. I tried to overpower her misery with love, but she would not let me touch her.

I already knew the dread plaint "you don't love me" from my years with Michele. Sarah insisted her true feelings were blacker still. I believed her truer feelings were love, tenderness, and understanding: when she let go of the anger, the good stuff was right there. Gurdjieff recommended "stopping the expression of negative emotion," a useful idea she rejected as denial. I told her I had a big heart and there was room for all, but she did not believe me. Exhausted to begin with, I eventually lost patience, ran out of compassion, lashed out at her for being such a drag. What a way to spend our time, arguing in the suburbs! Her suffering was too much like Michele's not to be my fault. What was I doing to drive women crazy? Why?

The boys were competitive too, Alfred demanding more things, Julian more attention. I took them to Charlemont for a weekend to take the pressure off Sarah. At the cabin Julian told me two dreams: 1) that he was hugging me and I disappeared; 2) that he was walking on bits of ground in the sky, missed one, and fell.

The next week, to give Sarah and me some private time together, I sent Julian to the Catskills with Johnny to work on lighting a show and drove Alfred across Connecticut to stay with his friend Russell Folger. Two days later Julian phoned to say that Johnny had thrown a tantrum and gone off to the theatre with the car, leaving him stranded in an isolated house with Johnny's driver and nothing to do but play Monopoly. He was upset by Johnny's rage mode, as anybody would be, and wanted to come home. I would have driven up to fetch him, but it was pouring rain and nearly dark, and I was fragilely recovering from a demolishing cold. So he had to stick it out.

Sarah and I went up on the weekend to see the show, *That Dada Strain* by Jerome Rothenberg, directed by Luke Theodore, a fabulous poetry-jazz extravaganza celebrating Tristan Tzara and the pioneers of Dada, with

Rothenberg chanting and preaching the brilliant, delirious words, musicians wailing and actors physicalizing, crazy and gorgeous in Johnny's lights.

We moved back to the city over Labor Day weekend. I felt useless and superfluous at the office, sick of working all day. It would be better to earn my livelihood from a series of projects. I had plenty of ideas; no telling what I could accomplish if I gave them my time and energy. I completed a first cut of *Milarepa*. I wanted to start a magazine, a pocket events guide like the ones you can buy on every newsstand in Paris, call it *New York This Week*. Freelance writing was theoretically possible. I wanted to write and direct more plays. I had good ideas for a movie and a television series. None of it would make me any money right away—or ever, unless I did it.

The night after Alfred's first day of school, Sarah went to bed early, turned out the lights, then got up and stormed "out" when I went up to my study. By the time she came back, I was in bed reading. She cornered me there, in a rage. I tried to get away. She jumped on me, hit me, made me so mad I hit her back. When I pinned her arms, she bit my leg. I fled naked to my study. She chased me, saying she was going to kill me. I was afraid she had a knife.

I ESCAPED FROM THE PRESSURES of the Press Office when Diane Fisher, my former colleague at *The Village Voice*, who had been writing speeches for the Mayor, was fired. Clark Whelton, the Mayor's chief speechwriter, a friendly, smart guy and former *Voice* reporter, hired me to take her place. As one of Clark's three assistants, I was to produce mayoral speeches, messages, and letters as assigned, plus the two columns for neighborhood newspapers that I already was "writing," leaning on drafts from the departments. Koch preferred to ad lib and rarely read from the scripts we wrote for him, but he liked to have one in his pocket. Dan said the work would only take me twenty hours a week; I could use the rest of the time for writing of my own. Relieved of nights and weekends catching press inquiries and chasing around with the Mayor, I would have more time for "life." I was weary of being on display in the madhouse of the Press Office and looked forward to privacy at my new desk behind a maze of filing cabinets in a former courtroom in the Tweed Building, just in back of City Hall.

In a dream Judith Malina said it was too bad I had given up my work, which was starting to be something. I said, "What work?" "Playwriting." I said I never thought it was real. "But it was," she said. Awake, I had the same thought: it was a cop-out not to pursue my métier. Something essential was being lost to the universe, of which I was charged to be part of the consciousness.

I had almost forgotten the theatre, which may have been objectively declining, too. It was down to a handful of columns in the *Voice*, where it had once been half the paper. The theatre section of the *Times* was now called "Arts and Leisure." It would take a major push to reassert my credibility as a theatre worker. My new work hours did not utterly preclude directing a play, but Sarah said she declined to look after my children.

I longed for a sense of moral coherence—of doing "write," as I miswrote in my diary. Moral action was loving and looking out for Julian and Alfred. Making Sarah so angry and embittered was clearly wrong. "Aren't you afraid to get so close to a dangerous lunatic?" she said. "Go back to your sweet little family!" This *was* my sweet little family, as I had thought she wanted it to be, and I kept trying to have the good prevail, keeping myself balanced with moderate, steady doses of coffee, aspirin, marijuana, wine, reading, writing, music, and sex, solo and with Sarah.

In another dream I took my pet lion for a walk down a wide red construction road cut through the woods near a beach. Thrilled to get out, the creature bounded off, chasing a shadow; it was gorgeous to see his lithe body stretching out, bounding over the ground. The road went nowhere, and we headed back. Beside a house on a hill up ahead was a blind man holding in his arms an enormous seal—a seeing-eye seal. I held my lion back with difficulty and kept us walking past. He had been impeccably benign so far, but he still was a lion.

Asked to contribute to an evening of one-act play readings at Theater for the New City, I had written two fantasy scenes about the Bess Myerson scandal; a couple more and I would have a play. I would have to deny I wrote it: I billed my contribution as *Any Time, Babe*, from *Trouble*, by Vernon O'Ray. Alas, the reading was lame. Marilyn Roberts was great as "Tess," but the actor playing her lover had a reading disability and stumbled through the words. Still, it was a start. I would feel better about the City Hall experience if I got some writing out of it besides the non-texts I was paid to write: speeches the Mayor did not deliver, letters he had not written, ghosted columns that did not say what either of us really thought.

4

MY BIG PINK HARPSICHORD came back, and I was glad to have it. Playing music every day preserved my sanity, and hearing me play Bach, Scarlatti, Couperin, and Rameau represented continuity for Julian and Alfred. Sarah loved to hear me play. Ken Wollitz came over with his recorder, sweet and fleet as ever. Mary Frank, a painter friend of Sarah's, and Susan Willmarth, a new friend, began coming every week to play their recorders with me, and we developed a lovely rapport.

Between my big pink harpsichord and the piano, there was hardly room to sit down, so I loaned the piano to a friend on the ninth floor, and Alfred, who was taking piano lessons, went up there to practice after school. He played charmingly in his first recital, his smile at the audience a special gift.

I had been writing on a Brother daisy-wheel typewriter with a tiny, awkward memory. I finally bought a proper computer, half for myself, compatible with the ones at work, and half for Julian, configured for his desires. It was my computer, and I set it up on my desk—which meant that Julian too now invaded Sarah's studio, slipping in the door and up the little ladder to the loft, sometimes wanting to bring his friends. He was into it, linking up with nerdy "bulletin boards." Sarah minded, but there was no alternative. She had the whole day to paint: the boys were at school till after three, when the light was fading anyway; Julian came home later still when he had basketball practice, and Alfred immediately went out again to play with his friends in the building. Sarah was home all that fall, then resumed teaching at Smith in the spring semester.

I witnessed Judith Malina's marriage to her longtime lover Hanon Reznikov in the Municipal Building, a year having passed since Julian Beck's death. She was sixty-two; he was thirty-eight. They were dressed up, romantic, serious, Judith glowing like a wise maiden, Hanon a man fulfilled.

Judith and Hanon

I loved walking Alfred to school every day, watching crocuses bloom in front of the Village houses, a magnolia, tulips, forsythia. After I dropped him off, I might squeeze in breakfast with Johnny before going downtown to work—nobody noticed when I came in late. With Johnny I could be myself in a way that was scarcely possible with anyone else except the boys, who were still children; it was amazing to be close again.

Johnny was grappling with mortality, his two oldest friends both ailing and failing. Kenny Burgess had been hospitalized with AIDS, recovered, then lost his loft on the Bowery, crammed with twenty years of his art. Johnny helped him move to a little upstairs place in Brooklyn; he took me out to visit, and I bought a collage.

Michael Wiley had stomach cancer, then a heart attack, and was desperately ill. Johnny's knees buckled the first time he went to see him in New York Hospital, suffering terribly, tubed up, tied down, raving. Johnny mastered his fright and calmed him when he was jerking uncontrollably by putting a hand on his heart chakra. Visiting Michael Wiley and looking after his affairs, Johnny broke through to a new openness and warmth. He was extraordinarily kind to me, welcoming my visits whenever I had the time, regaling me with marijuana, opera, and lively talk.

Sarah said we had maybe fifteen good years left if we kept our health and gave me an ultimatum: if I was not prepared to stay with her for fifteen years, we should split up right then. I was more concerned about the years after that, and the immediate present. Typically, she launched such confrontations late at night in bed, lying flat on her back ready to explode, too tense to touch and melt into love, me propped up on an elbow facing her from inches away, longing for embraces or else wishing I could read my book and go to sleep. These scenes hardly inclined me toward a marriage-like commitment, but I felt her distress, as they say, and tried to be compassionate and loving. It would not be simple to leave, with Julian and Alfred in the picture. I loved Sarah, but too often she was possessed and virtually erased by another being of appalling, mythic force that I took to be her mother, and I was not capable of playing her saintly rabbinical father. Her agitation had nothing to do with me, the Sarah I loved almost entirely absent. Such a fury or harpy would unman a satyr. My sense of failure sank me deeper in passivity.

In the wake of the presidential primary, the Mayor's Office was in shock. Koch had campaigned with Al Gore and attacked Jesse Jackson, stirring up the press and other politicians to a frenzy of outrage. The papers were dominated all week by stories about how the Mayor had hurt the city and himself. Sane people believed he was berserk. I thought he should endorse Jackson, but nobody asked me. Koch had lost his timing and sense of how things were playing to others when he lost Bill Rauch.

My left hip was so sore I could barely walk. A surgeon recommended two aspirins three times a day. I limped over to City Hall to hear the Mayor do one of my speeches at an Art Commission press conference, and he seemed barely able to read it, stumbling, slurring, incoherent. Was this a result of the tiny stroke he had suffered the previous fall? Nobody suggested it. Was he demoralized by the endless scandals? Burned out? The press could not believe his behavior; he called one reporter a "dog." George Arzt talked by the hour to reporters, who wrote that unnamed advisors (presumably Dan Wolf) had tried to restrain the Mayor to no avail.

I had two or three hours of speechwriting to do every day at most and cranked out the work well enough; Clark said I was good at it. I had privacy in the Tweed Building and time on my hands, but there was no way to distance myself from the Mayor show enough to do any writing or thinking of my own.

Back from Smith, Sarah was freaked out and blamed it on me. We needed help. Mary Frank recommended Girard Franklin, the analyst of her musicologist lover, Leo Treitler. "It's obvious that he loves you," Dr. Franklin boldly told Sarah at our first session, which helped immediately. Skillfully, he turned on me the following week.

Once we had both affirmed our choice to stay together, I treated myself to a few sessions of my own on the subject of work and livelihood. Dr. Franklin said I had left the theatre long ago, when I went off to work on harpsichords, and it was no longer a career option, a linear view I was not sure applied to artists. He said I needed a much better understanding of my parents' influence or I would not be able to change the patterns of a lifetime. My life had been predictable, he said; I was not my own person. I said he was being very provocative; he said he had to be, he did not have the luxury of just listening to me. I thought he was probably right but at $90 a session could not afford another open-ended analysis.

The boys left when school ended to spend the summer with Michele. As always Sarah wanted to go to the country to paint. My job would keep me in the city. I suggested she go on her own and I could come on weekends, but she wanted to be with me. So we stayed home, worked all day, and dedicated our free time to enjoying the city. She liked to go out after a day in her studio painting; we saw the latest movies, went to the country on weekends to visit friends, and had a very good time.

Julian, now thirteen, had been shaking the bunk bed and keeping Alfred awake. So I designed a complicated unitary structure to make their one room into three: a loft for Julian, an alcove for Alfred next to the window, and a television cave with sofa under Julian's room, though we hardly ever watched tv. With a full-bore teenager living his life on it, the structure had to be solid: I drew it out in detail, nesting the spaces together, with built-in

MICHAEL SMITH

beds, bookshelves, even a triangular laundry bin. I felt I was inventing a new field, design therapy, fixing the family through architecture. I might go into the business.

I took a few days off from work while the Mayor went to Europe and built the new room. Sarah helped, and Stefan gave us a day of carpentry. Doing architecture again was fun but physically miserable, the city horribly hot, the house a mess, sawdust sticking in our sweat.

5

MICHAEL WILEY DIED. Johnny disappeared, no longer answering his phone or doorbell or returning messages left on his machine. His marijuana office claimed not to know where he was. I thought he must be mad at me, or sick of taking me out to expensive dinners, or out of town: it was not unlike him to take unexplained trips. Finally Kenny Burgess phoned, in the middle of a festive dinner party celebrating Sarah's fifty-sixth birthday, to tell me that Johnny had AIDS and had spent the past month in the hospital with pneumonia. He was out now, staying at a midtown hotel. I called him and made plans to visit the next day.

I found him shockingly weak, unable to walk across the room to open the door, which had been left ajar. He was gaining strength day by day, he said, but would not be able to make it up the stairs at Cornelia Street. He was being moved to a new apartment in an elevator building.

A few days later he was strong enough to go out, and I took him for a ride in my car. Then he moved to his new apartment, a couple of blocks up Washington Street from Westbeth, and I began visiting him there.

The boys flew in full of energy, Julian wildly delighted to be back "home" in New York City. He had grown three inches, and his energy was overwhelming. Alfred was composed, tender, thoughtful, funny, eager to see his friends in the building. They loved their new rooms.

The following weekend I took them to Charlemont to help me reroof the cabin, which had leaked in the summer rains. Fred Katz trucked rolls of roofing up the hill for us. At thirteen Julian was great to work with, patient, energetic, focused on getting the job well done; Alfred, almost eleven, leapt from the woodshed roof to the cabin roof and back again. When they were little we sometimes went naked in the heat of the woods, which I always liked; they were too old for that now.

At the urging of both Michele and Sarah, I had divorce papers drawn up. Michele had settled down

Julian and me reroofing the cabin

with a solid, thoughtful partner, Joy Alesdatter, and stopped using my name; and I could understand Sarah's discomfort, not that I was not married to her, but that I was still married to someone else.

Dan Potter too had been signing divorce papers, Melisande having run off with a Jamaican. Devastated, Dan phoned and read me angry poems he had written about their breakup. I published them in a hand-sewn edition of seventy-five for him to give away, doing all the work myself. Sarah thought I was crazy to work so hard for nothing, but it gave me great satisfaction.

I turned fifty-three, and we had a dinner party for a dozen special friends. After dinner, before the champagne and cake, Susan Willmarth and I played Handel and Quantz on recorder and harpsichord. On Alfred's eleventh birthday, we took his best friends ice-skating at Rockefeller Center. Julian gave a party for his classmates in the apartment; Sarah hid out with a friend on the fifth floor while I maintained a parental presence from the other

MICHAEL SMITH

room. On Halloween Johnny married Patti Walsh so she could have his rent-controlled apartment on Cornelia Street. Bush was elected president—what a fiasco! We had an elegant, fun, sophisticated birthday party for Stefan, Sarah's son, who turned thirty. He and his girlfriend Jenny, who was writing Nancy Drew novels, had moved to Green Point; Stefan invited me out to see his new studio and the luminous street scenes he was painting.

L IFE WAS A CHAIN OF PLEASURES—dinner with Julian and Alfred, music with Mary and Susan, Becker playing Lendl on tv, sleeping with Sarah, breakfast en famille, walking Julian and Alfred to school, breakfast with Johnny, swarm life at City Hall. The Queen of the Night, an exotic plant I had brought with me from Westerly, bloomed in Sarah's luxuriant menagerie of house plants in the big south windows, the bud swelling for days, then opening late in the evening, its huge, intricate, ivory, lotus-like blossom emitting a potent perfume. We summoned friends in the building to admire it: by morning the flower would droop like a spent love-wand.

Jean-Claude was staying in Joe Chaikin's apartment on the ninth floor and invited up me to his private yoga classes with Ravi Singh. Sarah and I went to movies, ballets, plays, concerts, art shows, book parties, drove to Brooklyn or the country on excursions on beautiful days with and without the boys and their friends, enjoyed wonderful friendships and community. I was pleasantly busy at City Hall, going in late and sometimes leaving early, working without fret or friction.

Johnny gradually grew stronger and started going out again. In December he creating gorgeous lighting for *VKTMS*, a bizarre rendition by Michael McClure of the murder of Clytemnestra by Orestes, staged by the Living Theatre at Theater for the New City, directed by Judith in an extravagantly mannered style. I liked feeling I was the only person in the world who actually liked it. Kenny Burgess had a show of paintings of Morocco from the trip he took after his recovery from the first round of AIDS. Johnny, more tired than he was letting on, went to the Mamounia in Marrakesh for Christmas.

Sarah said her deepest desire was to live with me, but by January, when she resumed commuting to Northampton to teach, her mood had changed. She catalogued my turpitude, denounced my failure to satisfy her needs, cold in bed, treated my amorous eagerness as an imposition, saying if I was going to leave eventually I should leave now. Breaking up seemed stupid. I had made an elegant sliding shoji screen to close off our bed; we were finally comfortable. Koch was losing his grip, comparing the Controller, Jay Goldin, to Goebbels; my job was sure to end with the coming election. Putting the boys through another breakup was the last thing I wanted to do. Sarah knew what it was like living with them; the time to change her mind was not in the middle of the school year. She was kind and generous to them; they loved and needed her, and so did I. At the same time she was tormented and miserable, mad at me, rejecting me in bed even as she cooked us exquisite dinners, frustrated not to have enough quiet and solitude to paint even as she kept producing amazing, beautiful pictures, moving ahead with her work decisively.

Queen of the Night

6

SARAH SELDOM SAW her Orthodox younger brother Bernie and his family, thinking he did not approve of her being with me, a non-Jew. Bernie denied it: I was invited to dinner at their house in Queens and royally feasted. "Religion" increasingly became an issue between Sarah and me, although it was manifestly false. She had been secular since leaving home to study art at Cooper Union when she was eighteen. Brought up Episcopalian, I had long since given it up. To her I was still a Christian, and she became more Jewish in reaction, asserting her identity and integrity. She cooked a chicken the way her mother used to make it, plain boiled. For Passover she made us a seder—because of the boys, she said, because she had not done it for Stefan when he was a child. He and Jenny came, which made it fun. Coincidentally, Klaus, whom I liked to think of as my German son, was there for a visit. The evening was such a success that we basked in its afterglow for days.

Too often, though, the vibes on her days off from Smith were tense. She believed in confrontation, insisting on her "heavy," "dark," "Jewish," "peasant" nature. I made us another appointment with Dr. Franklin, hoping to get through the months until school ended and the boys went west without more fights and bitter feelings. After that, if we could not get along, we did not have to stay together. This time Franklin took the tack of he doesn't love you and I can help you learn to live with that.

Ondine died, dear, mad friend, amphetamine pioneer, world-class Callas queen. He was one of my favorite actors and the star of my little floating stock company: Scrooge in *Christmas Carol*, Jack in *Captain Jack's Revenge*, the King in *Prussian Suite*. It was not speed that killed him but alcohol. I had wanted him to play Marpa, Milarepa's irascible teacher. I wanted him to play Randy, Tess's Italian plumber lover in *Trouble*. I wanted to write an opera about Joe Cino, with Ondine as himself. I wanted to write a play about David Way and have Ondine play him as a raging fairy, my ultimate revenge. But it would never happen. A memorial gathering at Judson Church brought out some of the great rats.

Judith and Hanon opened a new Living Theatre on East Third Street off Avenue C. I took Julian and Alfred to see *The Tablets*, a gorgeous abstract work of Hanon's that Johnny lit spectacularly in the claustrophobic space. We lingered afterwards for Judith's birthday party. Pot was smoked. Julian was sorry he would not be around in the summer to join the Living Theatre and do anti-war street theatre.

He finished up well at Village Community School, intensely caught up in friendships with his classmates. He would return in the fall to attend the prestigious Bronx High School of Science. I was not quite sure how he had chosen Bronx Science and gotten himself in, but I was impressed. Alfred intended to stay in New Mexico with Michele. Sarah gave them a going-away party on the roof of Westbeth.

I thought about moving. Donny Nardona, back in touch after twenty years, urged me to come to Florida. "You'll fit in anywhere," he told me, and I knew he was right. New York was dirty, noisy, relentless, unhealthy. But I had to stay for at least another year or two because of Julian and also Johnny, now that he was ill.

Julian in 8th grade

Sarah told Dr. Franklin not just that she loved me but that she wanted to live with me and Julian the following year—I had thought she definitely did not. It made all the difference to be wanted. If I did not have to move, we could go to Spain again: Susan Willmarth had a house in a village in Catalonia and had invited us to visit. We were even making love.

I FLEW OUT TO SANTA BARBARA to visit my parents. Dad, escaping from the Medical Center, had reinstalled himself at home in spite of Mother's opposition. Coming back from Jerome Lowenthal's piano master class at the Music Academy of the West, she led me to the door of their apartment,

MICHAEL SMITH

Mother and Dad

looked inside, then suddenly took me away again, full of feeling. "What do you do when you can't sleep?" she wanted to know. I said I turned on the light and read a book. She said, "I can say the alphabet backwards"—and proceeded to do so. I navigated us onto a bench. She said she knew the books of the Bible and proceeded to name them, first the New Testament and then the Old, saying the names boldly, trembling with excitement. She said she knew a psalm. Then she lost it. I appreciated the moment of intimacy, though it was not exactly an exchange.

It was difficult being with my parents together but precious to be with either one of them individually. Dad asked me to play the piano for him, accepting now and plainly glad to have me there: now that I was a father, I recognized the same primal pleasure I felt with my own sons. He could barely get out of the chair and up on his walker, barely get the food to his mouth, raising the fork in hesitant extreme slow motion. He said he wished it was over: he had asked his doctor to finish him off, but he refused.

He reminisced, saying that he had feared his own father, feared his moods, feared his disapproval, defied him in order to defy his fear. He said, "I was afraid of my father because my mother made me afraid of him. Actually he was rather a mild, gentle man." Was he talking about himself? Had Mother poisoned me with her complaints about him? I too felt mild and gentle, unable to comprehend that I could sometimes be intimidating, that my sometimes desperate desire to communicate might look like fierceness, my wobbly stabs at a personality come across as confidence and self-sufficiency. I could never gain Dad's full respect; he was not that interested in me. But it was mostly my own insecurity and misunderstanding that stood between us, the past like a blurred erasure obscuring the faintly written present.

In July Sarah rented Mary Frank's deceased aunt's house in Woodstock and went there to paint; I would pay the rent at Westbeth. Alone in the city, I seized two hours in the morning for writing, swam at the Carmine Street pool on the way home from work, socialized or played music in the evenings or stayed home and goofed off. I bought a VCR and a few videotapes of young men masturbating, which I liked to watch when I was alone with Cat. I collaborated with Oren Jacoby, a friend from Westerly, on a musical version of *The Beggar's Opera* we called *Bum Rap*. We had a reading, and a musician started putting together songs we could take to producers.

Johnny, running low on stamina, proposed that I take over lighting the next play at the Living Theatre; that was something to look forward to. Kenny, back in the AIDS ward at St. Vincent's, was losing his mind. John Albano had the skin spots and was going blind. The city was beastly, the heat violent on subway platforms, malevolent inside the stainless steel elevators at Westbeth, my City Hall suits wilting. I joined Sarah in Woodstock on weekends for dinners with friends and hikes in beautiful nature, close and at ease. One weekend we drove up to Charlemont, where Stefan and Jenny were staying in my cabin. It was gorgeous there, sunny and sparkling, cool and breezy: I had never seen greens so green.

Sarah came back from the country with a stack of watercolors and pastels. Having sated myself on pornography and masturbation while she was gone, I was happy to have her back. She was unexpectedly touchy, though, treating me like some kind of dangerous wild thing she was afraid of setting off, delaying coming to bed till I was half-asleep. Or she was in pain and wanted only stillness. Or it was too hot. Or we were both awake but she did not want to talk about it. She kept bringing up marriage. Jenny wanted to get married; Stefan did not believe in marriage but loved Jenny and wanted her to be happy. Sarah appeared to have the same ideas about marriage that put Stefan off it: the institutional or Doxa view, in Barthes's term, that takes over for the actual practice and compact of two people. Why should we get married when our sex life had broken down? Was I to learn to be satisfied with less, like my poor father?

7

SARAH AND I FLEW to Barcelona and took the train to Gerona. Susan met us in her Deux Chevaux and made us welcome in her tall, narrow house in Monells, a medieval stone village in the pastoral Baix Emporda. Susan liked to get up early and paint the fields of sunflowers before the heat of the day. Then we would go to one of her favorite Costa Brava beaches, where I swam naked in the soft, cool Mediterranean,

Susan Willmarth in Monells

the pleasantest water I had ever felt. We saw beautiful buildings, towns, and cities, went to markets, ate delicious, unfamiliar food. I befriended a Catalan neighbor and tried but failed to fix his small, square, antique piano so Susan and I could play music together. Sarah and I rented a car and drove up into the Pyrenees to look at Romanesque churches and mountain scenery.

Susan was going home at the end of August. I urged Sarah to stay on in her house for a month so she could paint all the time without having to deal with Julian's return (also to leave me free to do lights for the Living Theatre). First we would spend a week in Barcelona. My Catalan friend

Joan and his wife invited us for lunch on the way to the city at their rustic mountain farmhouse. Afterwards we drank coffee and ratafia, a special wine made with secret herbs gathered by mountain women on Saint John's Day. So we were bewitched, not to mention exhausted, by the time we drove into Barcelona in a downpour. We found our way to the Hotel Apolo, remembered fondly by Judith from a Living Theatre tour, which turned out to be upstairs from a pornographic movie theatre. Shades of the Changing Scene! Sarah was not amused.

Walking out to find dinner, we turned off the seething Ramblas into one of the quieter, narrow streets leading to the Plaça Reial. Hungry and spaced out, I looked for a restaurant while Sarah walked on the other side of the street, not quite connected. I am borderline hypoglycemic and get spaced out when I am hungry. Hearing her scream, I turned to see two young men pushing her into a side alley. They were trying to take her big leather purse, which contained both of our passports as well as Sarah's money for the month to come. Two more young men jumped in, and the four of them hustled her up the alley. I ran after them, yelling. They had her down on the ground, leaning over and pulling at the purse, which she clutched to her body with both arms, wild-eyed, screaming piercingly again and again. I ran up and yelled and pulled at them, she kept up her terrifying shrieks, and they ran off.

I helped her up and led her back out to the lighted street, held her and tried to comfort her. She still had her purse and was not seriously hurt but could not immediately stop screaming. A crowd gathered. Eventually she quieted down, still shaking with fright and shock. The police wanted us to help identify her attackers, suggestively asking if they were Moroccans; but we had not really seen them.

Back on the busy, brightly lit Ramblas, we ate supper at an outdoor café, feeling threatened from all sides. Across streaming traffic we watched a young tourist put down his suitcase on the sidewalk and step off the curb to hail a taxi; someone promptly picked up the suitcase and melted into the passing crowd. It was gone when the kid turned around: we watched him realize what had happened. At our hotel, the halls were full of noisy Danish students. Sarah insisted on barricading the door with furniture and tying the terrace doors shut. It was a beautiful night, I was excited by the throbbing city energy, but Sarah had a bump on the back of her head and bruises and was deeply freaked.

In the morning we moved from the low-life lower Ramblas to the bourgeois Diagonal and the comfort of the well-run Hotel Wilson. For several days we devoted ourselves to enjoying Barcelona. I checked out Mies van der Rohe's iconic Barcelona Pavilion, still there after all these years, and we marveled at the Romanesque frescos in the Museu Nacional. The Picasso museum reminded us how great he really was. Sarah flinched whenever she saw slim, dark young men approaching, and there were a lot of them in Barcelona. On her birthday morning we took in a beautiful Zurbarán still life in one more museum; then it was time to part. Sarah would have Susan's car and house for a month, with nothing to distract her from painting, and I flew back to New York.

THE ATMOSPHERE AT THE LIVING THEATRE was intense as we struggled to realize *I and I*, a phantasmagorical play written in 1940 by Else Lasker-Schüler, a German Jew living in Jerusalem. *I and I* scrambled the Faust-Mefisto story together with the thuggish Nazis into a nightmarish philosophico-poetic Expressionist epic set in hell. It was a huge play to try to stage in a tiny space. Judith, directing it, asked me to make the stage glitter darkly. She wanted every special effect she could get.

Johnny had given the dimmers to Julian personally, he said, bringing in the cable and lights when he lit *The Tablets*, the first show in the new space. Before *I and I* he had light pipes put up. I thought they were too low and obtrusive, but he did it his way. He took no hand in my lighting design but sent over a crew to hang it, rewarding them with little "bribe bags" of pot as well as cash. "Just tell me what you want," he said. The Living Theatre couldn't pay, but that was the point of Johnny's lighting company, to be able to help theatre artists he believed in.

Tom Walker and Michael Saint Clair in *I and I* at the Living Theatre

The set was nowhere near finished, the pace maddeningly slow. Judith blowing weed made everyone stop and listen to her speculate and theorize when we needed to work on our many tasks. Technical rehearsals started hours late and dragged on into the middle of the night; all the while we were under pressure to open and start taking in some money from the box office. I had lifelong respect and love for Judith's art and was thrilled to be part of it. Whatever it took was okay with me.

I spent days at City Hall and nights at the Living Theatre. Ignoring Johnny's advice to be more "professional," I kept climbing a ladder, moving, adjusting, recoloring the lights one at a time, crafting a handmade style of my own, lighting the play's beauty, meaning, and structure. Vertical red and orange strip lights on either side brutally flooded the stage with color. A soft spotlight stayed on Michael Saint Clair, the black Mefisto, to make him visible next to Tom Walker, the pale, blond Faust. Tiny red Christmas lights all over the pipe-scaffold set made it "glitter darkly," per Judith's request. I kept myself relaxed and cheerful with pot, occasional beers with the boys, now and then a cigarette, home just enough to keep up with the laundry and housework, water the plants, and feed Cat, crawling into bed exhausted.

I loved working with Judith and Hanon, but they were barely able to pay the rent on the pitiful theatre on Third Street. The roof leaked: a downpour in the middle of tech week flooded my wiring and blacked us out. The ceiling was so low that Faust and Mefisto, elevated on scaffolding, bumped their heads on the light pipes. Tall actors could not stand up straight in the basement dressing rooms. The funky neighborhood scared respectable theatregoers away.

I romanticized these jagged weeks by cultivating a beautiful, lanky, sensitive boy just out of Bryn Mawr who was helping out with *I and I*. I spotted him sitting on the sidewalk in front of the theatre painting pieces of cardboard black, snagged him for one of my follow-spots, and let him sleep in Alfred's room while he looked for an apartment. I could barely keep my hands off him as we sat channel-surfing on the couch in the tv cave, both of us petting Cat. I wanted to pet him too, stroke his long back, kiss his wide mouth, suck his cock. He showed me his college performance of Beckett's *First Love* on video, stripped to underpants. He spoke of the "masculine" narrative tradition of peeling away masks to get to core identity versus the many-faced "feminine" way. He seemed to be flirting but didn't cross the line, and I kept my hands to myself.

During previews I kept refining my lights and tuning up the lighting crew's performances. They had trouble paying enough attention to get it exactly right. I would have loved to run the dimmers myself, but Sarah was coming back and would not put up with my being at the theatre every night. Julian, returning from New Mexico on the night of dress rehearsal, made his own way from Newark Airport to meet me at the theatre. I was happy to have him back, proud of his growing independence.

Johnny, thin, haggard, and unwell, came with me to the opening night performance. He would have lit it differently, he said, but acknowledged the do-it-yourself gorgeousness of the whole effect.

JULIAN STARTED HIGH SCHOOL at Bronx Science. He had to be out of the house at seven for the hour-long subway trek. Sarah flew from Barcelona to Boston and went directly to Smith, then came home for weekends, and I eased back into my normal routine of work, music, friends, and home life, with periodic look-ins at the Living Theatre to keep my people on their toes. City Hall was obviously ending, and about time! I put an ad in *The Village Voice*: "Obie-winning director seeks project for Jan.-Feb. Michael Smith, 691-0249 eves." The sole response was a man in New Jersey who wanted to dramatize Brahms's "Liebeslieder Waltzes." I liked the idea—bought a recording, listened to the songs closely, worked through them at the piano with a singing friend, and concluded that they were better as a ballet. Such a project would not solve my immediate problem anyway. Like *Milarepa* and *Bum Rap*, it would drag on for months or years and probably never happen. (*Bum Rap* had lost its momentum: with Koch on his way out, the moment had passed.) How I wished someone would hire me to direct a play!

8

KOCH LOST THE MAYORAL PRIMARY to David Dinkins, and I was offered two jobs the next day, one as a clerk in Johnny's marijuana shop, which was illegal, the other as general manager of the Living Theatre, which was insolvent. Selling pot for Johnny would bring in the cash I needed to keep going, but Sarah would be appalled, and I worried about getting busted and damaging my sons' lives. I agreed with Johnny that there is absolutely nothing wrong with marijuana, but I was not prepared to go into the business.

Johnny had been complaining for months about the manager of his stage lighting company, who was more interested in clubs than the art dance and DIY theatre the business was meant to serve. In October he fired him, changed the padlocks on the steel shutter that rolled down over the only entrance, and asked me to come work for him. I said I needed to take home $500 a week. Done.

The lighting company was entirely separate from the pot business, with its own location in a former meat locker on Washington Street, a few blocks from Westbeth. It was nicely set up, with a tidy front office and a big back room for equipment storage and repairs. An electrician was on duty to maintain the equipment and deal with rentals. By November I was opening up the lighting shop every morning before I checked in at City Hall, where there was practically nothing to do.

I couldn't help worrying about the lighting company's relationship to Johnny's pot business. He rested on his record: it had been running smooth and steady for years. It was not yet profitable but could be. Investing cash in it was perfectly proper, he said; taxes were paid on everything. Sarah was strongly opposed to my working for Johnny, bitterly jealous of our friendship and dire about the drug connection. She disapproved of Johnny altogether. Whatever the legalities, I felt this was less fraudulent than working for the city, where I was paid to sit at my desk in a stupor most of the day.

My immediate problem was solved. Practical work is a good fit with writing, and it would bring me back to theatre. Johnny said we were at the barricades together. We could supply the lighting needs of our theatre and dance friends and allies, who were many and active, and make it a profitable, useful little rental business, augmented with mail-order light bulb and dimmer sales. Johnny wanted the business to succeed, and I was just the one to rev it up.

I hung in with Ed Koch nearly to the end, as a gesture of solidarity and to keep getting paychecks. Sensible people like Sarah and Bicky said I should talk to my cousin Betsy Gotbaum, a top fund-raiser for the Dinkins campaign, and line up a better job in the incoming administration, as a deputy commissioner or the like. But I hated working for the government, once the glamor wore off. Paid by power, I felt co-opted and compromised. I was part of the counterculture, not the mainstream. It suited me to live and operate on the fringe, play chamber music, do chamber theatre. I liked people who lived outside the standard forms.

Finally it was too much to run back and forth between City Hall and the lighting company, and I handed in my resignation. When Clark Whelton asked me, "Are you landing on your feet?" I could say yes.

T HERE WAS A SLOW, steady trickle of rental activity. Johnny had business systems in place, and I enjoyed that sort of puzzle. He urged me to take charge and talked about making the business my own. But it was barely breaking even, as far as I could tell, and sustaining it without his personal support (from pot profits) was hard to imagine. In practice he made all the decisions and proved to be a problem boss like many another, insisting that I come in at nine and work Saturday mornings, which for some reason infuriated Sarah, making things happen by a flurry of demands, rattling on about opera or the Irish revolution when I had work to do and needed to think.

I liked the work without imagining I was really a techie-businessman. I needed creative projects. I was in touch with Pascale, finishing up the last pages of our *Agatha* translation and offering it to a producer; discussing *Milarepa* with Judith; writing a piece for the Changing Scene, Uncle Al having asked me for a text for a dance. It was not nearly enough.

Julian left on time for school every morning, saying his homework was done, everything under control, and I wanted to believe it, though I never saw him working. When his math teacher got in touch to report that he was often late to class, missed homework, did badly on tests, I confronted him; he said he had been inwardly tortured about lying to me. He was also behind on lab reports for biology, needing more guidance and help with discipline than I had been providing. I resolved to try harder.

Julian went to New Mexico for Christmas, leaving Sarah and me alone. She had the flu and then a frightening migraine that hung on for days. There was not much she would let me do for her. When we were not fighting, I loved her and liked our life together; but we could not stop fighting. I felt heartbroken not to be able to quicken our love affair into something sustaining and affirming for us both. She was mad at me in the morning and mad at me at night, no matter what I did. My resolution for the new year was to reclaim my autonomy and break free of my dependence on Sarah. If we were not able to be happy, there was no point in being together.

JANUARY FOUND ME WORKING LONG HOURS, selling dimmer packs to Japan and Argentina. I looked at a two-room apartment on Washington Street. Julian could have the bedroom for the rest of the school year. After that I would make it my own; the boys could camp in the living room when they came to visit. The rent was $1,000 a month, four times my share of Sarah's. I would manage. I had to get away from her misery, bitterness, and anger.

Julian came down with a bad cold. In the morning on the way to the doctor I told him what I was thinking of doing. He was a pillar of strength. He said he was tough, I should not worry about him. Westbeth was home and he loved Sarah, but he was accustomed to change. He said things do not get better: "If you leave bread on the counter it gets moldy."

That afternoon I went to the landlord and said I would take the apartment. I had my checkbook out, but he told me not to write the check until he had verified my references.

When I told Sarah I was moving out, she was literally floored. We talked for two hours in her tiny kitchen, I on a chair, she on the floor in the corner by the sink. She should have seen it coming: I had told her repeatedly that she was driving me away with her relentless hostility. She said it would kill her if I moved out. I hardened my heart and said I could not do that level of discourse. She said it would ruin Stef and Jenny's wedding, which was coming up in a couple of months. She wept, softened, begged me to stay, implored me to try again. She said she would drop it all—the mindset of anger, disapproval, taking my detachment personally. She said things would be different, she saw the light, she would change. She did change, then and there, opened to me and was beautiful and lovable again. I tried to hold onto my hard-won decision, but moving out really had no attraction. The next day I let the apartment go.

9

JULIAN WAS TOO SICK to go to school, and his mid-year exams were coming up the following week. He needed me to help him. Instead I had to go to Santa Barbara for my mother's eightieth birthday. She was back in the apartment after three weeks in the Casa Dorinda Medical Center, having fallen and sprained her back. Dad had been sick too. Mother was trying to keep him in the Medical Center for good, but by the time I got there, he too was back in the apartment. Bicky had arrived the day before. Dad persuaded her to take him home for lunch, settled into his comfortable chair in his well-arranged room for a nap, then refused to leave.

He was about the same as the last time I had visited, in the spring, and clearly happier at home. The Medical Center, he said, was "a hellhole." He was driving Mother crazy, though, and Bicky was mad at them both. At dinner Dad made a petty scene about Bicky's opening a bottle of red wine— "That's *my* wine!"—which made her furious in turn. Mother wondered aloud why Bicky did not play the piano as well as I did. We left early. Dad wanted us to stay, but Mother was intoxicated and blithering.

I told Bicky about my latest dust-up with Sarah, then regretted it. If it was not a turnaround, it was only a delay, and I did not believe in turnarounds: people stay the way they are, they do not suddenly change even if they want to. If I patched it up with Sarah and stuck it out, I was afraid I would start acting like my father. His coldness could be hideously cruel. So what if Mother provoked it, denying she had a drinking problem but out of control and wreaking havoc. Dad had kept her in his power for five decades. Now that he was weak and helpless, she was getting her revenge. It was pitiful and appalling.

Aunt Ginny came for Mother's birthday and added buoyancy. I appreciated her positivity, and we were very fond of each other. A lifelong Christian Scientist, Ginny joined Bicky and me for an energetic swim in the Casa pool.

All I could give my parents was my loving presence. No longer struggling to win their attention, I treasured their love and had no problem enjoying them

MICHAEL SMITH

individually. Dad was losing feeling in his legs and feared for his mobility. Mother's knee was so painful she could hardly walk. I urged her to resume doing aquathenics in the Casa's swimming pool and suggested an aspirin regimen, which had helped my hip, but I was not sure I was getting through. She had been hard-of-hearing ever since I was a child but denied that too, pretending to hear when she did not, pretending not to hear when she did not want to.

With Aunt Ginny

Mother cried when I left. Dad said, "Come back while I'm still here."

JULIAN FACED EXAM WEEK bravely, knowing his preparation was spotty, and got his grades a week later: he was passing English, French, Global Studies, and Literature, failing Art Appreciation, of all things, and conditionally failing Math and Biology—an insanely excessive course-load, it seemed to me—how had I let this happen? At fifteen Julian was making his own decisions, guarding his privacy and independence. Missing homework and cut classes were reported in all subjects. He told me he was more interested in what he could learn on the street. Bronx Science was a touch-and-go proposition, but he resolved to stick it out. Clearly it was not the right school for him. He said the teachers were only interested in the math and science whizzes. He told me about the Friday afternoon keg parties as if he didn't partake. The next year he would go live with Michele and Joy, who were moving to Pullman, Washington, where Joy had been accepted into veterinary school.

Sarah tried to let go of her rage, but we still were not connecting, unable to respond to each other, in the grip of a profound malaise, which seemed less personal than a sadness of the world. Sarah bounced in and out of the city all spring, four days home, three in Northampton, rocking the boat violently with every departure and return. This was her last year teaching at Smith; she had interviews lined up in Chicago and Maine. She spoke of not being around the entire next year—I could have the place to myself. I kept thinking there must be another, better way to live.

Whether Sarah was there or not, I was depressed. I had lost the rhythm of writing and struggled to get it going again. I wanted to write but didn't know what. Johnny said it was terrible that I was not doing plays, I should immediately start. I said I felt burned out and did not want to do it anymore. Johnny said it was the only thing I did want. Nothing else mattered. Everything else was downhill into decrepitude, suffering, and oblivion.

I made lunches for Julian and sent him off on time every morning. In March he confessed that he had been cutting school, spending his days in Central Park, hanging out with pot heads and acid freaks. He wanted to stop going to school. It was pointless: he could not possibly succeed at this juncture; he wanted to write off the year and start over in Pullman with a clean slate. He had the idea of working at the lighting company, which sounded good to me: I needed help and knew he would work hard. But the grownups I talked to, as well as my inner parent, made me feel I had to play out the parental role of trying to keep my child in school. Johnny said he wished he'd had me for a father.

I went up to Bronx Science with Julian and we met with his guidance counselor, who saw herself as an enforcer and freaked us out by talking tough, telling Julian it was illegal for him to be out of school, he had to go. He came out of this meeting enraged, as I was, but after thinking about it for a few days, he went back to school on his own initiative, talked to his teachers, and told me he could pass their classes. The chairman of the biology department allowed him to drop biology—his favorite course but the one that was overwhelming him—and work in the lab instead.

With Johnny in front of the lighting company

JOHNNY WAS THIN, frail, and vulnerable. He wore himself out working in the lighting shop until one day he could hardly move. He said he was hallucinating like the beginning of an acid trip. Patti, whom I barely knew, came to take him home and put him to bed. But by Good Friday he had rallied and took me to *Siegfried* at the Met.

Sarah was fully occupied with preparations for Stef and Jenny's wedding. She was doing the flowers herself, which entailed scouting trips to the flower market and complex logistics. Julian and I helped her collect them in her studio, transport them to the elegant old social club on Grand Army Plaza in Brooklyn, and arrange them for the occasion.

The wedding party was wonderful. Sarah was in seventh heaven. She had worried that Bernie and his family would not come because Stefan was marrying a gentile, but they did, full of fun. I wore a white suit from Saks. I loved Stefan and Jenny, who were admirably respectful and considerate of each other. The whole affair was beautifully affirming. I felt like a normal person.

An income tax refund spared me an immediate run on my savings, but working so many hours at the lighting company seemed pointless. There was not enough money coming in to keep the doors open, and Johnny, who was having major dental reconstruction, cut off his support. Bills piled up; I had to lend the business $500 to pay the electrician.

I TOOK THE TRAIN up to Northampton for Sarah's final weekend at Smith, thrilled to be going somewhere. We had a sublime picnic in a blossoming apple orchard, ascended a mountain for tremendous views of the valley, swam by ourselves in the enormous, gleaming college pool. She said goodbye to the art building after four years teaching there, and I drove her back to the city with her stuff. I had left Julian alone in the apartment for the first time, and he had hosted a party. He had worked hard at cleaning up the house, but it was still a bit sticky. One of Sarah's favorite bowls never reappeared.

With the wedding behind us, we fell back into bad habits, Sarah cornering me late at night after Julian was in his room, griping, blaming, keeping at me until I snapped, got angry, said ugly things. Then we went to bed not touching.

I went to up Charlemont with Julian for Memorial Day weekend. After dinner at Jean-Claude's, we all sat out on the porch in the ecstatic nightfall smoking pot, playing drums, clapping rhythms, and dancing on the grass. I noticed Julian toking too, not really surprised. I drummed to images of my exuberant son doing flying somersaults on the lawn and running across the meadow in the twilight with the cows.

He told me he had taken LSD with his girlfriend, Heather, in Central Park the previous Friday and it was very strange. I was not encouraging him to experiment with drugs, but everything was available in the Sheep Meadow. There was little point in setting myself against what he was going to do anyway. I advised him to be cool and not to tell Sarah.

In early June I flew to Denver, stayed at the Y, went for a swim, and made it to The Changing Scene just in time for the opening performance of *Sameness*, a fifty-three-minute dance work choreographed by Al to a spoken text I had written for him. It seemed to me very slight, barely an anecdote, about three sisters based on my mother, Ginny, and Viv. He paid me $400 for it. I stayed up late talking with Al and Max, whom I dearly loved, now both in their seventies. I was their heir, they said, but I could not imagine keeping their theatre going without them.

Alfred, his school year over, came to Denver from New Mexico on the bus, watched a performance of our odd little dance-drama, and flew back east with me for a visit. Sarah met us at Newark airport and made him a welcome-home party in the loft. He told me he loved the city and wanted to live there when he grew up.

10

HANON AND JUDITH disrupted this fragile equilibrium by inviting me to come to Europe with the Living Theatre for seven weeks to do lights for their tour. Many people in the company urged me to come. It sounded so exciting it scared me. I said I'd go.

I was so happy when I got home that night that I immediately made love to Sarah. She despised the Living Theatre, and I hesitated to tell her what I had decided. In the event her reaction was far worse than I had anticipated, a major freak-out that did not let up till five a.m., when she allowed me to make her a cup of tea and we sat quietly drinking it, watching dawn come up on Manhattan. I went peacefully to bed for forty-five minutes before it was time to wake Julian for school.

In the heat of another sleepless night Sarah told me to take my things and move out. "I may take it all apart while you're gone," she said. "When you come back there may be nothing here." I said I could be gone by the first of July, put my things into storage, take Julian and Alfred to Charlemont till I left on tour and send them to Michele and Joy a couple of weeks sooner than planned. At this, a terrifying blackness descended on Sarah. She threatened my harpsichord with a hammer and her beautiful new painting with a knife. She said she would die. So I backed off again, hoping to give our love another chance in the fall sans children.

Michele was not ready for the boys to come back early so I arranged for Alfred to visit his best friend, Peter Bassett, in the Catskills between my departure to Europe and his flight west. I proposed to take Julian with me on the tour. He would be helpful and learn a lot. He said he did not deserve it, having messed up the year in high school: I had promised him a trip to Europe if he did well. He wanted to be with his own people, to be turned loose in New York, not to leave Heather sooner than he had to. Sarah had declared, fiercely, that Julian could not stay at Westbeth after I left, that she needed to be alone. Unless he came up with another place to stay, with a parent at hand, I meant to ship him off to Michele at the last minute, hoping to spare him from being overwhelmed by the wildness of the city, where he was having terrific adventures but overstressed.

Then Sarah changed her mind, unilaterally telling Julian he could stay after all, be at home or not as long as he kept in touch with her. I was dubious but glad he was getting to do what he wanted. I would have arranged something for him, but he insisted he did not want packaged experience, he wanted real. I hoped Sarah would be able to handle it.

Johnny, suddenly bitter, told me not to come back to work at the lighting company after the tour. He said I was "too tricky," he declined to "subsidize your writing, life, and cock," he wanted a divorce. I said okay, relieved in fact, but it was very sad. He was thin, weak, unable to eat. I had been happy to be close to him again these past few years, and he had been exquisitely generous to me. As an employee, however, I hated his fanaticism and power trips: he made me feel guilty if I went out to lunch, if I did not work six days a week, turning me into one of his minions, who had to put up with his overbearing personality because he paid us. Now he was ill, and his team of care-givers were moving him to a new apartment, out from under the tormenting heels of his upstairs neighbor.

Working for Johnny had kept me going from the wind-up of Koch's

MICHAEL SMITH

mayoralty to the end of Julian's school year. The period in the late fall when I had been working two jobs had boosted my savings to $10,000, three-quarters of which would still be left when I got back from Europe in the fall. I had no job to return to, but I was not too badly off.

Sarah, savagely jealous, continued to oppose Johnny in every way. She phoned repeatedly on my last morning at work, saying, "Get the fuck out of my life!" and slamming down the receiver. It felt like two divorces in one day.

As I tried to ignore our incessant fighting and move ahead with life, my aplomb made Sarah so mad that she threw a baking dish full of freshly cooked rhubarb at me in the long entrance hall of her apartment. In a way I admired the act, so flamboyant and poetic, though I regretted the rhubarb,. But I was terrified that she should be that much in the grip of her anger, now a palpable presence. The immediate problem was to keep our conflicts from escalating to the point where she would actually throw me out or trash my stuff. I took the manuscript of my memoir to a friend for safekeeping.

I felt I had gained a certain wisdom with the passing years and accumulation of experience, but there was no way to express it with Sarah. It was wrong for us to fight, harmful to us both, bad for the environment. I longed for harmony. She said, "I will never be acquiescent."

When school ended, Julian went on the road for a week with the Mystic Paper Beasts. It emerged that Dan Potter had been buying acid from him. I took Alfred to Charlemont, staying in Jean-Claude's house while Jean-Claude finished a month-long retreat in my cabin, gratefully moving up the hill when he came down. The Fourth of July was iconic at the neighbors' hand-built house in a clearing, Jean-Claude and I the only gray-hairs. Alfred at twelve was restless in the woods, and we ranged far and wide for amusements. He practiced skateboarding in Harvard Yard, trying to land a "backside one-eighty," jumping the board off the ground (an "ollie"), turning it and himself 180 degrees in the air, and landing on it, still moving forward. We saw my sister Dinny act in Christopher Durang's inspiring play *The Marriage of Bette and Boo* in Williamstown. At the cabin I read to Alfred from *The Hobbit*, and we slept together sweetly in the big bed. The unsaid text was the passing of his childhood.

Peter Bassett's mother brought Peter up to the cabin for a visit; then I took Alfred to New Paltz to stay with them until his flight back to New Mexico. He would have a good time—and so would I. Even so we were both in tears in the car as it came time to part.

JULIAN TOLD ME he had taken acid again and turned into a puddle on the floor. Sarah insisted he was "in trouble," but Julian seemed to know what was what. I took his word that he was all right. He would have two and a half weeks before he was to fly to New Mexico; I hoped he would escape disaster and have some interesting times. This free space was what he wanted for himself, to use and misuse in his own way. All I could tell him was don't do heavy drugs, don't get anybody pregnant, don't expose yourself to AIDS, don't get hurt or arrested. It was only a little space of time and then goodbye New York. I did not share Sarah's fearfulness or low opinion of Julian's sense of self-preservation; but it was hard to keep my own judgment balanced while fending off her negative mind-set.

Sarah would depart in mid-August to visit friends on the way to her new teaching job in Maine, leaving the apartment empty for two weeks before I came back from Europe. Bicky, who was moving to New York so

Alfred with Peter Bassett

Ben could go to a better school, needed a place to stay at just that time. When I suggested that she could water the plants and feed Cat, Sarah blew up, saying there was a weird closeness between my sister and me, she was offended by our sense of entitlement, she was on the losing side of a class war with me and my whole family.

In many ways Sarah was tremendously loving. Cat was getting old and had a bowel obstruction, and Sarah had been giving him suppositories. She concerned herself with my children. She gave me lovely presents, her taste infallible. There was no one better to look at art with. We had wonderful times together. But it was too painful that we could not get along. I could hardly ever get through the raging static of anger, fear, and despair I unavoidably provoked. I hated our discourse. I was sick of analyzing our emotional situation. I intended to stop thinking about it while I was in Europe, then deal with it decisively when I came home.

I wondered if Johnny would still be alive.

11

IN THE SUMMER OF 1990 the Living Theatre was booked for twenty-two performances at a dozen festivals and theatres in Italy, Spain, Germany, and Czechoslovakia, performing *I and I* and *The Tablets* in alternation. There were twenty-one of us on the tour. We assembled at the theatre on East 3rd Street and flew from New York to Frankfurt, where Hanon rented two vans for the actors and a third to carry luggage and the set. I traveled with Hanon, Judith, and Isha, Judith and Julian's twenty-year-old daughter, in a fast, comfortable car. They were at home in Europe, having lived in Rome for years and toured all over. The little kilometers zipped by, Germany out the windows looking beautiful and perfect. "This is its moment," said Hanon, passing the hash pipe. "They won the World Cup, and they're reuniting."

We went first to Augsburg in Bavaria. After the condescending disregard our work had met with in New York, it was heady to be honored as artists, fed and feted, put up in a comfortable hotel and met by a curious press, in front of whose flashing cameras Judith made fine revolutionary gestures. Accused of "infantile utopianism," she invoked Brecht and Piscator, ideas pouring out in German, heads nodding, pens flying. Hanon announced that in addition to its performances, the Living Theatre would give a workshop in Augsburg and create a street-theatre piece on the subject of "the total degradation of culture by materialism."

At Chieri, in Piedmont, the stage was outdoors, in the courtyard of a palace; I had to work all night to get the lights up and focused before the sunrise. Besides recreating *I and I* on a grander scale, I was also attempting to reproduce Johnny's lighting for *The Tablets*. The technical director of the festival told Hanon that *The Tablets* with its three follow-spots and splintered shards of silvery light was the most beautiful thing he had seen in ten years. The exuberant, sexy young Italian light crew made me an honorary member of their collective. What a rush!

I was playing ping-pong with a Dutch boy from the company when Sarah telephoned from New York, telling me she had not seen Julian for two days and was desperate with worry. I was sorry to hear it, but there was nothing I could do about it from Italy. I tried to comfort and reassure her: Julian would be all right. I hoped it was true.

I sent a master light plot ahead to each presenter, but we were booked into every kind of theatre from a circus tent to an opera house, and in practice I had to reconceive the plan for each new situation. Arriving at a theatre, I joined in scoping things out with Judith, Hanon, and the crew leader, Gary Brackett, placing the play in the space, my favorite part of the process. Then I drew a new light plot and worked with local techies to set it up while Gary and half a dozen of the actors put up the pipe-scaffolding set. My reward was running the performances. It was empowering to rise to the challenge of this demanding work. Audiences were avid and enthusiastic.

We drove three days to Malaga, in southern Spain, where the grand Teatro Cervantes had an incomprehensible computer dimmer board and the head technician spoke no English. Judith noticed that I was getting tense and advised me to take a break. "Remember," she said with twinkle, "it's always like this." I walked out into the sunlit plaza, had a small beer and tapas at an elegant sidewalk bar, and relaxed. I was not the only one committed to putting on a good show; impatience would not speed up the process—an important lesson.

I skipped the drive back north, flew myself to Paris, spent a couple of days with Pascale and her girlfriend Simone, and took the train to Berlin. Word came from New York: Julian had survived his independence and gone west to Michele and Joy.

The warehouse theatre in Berlin was filthy, the American tech director listless. I had to sweep the theatre myself. "Don't get nervous, Michael," said Judith, "you're our rock." *I and I* was a triumph in Berlin, where the size, shape, and ambience of the theatre finally supported Judith's staging and the audience resonated to the play's lurid vision. In Italy people had said the evil that manifested as Hitler was too evil to be mocked, that identifying it as Hitler was superficial at this late date, this play not proper for the Living Theatre to do. In New York it had seemed incoherent. In Berlin everything fell into place. We were selling out the house, and Hanon, admitting he had been worried at the beginning of the tour, said the gamble was beginning to pay off. Judith said, "We're not at zero anymore."

I was exhausted, smoking too much hash, even cigarettes, since everybody did, staying up too late, working too hard, too lonely and unsnuggled. Fans and groupies offered themselves at one stop after another, but the personal click never happened. It was a cop-out not to get it on with someone, fidelity to Sarah a mask of virtue worn by cowardice. Attractive women in Berlin would have welcomed a friendly overture, but I had nothing to give. I ogled boys but had no interest in doing anything with them, or they with me.

My German son Klaus came from Frankfurt to visit me, and I drove us out to Potsdam in one of the company vans to see Frederick the Great's palace, San Souci. Driving out of Berlin on the Grünewald autobahn we listened to Beethoven's Ninth Symphony on the radio, the very music that made Germans imagine they could conquer the world, which climaxed as we snaked through a huge, once fearsome border station, now abandoned, the East German government having collapsed. Muscle-bound titans held up the cornices of Frederick's fanciful palace. The day was hot, Russian soldiers wandering about sweating in their heavy woolen uniforms.

In cold, rainy Prague, I set up in three hours and felt undauntable, despite a miserable cold. In Brno we squeezed *The Tablets* into a small experimental theatre, one of the cradles of the Velvet Revolution, then moved for *I and I* to a big, elegant, "conservative" theatre with a revolving stage, each show so intense it eclipsed the previous intensities.

Playing the Poet in *I and I*, Judith was a dumpy old lady with a hump. Hanon suffered the stress of keeping the company afloat. In the hotel in Tarvisio, heading back into Italy, I knocked on their door at nine in the morning and found them together in the bed, covers up to their chins, windows open to pines and Alpine peaks. In the clear, romantic light Judith looked like a girl, pretty and fresh, Hanon like a beautiful boy. She had a deep fount of energy and will, kept going doggedly, shined seraphically when she led a workshop, no matter how tired she was, and rose to every occasion, remembering the higher thought behind the act, articulating the aspiration. Hanon too had the philosophy and soul to rise above the plague of pressures, laughed when he could, always generous, tolerant, considerate.

In Berlin I went twice to the Pergamon Museum to see the carvings from Nineveh, the lion gate from Babylon, the naked Greeks and Romans. Taking time to enjoy the trip, we stopped for lunch in Padova and saw the sublime frescoes by Giotto in the Arena Chapel. In Arezzo I went every day for a week to look at the great frescoes by Piero della Francesca in the Church of San Francesco, five minutes from our convento. I drove a busload of actors into Florence to visit the Uffizi, packed with masterpieces. At a street performance I put on anarchist red and black for the first time and played recorder and tambourine. On the way back to Germany to fly home, the four of us stopped at a grand luxe hotel in Merano, the Alpine town where Judith's grandfather was buried, and searched the Jewish cemetery for his grave. They invited me to join another tour the following winter.

12

JOHNNY HAD NEARLY DIED while I was away. I immediately went to see him in his new ground-floor apartment in Chelsea, where Patti was taking care of him. He lay in the bed naked, curled up on his side with a sheet bunched around him, emaciated like a concentration camp extreme case, so weak he could not sit up, neck hollowed out, arms shrunken, hips and legs big bones, no flesh. His mind was fairly clear, but he barely had breath to speak. I said I would come often; Patti gave me keys.

Patti was quiet, self-effacing, and seemed peculiarly innocent, as if she knew nothing of the world; yet she was remarkably strong and focused in the face of Johnny's physical collapse. He could sound as querulous as my father, but she remained solicitous and friendly; responding to her sincerity, Johnny took the medicine she brought him and ate the food she prepared. He had railed against emotional entanglements that cost him more than he could afford. Now his need seemed perfectly matched to Patti's willingness to give and serve, and the atmosphere was full of love.

I had thought I would have to find another place to live when I got back. But when I imagined a place of my own, it was exactly like what I already had, a loft with high ceilings and big windows, full of art and plants, books and music: there seemed to be no point in moving. Sarah would be away for months; we would only see each other for a few scattered weeks. It helped us both to share expenses. Anyway, I liked living with Sarah—loved it when we were harmonious. She might be less tormented absent the boys; we might be able to get along.

It had come clear while I was driving around in Europe that I did not want another full-time job that left me no time for theatrical work. I needed to be actively involved in the things I aspired to do well: writing, theatre, music, love. Better I should hold down my expenses than be taken over by work for money, which is only a convenience, after all.

Alone in the city, I walked up to Chelsea to spend two or three hours with Johnny almost every day, relieving Patti so she could shop and go to her tai chi class. Johnny gradually gained a little strength. It was not sad to visit him but often fun, our mutual affection strong and sweet. Patti brought us food and said funny things. I put up racks for Johnny's vast cassette collection, and we listened to one Callas *Lucia* after another.

I had a few thousand dollars in the bank, enough to send child-support to Michele and keep myself going for a few months, paying the whole rent at Westbeth while Sarah was away. It was hard to worry. Something would happen. It would all work out. Sarah's fretting about money was not helpful. She said, resentfully, that the reason I could be so nonchalant was that I had a rich father; but my father was not rich. He apparently had a little over a million dollars to take care of himself and Mother for the rest of their lives; whatever remained would be divided among four children. He was never going to leave me enough to live on.

Theatre work is naturally sporadic. In the meantime I had assignments for stories about the Living Theatre tour from the *Village Voice* and *Lighting Dimensions* magazine. Diane di Prima asked me to write an introduction to her collected plays, exactly the kind of thing I should be doing. I had reams of memoir drafted, waiting for me to make something of it.

SARAH INVITED ME TO MAINE for my fifty-fifth birthday. She was teaching at Bates, living in a big old farmhouse on the main street of a village forgotten by time, turkeys in the barn, pens and outbuildings out back sloping down to long, narrow fields—a perfect New England scene, winter coming but not there yet. She cooked me an outstanding birthday dinner—fried green tomatoes, Indian stew with stuffed Hubbard squash, tarte tatin—which we enjoyed with a group of people I had never seen before. She took me to a distinguished potter to choose my birthday present—I chose a tall vase like the trunk of a birch tree—and showed me around the college. It was Indian summer, hot in the sun, the trees changing, green filling with red, orange, gold. I took my shirt off as we walked in the woods and fields behind the farm, and we spent a day on the beach. As we were returning to the car, Sarah tripped and broke her little toe, these little curses haunting our happiness.

On the Monday she went to work and I drove to Charlemont through the White Mountains, my body tingling to the swaying and vibration and the flashes of color that lined the road. I had looked forward to a few days of serene nothing in the woods, but the weather turned gray and rainy, and the cabin was dreary. Golden when freshly sawn, the boards were now gray with age. I felt vulnerable and forlorn, the radio my only companion. Smoking a joint helped, but my neck was stiff. In the night I couldn't bear listening to the trees dripping on the roof above my head; I opened the window beside my bed to drown the sound in the hiss of the rain on the forest.

In the morning I felt shaky inside, as though I might cry. I felt a great urge to redirect my life to some purpose. It was heartbreaking to be so far from my sons. Nothing made sense. What was I doing? Nothing! I felt lost and terrified, barely Buddhist enough or gentleman enough to maintain my inner calm and air of competence. The world was in trouble, and I was frittering my life away. Gurdjieff ignored history in favor of inner development. The best course was active compassion, but feeling so meager I did not have much to spare. It was not good enough to be happy with what I had; I needed to get real. If I faced the facts, I needed to reform my life.

I headed home a day early, lingering over my rituals of departure, leaving everything just so, the cabin unchanging except for the slow accretion of pictures and objets trouvées and the blackening of the wood. It was more beautiful out and about than inside the forest in the wet. The sun emerged in Connecticut. Complaining about the weather is stupid, but there's no denying it affects one's mood.

13

Cat was old, bony, stiff, not eating well, but we still took pleasure in each other's company. Dignified, no longer snappish, he was handsome as ever in his sphinx pose, paws suavely crossed, gaze averted. He liked sitting beside me on the bench as I played the harpsichord; wanting attention, he bumped up under my right wrist with his head as I played, or stretched out across my notebook as I wrote. He could no longer manage the ladder to my study; I lifted him up to be with me as I worked. He kept me company in my video cave and smiled at my self-indulgences, accepting me without judgment, sleeping close to me in my lonely bed.

Not going to a job, my time my own, I felt like a different person: my actual self. I went to Brooklyn with Sarah's friend Vera Williams to see Mark Morris's ballet to Handel, *L'allegro, il penseroso, ed il moderato*, which renewed my faith in art. Everybody said I was more relaxed. When Sarah came for a few days, I was glad to have her home. We made love more often, with more affection, a new openness between us.

I needed a writing project that would come to fruition in a timely way and bring in some money—perhaps a contract to write an "as told to" book, or a biography; I would be good at it and yearned to write about someone else's life for a change. But I no longer knew what a good idea would look like. Everybody had the same stale ideas. No one had any investment in my talent.

Bicky gave me a Frequent Flyer ticket to California to visit Mother and Dad, and within a day I was bored silly, try as I might to be nice. Mother had me drive her around Montecito to admire the multiplying mansions; I wanted to scream. Dad had too much time to think and held me hostage to such arrant nonsense that it made my head spin: pronouncements about the coming depression, complaints about long-haired waiters, on and on. I wanted to show him I could love him and never mind his opinions, but I told him to lay off the "Jew-boy" remarks. Old and weak, he contrived to capture me for himself and shut Mother out; she took her lunch and dinner into her bedroom, leaving us to each other, and drank herself silly, while Dad co-opted me into man-talk, invidiously disregarding my actual situation, expecting me to sympathize with the fallen rich, although I had never had any money—which he despised me for. Being feeble and helpless did not stop him from being a hateful bully. I had forgotten how painful it was to be there and hoped I never had to visit him again.

I stopped for breakfast in Santa Monica with Paul Sand, who said I should write a play about my visit to my parents. He would play me. That seemed like a good idea, both as a play and a way to work through my bottled-up feelings. Paul was in love again. He was always in love and told me he always fell for straight guys. I said, "I wasn't straight when you fell for me." He said, "Yes you were."

Around the fringes of my visits to Johnny, I made music with Irving Reid, my dentist, who lived close by. Thrilled with newly discovered possibilities of his big, beautiful voice, Irving sang higher and freer than ever as we explored the rich literature of lieder. The feelings got very intense, and after the music, a couple of times, he kissed me on the mouth and said he loved me. Irving was big when I hugged him, his physical impact overwhelming: I loved him too but not that way.

I went up to the ninth floor and worked out with Joe Chaikin on his Total Gym. I went to Jean-Claude's apartment for Ravi's yoga classes. Twice a week I took a movement class with Sally Gross in her studio down the hall. I felt good as the year wound down, not quite so old and lumpy, although my left hip was hurting and weak. I wondered how it would handle another Living Theatre tour; it had just barely seen me through the last one.

I applied and was accepted to MacDowell Colony for a five-week writing residency the following spring. I was over my depth in my memoir, but I put in two three-hour sessions of writing every day, visiting Johnny in between, attempting to finish a draft, hoping to send it out and be free of it. I hoped to write a play at MacDowell and produce it at Theater for the New City in the fall.

This time I would come back from Europe with nothing. How was I to pay child support while I was at MacDowell? I would be broke at the beginning of the summer, when I wanted to see my children. I wrote to Bill Honan at the *New York Times* proposing a couple of theatre articles. Surely somebody would want a travel piece about driving in Europe if I wrote it. I encouraged a production of *Agatha* in Denver and planned a Modell-büch of *Milarepa* for presentation to potential composers. If I set some projects going, money would follow, and all would be well.

14

On Sarah's winter break from teaching, we went to Washington for the museums. Never had I so enjoyed looking at art—Renoir's *Luncheon of the Boating Party*, Van Gogh's *Road Menders*, Cezanne's house in the forest on a lake: I wanted to live there! Back together in Westbeth, we had a sweet Christmas breakfast and presents by ourselves, with a Christmas cactus in blossom for a tree. Later in the day, Jenny's rambunctious family was too much for us, her brother carrying on in a strange, loud, drunken mix of crudeness and sentiment. It gave me a headache, and Sarah's cold came back with lethal ferocity.

Walking up frigid, gray Bethune Street to D'Agostino's, I passed a man sitting on a stoop in the snow holding a snowball in his bare hands. On the way back I stopped in front of him, holding my bags. "Aren't you getting cold sitting there?" He looked at me with red eyes. "Shouldn't you get inside somewhere?" He looked slowly around at the shuttered house behind him. "Do you need something?" He slowly shook his head.

Johnny grew sicker and weaker, his various afflictions treated by massage, acupuncture, herbal medicine, injections. AZT was the only remedy for AIDS and didn't really help. Hiccups could only be stopped with Thorazine, which wiped him out for a couple of days. He was in and out of his mind but seemingly serene, and I loved seeing him.

I was writing about Johnny in my memoir, and he gladly answered my questions as they arose. When that section was finished, I read it to him. He could hardly talk, only moan a little—little affirmative moans as I read—not pain but a kind of amazement—a few times said "Wow!" He tried to speak but lost the thread. He liked my reading to him, though, and later would fill me in on some details of his life that I did not know or had forgotten.

Suddenly Sarah's brother, Bernie, was in Long Island Jewish Hospital for emergency surgery, ostensibly for diverticulitis. She rushed down from Maine, and I went with her to visit him several times. In contrast to his usual

Michael Smith

warm ebullience, his post-operative daze was shocking. Sarah wept in my arms; she said, "I wouldn't be able to bear this without you." After a few days Bernie appeared to be healing, and I took her to the airport to go back to Maine.

I went straight from there to a rehearsal of *Rules of Civility*, the Living Theatre's new show, which I was lighting, then to Johnny's house after that, to help him go to the bathroom and brush his teeth. *Rules of Civility* was Hanon's adaptation of a text by George Washington. I lit it in washes of red, white, and blue, with a grid of downlights that shifted patterns in sync with the choreography, an effect I called "geometry." When the action moved out into the audience, the light came with it. The initial lighting setup took a couple of full-out days and left me all but paralyzed with weariness, a familiar feeling from years of setups.

My patriotic palette was pointedly sarcastic. Iraq had invaded Kuwait, and Bush was pitching the country into another war. I was horrified that my country would initiate more killing. Grace Paley, Vera Williams, and a group of admirable Village women silently marched against the war every Saturday for months. At Leo Treitler's sixtieth birthday party, his son the minister-to-be called for silence in consideration of the war, then asked people to voice their fears and anger. Many spoke up, movingly and sincerely. All opposed the war, hated the waste and destruction, feared the consequences, that the wrong lessons were being learned, the wrong national policies would continue. Stef and Jenny and many of our friends went to Washington for a peace march, for which Mary Frank made many signs; I was dismayed by the minimal coverage the media gave to the large demonstration, how irresistibly the press lined up behind this catastrophic policy. Each night at the end of *Rules of Civility*, the cast took the audience out of the theatre, led by two George Washingtons, for a brief candlelight vigil against the war. The Puerto Rican grocery on the corner put a flag in the window.

Word came from Santa Barbara that my father had fallen in the night and broken his hip. Mother refused permission for him to have surgery, falsely declaring that Bicky and I were against it. Dad signed for it with an

X, no longer able to write his name. I felt old, gray, frayed. The night I heard about my father's surgery my own hip cricked so sharply that I could not get up off the television couch: I had to roll down onto the floor and straighten the joint with a wrench and stab of pain that left me dazed, kneeling, half lying on the couch, stuck for several minutes.

Dad was in the Casa Dorinda's Medical Center refusing to get out of bed or eat. Mother had washed her hands of him. She was in the Medical Center too, having fallen again, and would not go down the hall to see him. They both told me not to come out; and I had no desire to be in on this agony if I was not wanted. Bicky would go at the end of the month.

15

JEAN-CLAUDE OFFERED ME a timely job lighting his new play, *Ancient Boys*. Reading the first version, I found the "fairy" stuff embarrassing. Revisions had made it shapely, and if it flowed as it should, it would be beautiful and affecting. It was certainly sincere, Jean-Claude's heartfelt effort to engage the AIDS emotions and a tribute to his friend Robbie Anton, the puppeteer, who had died of AIDS, ashamed and denying it to the end. I was grateful for the $1,000 fee. *Ancient Boys* was set to open at La Mama Annex the same day the Living Theatre company was flying to Zurich, driving from there to Rome to open the winter tour. I could fly directly to Rome, have my cake and eat it too, open *Ancient Boys* on Saturday night in New York, *Rules of Civility* on Tuesday in Rome. Now I was cooking.

Jean-Claude's hero was a maker of giant environmental sculptures, and Jun Maida, a visionary artist-designer, had made an enormous, fantastic bird of twigs. Regrettably, the director pushed the bird upstage, into the background, weakening the image, so the artist's work seemed secondary to his unsatisfying love life. Lighting the play in the big space, finding ways to sharpen the action and ease the flow, was taxing and rewarding. War with Iraq hung over the future, a nightmare vision of the good world ruined.

Sarah and I could not agree on a plan for the summer. She argued against my going to Europe again, saying I should stay home and make some money, not acknowledging that the Living Theatre tour was the only gig I had. She read the draft of my memoir, said she found it gripping, but made me feel it was unpublishable in anything like its present form.

Ancient Boys opened. I was on my way out the door when Lou Zeldis, a friend who had worked with Peter Brook, remarked how beautiful Jun Maida's great bird of twigs looked in the work lights. In my lyrical colors, I realized at that moment, it was never clearly seen, the obsessive Zen sublimity of its making never registering to authenticate the play's hero as an artist. From the airport, waiting for my overnight flight to Europe, I sent back word to pull all the gels. I never learned whether they did.

On tour, every new city would be a new chance to get it right.

FRENCH SECURITY practically dismantled the plane in Nice, fearing Arab retaliation for France's part in the incipient Gulf War. From Fumicino, I shared a taxi into Rome with an admirer of Mussolini, climbed four long flights of stone stairs to leave my suitcase at the pensione, stopped in a caffè for a coffee and pastry, trudged up the Palatine hill to the elegant small theatre where we were to open the following night, and worked hard all day to get ready for rehearsal.

The programs said "luci John P. Dodd," and Isha, who was playing one of the George Washingtons, was not named. I didn't care, but Isha threw a fit, and the rehearsal was a mess.

The next night's opening was fine. I ran the dimmers from a balcony close to the stage, feeling more than ever part of the performance, my lights immaculate. At the end the cast passed out candles, and the two George Washingtons in perukes and ruffles led most of the audience to the Via Veneto for a five-minute silent vigil across the street from the American Embassy. It was moving to stand together in the lively Roman night, gazing at the hulking, darkened embassy, thinking about the brutality of power and the wrongness of war. Police converged from all directions, winking blue lights atop their cars (not the brutal blinding strobes of American cop cars).

The five minutes were up, the audience dispersed, and the company walked back to the theatre. The next day I accompanied Hanon to a meeting with the chief of police, who, all the while toying with a large knife, denied us permission to demonstrate anywhere but in the quiet street in front of the theatre. If defied, he would close the show.

The next level of horror had started in Kuwait and Iraq. News headlines declared "il giorno di Bush." Oil wells were burning. Marines were invading. Gas attacks were rumored through the news blackout. It was weird to be an American.

We played in Rome for a week, and after the opening my days were free. At the Capitoline Museum I touched the statues when the guards were not looking—caressed Hermes's cheek, Hercules's balls, Antinous's ass. You can feel more subtle contours than you can see. Touching the cool stone was sensuous, erotic—made me want to touch a real person.

Judith missed this tour, stuck and suffering in Hollywood, acting in the movie of Oliver Sacks's *Awakenings* to support the theatre in New York, where a second company was performing the same play. Hanon managed the bookings and money and fended off the demands of the performers, who bickered and acted like babies. I got high and hung out with them, but I was not attracted to any of them, except maybe Sander, the Dutch boy, who was drinking and flipping out and basically straight. Decades older than anyone else on the tour, I was getting to be a solitary person.

Sarah telephoned on our last day in Rome. Her brother had been diagnosed with an ominous cancer, and Cat had taken a turn for the worse. I was sad about Cat but not too sad: he was winding up a full, splendid life. But Bernie was forty-one, with a fine career as a lawyer, a wife and three wonderful daughters, important in his community, loved for his warmth and generous spirit. Bernie should live long and enjoy wisdom.

Touring *Rules of Civility* was much easier than the previous summer's double-header. I had made a more doable lighting design, and the set was simple: tall curtains painted by Julian Beck that folded up into a single trunk. The tour schedule was strenuous but not without breaks, one-night stands

MICHAEL SMITH

alternating with week-long stays in several cities, reasonable drives from one to the next. I was happy to be in Italy doing theatre.

Rules of Civility was funny, jazzy, serious, and the loyal Living Theatre audience of students and radicals flocked to our performances. In Salerno the electricians kept blowing out the whole theatre until, minutes before the performance, I triaged a third of the dimmers. In Naples sixty people from the workshop performed Hanon's street piece against the war. The lighting crew from Chieri came to cheer me on as I set up in Torino's elegant Café Voltaire. Leaving the ferry from Genoa to Sardinia, our vehicles were searched by the police, sniffed by dogs; but we had eaten our last crumbs of hash as we rolled down the ramp from the boat and saw what was about to happen.

My translation of Marguerite Duras's *Agatha* opened in Denver while I was in Sardinia. I telephoned and spoke to Maxine, who said it was very good but not much audience was coming. I was sorry to miss it, curious whether the play's extreme slowness was tolerable, whether the impossible desire between brother and sister could generate sufficient energy in the absence of movement, action, stars. Could another director see the point? *Agatha* would be boring unless it was charged with erotic tension—itself a kind of boringness, but pleasurable.

Urbino had the most beautiful theatre, a plush, sparkling little opera house atop the city walls, with a sunny caffè where I made the acquaintance of grappa. When the Living Theatre actors chanted, "Break the rules," half a dozen students came on stage, wandering among them for the rest of the performance and joining in the bows. In Padova the theatre was a bare, neglected church; spectators packed in and cheered us at the end.

Spring came as we finished in Italy, cherry trees in blossom on the hillsides above Modena. We plunged back into winter as we drove through Austria. Budapest was cold and wet, our housing a student camp on the desolate edge of the city with wretched showers and food. Accustomed to Italy, everyone was paralyzed with dreariness, hapless in Hungarian; a visit to the public baths cheered us up, huge, grand, wet, and warm, with a dash of gay cruising and display. We played at the Szkene, a well-used black box at the Engineering University, which was jammed for the performances, spectators flowing onto the stage, blocking my footlights, pushing everything upstage. That was all right with me: I loved it when people crowded in to see the work. We held a Living Theatre seder, Hanon officiating beautifully.

The company was flying home from Zurich; for some reason my ticket was from Milano. Hanon dropped me at a hotel, and we parted on the best of terms. A *piccola birra alla spina* calmed my paranoia at finding myself suddenly alone, and I walked over to the Duomo, magnificent on the outside, hugely stern and gloomy within. The piazza was seething. I strolled through the Gallería to La Scala and bought myself a balcony seat for that evening's opera, *Adriana Lecouvreur* starring Mirella Freni. La Scala and La Freni did not disappoint, though I was unable to deduce what was going on. It was silly of me not to know Italian.

C AT HAD DIED with his paws crossed ten days after I left on tour, discovered by the tenant after Sarah left for Maine. Claire Rosenfeld, our friend on the fifth floor, consigned his body with appropriate ceremony to the Hudson. I had the idea of writing Cat's life story, wondering what he thought of all my carrying on? Cat was a person of great dignity and self-possession; I loved him, it would be a pleasure to memorialize him. People are crazy about cats. A comedy romance from Cat's point of view might sell!

Based on which classical statues I wanted to touch, which young beauties my eyes were drawn to on the street, the images that turned me on, what gender I chose to hang out with, I took the lesson this time in Europe that I would be better off gay. So when I got back together with Sarah, it was a happy surprise to find myself making love to her with untrammeled naturalness and passion. Unfortunately we found no such satisfaction in verbal intercourse, the question of the coming summer still fraught. I might be able to coast through it at Charlemont, which was there for nothing, but she needed a studio. Sarah urged me to take a job with an international aid or human rights organization, which appealed to me theoretically.

The week in New York before I was due at MacDowell Colony felt like another stop on the tour. Bernie's recovery, at first assured, was now uncertain. Johnny was the same. Sarah, finished in Maine, rode waves of depression as she reordered her studio and home, tenant gone, Cat gone, boys gone, me going for five weeks, both of us thinking about going away again in the summer, perhaps in separate directions, and coming back to no jobs.

16

THE DAY BEFORE I LEFT for MacDowell, Patti and I dressed Johnny and took him out for a ride. He was gallantly cheerful, but his left arm and shoulder were sore, and I hurt him as I lifted him out of the wheelchair to put him into my car. I thought he could shuffle back a step so I could set him down onto the car seat, but he could not move his legs at all. I lowered him into the seat, lifted his legs in, and set him up as straight as I could.

The day was bright and blustery. I drove up through Riverside Park, the trees in bloom, to Sakura Park near Riverside Church, where Denis Deegan had planted hundreds of bulbs, not yet emerging. Patti was magnificently lively and funny. Johnny sent her into a deli for coffee, and we parked by the park. He asked me to crank down his window, and the fresh, chilly, living air felt good. But he was not doing well. He had sores in his mouth and difficulty swallowing. Some of the coffee came up, and the hiccups returned. Back at his house he put his good arm around my neck, I lifted him out of the car seat, lowered him into the wheelchair. Patti and I lifted him easily and set him up in bed. As I was about to leave, he thanked me, saying it had been a wonderful day.

And off I went to New Hampshire, thrilled by the clear American sky. MacDowell would be an opportunity to settle down and write undistracted, everything provided, nothing to do but work.

I slept in a clean room in a quiet house near the main building. Every morning after breakfast I walked out to my personal studio, a rustic cottage isolated in the woods, and stayed there alone until late afternoon. I had two big work tables, one for my computer, one for editing and writing in longhand. There was a rocking chair in front of the fireplace, a cot for naps, a piano for breaks from writing. Lunch was brought in a basket and discreetly left on the porch. Otherwise no one came by all day.

I saw the other colonists at breakfast and dinner. We all agreed that MacDowell was heaven, giving us not only precious time to work but affirmation and respect as artists, hard to come by in the real world. We felt lucky to be there, and I was impressed with how diligently every one of us pursued our work.

Spring was about to enter, buds appearing on the bare branches, the woods still open to the sky, soft and brown underfoot. My Italian spring with its hillsides of cherry blossoms seemed like another year. I kept a fire going most days, and the nights were cold. I would have liked some hugs and snuggles, not to mention sex. But I had no knack or heart for fleeting encounters—wants, needs, but nothing to give. Donald Antrim, who had been hopping from one artists' colony to another working on his novel, pooh-poohed the myth of affairs at colonies, which he said are like monasteries. I had always secretly fancied myself a monk.

Ping-pong competition was fierce among the male writers, including me, Donald, Chris Noel, and P. David Ebersole, a screenwriter from Los Angeles. Chris, a boyish Vermonter whose first novel Knopf had published, had submitted his second book and not heard a word for eleven months, could not get through to his editor, letters not answered. When I asked Donald what he had published, he said, "That's the kind of question an older writer asks a younger writer, and the answer is, nothing."

It improved my state of mind to be taken seriously as a writer. Needing to get somewhere with my memoir, I pressed ahead, cutting, editing, writing new, revising day after day. At Dan Potter's suggestion I focused in on the years I lived with Johnny,—coincidentally the early glory days of Off-Off-Broadway—and by the end of three weeks I had finished a tight version of that story, which I called *Wild Dogs*. I gave the manuscript to Jill Claster, a

Ping-pong at MacDowell Colony

historian from New York University, who brought it back a couple of days later with wonderful praise: she found it moving, engaging all the way through, "very visual," professional, without a jarring note. She criticized the last two paragraphs, which I fixed.

A couple of nights a week resident artists would give presentations of their work for fellow colonists in the library. At the last minute two painters who would be showing slides invited me to read something to fill out their evening. I could not remember ever having read my work to an audience before.

I decided to read not from *Wild Dogs* but from an older manuscript I had brought along called *Names and Events*, an obsessively detailed log of everyone I saw and everything I did for two and a half months in the winter of 1964-65. I was living with Johnny, madly in love with him, the story rife with gay sex and drugs. Reading about this to my peers would in effect be coming out, an odd thing to do if, as it seemed, I was not gay anymore. I had finally accepted the reality that my own life was the main material of my personal writing. To be honest, I needed to come out in my writing even if actually, actively being gay was behind me.

I timed off fifteen or twenty minutes' worth, beginning at the beginning, and after dinner I did it, willing myself not to act shy or apologize but straightforwardly present what I had written thirty years before. The response was positive, each of the writers making a point of saying it was good, Chris Noel delicately referring to the fact that "the narrator is gay." Afterwards we played ping-pong. Chris won, but not before some blazing exchanges we both mightily enjoyed.

I sent *Names and Events* to Allan Kornblum at Coffee House Press, who was publishing Diane di Prima's plays, and *Wild Dogs* to Karen Rinaldi at Turtle Bay Books, a friend of Donald Antrim's, feeling I was coming back to writing after a fifteen-year hiatus. Groping and struggling is part of it. It was time to hatch the eggs, show my stuff, be good.

Alone in my woodsy studio, after the first rush of work, I was obscurely "under the weather," trying to get started on the play about my father that Paul had suggested, which I called *Life Before Death*. Confronted with the dread blank pages, I found myself pacing like an animal in a cage. I was also trying to finish a fictionalized story, *Serious Eyes*, about the boy I had fancied during *I and I*. Chris Noel read the story in his writing teacher guise and wrote notes all over it suggesting major revisions, reminding me that writing is not easy. *Life Before Death* came hard. It was not the moment to write about my parents when feelings were so raw and changing. But I had to write. Writing was my salvation, my medium of meaning, and I kept at it right up to my last day there.

17

I LOOKED FORWARD TO BEING HOME after months of strange beds and no honey, which was worth the stings. I intended not to rock the boat but stay positive and deal with what came. Again feeling that Sarah and I could make it work together, I resolved to give more, be confident, and somehow avoid being emotionally jerked around.

Bernie's illness was worse than thought, cancer in his liver, pain all the time. Sarah spent whole days at Mount Sinai Hospital with Bernie's wife, Hannah, meeting with the doctor to work out how to talk about it with him.

Johnny was still thinner and weaker, even less able to talk or move. He had long ago told me not to be sad about his illness, and I was not, although it pained me when he suffered. I felt great tenderness for him, and peaceful being close to him—happy, even. Patti was at the end of her rope; I promised to come for a few hours every afternoon.

Dad telephoned Bicky and asked her to fly to California and intervene to get him out of the Casa Dorinda's Medical Center, where he was trapped in a small room with a dying man, miserable, hating the nights. She felt awful that she could not do it. Mother would not have him back in the apartment, claiming round-the-clock nurses would cost too much. "It's my money," he said. He offered her $30,000 cash to let him come home to die, but she was immovable. He tried to persuade Lotte, the good German woman who had been helping him every morning for several years, to take him home to her house. He needed someone wholly devoted to his care, as Patti had been to Johnny's these many months. I had the time free and might have taken it on, but on my last trip to Santa Barbara I had not been able to stand him, and Sarah needed me, and Johnny needed me, and Patti needed me, and I was looking forward to visits from Julian and Alfred, whom I had not seen for almost a year, and Dad had not called me, he had called Bicky.

By late May Johnny was hovering on the border between life and death. He could only move his right arm and hand, lying crumpled on his pillows with his head at an angle, too weak to speak, his bent, loose-hinged legs slowly opening and closing like a butterfly drying its wings. Any movement of his left shoulder and arm hurt him. His look was sometimes alarmed, sometimes loving, eyes bigger and more intense than ever, then glazing and drifting away, his few words endearments. I had little to tell him that was not boring or depressing, not wanting to go on and on and be annoying. I reported that Sam Shepard's new play, which Bill Hart had directed at the American Place Theatre, was not very good. He said, "Who cares?" I rubbed salve on his bed sores, changed his diaper, read him Whitman's glorious *Calamus* poems. Much of the time I just lay with him, close to him, my hand on his body, drifting off.

I was worried about my own health, too. I would need a new hip before long: the ten-block walk to Johnny's and back was my limit in a day; and my city health insurance had lapsed. My Toyota was making ominous tapping noises, smoking and burning oil. If I did not find a good mechanic I would have no car . . . and no money . . . What should I do? What could I do? An office job? I could not commit to anything right away; Alfred was coming. What office? Who would have me? The economy was sagging even for people who wanted jobs. Whom could I serve? I no longer had a sense of having any skills. Could I not stay home, write what I liked, and sell it? Why on earth not?

Jed Mattes, Donald Antrim's agent, found *Wild Dogs* "not at all involving." His criticisms rang too true. When I talked to him about my other writing projects, he said, "You need focus." He liked the idea of a biography of Richard Barr but said theatre books were the hardest sell: no way could he get me enough of an advance to pay for the time it would take to research and write it. Bisexuality was a hot topic; he suggested a magazine article. My life of Cat had some appeal; I should write it and see how it went. Publishers rejected both my manuscripts.

It was hard to concentrate given the desperate plight of my loved ones and the inevitability of interruption. Writing is not a job but a practice like meditation and needs to happen in its designated time. How could I bring personal enlightenment to bear on loved ones and the suffering of the world? I did not want to tell the story of what a miserable failure I was but how I became so wise and joyful.

One of Sarah's nieces, defying her dying father, suddenly announced that she was marrying her Chinese boyfriend, saying she could no longer lead a double life. Sarah persuaded Hannah to let her spend some nights with the boy, and the wedding was postponed. At least fifteen people said Bernie was their best friend and they were devastated by his illness.

My tender feelings were strong and spontaneous as the disintegration of Bernie's life shook Sarah's world. Her brother had seemed rock-solid, his fidelity to Jewish life balancing her own escape. The intensity of her compassion for him was so sharp and actual that she said it made her other upsets—with me, for example—seem like nothing but ego. I was glad to stand by her. Hannah said I was a mensch.

Wanting to paint in the country, Sarah found and rented a house in Shady, near Woodstock, New York, for the months of July and August. The Westbeth loft could be sublet again to cover the rent. She invited me to come for the summer with Alfred, who would arrive on the first of July.

I drove up with her on the first of June to look it over—a two-story house in a clearing on a hillside with a studio for her and a writing room for me, bedrooms for us and Alfred and Stef and Jenny's weekends, less than two hours from New York. It was even furnished to my taste, hung with Buddhist art, stocked with books about Gurdjieff, music and video systems hooked to all the channels. We planted tomatoes to stake our claim. With a getaway place like this, life in the city made sense: we should have it all the time.

Sarah was with her brother when he breathed his last. That day Johnny was very still, and I wondered how long he would live. The day before, Patti said, he had told her to take $2,000 out of the bank and buy candy. He wanted to roll out of bed onto the floor so the nurse and supervisor would come and take him back to his room. Patti stayed calm and sweetly reassured him.

Bernie's funeral took all day. The Orthodox Jewish service at a mortuary on Flatbush Avenue was intensely moving—the rending of the garments, his closest friend sobbing desperately, speeches about how good and special a man he was, "the epitome of integrity." Everyone felt better when they were with him. He gave and never took. He was the same everywhere and never expressed regret. But the burial, after a long drive out to the cemetery on Long Island, was horrible. The men took over and turned their backs on the women, stopping for prayers every few steps from the hearse to the grave, lowering the coffin into the ground, piling worn-out prayer books on top of it, then shoveling in dirt until the hole was filled, walling off the women from even being able to see the grave.

18

Julian came from Pullman for Heather's high school prom, having spent the past two months in Spokane in rehab for alcoholism and drug abuse. His account of his year at Bronx Science surprised me—I had no idea he had been drinking, for one thing, buying beers in delis all over the city. His real friends were not dopers, he said, although they sometimes got high; the serious druggies were the other kids from Westbeth and the people he met in the Sheep Meadow in Central Park. He had loved most of the year's adventures, although school was a disaster. He only started to get unhappy in the summer, he said, after I left for Europe. Then in Pullman, repeating the year, he realized he could not control himself. He made a good case that I was addicted to marijuana, although privately I did not buy the addiction model. His rehab

Julian and Heather

protocol rewarded good behavior with cigarettes!

I took him to Charlemont, where we still had two little roofs to do, and we worked together well, each cheerfully taking on jobs the other found onerous. He had no end of ideas for fun—picking wild strawberries, catching fireflies, leading each other blindfolded through the forest, "getting lost."

On the way back to the city the Toyota's engine blew. We limped to a repair shop. There was talk of a new engine, but I was not sure it would be worth the cost, which I could not afford, whatever it was. We took a bus into the city in time for Julian to rendezvous with Heather at the Port Authority bus terminal for a Grateful Dead concert in New Jersey.

I was sad about the Toyota, which I had always liked. I had only kept it in the city because I had it—most of the time Sarah had been the one who needed it. Still, it had been nice to drive it uptown to the movies, as if we lived in real America. Now, though, we needed a car; the house in Shady was miles from the nearest store. So we set about buying another one, falling into the clutches of a dubious character who lived down the hall and had a tiny car lot in the Bronx. I could not afford to buy a car, and Sarah did not want to own a car; I wound up buying a second-hand Nissan with money she supplied, intending to sell it in the fall and get her money back.

Alfred came, just wanting to have a good time, overlapping Julian by a week, and with both boys there, Sarah and I were back in the old tense standoff. During the crisis with Bernie, she had needed me and let me comfort her as best I could. Two weeks after his death, devastated with grief, she was cold, remote, touchy, angry, unreachable. She had planned to be up in Shady the week the boys were in New York, but we still did not have the car, registration delayed by a missing title.

Running around the city made Julian too desperate, and seldom seeing him, we worried. When I put him on a plane back to Pullman, it seemed too soon but also just in time; he said it had not been easy to get his case manager to let him stay so long.

My need for money was starting to make me crazy—not that I actually needed it. I could float the summer on credit cards if I watched my pennies. But Sarah kept at me relentlessly about the need to take action. It was dangerous to count on my father's money to bail me out, if that was what I was doing. She said he was not going to die until he had spent it all.

I parked our new car the first night I had it around the corner on Bank Street, and somebody smashed in a window. I had it replaced without mentioning it to Sarah, for $75. She went to Shady for a few days by herself, phoning to say that once she was there she felt tenderness for me for the first time in weeks. I certainly had felt its lack and hoped things would be different when we were together in the country.

I wrote to my parents asking for $2,000 to help me get through the summer, much of it for air fares so I could bring Alfred out to visit them in Santa Barbara in August. Dad told Mother not to send me anything—"He should earn it." She said she would send $1,000. The last thing Dad had said to me when I was there the previous year was, "If you get in trouble, let me know and I'll send you some money." Mother had often said, "You can count on us." Apparently my present situation did not qualify as trouble. Alfred, who always knew exactly what he wanted, induced me to buy him a bicycle. I had an anxiety attack about the money that required a walk around the block and a heart-to-heart on a park bench, but he did not give up. Ultimately Mother sent $2,000, and everything worked out, as, after all, it must.

Sarah came back to town for the last night of sitting shiva for Bernie and a memorial service, and we made love at last. She would stay to manage the renting of the apartment; Alfred and I would leave for Shady the next day for the rest of the summer. I went for the last of my daily visits to Johnny. He said it was time for a warm body, so I lay close to him; then he wanted a back rub; then we had a tiny nap; then he had me dress him, in a pink Chateau Marmont T-shirt and Bergdorf khakis, saying he wanted to go to Paris; I said we could bring Paris here, and put on "Callas in Paris." Johnny said, "What are we waiting for?" Carolyn Lord came and tried to distract him with dinner, but he fiercely refused. He was ready to leave for the airport. I told him I regrettably could not go to Paris with him and took my leave, Carolyn calmly preparing to give him a tranquilizer.

On the Fourth of July, Alfred and I drove over to Saugerties, on the Hudson, to picnic in a park with thousands of other Americans; but as twilight fell, before the famous fireworks were to start, the festivities turned chauvinistic, making Independence Day a celebration of victory in Kuwait, and I found it too painfully out of tune with my own patriotism. Alfred agreed so we left, went back to Shady, and happily shot off our own little fireworks in the clearing in front of the house, taking turns lighting them on the gravel driveway, sitting close together on the concrete steps to watch.

I set up my computer in the little upstairs study and burrowed into my usual struggle to write, shutting myself in until lunchtime, then having a nap, doing something with Alfred later in the afternoon, and with Sarah once she arrived. Irritated that Alfred slept late and watched movies on television, Sarah tried to make me feel guilty for not arranging "constructive" activities. I thought it was better to let him do what he wanted to do. She said she could not paint while Alfred was watching television, although her studio was upstairs in the other wing of the house.

Alfred was thirteen, quick-witted and funny, and I loved having him around, our bond a reliable pleasure. Sarah and I had all the time we wanted to paint and write. The Catskills are famously pleasant in the summer, and we had good friends in the neighborhood. We went on delightful outings—hikes, picnics, swims, scenic drives. There was a spectacular swimming hole in the creek five minutes from the house, with a deep pool under an overhanging rock, overlapping ledges, pools, and falls drawing an explorer upstream through the woods.

Alfred at Shady

In my writing room I pressed on with the play about my parents with a heavy feeling; it was no fun at all. I reread a series of letters about writing from Elizabeth Hawes, who had befriended me at Riggs when I was twenty-one and first imagining myself a writer. She spoke of my "creative power": "It is all around you and one can smell it… It is why I care about you." Where was it now? Dead? Killed? Sapped by years of pot smoking, masturbation, misplaced love? Lost? Wasted? Bottled up? Or still alive and wild to get out?

19

JOHNNY DIED ON JULY 14, 1991, at six in the evening. Patti called me a couple of hours later. She and Magie Dominic were with him when he died. Patti had taken him to the hospital earlier in the afternoon—his temperature had gone up to a hundred and six. She said he smiled at the end like an angel. Magie said he floated up off the bed for a moment.

I had taken Alfred to see Johnny a few days before he died. In the aftermath we drove into the city and spent several hours at his apartment with Patti and others who had been close to him. Only Patti expressed spontaneous emotion, tearful, overwhelmed.

For me, Johnny's death was the end of a thirty-year arc from youth into middle age. He was six years my junior, twenty when we met, but always the stronger will—decisive, opinionated, fiercely stubborn, because he felt he had to be. Loving him, I was compelled to open myself to his defiantly untamed and contrary values. Our affinity showed me a different way of being. His influence, amplified by drugs and exciting times, pushed me out of the narrow smugness of my class and sex and changed me forever. Long after our love affair was over he remained my great lost love, often present in my dreams, and my principal link to New York, the one person I always tried to see when I went to the city. After a five-year break, we had met again in 1985—the same night I reconnected with Sarah—and since then he had become my closest friend, tricky, elusive, but unfailingly generous and warm. Now that he was gone, there was nothing keeping me in New York.

Alfred was sensitive and simpatico, letting me take my time at the wake. Afterwards we drove deep into suburban New Jersey looking for miniature golf, finally finding a lame, flat little course upstairs from a video arcade, which Alfred preferred.

Sarah was not very sympathetic. She had been jealous of Johnny, saying I was still in love with him, which was true in a way. Once I loved someone, I was not going to stop, although Johnny brooked no illusions. To me this was a good thing—love is good—but Sarah was bitter about it. "Don't be nasty,"

I pleaded. She countered, "I'm a nasty person. Nasty nasty nasty."

My dependence on her was humiliating. The week after Johnny's death we reached a new low. "Are you just being your friendly, polite, rational self this morning? Irreproachable? Perfect?" This was the way she talked to me. Breaking up might be a moment of exhilaration, but there would be nothing good in losing her esteem and affection, her virtues and generosities, in failing again at love. When she let go of her unhappiness, the weather cleared completely.

I wrote a memorial piece about Johnny for *The Village Voice* and a story for the *Woodstock Times* about Joe Chaikin, who was coming up for a reading of Jean-Claude's new play. I borrowed the car for the weekend, left Sarah to herself, and took Alfred to the cabin at Charlemont, which was even more peaceful than Shady. Sitting on the porch of my woodshed I was visited by Johnny's spirit in the form of a large butterfly, velvet brown with a row of iridescent sky-blue spots and a cream-colored band along the irregular trailing edge of its wings. It fluttered about me for a long time, coming and going, landing nearby, opening and closing its wings with a steady movement. It touched me once, fluttering against my thigh, then led me inside to my writing desk and trapped itself against the clear, clean, high trapezoidal window. I freed it using Johnny's gnomic light plot for *The Tablets*, which happened to be handy.

Back at Shady, Alfred exchanged visits with Peter Bassett, and we all had fun tubing on a nearby river. A houseful of friends came for the weekend. Sarah was painting a remarkable large picture based on a photo of the Stealth bomber that I had cut out for her from the newspaper: the ominous, weirdly unnatural silhouette of the plane dominated the space, with flowers coming out all around it into luminous, heavenly light. Painting it was an exercise in frustration. The hard-to-find white flowers Sarah needed as models wilted before she could finish painting them, or the day was dark.

Alfred and I departed for a spin through California: a day at Disneyland courtesy of Anne Millitello, who was working at Disney as an Imagineer; a night with Paul Sand in Santa Monica; and so to Santa Barbara. Alfred loved

California. He said I should move out there so he could go to a California university.

My father was on his back in the Casa Dorinda's Medical Center, well-pillowed and angled up, immobile except for his arms, continually rubbing his hands and fingers. Happy to see us, he talked energetically, and I let go of the anger and bitterness that had overwhelmed my previous visit. Dad retold a bizarre story about his "neurotic" mother: in later years, wanting to have something wrong with her, he said, she went to a doctor in New York who said her stomach was upside down (in previous versions it was her uterus); she had surgery, suffered a coronary, never got out of a wheelchair in her final years, smoked like a maniac, and died by setting herself on fire. His brother John had invited him to view her remains, but he declined.

Mother was recuperating at home from the replacement of her right knee: she showed us the scar. Now her left was giving out. She walked unaided, but slowly and unsteadily. She showed us an afghan she was making for Alfred. Her dinner came on a tray, and we kept her company until she started choking, her nose running. She said this happened when she talked too much. Then she seemed to be crying. We hardly knew what to do.

Mother said she had "had it" with Dad and seemed to have given up on herself as well. Isolated in her apartment, she was drinking more, according to Lotte, who was still taking care of Dad, and several times had injured herself by falling. Julie Bates, her closest friend, spoke of a total personality change: spending her days smoking and drinking alone, Dot, who had been so much fun, was not only physically declining but mentally blurred and lost, cut off from her friends and the outside world, her special warmth, charm, and kindness sadly faded, her conversation repetitious and vapid. She sent me to the store for gin and vodka. I mindlessly complied.

On Lotte's night off, I liked caring for my father, feeding him his dinner, afterwards cleaning up the B.M. in the bed, wiping his bottom, rubbing salve on his poor sore skin, red from lying in the bed all day, more often wet than not, changing the sheet folded under him. The redness and soreness extended to his no longer private parts; he asked me to put salve and then

MICHAEL SMITH

powder on his cock and balls. I treasured such intimacy even in this extremity, trusting and direct on the most basic level.

It began to seem like a good idea to move to Santa Barbara. It would cheer up my parents. Alfred wanted to live with me to go to high school a year from now; there was no way to make that work in New York, and he loved Santa Barbara. I went to see Audrey Berman, an editor I knew from *The Village Voice*, in her office at the *Santa Barbara Independent*, a *Voice*-like weekly newspaper, and asked about a job. She said in a general way that they would love to have me.

Alfred was patient and tender with his grandparents and fun with me. He learned to dive in the warm pool at the Casa Dorinda. I bought him a pair of Nike Airs to wear to school, shoe-buying one of our precious rituals. From Santa Barbara he was going back to Michele, and we would be apart for another school year. We walked on the beach late the last night after we were packed, a long, steady walk in the misty full-moon night, wave foam glowing in the crash.

20

I HAD SENT *Wild Dogs*, the story of my romance with Johnny Dodd in Greenwich Village in the sixties, to Wolfgang Zuckermann in Paris, who responded with a long letter full of constructive criticism. When I got back to Shady I found a second letter challenging me to make good on my book by turning it into a novel, offering to stake me to three months in his house in a village near Montpellier in the south of France to work on it. He suggested I come *tout de suite*. What did I need money for if the boys were with Michele? I could use his computer, car, and piano. If I went back to New York, I would have to get a job and not have time to write. He said my story was a hot property but I needed to bite the bullet and do the work to tell it right. This was a once-in-a-lifetime opportunity, he said; if I let it pass I would never write anything but little newspaper pieces. That stung.

Air fare to Lyons was $800, which I didn't have. Wolfgang wrote again, suddenly doubtful. Sarah would not stay on hold. I did not want to be uprooted, homeless, with no place to leave my meager possessions, and I was worried about the news from Santa Barbara. My father, jolly while I was there, had grown angry and desperate after I left. They had him sedated because he had kicked one of the nurses. On the phone he sounded weak and faint: "I'm thinking of you"; "I'm thinking of you too"; "I love you"; "I love you too"—I thought that was what

Wolfgang's at his house in France

he said, and he put down the phone. Meanwhile Mother was about to have surgery on her other knee.

I slowly came around to going back to New York and novelizing my story there. I had already started opening up the first-person narrative into scenes, with myself as a third-person character, and it went right along. Eight pages sprang from the first sentence, the first chapter turned into two. I could sharpen the focus much more and make it twice as long.

Shady days were so heavenly that it made no sense to leave. Every day I did a little meditation, wrote for hours, then swam in the stream, though the water was getting cold.

BACK IN THE CITY, I blended right in, not missing a single day's work on my book. My old friend Dennis Pinette, who had been painting industriously in Maine, had a show at a Soho gallery, and his dealer hosted a big dinner party after the opening. Dennis said money comes when you need it and I had nothing to worry about. That had been my basic feeling all along, and so far it had been working—I had had a very good year with no job or money coming in. At this point, though, I was several thousand dollars behind, my credit cards maxing out, leaning too much on Sarah. Then her teaching job in Vermont fell through, and she started worrying again.

She was still deeply mourning her brother, sad all the time, and the Jewish holidays made matters worse. We had good times with friends, soaked up the cultural riches of the city, but it was hard to say which of us was more withdrawn. If I drew her out, I found sorrow over Bernie, Jewish confusion, worry about Stefan, her nieces, her own future, despair about her work. If I opened up, it was about my wasted, directionless life.

It was great when we made love, but that only happened every ten days or two weeks, no matter how much I pressed or obsessed. Wanting more was distracting, frustrating, humiliating. Sarah was not in the mood, saying how tired she was, subtly flinching from my touch, stiffening, lying inert. After a few days I would love myself if she was not going to. I didn't really want to give myself an orgasm, preferring to stay ready and open to love-making, but it was forever on my mind, my head in my pants, sneaking time with my j.o. video pals or dipping into peep shows to the point of silliness. Better just do it; then I could think about something else. My hay fever had never been worse, even with antihistamines. I was zonked and overwhelmed with symptoms. On bad air days, when the World Trade Center disappeared into the poison murk, I knew I could not go on living in New York.

WON, THE ONE NURSE Dad liked, reported that he had not had anything to eat or drink in three days and his fingers were blue. I decided to go immediately. Then Bicky called to tell me he had died—Mother had called her. The next morning I was on my way to Santa Barbara.

Lotte, Dad's caregiver, best friend, and a great comfort to him in the final years and months, told me the nurses in the Medical Center had been giving him sedatives to calm him down: he was still fighting to go home to die. He could perfectly well have been moved back to the apartment three weeks earlier, when Mother went into the hospital for knee surgery: she was not even there. I had urged it, but she refused to discuss it. Dad must have finally realized he could not win, and they helped him let go.

Bicky and I went downtown to the funeral parlor to arrange for the cremation. I asked if we could see the body, and they laid him out for us in the chapel, wrapped to the neck in cloth like a corpse in India, head on a pillow. From across the room he looked colorless, minus the glow of life; up close we saw his beak of a nose, the flesh wasted away, his closed eyes reddish and sunken. He looked peaceful, dignified, and surprisingly small. I wanted to put my arms around him to warm him up—he was being refrigerated until time for the fire—but I was reluctant to kiss him and feel cold flesh on my lips. Anyway it was not him, his spirit gone. I laid my hand over his hands, folded on his chest under the sheet. Bicky touched his hands and jumped back, thinking he moved.

Lewis and Virginia came, and Chuck Willey, the family lawyer, briefed us on the will. Dad had left $50,000 outright to Lewis, saying, "You'll know what to do with it," and $5,000 to Lotte. The rest was divided into two equal trusts, one for Mother, the other split two-fifths for Bicky, two-fifths for me, one-fifth for Virginia, a noticeable snub, ostensibly because we had children and she didn't. We would receive only the interest until Mother died, in case the capital was needed for her care. The income from my share would be around $1,000 a month, once the will was probated, probably a year.

Forty or fifty people came to a memorial service for Dad at All Saints-by-the-Sea, which was dignified and impersonal. Mother asked her friend Geoffrey Rutkowski to play the cello, but there was no opportunity for any of the family to speak. She was frail and shaky, walking to her pew from the back room, supported by Bicky and me, then up the aisle at the end of the ceremony, receiving condolences in a wheelchair on the lawn. We four children talked about our father among ourselves the whole time we were together. After the service, many people said how wonderful Mother was but nobody said anything about Dad. I wanted to remind them how charming he could be, how dashing, handsome, and glamorous, how much fun, what a good father he was to me.

MICHAEL SMITH

I decided to stay in Santa Barbara for a while to help Mother until she was stronger. For one thing, she had lost track of her bills. Someone needed to straighten out their financial affairs in order to settle the estate. Bicky was Dad's executor—he never thought I had any sense about money. She offered to split the $20,000 fee with me if I would do the legwork in Santa Barbara. I gratefully accepted.

I had to make a conscious effort to forgive Mother for her cruelty to Dad at the end of his life. After that it came naturally to be patient with her, spend time with her, slow down to her tempo. She was often remote and hard to reach, but our original affinity was still there somewhere: we enjoyed being together. Sleeping in my father's bed, I liked remembering him and feeling close. I attended Friends Meeting every Sunday, comforted by the right thinking, shared silence, loving gentleness, faithfulness, acceptance. I started seriously thinking I should stay.

Mother was still in the Medical Center recovering from knee surgery so I had their apartment to myself. Paul came to visit. We laid out mattresses on the living room floor so we could sleep together, smoked a joint, lay around and talked, hugged and tussled, getting quite turned on in our underpants. Paul asked me if my heart had ever been broken; I said yes, by Donny, Alfie, Johnny, and Michele. Paul said I was one of the three people who had broken his.

I THOUGHT ABOUT MOVING to Santa Barbara, but it was daunting to think of starting over in a new place. Lewis, perspicaciously, said I would not be starting over but going on with what I did, which was writing and editing. Was this true? I had completely lost track of any such career. Music reviews for *The Day*? Harpsichord construction manuals? Speeches for Koch? What a joke! I had not done a play in years, and my "novel" was wallowing in confusion.

Still, I felt a rush of possibility in the idea that I could have a new life there. Everybody I talked to encouraged me to make the move. Audrey Berman introduced me to Marianne Partridge, the editor of *The Voice* after my time, now the owner and editor of the *Santa Barbara Independent*. All she had for me to write was a dance review, for $10, but at least we were playing the same game: to her I was an old pro.

Audrey threw a dinner party in my honor and introduced me to a few people. One of her guests was a Plantagenet. Another was Lucy O'Brien, a friend from Taos; her son Simon had played with Julian when they were two. Lucy worked for the County Arts Commission and knew all about the reality of making a living as an artist in Santa Barbara. There were not many opportunities, she said, but getting access to them was easy. Everything would be easy in Santa Barbara compared to New York, where I had felt paralyzed, blocked at every turn, disempowered. I did not hesitate to pick up the phone and call anybody who might have an idea for me, and they passed me on to others. Lucy said it would take me six months to figure it out.

A plan evolved: to go back to New York in December, light the Living Theatre's 40th anniversary benefit at Cooper Union, light Hanon's new play, *The Zero Method*, at the Living Theatre on East 3rd Street, then pack up my scrappy possessions and move west. A scene in the benefit show featured angels on ladders; observing the sunlight reflecting off the swimming pool at the Casa Dorinda, I had a vision of bouncing light off mylar on the floor to make the angels float. I would have liked to go on tour to Europe with Judith and Hanon in the spring, and move after that; but I doubted that Sarah would stand for it. My mother would think I was gone again for good. Without me she had no one.

I tried to be straight with Sarah on the phone. She said if I was not coming back with hope, open-minded, not to come at all—"Send Bickley with a truck." I wanted to go back and leave in my own way, not be thrown out. When we spoke as two souls in the predicament of life, I felt deeply connected; she lost me when she reverted to ultimatums, denunciations, threats, and insults: "You're a monster! You're a fucking monster!" (slam). I feared for my possessions.

Once my mother moved back to the apartment, I quickly tired of living in the old folks' home. It was hard to be with her later in the day, when she was often blotto. Manny Peluso, now a substance-abuse professional, suggested an "intervention," something Michele's family had successfully done for her mother, who was also an alcoholic. I tried to talk to Mother about it, at least get her to acknowledge that it was a problem, but she flatly denied it. I went to an Al-Anon meeting, traced alcoholism back through the family, acknowledged my own addiction to marijuana, although in fact I hardly minded not having any.

Bicky did not think Mother should be alone on a holiday. I agreed to stay through Thanksgiving and go back to New York in early December, in time for the Living Theatre benefit. Bicky would come out to

With my mother

help Mother move to a smaller unit and stay for Christmas. Audrey would rent me a room in her house for $400 a month when I came back. I could store my possessions in her garage until I found a place of my own.

I asked John Lucas, who was working for a big-time architecture firm in New York, for a loan of $9,000, on top of the $1,000 I had borrowed the previous spring, to be paid back with my half of the executor's fee when the estate was probated. He generously agreed. That would clear my credit cards and give me a few thousand dollars in the bank until I found work in Santa Barbara. Mother would help me with the move.

On Thanksgiving I thanked God for life, music, the blue sky, and the wind. At dinner in the Casa dining room Mother charmed a table of friends by sing-speaking "I Wanna Go Back to My Little Grass Shack."

She was barely back on her feet, walking with difficulty. I was glad I was moving to Santa Barbara: it would be too forlorn to leave her alone. The next day I took her to the hospital for an ultrasound exam, and they found a life-threatening blood clot in her leg. After a few days in the hospital the treatment was working. She would be back at the Medical Center for a while, well looked after. I could go.

I was barely getting over a cold. Badly unnerved, I hardly felt I had the strength to make this major change with no one to lean on for moral support and reassurance. My last night in my father's room, soon to be dismantled, I was kept awake by mild, constant pain in my left hip, which was only going to get worse. No relationship, philosophy, pharmacology, or change of scene could save me from the nights I no longer expected to sleep through: my father's nights. I sympathetically shared my mother's pain and what Dad had gone through for ten years in this very room. In my dark night thoughts I was scared to death.

21

I REAPPEARED IN NEW YORK just in time for the Living Theatre's benefit in the Great Hall at Cooper Union, rehearsals one day, setup and show the next. My swimming pool effect was subtle and pleasing, my lighting nothing like Johnny's, the whole affair successful. Sarah was painting all day. I was back in my cozy study. Every evening we had artistic and social engagements with warm friends as the season revved up toward Christmas.

From this vantage, my plan to move to California seemed fantastic, perverse, loony, bizarre. My personality was crazily split: I was happily living my life in New York, at the same time planning to abandon it and start over in Santa Barbara. To Sarah's mind, I was not leaving the city but her, and she was half right. She said I had a pattern of tearing down my life, and the "free" thing to do would be to break the pattern and stay. But I did not believe she could break her pattern, or wanted to.

Perhaps, like George Cukor, I simply "preferred the sybaritic delights of California to the ascetic rigors of New York," although that sounded ridiculous to a born New Yorker. "You're moving because it's *pleasanter*?!" If I did not move, what about my mother, and Alfred, and my own health and well-being? I had bloody crusts inside my nose.

Wishing I would get a job in New York doing something worthwhile, Sarah took me to an inspiring Human Rights Watch dinner, where I ran into Betty Rollin and talked to a man who had known Trotsky. At Friends Meeting on Stuyvesant Square, a woman observed that fifty million people have been murdered in the past century by psychoanalytically normal men. Men's power is not working: it is time for women to rise up and take the power that is theirs. I heartily agree. A man said Earth's originally poisonous atmosphere was gradually made breathable by the release of oxygen through photosynthesis; similarly, he said, little acts of love can gradually counteract the cruelty and suffering and eventually make the planet habitable. I wish it were true. How I would have liked to work at an organization like Human Rights Watch, maybe in publications, striving to counteract the evils of violence and exploitation! But I had taken another road, devoted to making personal meaning in equal parts from love and art, another kind of usefulness, possibly. Was I kidding myself? Did I have to become a different person? Was not this self salvageable?

I let the days go by as if nothing had been decided. I heard myself telling people outside Sarah's circle that I was moving to Santa Barbara, to see if it sounded real, and it did. I dreaded the breakup, dreaded destroying the love between us, dreaded hurting Sarah by rejecting her, leaving her, "deciding," dreaded taking our life apart, my study so cozy and complete, dreaded the whole process of packing and dismantling, especially under the cloud of her sorrow, still heavy with Bernie's death, feared the transformation of her sorrows into rage.

I wondered how little of my stuff I could take—or was that a cop-out, a postponement of parting absolute? To preserve a modicum of peace we both had to stop ourselves from saying what we thought and felt. That was no way to live. Choking on swallowed words, I could hardly think about writing.

Bicky wrote from Santa Barbara assuring me that I would find love, happiness, and satisfying work there. I sent Audrey the January rent.

T*he Zero Method* OPENED two days after Christmas in my carefully crafted lights. Hanon's two-character play combined Wittgensteinian philosophy, film noir, and the true story of his romance with Judith in the Living Theatre. I used light to define zones, help move the play through time amd space, clarify the structure, and make Judith look beautiful. Hanon was a joy to serve, intellectual and fervent, his vision pure, honest, passionate, our collaboration challenging and fun. At one point his script called for "waves of light," which I realized with pairs of crosslights in planes moving up the stage, gelled in peacock colors, at Judith's suggestion, surging and crashing in sync with the mental energy, like Johnny's lights at Judson in the sixties.

Hanon and Judith in *The Zero Method*

The Zero Method was to play two weeks into January. I would have liked to run all the performances myself, for the matchless pleasure of performing with Judith and Hanon; but Gary Brackett would tech the tour, and I turned the dimmers over to him after New Year's, as soon as he had learned the cues. The work was poignant and would play better in Italy, where audiences were willing to think. My New York friends disdained it.

Bringing boxes into the house sent Sarah into a tailspin. I tried to keep my packing activities out of her face; but that made it hard to get much done. We went to parties, had dinner with friends, spent friendly time together, but violent emotion regularly broke through. One night she got drunk on Armagnac, trying to drink herself unconscious, and went through an amazing trip: throwing herself around on the floor of her studio in grief, my leaving, Bernie's death, and Stefan's imagined vulnerability scrambled together in her mind, displaying grief so intense that I felt what I was doing had to be a mistake, nothing could be worth this; moving on to happiness and clarity, drunkenly telling me to "go in peace," describing my life as a comic Oedipal spectacle about to culminate in my marrying my mother, now that my father was out of the picture; then sick. I sat with her like a loving nurse or mother. I felt her pain and would have done anything to lessen it short of giving up my resolve to reclaim my autonomy. When it was good between us, I could not see the sense of tearing our relationship apart. It was always thus: when good, good enough to keep; but when the bad side came around, as it did several times that week, and always had and always would, I could not stand it another minute, not one more time!

I put off my departure for a few days at Sarah's request so she could finish her job applications by the deadline and helped her by typing letters. Then Jenny had a miscarriage, one more depressing blow. We went up to the hospital to be with Stef and Jenny. I loved and admired them, and though this felt like a terrible loss, I was confident they would go right on and have the children they wanted, the grandchildren Sarah wanted, and they did.

Sarah described herself as an "old Jewish hag," as a "Jewish peasant," as "ugly," never as the beautiful, strong, independent woman she was, an exceptional teacher, a unique and splendid artist working at the height of her powers. Her friends told me not to worry, she would be all right; she could concentrate on painting, not squander more time, energy, and spirit squabbling with me—which in fact is the way it worked out. Once she accepted that I was going, it was strange not to have the pressure of her opposition. I felt so "there" that it was hard to believe I was leaving. I was frightened by the void ahead, and thrilled.

MOVING OUT OF WESTBETH was a long day of hard work. Sarah went away in the morning and left me to it. I took the subway to Rego Park and brought back a rented truck. Bicky, Steve, and Ben offered to come help me, but Sarah did not want them in the house. Instead my friends at the lighting company sent over a crew with two rolling bins and a dolly. It was amazing how much stuff I had! By evening we had most of it in the truck. I left my piano where it was, up on the ninth floor, where the apartment was sublet, the new tenants unreachable. Sarah had filled a big box with kitchen stuff she did not want. She asked me to tear down the loft I had built in the boys' room, but that was beyond me—I couldn't even think about it. I later regretted leaving her the fine bed Hinrich had made for Michele and me, not wanting to leave her sleeping on the floor.

John Lucas came down after work to help with loose ends. It was late by the time we swept up, shut the door, and drove uptown. Bicky had made soup. I had intended to hit the road that night, but I found a parking space right in front of her building, and the doorman said he would watch the truck. So I gratefully went to bed, going to the kitchen window several times during the night to look down on the truck filled with the texts, machinery, instruments, props, and costumes of my life.

Returning to New York, I had hoped to get back to theatre, and finally had, after four basically meaningless years at City Hall. But obviously I couldn't support myself on sporadic lighting jobs and occasional Living Theatre tours, however enjoyable they were. Thanks to Sarah, I had been able to provide a home for my sons as they were growing up, but it was too hard on her to contend with them as well as me. All she really wanted to do was paint. Not having directed a single play or made any headway in getting mine produced, I was as frustrated as she was. We had years more of life to make good, and fighting with each other was not helping either of us to move ahead. In some ways I was at a low ebb, homeless, jobless, loveless. On the brighter side, I was free again, released in different ways by the failure of another relationship and my father's death and Johnny's death, ready to start a new cycle in a new place, hoping I had learned some useful lessons in all this turmoil and confusion, my energy and optimism good as new.

Reset West

1992–2003

With Carol Storke in a field of fowers

MICHAEL SMITH

1

THE SUNLIGHT AND BRIGHT COLORS of Southern California were a welcome improvement. In balmy, sweet-smelling Santa Barbara, it was hard to remember the grit, grime, and grim determination of Manhattan and the biting winter wind off the Hudson. I unloaded my possessions into Audrey Berman's empty garage, returned the truck, and set myself up comfortably in her guest room. Opening the big garage door onto the sunny sidewalk, I played my harpsichord to infrequent passersby until Audrey persuaded me to move it into her dining room. She liked hearing me play.

Audrey was pursuing a love affair with a professor at Cal State Northridge and away for days at a time. I could pretend this was my own nifty bungalow, play ball with her dog in the flowery backyard, ogle my gay guy videos in her comfortable tv room and masturbate to my heart's content. It was relaxing to indulge myself without feeling I was cheating on anyone.

Reeling from another breakup, I was far from clear about what I wanted to do next on the love front. Otherwise I felt newly empowered to act, a change from my recent paralysis in New York. I attended Friends Meeting on Sundays and appreciated the good Quakers, especially when no one spoke. I went on a few friendly dates with Lucy O'Brien. I met with the board of a local theatre company and proposed that we start a playwrights' festival; alas, their leading actress was leaving for New York and the group was falling apart. In February bright yellow mimosa blossomed all over town. My mother needed me every day but not for long. Her new knees were bothering her; the doctor prescribed walking.

There was a potential editing job for me at the weekly *Santa Barbara Independent*, but it would take a while to materialize. In the meantime I observed that the daily, *Santa Barbara News-Press* glaringly lacked a music critic, which seemed inexcusable in a town so rich in classical music. I kept at them until they let me review a few concerts. The money was pitiful—$35 per review—but doing it cheered me up. I don't feel like myself unless I am writing and being read.

The question of livelihood was pressing, but I had deeper concerns: production of expression—fathering—finding and giving love—love and creative work—being a better person generally and leading a better life. With all my advantages, it was sinful not to be happy.

Lucy O'Brien, friendly and busy with her work at the city Arts Commission, suggested I check out what she described as a "networking event," which turned out to be a gay men's reading group.

"I don't know if you'd be interested," she said.

"I don't know either," I confessed.

Did she think I was gay? Was I? Another major love

With Lucy O'Brien on State Street

failure with another woman suggested something was screwy; but I was not the cause of Michele's coming out as a Lesbian, and Sarah's prickliness and grief predated her affair with me. Were we helplessly reenacting our parents' marriages? Lucy was wise, beautiful, sympathetic, and refreshingly straightforward, but I was in no condition for love-making, too needy and emotionally empty to feel ready for another relationship. She gently advised me that her spiritual teaching was not to take on more than she could handle.

The mere sight of a beautiful boy sometimes seemed to redeem the world. I should be looking for a man, I thought. But I could not be more aggressive than I felt, no matter how much I hungered for intimacy. Functionally satisfied with solo sex, I still wanted love. Why was I alone when I didn't want to be? A friendly, affordable young therapist at the Gay and Lesbian Resource Center, attentive to my confusion, assumed I was gay and ashamed to admit it, which limited his usefulness. I was not looking for permission to come out and embrace my gayness. I had done that years ago. I was way ahead of him.

I had been driving Mother's Nissan while she was laid up. Wanting it back, she cosigned on a loan, and I bought a zippy red Honda hatchback that was practically brand new. Mother at eighty-two was walking with difficulty and hard of hearing, but brave and cheerful in the Pew family tradition, saying she hoped she would not get grumpy (like Dad) when she got really old. She was much less active and outgoing than she used to be, but still regularly played the piano for tea parties at the Casa Dorinda's Personal Care Unit, which housed elders who were no longer up to living alone. "Somewhere Over the Rainbow" showcased her sunny nature and graceful arpeggios. I was glad to be there for her, gratefully repaying with my presence the love she had given me all my life.

Mother loved to play the piano.

I tried to get back to work on my memoir, but I was discouraged with the way it was written. Sarah had perceptively observed that my narrator lived a ghost life in the present that was seldom if ever referred to even peripherally. I had been hiding my present-day self because it was such a disaster. As the story of youthful promise come to nought, the book was a downer, the stalled narrator stalling the book. Well, the past was over, that story finished. I was not interested in nostalgia, canonizing friends now dead, or memorializing my earlier self, which had fallen away. The old stories reawakened misunderstandings and ignorance I wanted to leave behind. I wanted to think as I never had.

I cooked for the homeless at an Episcopal church and played ping-pong with an over-forty group at the Rec Center. I gave out leaflets with the Quakers at the Goleta post office on tax day. I reported my actual 1991 income, $1,600 for scattered newspaper writing, and paid $165 in self-employment tax. I did an orientation course in television production at the public access channel. I reviewed concerts for the *News-Press* and chased after other writing gigs, struggled with my book, wondered how to keep going and how to make room in my new circumstances for my sons.

2

ONE DAY MOTHER chanced to mention that Carol Storke, whom I had known in Santa Barbara in the fifties, was divorced and back in town. Our parents had been friends; we lived a few blocks from each other in lower Montecito. Carol and I had played tennis and gone to the same parties. We hadn't seen each other since college, although we had both been living in New York. Knowing no one else of my generation, I called her up and invited her to lunch.

We arranged to meet at the dolphin fountain at the foot of State Street. As I waited, I wondered how old she would be. I was fifty-six, my hair long gone white. I peered at a dumpy, gray-haired woman sitting on a bench and wondered if that was Carol; then Carol herself came striding across the boulevard, tall, vigorous, dark-haired, instantly recognizable, looking fine. We poured out our stories over lunch, went together to a play the next night and a forward-thinking lecture the night after that. We had both been reading Fritjof Capra and thinking about new paradigms.

Carol and I were delighted to find a fellow New Yorker with common points of reference, and we were powerfully drawn to each other. I was hesitant, not trusting my feelings. It was too soon. I was not over my breakup with Sarah, and Michele before that, or the deaths of Johnny and my father. But Carol was too good to lose, the moment too exciting to let pass. Bicky had said I should find someone who would be good for me, a criterion that had never occurred to me before.

We started seeing each other every day, stimulated by each other's company. Just as I was working up the nerve to get physical, an outbreak of herpes on my penis made me feel weird and untouchable. Carol was disconcerted by the unexplained loss of momentum, and

With Carol Storke

so was I. A month after our first lunch I was all better. She took me to the top of Figueroa Mountain, ever after one of our favorite spots. I sat beside her on a boulder gazing out over the rugged wilderness, put my arm around her, drew her to me, and at last we kissed. We drove down into the canyon to Davy Brown campground for our picnic and kissed some more, rolling around on a blanket spread in the dry grass, passionately pressing together. Back at her house, we picked off the foxtails and went to bed.

After that we wanted to make love all the time. I had never in my life had so much sex. She liked it as much as I did—called it "fun." My sexuality was entirely taken over by my intense, deliciously exciting attraction to Carol. We spent every night together, in my bed or hers.

That ended my need for therapy—or pornography. At my final session I tried to give my therapist a shopping bag full of gay porn tapes as a donation to the Gay Liberation Resource Center; he declined, and I left them in a dumpster out back. Love and sex would not be a problem with Carol. We were good for each other, we knew it right away.

Julian and Alfred in Pullman

JULIAN CAME FOR A WEEK while Audrey was in Europe. Having Carol in my life had renewed my hope, heart, and happiness, and Julian's visit was joy untrammeled. Mother loved seeing him, and he was sweet with her. Now seventeen, he would have liked to stay in Santa Barbara and get a job but agreed to go back to Michele and finish high school in Pullman, Washington, where his second mom, Joy, was in veterinary school. I drove him up. It was terrific to see the two boys together, so different in their natures, both so close to my heart. I loved being a father and treasured every bit of time with my growing-up sons.

As planned, I brought Alfred back with me to Santa Barbara to live with me and go to high school. There was no room for him at Audrey's, and Carol had tenants sharing her house. So I arranged to rent the upstairs rooms in Lucy's house near the beach. Carol came over to sleep with me, but there was not much privacy, the shared bathroom down a flight of stairs. She preferred her own big bed, and so did I. She had given me my own garage door opener and a drawer in her bathroom, a clear signal that she wanted me there. Barely a week after we had moved in at Lucy's, Carol's tenants moved out, and Alfred and I moved to her house in Goleta. Initially taken aback, Lucy found two German students to take up the slack, and everything worked out.

Carol and I both felt we had found the right other person at last. We decided to stay together for the rest of our lives.

CAROL WAS a ninth-generation Santa Barbaran, descended from José Francisco Ortega, the first comandante of the Santa Barbara Presidio. Her grandfather, T. M. Storke, the publisher of the *Santa Barbara News-Press*, was instrumental in bringing Santa Barbara a new Art Deco post office; constructing Cachuma Dam in the Santa Ynez Valley, which gave Santa Barbara a reliable water supply and enabled its growth; and establishing the Santa Barbara campus of the University of California. T. M. received a 1962 Pulitzer Prize for his editorials against the John Birch Society. Her father was also a leader in the community.

Carol's father, Charles E. Storke, leading the 1954 Fiesta Parade.

Carol had gone east to college to get away from her mother. She was at Smith while I was at Yale, and we evidently went together to a football weekend at Princeton, little as we were interested in football—she knew my Kansas City pals Jim Scarritt and Jim Starr, must have met them through me. Carol majored in history at Smith, moved to New York after graduation, married and started a family with Sidney Whelan, a respectable young lawyer. They lived on upper Fifth Avenue and had three children; another child came to term but did not survive. Leaving law, Sidney became vice president for development at the American Museum of Natural History. They had a busy social life cultivating donors—an ordeal for Carol, who never liked dressing up à la mode and performing polite conversation. She was sick of cooking and wouldn't dream of ironing my shirts. I was the anti-Sidney, free to be myself.

Her husband minded her working for money, so Carol did volunteer work at first, then segued into a job. After their divorce she worked at the Vera Institute of Justice, later running the New York City office of the New York State Commission on Corrections, focusing on criminal justice issues and prisoners' rights. She moved with her youngest child, Sid, to a loft near City Hall and worked on productivity for the Deputy Mayor for Operations. We overlapped in the Mayor's Office—used the same subway stations—but didn't know it. We hadn't seen each other for thirty years.

Driven out of her city job over policy issues, Carol had other jobs, earned a master's at Pace University in information technology, and worked as a consultant. Once Sid went away to college, she decided to leave the city for much the same reason I did: a better life awaited us elsewhere.

Carol was solid, clear in her values, free from the insecurities and paranoia that had troubled my previous relationships. We thought differently, but our minds worked at the same speed. Falling in love, we marveled at how well-matched we were. I was strong enough for her, she said, and she was strong enough for me. I no longer had to hold back or watch my step. Any qualms I had, with nothing to feed on, melted away. I was thrillingly attracted to Carol and felt lucky to have linked my life with hers. Her openness was exemplary, her intelligence bracing and companionable, her steady love the support and affirmation I had always longed for. It made everything easier that she had a house.

Carol's father, Charles Storke, lived in Montecito with his third wife, Lib. Now in his early eighties, he was a formidable character, smart and deeply knowledgeable about his city. His humor could be sharp, but he was unreservedly generous to me. Not long after I moved in with his eldest daughter, he said to me, "Welcome to the family."

In Santa Barbara Carol had been working as a computer systems designer, but the economy was shaky and she had been laid off. Not working gave us precious time to get to know each other—and Alfred, who had arrived with me. That first summer we took a trip to New Mexico in Carol's Jeep,

MICHAEL SMITH

Carol and Alfred with her Jeep in Monument Valley

camping in two tents along the way. Alfred visited his cousin Francis in Taos while Carol and I went to Madrid, an old mining town south of Santa Fe, to visit her daughter Lora and her husband Eric. We drove home by way of Monument Valley and the Grand Canyon.

3

THE ARTS EDITOR OF THE *Santa Barbara Independent* was moving to New York. I told Audrey I wanted his job. Marianne Partridge, the editor, said they would be thrilled to have me. While I was waiting to start, they asked me to put together a multipage section on Old Spanish Days Fiesta, an annual Santa Barbara blowout in early August. I still remembered sitting on folding chairs at the curb in front of my father's store on State Street watching the Fiesta parade in the summer of 1954, seeing Carol and her family ride by in a carriage in their florid Fiesta costumes. Her father was El Presidente that year and led the parade on a palomino stallion. I got into the spirit with Carol and dressed up in style for my first Santa Barbara Fiesta as a grownup.

In fall 1992 Carol was rehired by her old company; Alfred enrolled at San Marcos High School, a ten-minute walk from home; and I took over as arts editor of the weekly *Santa Barbara Independent*. The job was half-time, the pay laughable, my office a windowless cubbyhole; but in other ways it was ideal, giving me a voice and a pretext to poke into everything I cared about and an instant identity in my new hometown. The paper threw a party to present me to the local arts community. Before long I knew all the theatre and dance companies, musical groups, and gallerists in town. I was the one to talk to when they wanted publicity or reviews.

Fiesta spirit

We had a memorable Thanksgiving in a wild stretch of Paradise Canyon. Lib, Charles's wife, served a traditional turkey dinner on a long table on a gravel bank beside the creek. There were a dozen of us, including Lib's children and grandchildren, Carol's aunt Jean Menzies, a historical scholar, and my frail mother, who sat in the car while the rest of the party hiked up the creek and looked at fossils in the rocks.

MICHAEL SMITH

Carol's children: Sid, Tensie, and Lora

CAROL'S CHILDREN came west to spend Christmas with us. Tensie, the eldest, lived in Manhattan with her three-year-old daughter, Lora-Faye, born after her young Swedish father was killed in an auto accident. Lora-Faye hid behind her mother and wouldn't speak to me. Sid lived in upper Manhattan with his African-American wife, Lisa. She was a graduate student in history; he was a guitarist, led an Afro-pop band, and had a day job promoting classical music. Lora and her husband, Eric, both writers, were thinking of moving to Maine. Carol's children were suspicious of me at first but could hardly fail to see that their mother was happy to have me in her life.

Carol was a good sport about my arriving with a teenage son. I knew it wasn't easy for her, but I loved having Alfred in my life. We were naturally harmonious and pleased to be together. He was friendly and loving but rarely forthcoming about his inner thoughts, claiming he didn't have any. It must have been extremely difficult for him to keep adjusting to different women and moving and changing schools, but he didn't want to show it and played cool. I regretted putting him and Julian through all that. I preferred stability myself, but so far I hadn't been able to hold onto it. We bought a ping-pong table and set it up on the patio, and Alfred and I embarked on a competition that continues to this day. I bought him a drum kit, which he set it up in his bedroom. He practiced diligently and became a drummer.

A LTHOUGH MY OWN THEATRE CAREER seemed to be over, I was glad to find an energetic, creative theatre scene in Santa Barbara. UCSB and Santa Barbara City College both had vigorous theatre departments. There was a good small professional theatre company downtown, and a new black box theatre for independent groups. Lovingly detailed, imaginative, strongly acted productions played for two or three weekends, then disappeared without a trace. I thought an annual awards ceremony would bring the theatre community together and reinforce the best work. Marianne and Audrey liked the idea, and the *Independent* gave it full support. I knew how to do it, having produced the Obies for *The Village Voice* in the 1960s.

The art director of the *Independent* designed a handsome, witty award statuette in the form of a chunky lower-case letter i, with a ball for the dot. I found someone to carve the model out of wood, someone else to cast them in resin. They were satisfyingly heavy, lacquered a vivid purple, with the winner's name on a small brass plaque. (The color would change each year.)

It was a challenge to find jurors who had seen enough of the many plays that had been done during the season. I avoided reviewing plays in Santa Barbara but saw just about everything, seeking to get the measure of my new arena. It added credibility when Philip Brandes, the chief critic of the *News-Press*, agreed to be one of the judges. (The *News-Press* normally pretended the *Independent* didn't exist.) Lucy O'Brien came on the panel and suggested an older man named Dick Spahr, who loved plays and got in to see them by volunteering as an usher. "Are you sure his name isn't Dick Spahn?" I asked. In fact, by an amazing coincidence, it *was* Dick Spahn, my directing mentor from Riggs, who had sent me to New York to get started in the theatre. Dick had retired to Santa Barbara because it had a good bus system and he could get along without a car.

The first Santa Barbara Independent Theatre Awards, immediately dubbed the Indies, were given out on a Monday evening in May at Center Stage Theater. I worked with the tech director to make the lighting theatrical and emceed the presentations. A crowd came and contributed to the upbeat atmosphere. The award winners were excited, the thank-yous entertaining, and the paper hosted a party on the terrace afterward with food, music, and excited theatrical voices. Someday I wanted to win one myself.

With Indie statuettes

Giving an Indie to Karyl Lynn Burns

CAROL LED US INTO a curious group activity called "dialogue," devised by the physicist David Bohm, which she had picked up from her former roommates. Every couple of months we drove up to the Bay Area, stayed two nights with her brother Charlie and his family in San Rafael, and spent all day Saturday and most of Sunday in a house in Marin County meeting with c. twenty other people for a special kind of group conversation, an attempt to let go of our self-conceptions and "think together." A topic would spontaneously emerge. Most of the participants were human resources people from the corporate world. The effort to be serious, not trivial, made the process engaging, and I liked the people. I had only ever been around artists; regular people were a novelty—exotic.

Alfred departed to spend the summer with Michele and Joy. Carol and I were happy to have the house to ourselves. If we liked, we could leave doors open, walk around naked, frolic in the living room, though now that we were both working we had less time to be together. After one dialogue weekend, we took a romantic vacation jaunt up the northern California coast. In the Napa Valley we squeezed into a glider together for a thrilling ride: it was either that or a mud bath. We went to San Diego to see *King Lear*. It was a joy to be together, whatever we did. I went to New Mexico for a week to light the Living Theatre in Taos and Santa Fe and hurried back.

JULIAN HAD LEFT PULLMAN, where Michele and Joy could not stop worrying and keeping after him, and moved on his own to Bellingham, Washington. I flew to Seattle, rented a car, and drove up to see him. He was living in a downtown SRO and working at a Mexican restaurant. I slept on his floor. With his curly dark hair bleached yellow, he was a charismatic kid. Everybody seemed to know and like him.

Alfred decided to stay with Michele and Joy in Pullman for his second year of high school. But Carol and I were not alone for long before Julian, now nineteen, came hitching down the coast. Moving into Alfred's room, he quickly found a job at a public-interest phone bank, raising money for environmental groups, bicycling back and forth to town.

I took Julian to Big Sur for a weekend in the fall. He brought out magic mushrooms as we hiked down into a canyon, and we spent the afternoon blissing out on the high cliffs above the wide Pacific. Angels came to visit us in the form of clouds, beautiful and benign, sailing in over the ocean. Angels are real energy-forms but insubstantial: it makes perfect sense for them to manifest as clouds. I still see them now and again.

I MADE IT A PRACTICE to visit Mother every two or three days. She was delighted to see me, sorry to see me go, eager for me to come again. I always liked seeing her, but the demands of my increasingly busy life made it hard to carve out time. I worried about her driving, although she rarely went farther than the liquor store. She had been a wonderful driver, and the habits lasted a long time; but one day somebody opened a door in her path, and she scraped the whole side of the car. Fortunately she was moving slowly. She had it repaired, at considerable expense, without telling me about it, but when it came time to renew her license, she failed the vision test. Carol's Jeep had been giving her trouble and was really not adequate for pulling her horse trailer. She bought Mother's Nissan at the blue book price and a pickup truck for the horses.

Julian in Bellingham

4

I ONLY GRADUALLY CAME TO REALIZE how important horses were to Carol, who was finally letting her equestrian passion flower after decades of being thwarted by circumstances. She had loved horses since she was a little girl, when her maternal grandfather had a hilltop ranch in Goleta, not

Carol on Rhea

far from where we lived now, and kept ponies and then horses for the children. She treasured her memories of riding with her sister Barbie through the lemon groves, long since replaced with tract houses, of competing in Santa Barbara horse shows and riding in the Fiesta parade, although she had never had a good horse of her own, riding lessons, or the opportunity to be serious. Grown up, living in New York, she visited good friends with horses on a farm in New Jersey. After her divorce, she and her boyfriend Bill Katz bought a place in Pennsylvania where she kept a horse, but that was hours away. Now she had the opportunity to ride and work with horses as much as she liked, and she wanted to make the most of it.

She had brought two mares from the East, her chestnut quarter horse, Rhea, and Rhea's unexpected colt, Surprise, now three years old. She kept them at a nearby boarding stable. She rode on weekends with equestrian friends and twice year went on camping trips with a women's riding club, the Sage Hens, a group my mother had ridden with. I of course was a dude ranch rider from childhood. She put me on Rhea and I took a short ride, but my lame left hip made it impossibly painful to sit in the saddle: the next day I could hardly walk.

Carol claimed that riding and training horses meant as much to her as writing, music, and theatre did to me. I insisted that art has more inherent meaning: art is privileged, to my mind, serious in a different way, higher, deeper. Art matters. The artist is not just having a good time but on a quest for transcendence and redemption. Art is more serious than anything but love, certainly more serious than a hobby like horseback riding, (That did not mean that I was more serious than she was: I have never been very serious.) This was as close as we ever came to fundamental disagreement. Ultimately I conceded the point and gave her the full respect for her passion that I wanted for mine.

I KEPT TRYING to find a way back into the theatre—direct, get my plays on, do lighting, have some fun. I had lunch with Pope Freeman, the grand old man of Santa Barbara directors. Pope headed the drama program at Santa Barbara City College, which had two theatres and staged five or six excellent productions a year with a mix of professional and student actors. He was friendly but said their budget was too tight to hire an outside director. I got to know people in the theatre department at UCSB, but I had no academic credentials. I took scripts to Robert Weiss, the director of Ensemble Theatre Company, who said they might let me do a one-act on their second series. They were all defending their hard-earned turf and preferred me as a journalist.

Jarrell Jackman, the executive director of the Santa Barbara Trust for Historic Preservation and a theatre buff, asked me to put together a historical reenactment of English explorer George Vancouver's visit to Santa Barbara in 1793. The occasion was a benefit dinner in the restored Presidio chapel, two hundred years later to the day. I wrote a playlet, *Entertaining Vancouver*, using contemporary accounts, and devised a bold staging, seating the hundred guests at two long tables running the length of the chapel, playing the action in the long, narrow space between.

In a second show I did at the Presidio Chapel, *Life Is a Round*, the third comandante, Goicoechea, materialized through a projection screen and magically transported the audience back in time.

For Halloween 1994 the Trust asked me to put together a spook house in the Casa De la Guerra, a large adobe built in 1821 and long the social center of Santa Barbara, which was in process of being restored to its original form. Visitors were ushered by a black-lit skeleton into the deconstructed sala, where amid the rubble five actors embodied the ghosts of historical figures, each with a brief monologue. In the next room Jerry Jackman, costumed as José De la Guerra, had children sign their names in a ceremonial book. A big corner room was beautifully set up for El Día de los Muértos by theatre activist Joseph Velasco. The spook house proper was classical, with a man in a bear suit, a cardboard tunnel, a wild man in a cage with rubber bars, a dead girl in a coffin who suddenly sat up, and a moving wall that closed in on hapless visitors. The teenagers operating the moving wall got carried away, their shrieks frightening younger kids so much that their parents had to take them back out the way they had come in. I was surprised it was scary; I had thought it was completely silly.

Robert Weiss invited me to do a short play on an evening of one-acts at the Ensemble. I extracted the Beckettish, dreamlike play-within-the-play from *Half Life*, calling it *Come In Here*. The character was meant to be about fifty, the age I was when I wrote the play. I cast my one-time mentor Dick Spahn, who was well into his seventies. I loved the opportunity to direct him in a play, completing the circle of our creative friendship.

Dick Spahn and Gwynne van Seenus
in *Come in Here*

5

In summer 1994 Carol and I took our combined families to Europe. Julian and Alfred flew with us to Rome. The first evening the boys went out alone, met some Italian kids on the Spanish Steps, and were whisked off on the back of a motorcycle (first Julian, then Alfred) to a rock festival on the outskirts of the city. After a couple of days in Rome we drove north by way of Orvieto to join Carol's family at a villa she had rented near Lucca, a beautiful big old house with plenty of rooms and a swimming pool. For a week that was our base for visits to Lucca and other excursions. Julian went to Florence with Lora and Eric while Alfred and I went to Siena and wine tasting in Chianti with Sid and Lisa. We all went to Cinque Terre, where the steep hillsides defeated Carol and me and the young people hiked to the next town. I consoled myself with a swim in the Ligurian Sea. Tensie's fiancé, Michael Peters, was there with his son, Luke, who was a year older than Lora-Faye. We cooked and ate together in the big, rustic kitchen and had a first-class bonding experience.

Then everyone went different directions. I bought Julian and Alfred rail passes and saw them off in Lucca, pointing them in the direction of Prague, telling them to meet Carol and me in Paris at the Hotel St. Sulpice in ten days. Carol and I drove north over the mountains to the Po Valley, but it was too hot in Verona, and the streets of Parma were deserted. We went up into the Dolomites to cool off.

It was a relaxed, altogether happy trip, apart from an attack of grumpiness I suffered at Bellaggio, something to do with a grandiose five-star hotel we decided not to spring for. Weeks of no writing was taking a toll. Leaving Carol napping at the modest lakefront hotel, I walked by myself to the end of the island, where stone steps led down into the waters of Lake Garda. There was no one around so I took my clothes off and dove into the lake. The cool, dark water felt wonderful; when I got back to Carol, I was fine.

Dropping off the car in Milano, we took a train into France to visit Wolfgang Zuckermann in Avignon, where he had opened an English-

Seeing Alfred and Julian to the train in Lucca: off to Prague

language bookshop. When we arrived at our hotel in Paris, to my great relief the boys were already there, asleep in their room. Pascale joined us for dinner. Julian was a vegetarian so we never did have real French food. The city was jammed with tourists. On Bastille Day Carol and I dined with the boys, danced in the street, then sent them off to see the fireworks at the Trocadero. Alone, we walked past our hotel and sat down on a bench in beautiful, austere Place St. Sulpice. A man and three young boys quietly appeared with small fireworks and set them off on the paving stones next to the fountain, our own private fireworks show.

By Amsterdam, my hip was so painful I could hardly walk. Carol and I rented bicycles; I kept mine, rolling slowly alongside as the others walked. I took her to meet Paul McNulty, my pianomaker friend from Stonington, who had set up shop in Amsterdam and was raising two young children. Julian and Alfred had wanted to stay in a hostel, on their own, but couldn't work it out so we got them a room in our canal-side hotel. We went together to the Van Gogh Museum and a glorious baroque organ recital in the Nieuwe Kirke. I got away by myself to visit a marijuana cafe, went back to the hotel, and made love to Carol, happy to be high. She got right into the spirit.

Julian in the garden

LATER IN THE SUMMER Carol and I flew east again for Tensie and Michael's wedding in Danby, Vermont, where Carol's first husband, Sidney Whelan, had kept his parents' summer place. Carol had spent many summers there when their children were little, Sidney coming and going from the city. There was a beautiful big old house with a barn and enormous meadows and a sweeping view across the valley to the mountains. Sidney and his second wife, Patsy, had built themselves a new house a little way up the hill and turned over the big house to the children, who gathered at Danby for holidays and treasured the time together.

I loved having Julian with us in Santa Barbara. We had fun together and separately. Julian, carefully following the instructions in a book I had on marijuana cultivation, grew a single marijuana plant in a pot, timing its exposure to light, monitoring its water and nutrients, pinching it back strategically. It turned into an astonishingly dense, vibrant plant, a compact, budding ball of thin spiky leaves, in striking contrast to the six-foot weeds I had grown out behind our house in Lower Ranchitos. Carol was worried that our hostile next door neighbor might turn us in so Julian had to keep it out of sight. I thought of it as his science project, and it would have surprising significance for his future livelihood.

Julian was good at his job, gained strength and confidence, and decided he was ready to go to college. Evergreen, a bastion of liberty in Washington State, would be affordable because of his still-established residency there.

MICHELE AND Joy moved back to New Mexico, and Alfred came back to Santa Barbara to live with Carol and me again for his third year of high school. Delighted to have him, I ignored the slightly chilly relations between him and Carol, both of whom might have preferred to have my full attention. They were very good about it.

San Marcos High School still didn't work for him, unfortunately, though he was a bright, energetic boy, full of good will. Trying but failing to get interested in his classes, he fell in with similarly disengaged peers. We didn't know any families with kids and couldn't help. Teachers looked at him funny in the halls, he said, and were not amused by his sense of humor. I regretted not sending him to a better school, where his individuality would have more chance to be appreciated. We looked at a desirable boarding school in the Santa Ynez Valley—I could have persuaded Mother to help pay for it—but he was not motivated enough to get in, not wanting to leave home. I helped him transfer to La Cuesta, an alternative public high school downtown, but that was no better. Finally he just stopped going.

At seventeen Alfred was reliably good-natured around the house, doing chores when asked, but not proactive, sleeping late, staying in his room, which I had regrettably encouraged him to paint black. He seemed withdrawn and perhaps depressed, although he said he was not. When a neighbor complained about his drum practice, I insisted that it was not noise but music. I refrained from criticizing his friends.

One of Alfred's phone conversations found its way onto the answering machine: plans to get together with a pal to smoke weed, discussion of an

Alfred praccticing in his black bedroom

acid trip with a girl who had freaked out, obscure references to sex, all in a kicked-back jargon I had never heard him use. As a writer I was so fascinated that I transcribed the tape. I could hardly hold any of it against him. I smoked pot and had taken acid and loved sex and never made much secret of it, but not until I was older and better able to take care of myself.

Nothing was happening for Alfred in Santa Barbara, and in the spring he decided to go on the road. If he couldn't keep it together at school, I didn't know what he should do and was glad he was taking action to get out of an evident funk. He took off with his friend Cengiz, hitchhiking up the coast as far as Santa Cruz, where they camped outside town near the ocean. There, during an acid trip, Cengiz disappeared. I only heard about it months later. Alfred searched for him on the beach in the dark and stayed with his stuff for a few days, waiting for him to reappear; then deposited his things at a church and went on north alone. Tragically, Cengiz was never seen again. His mother called many times over the following months and years. Detectives questioned Alfred, who was deeply freaked out about it. It was almost a decade before his friend's body was found.

6

MY JOB AT THE *Independent* had turned into full-time work for half-time pay, so I was immediately receptive when the owner of *Santa Barbara Magazine* began taking me to lunch. Dan Denton, a likable Yalie from Florida, had bought and revamped the magazine into a slick quarterly rich in high-end real estate ads, full of lavishly illustrated articles about nature, local history, and lifestle on the American Riviera; I had not been reading it, but I admired its quality. At our third lunch Dan wondered if I might be interested in becoming the editor. I said yes, indeed I might.

First I had to be approved by Kimberly Kavish, the art director, who grilled me over another lunch. The reality was that I had a sketchy career as a newspaper editor and writer and no magazine experience. But I was a smart, capable person, I could cope. Four issues a year did not look like much work compared to the *Independent*, though we would also be producing *Pasadena Magazine*. Dan said he had been looking for an editor ever since he bought the magazines. He offered me $40,000 a year, twice as much as the *Independent* paid me. After I had accepted, he said I was a bargain.

I came from a tradition of minimal editing. *The Village Voice* basically ran stories the way the writers handed them in. As a writer I appreciated this respect, and I followed the same principles at the *Independent*, where there was hardly time to do more than clean up the grammar and punctuation. My initial impression was that Dan Denton overedited *Santa Barbara Magazine*, muting the writers' individual voices. Once I started editing it, I found myself doing the same thing, often taking stories completely apart, restructuring them, sending them back for rewrites, rewriting them myself when the original research was inadequate or wrong. It was my job to make the writers sound good and present a polished face to the world. It was the first time I tried to be professional.

Dan was demanding; I resisted him at first but quickly learned not to. I liked his thoughtful analysis of Santa Barbara's unique charm. The magazine could do good by affirming the town's roots in ranching and later as a winter getaway for rich industrialists with a taste for art and civic betterment, countering the erosion of its identity by overbuilding, rampant commercialization, and invasion by overconfident newcomers from L.A. who thought it was a blank slate. I had been coming since 1953 and had a strong feeling for the place. Small-town journalists have to be boosters to some extent. My mother's energetic volunteerism connected me with a tradition of noblesse oblige; my father had been a prominent downtown businessman. Carol linked me with deep history, the land, and equestrian traditions. I was personally interested in fostering the arts. The magazine gave me an opportunity to speak up for what was real and special about Santa Barbara.

One of our many icnics

Carol had been laid off from her job again and was actively looking for another, meanwhile collecting unemployment and helping her father with paperwork, bills, and family business. Charles, in his middle eighties, needed oxygen all the time but was still vigorous and active. Carol joined him on the board of the Trust for Historic Preservation. She was as busy as I was, but we made time for picnics. Carol and I were happy to be together.

Before I left the *Independent* I helped her get started writing a column about horses and related subjects. Her experience was bureaucratic, and at first her writing was stiff. I showed her how to make information into stories and tell them in her own voice. She was an apt pupil and soon good at it. *The News-Press* having dropped its horse column, Carol's monthly column in the *Independent* became information central for the equestrian community. I helped her as much as I could.

7

ON MY MANY VISITS TO SANTA BARBARA through the years I had enjoyed plays, operas, and concerts at the beautiful Lobero Theatre with my mother. I used to say it was my favorite theatre next to the Odéon in Paris. In spring 1995 the Lobero was in trouble. The state had mandated seismic renovations that would cost millions, and the fund-raising campaign had stalled. I telephoned Nancy Moore, the executive director of the nonprofit foundation that ran the theatre, and asked her what I could do to help. She suggested I join the board of directors, which had not occurred to me: I was thinking of doing a story. My parents had both served on boards, but I had never thought of myself as board material—indeed had deliberately placed myself beyond the pale for many years. I was falling back into the middle class.

I began by arranging a benefit piano recital by Mother's good friend Jerome Lowenthal, a brilliant pianist and personality who taught at Juilliard and at the Music Academy of the West in Santa Barbara in the summer. In New York for a weekend to visit Bicky, I had a pleasurable breakfast with

The historic Lobero Theatre

Jerry, who was happy to be asked and readily agreed. I had forgotten how much I like presenting concerts. I worked with Nancy to woo sponsors and an audience, and we made more than $30,000 on the evening. That helped regalvanize the capital campaign, which went on to success, the Lobero saved. The board elected me vice president.

M Y LEFT HIP was increasingly problematic. I was reluctant to walk the three blocks over to State Street for lunch or to the back of the supermarket for milk. I was on a maintenance dose of aspirin, accustomed to the pain and limitation. Carol was more conscious than I of how much I was slowing down, walking slowly, carefully, as if fragile, as if I was getting old.

The first time I heard about joint-replacement surgery, when Alice Potter got new knees, I shuddered at the very idea. But I had been getting used to the idea now for several years, and after the Lowenthal concert, I went into the hospital for a new hip, feeling no real trepidation. Carol was a great comfort, sitting with me as I went under, there when I struggled back to consciousness. I had a nasty hour the first night when a young male nurse tried and failed to insert a urinary catheter; a senior urologist got out of bed, appeared, and briskly did it. I had brought along Proust and tapes of good music, and I was happy in the hospital, high on painkillers, looking out the window at the slowly changing light, although the nurses needlessly made me nauseous by giving me pain pills on an empty stomach.

I went home in a few days, and my recovery was steady and pleasant. I spent my days on the living room sofa, reading and listening to music, and faithfully did the prescribed exercises, essentially the ballet barre, slowly regaining strength and mobility. Within a couple of weeks I was back at work, walking with a cane; within a couple of months I was good as new.

T AKEN UP WITH JOURNALISM and getting my new life in order, I had not been doing any writing of my own. Not writing makes me antsy, that should be perfectly clear by now, I don't like the feeling or how it makes me act. So I made a fresh start on what would eventually become this book, resolving to work on it every day, if only for an hour, every single day, seven days a week.

Carol liked to get up early, and we did yoga together first thing every morning; I taught her what I remembered from Ravi's classes in New York, putting together a half-hour routine out of his book. After breakfast I went into my study, smoked a little pot, and wrote for an hour or so before leaving for work. I had told Dan that I would not come in before ten, and I was frequently later than that. There was hardly enough to do to keep me busy all day except in the last two or three weeks of each issue, when I was pushed to the limit. Kim Kavish was a good designer but very difficult to work with. Dan was spending more time in Florida but kept a close eye on my editorial decisions.

Fast Books, my publishing arm, published my experimental novel *Near the End* thirty years after I had written it. Presented as parallel texts on facing pages, the book is a loosely organized, impressionistic interior imagescape of a man who has slashed his wrists with a butcher knife and lies bleeding on the kitchen floor. It spookily foreshadows Joe Cino's grisly suicide: the book was finished two years before Joe's sad end. His mind wanders as he waits for the ambulance, which he may or may not have called. The left-hand pages include long lists of names, like a ritual invocation; the right side is more narrative. There are only fragments of story, though, with no linear coherence: the unit is the sentence. *Near the End* is an artifact of the sixties, pre-postmodern, ironic, defiantly obscure and disorganized. Despite my modest success as a journalist, this was the kind of writer I really wanted to be.

Michael Smith

Near the End

Near the End was the first real book Fast Books produced. I hired a designer and had 500 copies commercially printed and bound. The cover was a blow-up of the five-cent George Washington stamps Johnny cut up for his collage wall in my Third Street apartment, a handsome, privately meaningful image that made the text resonate with national history. I liked it a lot. Only when the books arrived from the printer did I realize that the back cover was blank, white, empty; the designer hadn't thought to have me write the promotional copy that belonged there, and I didn't know any better. Nor did it have a bar code. So the books were unmarketable. I gave away a hundred copies and stowed the rest on a shelf in the garage.

Reviewing classical music every week in *The Independent* meant we were constantly going to concerts. Carol enjoyed them as much as I did, counting

the flow of free tickets a substantial contribution to our domestic economy. I was interested in dance as well and served on a jury vetting choreographers for the annual Choreographers Showcase of the Santa Barbara Dance Alliance. I wound up producing the concert, which I dubbed *Choreosplash!* Instead of Center Stage Theater, the group's usual venue, I held out for the Lobero, where the work would be better-framed and get more respect. We did a publicity blitz, and on the night of the concert, there was a line from the boxoffice to the corner, the dance audience more numerous than anyone had realized.

Not to sound smug, I was doing pretty well in Santa Barbara. After less than four years, I was visible in the community, involved in public activities, part of respectable society, although neither Carol nor I was very social. We preferred our picnics in the hills. Carol was the key to my stability, the foundation of my happiness and relative prosperity, our love steady and growing. We casually referred to each other as husband and wife, not wanting to make people wonder about our relationship, although we were neither of us interested in tangling with the marriage laws again or having our union sanctioned by anyone but ourselves. We would love and take care of each other and stand by each other in every way. That was enough.

8

THE FIRST TIME I SAW CAROL'S HOUSE in Goleta, it was night, and I had taken the back way from town, imagining that I was going someplace beautiful out in the country. Only slowly did I come to realize that 4957 La Gama Way was a tract house in a generic middle-class suburb, albeit with a large extra living room and a big backyard. Carol had tried to find a place where she could keep horses, but Santa Barbara real estate was insanely pricy. The house in Goleta was what she could afford; the horses were at a boarding stable. Carol was better off than I was, but not as rich as I for some reason imagined, generalizing from our parents' Montecito lifestyle, I suppose. The Storkes were indeed a leading family in the town, and

Carol's house in Goleta

Carol's mother's father, Sellar Bullard, had been moderately wealthy. But little wealth and no property had trickled down to her generation. She had struggled to establish her independence after years lost to a conventional marriage. Carol was task-oriented and realistic about money. I kept good track of my personal finances but had never actually understood the concept of capital. You'd think my father would have explained it to me.

Carol had moved into her house the way it was, bland and dated. Once I arrived it did not take long before we started transforming it. We painted our bedroom a pleasing blue with vivid pink on the narrow trim around the doors. Carol adapted some bright chintz curtains she had from New York. We moved the piano to the other end of the room it was in and had a cabinetmaker build her a U-shaped work space, with shelves to her specifications, adding an ocean-view window.

Out back was a beautiful garden she was happily developing, with paths for strolling among flower beds and fruit trees, avocados, lemons, oranges, and kumquats, and vegetables up in the back. I contributed a Monet garden in a box bed and a garden of blue flowers along the edge of the wide concrete patio.

Carol in her new office and the backyard garden

In late 1995 we undertook a more drastic renovation. Crawling around in the attic, I had found a large volume of waste space above the low cottage-cheese ceiling of the added-on living room. The white tile floor was clattery, cold in winter, impossible to keep clean. The wet bar was tacky and useless, the fireplace bogus. We had a contractor tear out the ceiling, revealing a massive wood beam supporting the roof; demolished the bar and unboxed the skylight, flooding the room with daylight; reconfigured the arch beween the rooms, improving the feng shui; and removed the fireplace, which was never going to be used: Carol is sensitive to smoke. Mexican workers laboriously chipping away the white tiles thought we were mad to destroy such a fine floor, but dark-stained hardwood would be a huge improvement. We painted the walls a rich, deep pink, dramatic and warm, only later realizing it was the same color as my harpsichord.

I had felt trapped in the small child's bedroom with one high window

On the new little deck outside my office

that I had taken as my study, having to go through the house to get outside when I wanted to smoke a joint. A sliding glass door opened it up to the out of doors, and I built myself a little terrace for the sun and air. I painted the walls of my study Traffic Red, for creative energy.

We had both liked living in lofts in New York, and our main rooms took on the same kind of open, liberating feel. Our art looked great on colored walls. Carol had a collection of paintings by Mexican modernists, many from her mother, historic lithographs of New York, and early California and western drawings and prints. My own little art collection had languished in storage while I was living with Sarah, who didn't want other people's art hung in her house. Carol and I bought several paintings by Patricia Chidlaw, a local realist, and two very large abstract oils by Rafael Perea de la Cabada, a young Mexican artist living in Santa Barbara.

Carol gave me a mobile for a birthday present made of glass that changed colors in the sunlight. We picked out elegant fabric and she sewed long curtains for the living room. Her polished Empire dining table would fit better in the nineteenth-century house Tensie and Michael had bought in Brooklyn. The pine Shaker table I had made in Stonington was up on the rafters in the garage. I sanded and refinished it, and we dine on it to this day.

CAROL'S PIANO, a seven-foot Steinway she had brought from New York, had been muffled in the carpeted, low-ceilinged "music room." In the newly expansive living room it revealed itself to be a fine, powerful instrument. Carol had played chamber music at the 92nd Street Y in New York, accompanied a violinist and a singer, and had a good technique. We enjoyed playing duets, but tendinitis from hours at the computer and the rough work of gardening and horse care brought an end to her playing. After that the piano was all mine. I read through Chopin Nocturnes one month, Mazurkas the next, and worked my way through the Beethoven Bagatelles. I went back to the Scriabin Preludes I had explored in New York. I worked on Brahms Intermezzos, and children's pieces by Bartok, and kept coming back to the Mozart and Haydn sonatas, finding new favorites.

Accompanying baritone David Rubens, a knowledgeable musician, gave me a chance to engage with the greatest song cycles, Beethoven's *An die ferne Geliebte*, Schubert's *Die schöne Müllerin* and *Winterreise*, Schumann's *Dichterliebe*, Vaughan Williams's *Songs of a Wayfarer*, all new to me. The big virtuoso repertoire was beyond me, but this music was mostly within my reach. I adored playing tenderly, softly slipping in behind the voice, letting the piano sing, invoking an infinite gentleness of sensibility; I had more difficulty rollicking. In the real world, one has to be practical, rational, focused on goals; playing music took me into a realm of pure feeling, pure pleasure, restoring my balance and keeping me sane.

My harpsichord came to rest in the small, dark dining room between the entrance hall and the big living room. I kept it tuned and played Bach, Scarlatti, Couperin, Rameau, magic portals to the eighteenth century. Often when we had people for dinner, I overcame my shyness and played a little afterward. Music added another dimension to an evening, something to remember, a welcome break from having to talk. Few people you know play anymore.

Carol liked to lie on the floor and listen to operas. I had a large collection of Bach Cantatas and played them on Sunday mornings while I made pancakes—my nod to church-going. Music in the air helped me to write. Reasoning with words is a left-brain activity; music activates the other half. I try to keep both sides going. In my cabin at Charlemont I had practiced a simple exercise that lets you directly experience the two halves of the brain. Look at a candle burning in the dark; cross your eyes slightly and you will see two flames; without moving your eyes, move your attention back and forth from one flame to the other; as you do, you will feel the shift in your brain, behind your eyes: this I think is what Sam meant when he told me that attention is "material." You can move it at will.

ALFRED HAD FOLLOWED the Grateful Dead all over the country as part of a traveling kitchen, giving away food at music festivals. Eventually he landed back in New Mexico, holing up with Michele and Joy to recover. The loss of Cengiz weighed on him, and he was exhausted. After a couple of months, he moved to Santa Fe on his own, and once our

Alfred in Santa Fe

house was cleaned up from the onslaught of renovation, I went to see him. He had a job at the Wild Oats juice bar and a comfortable room a few blocks away.

I took him out for sushi, then spent the night with Michele and Joy in

San Juan, a village thirty miles east of Santa Fe, where they had bought an old adobe. Joy was practicing as a vet in Santa Fe. Their house was warm and welcoming, their hospitality a blessing. This was the way Michele and I might have lived if we had stuck it out in Taos. It was an ideal that still appealed to me: simple, close to the earth and the cycle of the seasons, quiet, with the possibility of long stretches of no distraction, nothing to do but read, think, write, be there. But life is never so simple; I am complicated and ambitious, hungry for the big world with all its temptations, in love with urbanity and performance—always looking for someone coming up the path to my hermitage.

No longer the lithe nymph who had first beguiled me or the insecure neurasthenic who had driven me nearly nuts, Michele was dear to me with her enthusiasm and loving spirit. Snuggling down in the guest room lined with books, handcrafts, art, and pictures of our children, I reflected on how long and hard I had tried to save our marriage. I was in every way better off with Carol, as Michele was with Joy, both of our partners strong, clear-headed, loving women.

The next day I drove up the canyon to Taos to help Julian celebrate his twenty-first birthday. He had spaced out Evergreen, dropping out in the

Julian, Taos man, 21

Michael Smith

spring of his freshman year to live rough in the forest. Probably feeling guilty, or at least embarrassed, he had largely quit communicating with me, and I was worried about him. I found him scruffy but full of energy and wide-ranging ideas, with friends and connections all over town.

9

Bob Potter, a theatre professor at UCSB, invited me to contribute to an evening of ten-minute plays by Santa Barbara writers that he was producing at Center Stage Theater. Delving in my journals to research my memoir, I stumbled on a short play, written to be done at the Changing Scene just before Michele's and my wedding, about a young couple hosting their first dinner party. *The Dinner Show* was slight and too weird for the occasion so I wrote *A Wedding Party* instead and had completely forgotten the other play, which had a wacky charm. Bob suggested having Maurice Lord, a student of his, direct it. I went to see Maurie's student production of Sam's play *Icarus's Mother* and thought he did a better job with the actors than I did at the Caffè Cino. A big, bouncy guy in his twenties, Maurie understood my intentions as no one ever had before. He cast *The Dinner Show* with talented kids he knew from school. Under the circumstances there was no way to realize the set I envisioned, but otherwise his production was wonderful. The play takes a turn into Ionescoish surrealism when the young bride transforms into Pocahontas and the dinner guests arrive carrying potted palms in front of their faces. A duo of groovy musicians stand in a corner and noodle along, then join the guests at the dinner table. Judith and Hanon happened to be in L.A. and came up to see it; I was glad to have friends from the real world see my tiny play, embedded though it was in a mostly amateurish evening, and frivolous as it was in relation to the Living Theatre's serious work.

Dan Wolf died, and I flew to New York for his memorial service at the Friends Meeting House. Ed Koch and many former colleagues were there. Afterwards I went to supper with David Gurin and several other veteran writers from *The Village Voice*, Jewish women buzzing with the self-awareness, irony, and intellectual energy I sorely missed in California.

I drove up to Charlemont for Jean-Claude's sixtieth birthday party. The day was classically gorgeous, pretty people dressed in white drifting around the meadow, everything perfect. I felt irrelevant, my heart elsewhere, few of this crowd dating to my time except Joe and Fred. At the end of the evening everybody gathered in the barn and took turns praising Jean-Claude. I retreated to my cabin, which seemed more forlorn than serene.

At Eaton's Ranch

WITH MY NEW HIP, I could ride a horse. I bought myself Levis and boots, Carol gave me a cowboy hat, I tied a bandana around my neck, and off we went. Carol was pleased with how well I sat a horse, although I really had no idea what I was doing. In June 1996 we spent a week at Eaton's Ranch in Wyoming, where I had honeymooned with Michele (and my parents) twelve years earlier. Eaton's is the only dude ranch that allows you to ride out on your own; at others you have to follow a cowboy in a long line of dudes. The first day a girl wrangler took us out, and after that we went by ourselves, riding every day. The rolling foothills of the Bighorns were green with young grass, vast unfenced stretches where we freely roamed. In the mountains above, at the top of steep, strenuous, rocky trails, was a gorgeous high country, flowering, unpeopled vistas of leas and peaks unfolding in every direction. The ranch offered an easy, unintrusive hospitality, and we kept to ourselves, making love in the afternoon, happily reading in our rockers on the porch as the sun went down.

Carol had terrible news: her youngest brother Paul had suddenly died in Florida, age forty-four, leaving his Guatemalan wife Elizabeth with three small children. Carol had been especially fond of Paul and felt the loss acutely. I comforted her as best I could. Her beloved sister Barbie, with whom she had ridden and played Mexican songs in her youth, had also died suddenly a few years earlier, which compounded the grief. Her father was devastated. My heart went out to them.

10

CAROL'S FATHER was facing his own mortality and looking to wind up his earthly affairs. He had begun giving away cash to members of his family, including $20,000 to me. (I bought stock in Santa Barbara Bank and Trust, which seemed like a solid investment; they subsequently overexpanded and went bust, and I lost it all.) He gave half a million dollars to the Santa Barbara Trust for Historic Preservation, to support the restoration of the Casa de la Guerra, and a substantial gift to UCSB, endowing fellowships and a chair in environmental sciences. Henry Yang, the chancellor, valued Charles's deep knowledge of the community, and UCSB thanked Charles with an event at the base of Storke Tower, a landmark given to the university by his father. Carol organized a family reunion for the occasion. T.M. had installed a carillon in the top of the tower. A carillonneur performed for us, and we were taken up a few at a time to see the console and bells.

The UCSB event was greatly enjoyed by all of us. Charles was gratified by the fuss and made a magnificent patriarch. His lungs were failing but his spirit was indomitable. He had a van modified so he could drive his electric wheelchair into it and keep going about.

The celebration of Carol's sixtieth birthday in September at Danby was appropriately festive. Afterwards we got off by ourselves for a day and night in my peaceful cabin an hour away. It was no use to me now: I might never come again. But I relished the timeless vibe and sharing it this once with Carol.

Carol on the porch of my woodshed, Labor Day 1996

MOTHER, NOW EIGHTY-SIX, spent virtually all her time in the recliner in her bedroom, smoking one cigarette after another, a favorite Rosamunde Pilcher novel open on her lap, drinking alone. Julie Bates, having attempted to rouse her from this alcoholic lethargy and failed, was broken-hearted and furious at her for letting herself go. When I stopped buying her gin and vodka, she had it delivered. I was keeping her checkbook and paying her bills, but I was reluctant to use the power of money to take away her autonomy. She periodically fell and hurt herself, and was in and out of the Medical Center. Gradually I became the only person she saw, apart from nurses who occasionally looked in on her and the people who delivered her meals. If I stayed away longer than two days, she got desperate, calling at all hours and begging me to visit. I urged the Casa Dorinda administration to move her to the Personal Care Unit, where there would be activity around her and staff to keep an eye on her. They kept putting it off.

In November Mother dropped a burning cigarette and set her chair on fire. A passing nurse saw the smoke, and a maintenance man helped pull her out. That was the end of living by herself. There was no room at the PCU so they moved her to the Medical Center for the time being. She hardly seemed to be aware of what had happened. In her abandoned apartment, the chair was gutted and everything stank of smoke; it was depressing, the life gone.

At the Medical Center, Mother did not seem to care that she could no longer drink and quickly adapted to going outside to smoke. In the spring she was moved to a pleasant room at the PCU, furnished with her own things. Bicky came from New York to help clear out her apartment. There was not much left from the houses we had grown up in. We took home a few things we wanted to keep and sold the rest. Mother had kept my baby book and a few photo albums. It was astonishing how little record my parents had left of their long and interesting lives.

CAROL AND I WERE GLAD to have her father and my mother at our house in Goleta for holidays, though these occasions could be touch and go as they aged. Old friends, they looked at each other with some dismay. In 1997 Julian and Alfred were both there for Christmas and helped make it festive. We put up a big tree in the expanded living room. We set out Carol's collection of small, carved wooden figures in a crowd on the back of the piano, and I displayed her Polish crêche figures in the greenhouse window beside the front door with twinkling lights.

We revived our annual New Year's Day open house, suspended the year before because of construction work, inviting our neighbors along with forty-odd other people we knew and liked. Carol and I often complained about the difficulty of making friends in Santa Barbara. We had repeatedly invited one or two other couples for dinner, but it never seemed to lead anywhere; sometimes we never heard from them again. People I wanted to be friends with related to me as the editor of *Santa Barbara Magazine*. Carol's horse friends only talked about horses, and just as well: most of them were right-wing nuts. As for intimate, personal friendships, she thought we had moved past that time in our lives, the intense connections made when we were young. This has some truth to it, but I had made good friends in Taos, Stonington, and New York, and would again later in Oregon. Maybe we did not want friends: we barely had enough time for each other.

We had, though, a growing aquaintanceship, and our party was lively and fun, starting in midafternoon in the garden, then moving inside as the chill of evening came on, clustering in the warm, glowing living room. A few lingering guests prevailed on me to play the harpsichord for them, which I was eager to do, having polished up a few Scarlatti sonatas just in case.

Julian stayed for a month, working at his old job to save up some money, then went back to Taos to start building himself a house on a quarter-acre he had bought way out on the mesa west of town. Alfred stayed, took classes at Santa Barbara City College, played drums with a band called Red Noiz 3, and got a job powder-coating outdoor furniture. When he felt ready, he rented himself a place downtown and left us to ourselves.

11

SURPRISE DEVELOPED A NERVE DISORDER and had to be put down. Her successor, Breezy, was spirited and athletic. Carol and I often went out on the trail together, with me on her mare Rhea. Rhea was a pill, though, grumpy and stubborn. I started to want my own horse. Carol's trainer friend Maggie Powell located some horses for us to look at in the desert, and we drove down in the truck with the trailer. We stayed with Maggie and her family at 1000 Palms, an oasis near Palm Springs that was now a nature preserve. Their cabin had been grandfathered in; we were the only ones there after dark. While the others sat around and smoked, Carol and I went for a walk in the moonlight, up the sandy arroyo to the majestic grove of palms, fallen giants lying where they had crashed to earth, and ponds of black water.

The next day we looked at horses. It was hard for me to read the situation: who was the owner of which horse, who the trainer, who had what interest

A horse of my own: Dancer

in selling them, accordingly how frank were they being about the horse's traits? Carol had been studying horsemanship with Pat Parelli, a legendary teacher who had developed new methods of working with the horse, asking for what you wanted it to do rather than forcefully bending it to your will. I liked watching her get into a pen with a horse to try out its personality and evaluate its condition. We were shown a couple of big, good-looking quarter horses and a smaller buckskin mare with one eye, which reared up and started to lunge at Carol when she waved the whip. Kids had mistreated her, apparently, and she was on guard.

We mounted up, me on one of the better-looking horses, and went for a ride into the sagebrush. I kept eyeing the buckskin and eventually asked to ride her. Dancer was her name, and she went right along, easy to steer; I liked her looks, chunky, with a short back and thick ankles. Carol kept having trouble with her horses going lame. Dancer looked strong, and I wanted a smaller horse so I'd be closer to the ground in case I fell off. She was also significantly cheaper than the others. So I bought her, and we took her home with us. Carol offered to pay her board, which would amount to much more. Whoever thought I would have my own horse?

ANNE SMITH, the Lobero board president, and Nancy Moore, the executive director, went to the Williamstown Playhouse in Massachusetts on a scouting trip. The director Peter Hunt had just been let go. Anne and Nancy came back with a proposal to hire Hunt and his partner, Bill Stewart, as artistic director and business manager of a new producing theatre company at the Lobero, to be called the Lobero Stage Company. I supported the idea because I wanted to see plays in the Lobero, although my own inclination would have been to do them ourselves. That was why the theatre was built in 1924: a bunch of artistically inclined rich people wanted a place to put on plays. Nowadays it was mostly a concert hall.

There were a number of doubters on the board. Anne hosted the crucial meeting at her very grand house above Mission Canyon, where her husband, Bob, owner of several television stations, and his ninety-year-old mother spoke up for the plan and pushed it through. The Smiths and another couple, Herb and Elaine Kendall, pledged $100,000 each, which carried the day. The Lobero Stage Company announced a season of four plays in spring 1997.

The folly of this plan was evident right away. Stewart's feasibility study projected an unrealistic number of subscribers. His budget was twice the size of the Lobero Theatre Foundation's; they set up a parallel administration, eluding Nancy's attempts at rational control. Hunt made all the artistic decisions, treating the board like a bunch of know-nothings; announced a season of plays of dubious interest and practicality; promised celebrity actors who never materialized; and cast and rehearsed the shows in L.A., alienating the Santa Barbara theatre community. I was vice president of the board, but money called the shots. We set a deadline for a minimum number of subscribers, which was not met. At a meeting at the Kendalls' I was prepared, indeed eager, to pull the plug; instead Herb and Bob came up with another $50,000 each, and the debacle went on.

Death Takes a Holiday was the first production. The set was striking, the lighting dramatic, the acting decent, but the play was dated and of little interest. Ticket sales lagged. Next on the schedule was Brecht's powerful *The Resistible Rise of Arturo Ui*; Hunt cancelled it as uncastable and too expensive, substituting a dramatic reading of *John Brown's Body*. It emerged that he had done both of these plays before.

We were getting deeper in the hole. At a crisis meeting of the Lobero's Executive Committee, Bob Smith took over, presenting a chart of the financial situation, arguing that we should cut our losses and close before the next production. I thought he was mistaken; the next show was Noel Coward's *Blithe Spirit*, with a popular young television actress in the lead, sure to be much more appealing to our audience. I thought Bob's numbers were wrong, that we might lose a little more but probably not, that it was worth taking the risk rather than lose face by canceling. I said, "Why are you here? You're not even on the board."

My position did not prevail. Word was sent to the rehearsal room in Thousand Oaks, where rehearsals had begun, and the actors disbanded. The next day Bob and the other big shots changed their minds and tried to restart the production, but it was too late. The star had accepted another offer. The scene shop no longer had time in their schedule. The Lobero Stage Company was dead.

It was a disaster for our reputation and finances. The Stage Company had preempted the theatre for four months, pushing our usual tenants elsewhere; there was no rent coming in, no way to fill the void. Hunt and Stewart had tried to jump-start a full-blown professional theatre from nothing, built up an office staff that was hard to sluff off, and burned through more than a million dollars. Bob and Herb had pressed their friends for contributions; donors felt ripped off, understandably, and turned their backs. Subscribers, initially stiffed, were furious.

We had not just failed, the way theatre is always likely to fail; we had copped out halfway through the first season. It was painful to me personally, every aspect of the enterprise contrary to my own sense of how to do theatre, which had never even had a hearing. I had let myself be intimidated by the rich people. It would take the Lobero several years to recover.

12

The 101 freeway, planted with palm trees and oleanders as it sweeps through Santa Barbara, can be stunningly beautiful. Driving toward Montecito to visit Mother, I was awestruck as I rounded the curve to face the mountains' majesty, the light intoxicating, the air exhilarating. I wanted to be out in it, not shut up in a rolling metal box. I had the idea of getting myself a motorcycle. Not knowing one motorcycle from another, I went to the Honda-Yamaha dealer in Goleta. They put me on a bike that wanted to leap out from under me. It was way more tippy than my Vespa!

I dropped in at Dyno-Cycle, a small, serious-looking storefront with intimidating Ducatis on display, and told the boss I was looking for my first motorcycle, something quiet to use around town. He said he had just the thing, a red BMW R650 that belonged to his girlfriend. He would bring it in for me in a couple of days. When I went back, he lent me a helmet and sent me off for a ride up a nearby canyon. I had only ridden a motorcycle twice in my life. It seemed smoother and better balanced than the Japanese bikes, and I loved the way it looked.

I had not mentioned this fantasy to Carol, who was startled when I did. I assured her I was not looking for thrills or danger, I would be careful, and she gave me her blessing, although she said she would never want to ride on it—and never did. So I got a learner's permit, bought the BMW, and brought it home. There was room for it in the garage in front of my Honda.

I was required to take a motorcycle safety course and glad of it. There are techniques for turning, stopping, staying out of danger, and I was glad to learn them, not a bit drawn to the risky aspects of motorcycle riding. Feeling shaky and alarmingly inept, I drove slowly at first, cars piling up behind me.

My motorcycle made driving to work fun, let me park free downtown, and surprised my friends. I improved with practice and rode it every day the weather was fair, which is practically every day in Santa Barbara—unless I was going to see Mother, who wanted to be taken for a ride and watched for my little red Honda.

Mother was doing better in the PCU, where the attendants grew fond of her and treated her well. My visits devolved into taking her out in my car so she could smoke. Only one store carried her cigarettes, Silva Thins; then they stopped, and it was a struggle to find a substitute. I calibrated her smoking at four cigarettes per ride; if there were more in the box, she tried to smoke them all before we went back, lighting two or three at a time and

puffing rapidly. I hated the smoking, but my visits meant the world to her. "You're the only one," she said, countless times; and, "I don't know what I would do without you." Packaged lines, no doubt, but how could I not be affected? She hated being taken back, sometimes almost cried, said she wanted to die. But she did not want a longer outing. As I was driving around scenic parts of Montecito to pass the time, she would think we were almost back and start asking, "When are you coming again?"

Carol hated the smell of cigarettes in my car. I bought a miniature vacuum so I could vacuum up the ashes.

Mother looked forward all year to Jerry Lowenthal's master classes every summer at the Music Academy. I parked her wheelchair up front on the aisle, and Jerry, who was very fond of her, stopped to give her a kiss on his way to the stage. She enjoyed the music but couldn't hear anything he said.

In August I went to Taos to see Julian, who invited me to stay with him out on the mesa near his building site. I flew to Albuquerque, rented a car, and met him in town. It had rained every day for a week, and it was raining as we drove west from Taos into the sunset; we stopped beside the highway and got out to look back at the rainbow. Beyond the gorge bridge, we turned off onto a dirt road heading west across the bare, open plain. The road was decent at first, then bumpy, then muddy. It was six more miles to our destination, much muddier ahead. Julian didn't think my rented Dodge would make it and suggested we leave it at his friend's junkyard and hitch the rest of the way; I was afraid it would be absorbed into the junk. A woman emerged from an RV, damaged as if she been beaten up, and said it would be okay.

It was nearly dark as we stood by the road in a drizzle and waited for a ride. A van came along, and Julian flagged it down. We sat in the back on a pile of tools and metal rods. The mud was deep and viscous. When the van slid off into the ditch, the driver just floored it and kept going.

Julian was staying in a once beautiful handbuilt house known as the Parthenon, where he had cleaned up a room for me and provided a comfortable bed. He cooked us dinner and played me a tape he had made of poetry and improvisations on a shakuhachi. Later a circle of kindred spirits gathered around a fire out front, got high, played music, sang, and danced under the vault of stars.

In the morning we walked over to Julian's house, half a mile down the road. He had the framework up for a single room with a peaked roof, vast views in all directions, the space around it exhilarating, opening up to distances you never see elsewhere. He planned to nail on scrap from the lumber mill inside and out, stuff the space between with newspapers, and mud over it on both sides. I helped him nail up a few boards on the back wall.

Back at the Parthenon, Julian proposed an acid trip, and I agreed to split a dose with him. We stayed around the house until the drug started coming on, then hiked up the small mountain that rose behind the little settlement, which was not as small as it looked. It was gorgeous up on the higher slopes,

MICHAEL SMITH

the vast view amplified, multicolored stones twinkling on the ground, tender moisture falling and sweetening the air.

On the way up we visited a woman friend of Julian's, a painter living alone in a big filthy mess of a one-room house. She was going into town to an art event and invited us to come; I was dubious but we said maybe. After enjoying the heights we rambled back down and encountered her again. If you were in costume you got in free so she put Julian in a knee-length dress. I was far from sure I wanted to go, but pretty soon we were in her four-wheel-drive Toyota churning down the muddy road. I urgently suggested we get out and go back to the house, but the momentum was too much for me. A kid from Minnesota had made a pot pipe out of mud, wet mud. I puffed on it hoping I would mellow out.

Julian and friend Ry Richards on the mesa

We arrived at sunset at a gallery near the flashing light a few miles north of Taos. I got as far as the door, saw a big room crammed full of people, twenty or thirty performance pieces on the program, music blaring, sharp lights, and couldn't face going in. Julian stayed with me. Now what? We were miles from anywhere without a vehicle. Darkness had fallen. We went back to the car and Julian changed back into his own clothes. There was a bar up the road, he said—we should get inside, have something to drink and eat. We walked along the side of the road, an occasional car passing out of the blackness. We sat in the bar; I drank a beer. Julian knew the waitress.

I was weirded out, panicky, my stuff unreachable on the mesa: my notebook worried me most. The place was a tennis resort, and I had my credit cards, so I rented us a room, thinking I would feel less awful if we could be alone. But no. I felt crazy, desperately isolated, lost in my miserable churning paranoia. Julian was loving and understanding, but nothing he could say or do was any help. I telephoned Carol; even her long-distance love could not relieve my distress. I had to suffer through it.

Eventually the drug wore off. In the morning I was more or less all right. We sat in the sun and watched people play tennis, ate breakfast, called a taxi, retrieved my rental car, drove up to Arroyo Hondo and soaked in the hot springs beside the Rio Grande. I headed for home without going back out to the mesa. Julian mailed me my suitcase.

I had never had a bad trip before. Maybe my liver couldn't handle it anymore. I told Hanon about it later; he said it was twenty years since he had taken acid. Julian and I agreed we had made a mistake going into town: the acid experience is conditioned by "set and setting," as Tim Leary theorized in the early sixties; we would have been all right if we had stayed on the mesa. I was badly shaken.

13

WHEN CAROL'S FATHER was not getting enough oxygen, he couldn't think straight. My mother was in a wheelchair and more and more remote. Being so closely involved with our parents' decline was a constant reminder of the indignities we had to look forward to. We were twenty-five years behind them, but being with Mother made me feel old, her noncommunication an agony; I wanted to be kind, but sometimes I could hardly stand it. I tried to visit her every other day, rushing over from the magazine, grabbing lunch in the car on the way, slowing myself down to her blanked-out adagio, then rushing back to work, or downtown to another desperate meeting at the Lobero. She had no one else.

So I was glad when Bicky decided to move to Santa Barbara, though sorry she was breaking up with Steve, difficult as he was. Ben had learned from an intercepted email that his father was having an affair with a graduate student and told his mother. She and Steve had been living in separate cities for years, what did she expect? Furious and hurt, Bicky arranged with her employer, a women's advocacy organization called Catalyst, to start a West Coast operation based in Santa Barbara, where she had grown up and always wanted to live. She arrived in November, rented a glamorous modern house high up in the foothills, and Ben came out at Christmas to help her settle in.

Mother and Bicky in our garden in Goleta

Bicky and Ben were having Christmas dinner with Mother, Alfred had gone to New Mexico to be with Michele, and Carol and I were happy to have a no-family Christmas for a change. She had a new horse, Chinita, Breezy having proved psychotic. On Christmas Day we rode Chinita and Dancer into the rugged Santa Monica Mountains and picnicked beside the trail. The wind came up and we were practically blown away. It was a memorable way to celebrate Christmas.

I SOUNDED OUT JERRY LOWENTHAL about doing another benefit recital, to help the Lobero recover from the Stage Company fiasco. I also asked his help in arranging a recital by Vassily Primakov, a brilliant teenage Russian pianist who had come from Moscow to study with him at the Music Academy the previous summer and made a tremendous impression on Santa Barbara music-lovers; he was now a student of Jerry's at Juilliard. Jerry was entirely helpful and everything went smoothly. I again found generous sponsors. Vassily's concert in March was a particularly brilliant success.

Joining the board of the Arts Fund, I became co-chair of the Individual Artist Awards, a program that channeled small sums of money directly to artists. In this role I emceed the annual benefit party. Robin Bisio, a choreographer and award winner, enlisted me to play music for a dance piece; I trucked my harpsichord over and played *Les Baricades Mystérieuses* as a young woman danced, brandishing branches. I

Emceeing the Individual Arts Awards, with Baroness Leni Fe Bland

also invited Jim Connolly, an exuberant bass player and composer, to perform with his irreverent ensemble, the Gove County Philharmonic, testing the limits of some of our more respectable supporters.

I REMARKED TO JULIAN that I loved my life in Santa Barbara, I was happy with Carol, I had decent work, I was saving money, everything was entirely satisfactory. All that was missing was that I was not doing theatre. He said, "What's stopping you?"

I kept imagining someone with a theatre would recognize me as a talented, capable playwright, director, and lighting designer and ask me to do something, but they didn't. If I wanted to do plays, clearly I would have to produce them myself. I had been learning how by putting on events at the Lobero and elsewhere. Making a budget is the key: the budget not only shows how much money you will have to spend but makes you think through everything that has to be dealt with. Nothing was stopping me. I was ready to produce a play.

I decided to put on *Trouble*, my fantasia on the Bess Myerson scandal, at Center Stage Theater in the Paseo Nuevo, a bustling downtown shopping mall, curious to see if my four vignettes would cohere into a play. Maurie Lord would direct. He loved my writing and was eager to work with me.

We had a terrible time casting the play. I wound up hiring three Equity actors, each of them costing more than $1,000. They were all three prima donnas, snotty to Maurie, hard to deal with, artistically frustrating, each of them impossible in a different way. Gloria Rossi had the big, brassy presence to play Tess Byerson but was distracted by thoughts of moving to Greece and refused to say the many "fucks" and other low epithets I had used to characterize her. (Myerson was known for her dirty mouth.) The Equity contract specifically required her to say the lines as written, but she did not want her daughter to hear her talk that way; I only got one "fuck" out of her. More distressingly, she neglected to fully master her lines; as a result her big monologue, which I thought was brilliant, never completely made sense.

Semi-famous Ben Bottoms would not consent to play Dickie, Tess's personal assistant, until I secretly agreed to do a story about him in *Santa Barbara Magazine*. Fortunately it was a good idea for a story. Then he refused to work with the costume designer, who wanted to take him to thrift shops, holding out for Saks Fifth Avenue, which had opened a tony branch nearby.

Maurie Lord and Ben Bottoms in the rooftop parking putside Center Stage Theater

I tried to stay out of this fracas, hoping Maurie would get it under control. On opening night, in a wacky protest, Ben came on in unmatched shoes and two neckties, his costume bizarrely inappropriate for the character. I had to give him $150 to go buy something more suitable that he was willing to wear. He refused to accept that Dickie was gay.

Laezar Schlomkowitz, doubling as Mayor Koch ("Big Boy") and, later, Tess's jailed lover, Randy, played his scenes so slowly that we had to put in an intermission. His refusal to wear a wig made it hard to realize that these were actually two different characters.

The supporting actors were fine, Maurie did his best directing, and the show was successful in its own weird way. The set design was misguided, but my lighting made it work. I loved the scene where Tess and Dickie were stuck in an elevator, trapped on the bare stage in a sharp square of bright light. The moment when Tess and Randy drifted out of his jail cell into a romantic neverland was theatre magic. The play didn't mean much, though,

MICHAEL SMITH

in Santa Barbara, where people barely knew Bess Myerson and Ed Koch and had never heard of the Bess Mess. It was a New York story

Not wanting to say I was producing *Trouble* myself, I made up a producing entity I called Genesis West. Although we did fairly well at the box office, I was out-of-pocket a little over $5,000. It was worth it. I was a producer! I had a theatre company! I could put on plays!

14

CAROL WAS DISTRESSED about Earl Warren Showgrounds, a state-owned complex of horse barns and show arenas that her father had helped establish. In the 1950s the Santa Barbara National Horse Show was a social event; I remembered going a few times with my parents and running into Carol and her family there. The showgrounds had been neglected for years. The current directors, political appointees with no great love of horses, were looking at redeveloping the site and building a hotel. If the showgrounds closed, that would be the end of horse shows in Santa Barbara.

With a few of her horse friends, Carol went into action, organizing the Friends to Restore Earl Warren Showgrounds, putting together an in-depth report on the situation, distributing Save Earl Warren bumper stickers, and using her column in the *Independent* to sound the alarm. Earl Warren had been a friend of her grandfather's when he was governor of California; I heard him speak at UCSB during the Vietnam War. When Gray Davis was elected governor, Carol saw the possibility of a more enlightened group of directors being appointed and put her own name forward. But Davis dragged his heels, leaving the Republican deadheads in place. When they carved out a piece of the horse show parking for a roller hockey rink, Carol and her friends sued. Over the next couple of years, what with writing her column, defending the Showgrounds, and struggling to put the Trust for Historic Preservation on a more businesslike basis, she was over her head in work and pressure.

Her father was much faded, not having entirely bounced back from a series of minor strokes, his breathing worse. I helped Carol move him into his study, close to the oxygen generator he depended on. Carol spent more time with him now, coming back from her visits drained and sad. His mind, always so sharp, was often foggy now, sometimes desperate.

When Lib called in the evening on December 6, 1998, we rushed right over. After dinner Charles had felt unwell, lay down on his bed, and died. He lay there now, dead, his bright spirit gone. Lib perched on a low chair in the middle of the room, stunned; I stood close beside her. We stayed as officials came, asked the necessary questions, and took his body away. I was glad to be there for Carol.

Family and admirers gathered for the obloquies, first a funeral at All Saint's Church, then a gathering in the More family plot on the crest of the hill in Santa Barbara Cemetery. Charles had been a presence and much loved, and a goodly circle gathered around his ashes. The cap he often wore, lettered AMO on the front, rested on the urn. Several people spoke movingly of how much he had meant to them, his specialness, his warmth and depth as a human being. I missed him too. He had been generous to me, buoyed me with his trust when I was at a low ebb, taken me into his family, given me his daughter. He was a gentle man, with an irreplaceable knowledge of Santa Barbara, a spirit not to be met again.

Already exhausted by her father's difficult final months, Carol was his executor, which would be virtually a full-time job for a year, with many difficulties to be overcome and a huge tax bill to be paid. In the end there would be about $4 million to be divided among his heirs. Investing her share would let Carol keep spending money on horses and feel reasonably sure of not running out.

CAROL AND I WENT RIDING TOGETHER OFTEN. At first she picked my horse's hooves, saddled for me, and did all the work, then taught me how to do it myself, which was pleasant enough. I would never care about horses the way Carol did, but I enjoyed being out on the trail with her, an interesting and relaxing way to be together. She trained our horses to go into the trailer without fuss, and there were no end of beautiful places to ride and picnic around Santa Barbara, cliffs above the ocean and ranches in the hills. Sometimes we went farther afield, occasionally on a group ride with a riding club.

Dancer was an excellent horse, touchy with the other mares but kind to me, calm and well-mannered on the trail. She was sometimes willful, though: at a certain point on one of our favorite trails, she invariably tried to turn left, back to the trailer, rather than right, down to the lagoon. I had a few riding lessons, saw the error in my dude-ranch tendency to let the horse decide which way to go, and gained enough technique to win the argument. But it always caught me by surprise.

In the course of writing her column and dealing with her horses' injuries, Carol encountered a range of innovative equine therapies, from chiropractic to crystals. Now she started applying these New Age ideas to herself. Every week Mujiba, a massage therapist and healer, dug deep into her muscles and her psyche, helping Carol work through pain to overcome her deep-seated anger at her long-dead mother and free herself from long-held tensions brought on by two muggings in New York. We both were Rolfed.

She took me with her to an animal communication workshop in Santa Ynez, where we gazed into the eyes of pictures of animals; mine was a toad, and indeed, with effort I could see right into its soul. It seemed preposterous to communicate with a particular animal by looking at a photograph of it, and expect to get communication back. But it certainly was possible to communicate with my horse: I understood Dancer's feelings and did not doubt that she understood mine, although she sometimes declined to pay attention. Cat had understood everything.

I tended to think of Carol as a rational, grounded person, myself as wild and intuitive, but these roles had curiously reversed, as they do in deep relationships. Now she was the far-out one, I the skeptic, struggling to stay open to where she was going.

My neck was so stiff I couldn't get comfortable in bed. My doctor said it was arthritis, age, I should get used to it: I would have to change doctors.

Carol sent me to her chiropractor, who applied methods that seemed like hocus-pocus, wiggling my feet as I lay on a table, testing my responses by pushing down my extended arm as I thought about my problem, e.g., stiff neck, touching me lightly on the temples and telling me, "Think *'field.'*" This was pleasant but did not have much immediate effect. Sleeping on my side or back relieved the pain. Still I could hardly turn my head. One day Dr. Brown tried something new: had me sit up, felt for the most tender vertebra in my neck, touched me lightly there and on the crown of my head, and when he told me to turn my head, it went right around, farther than it had turned in years. I felt some key relaxation occur: I had been stopping myself. From then on it was fine.

15

MAURIE AND I STARTED MEETING FOR COFFEE on Tuesday mornings at ten at the Café Siena on State Street, sitting on the open-air terrace out back so he could smoke. We talked about whatever was on our minds, vaguely thinking another project would eventually arise. I tended to get there ten minutes late; Maurie was always early.

One Tuesday he was bubbling with enthusiasm for Sam Shepard's play *Buried Child*, which he had just reread, saying he wanted to direct it more than any play in the world, that he could ace it. I had been puzzling over the question of how to bring plays to the Lobero in the wake of the Stage Company fiasco, feeling it should not be so very hard, so I said, without much forethought but aware of my boldness, "Let's do it at the Lobero." I had tried to read *Buried Child* in the late seventies, when it won the Pulitzer Prize, but found it depressing and put it down. I read it now and heartily agreed with Maurie that Sam's play was great.

So began the second production of Genesis West: first an impulse—then a detailed imagining—then it happens. The Lobero was a union house, and the budget penciled out at $30,000. The board, now hopelessly risk-averse, would not agree to back it; I would have to raise $20,000 to cover the probable loss, though I hoped the play would be a box office smash—I never learn. We projected six performances over two weekends in June, the first consecutive weekends the theatre had free.

In the next few months I raised nearly $23,000, and we went into production. Maurie liked me to be present at rehearsals, but I found it hard to sit still; if I was going to be there, I wanted to be directing. As producer, I had endless other things to keep track of—set design and construction, costumes, publicity, ticketing, paperwork, money—and wanted to keep living my life. Maurie was single and could put everything else on hold till after the play. I had other obligations.

Intimidated by the size and quality of the Lobero, I hired a professional to design the set. He promised to have it delivered to the stage door on the morning of load-in, ready to erect. In the event, he was in and out of town on other jobs, the set-builders he had in mind were otherwise engaged, and I wound up driving a rented truck to North Hollywood to pick up used tv flats for our fifteen-foot walls. The union stage crew at the Lobero would put them up. The designer thought he knew how to erect the set but didn't, which led to much costly muddling. He took over the lighting too, pushing me aside, to my regret. I would have done it better.

It was a good-looking production anyway. Maurie assembled a great cast and brought the play fiercely to life. Carol came to the first and last performances, encouraging and perceptive. The septuagenarian physician who played Dodge amazed me. In the third act he sat downstage on the floor, propped against a television set, and died while the audience's attention was elsewhere; I watched him do it.

Predictably, the box office fell far short of what I had hoped for, audiences peaking at around 200 of the 650 seats. The production lost more than $25,000, not counting months of exhausting unpaid work by Maurie and me, $3,000 of it out of my pocket, not too much to spend for a real good time.

Robert Biechel Jr., Rojan Disparte, Kinsey Packard. Michael Rathbone, Larry Williams, and Howie Lotker, actors in *Buried Child*

Doing the play had consumed my entire attention and energy for two or three months. I wasn't really there when I was doing a play, according to Carol, although I felt intensely present and alive, more myself than ever. Needing some concentrated time together after *Buried Child*, we took a ten-day trip to Portugal. After exploring Lisbon, we rented a car and drove up the coast to Coimbra, circling east into the mountains, south into cork oak ranching country. and back to Lisbon. I was reading Saramago's fanciful novel *Baltazar and Blimunda*, which followed our itinerary part of the way. Portugal is a scenically spectacular, fabulously interesting country.

Michael Smith

Carol liked it as much as I did, and we had a very good time, stumbling on many amazing sights.

B OB SMITH, the tv mogul I had tangled with over the Lobero Stage Company, called me at *Santa Barbara Magazine* to ask if the magazine might be for sale. I gave him Dan Denton's number in Florida. Dan called the next day to say he was selling—just as I finally had the job under control. I could do much of the actual editing at home and had privately decided, for my mental health, that I would only go into the office four days a week, designating one day as "off" in my personal appointment book and not thinking about work.

The sale did not immediately threaten my job, and so what if it did? I was basically sick of it and already tempted to quit. Still, I liked the cash flow, which made the whole system work, letting me spend money without worrying about it, help the boys, pay my way in the household, and blow a few thousand dollars a year on theatrical productions. Living on my salary from the magazine, saving the trust income my father had left and my music-critic earnings from the *Independent*, I had put away almost $100,000 since moving to Santa Barbara seven years before. I wanted to keep the job for another year, if I could stand it, until my sixty-fifth birthday, when I would start collecting Social Security. Longer if they made it pleasant.

Dan flew out to close the deal and said goodbye. Bob Smith came up to meet the staff, bringing along his twenty-four-year-old daughter, Jennifer. Rich on the stupidity of television and full of himself, Bob talked the whole time, telling us what he had in mind, not interested in anyone else's thoughts. Jennifer would be running the magazine: he had bought it for her.

Jennifer loved magazines and had worked for *Buzz* in L.A. With the best intentions, I imagined myself mentoring her, perhaps taking her on as assistant editor for a few issues, then turning the job over to her. It turned out she already knew what she intended to do. She wanted the magazine to cover fashion, interior decoration, weddings, society. She wanted to expand it, dress it up, turn it into a cross between *Elle* and *Town and Country*. Her father was ready to spend whatever it cost. I had always known the magazine had potential as a bigger brand. But try as I might, I felt an ineradicable antipathy to their whole outlook.

Bicky's husband, Steve, pursued her to Santa Barbara and talked her into going back to Ithaca. They left in July, halfway through another Music Academy season. I was again Mother's sole comfort.

I gritted my teeth.

16

DANCER WAS GETTING OLD, not quite lame but weak in the hind end, and Carol worried about her safety on the trail. Dancer herself worried when she went down steep grades, afraid her legs would give out, that she would fall and hurt me. Carol said she had to go and found a woman who promised to take good care of her. So we gave Dancer away, hoping for the best for her. I was relieved not to have to go out every day after work and clean her stall. But I was sad to say goodbye to such a fine horse. I talked to her at length the last day, told her how much I appreciated her, shed a few tears. As I walked away she went back to her hay.

Carol's idea was that I should ride Chinita, her gleaming coppery quarterhorse, and she would ride Martha, a plain, reliable horse she had acquired after a hair-raising experience with Breezy. Chinita proved nervous and competitive and was too lightly built for me, her ankles too elegantly slim. Carol loved riding Chinita so we switched. Martha was uncommunicative but steady.

BOB POTTER asked me for a ten-minute play about Santa Barbara for another omnibus production by Dramatic Women. I had an idea for a play about myself and my father, springing from the early morning moment in 1953 when my seventeen-year-old avatar arrived at Dad's motel room door in Santa Barbara after driving all night across the desert; but I was too busy to settle down to it. Carol was going to New York in November to see her children, grandchildren, and best friend, Marcia Goffin; I would fly to Newark with her, then go my own way, visit old friends and Village haunts, and write my play in the city. I was curious to meet Johnny Dodd's son, Fleming Lentakis, who was living in New York.

I stayed at a budget hotel on 11th Street, next door to Sally Kempton's old apartment. The neighborhood looked the same. I visited Patti, still living in Johnny's apartment on Cornelia Street. Gary Zarr, my literary pal from Mayor's Office days, took me to Babbo for lunch. I hooked up with Carol, who was staying with Tensie in Brooklyn, for an enjoyable rehearsal by the New York Philharmonic and lunch at the Museum of Modern Art. Fleming came to the Village to meet me, friendly and curious about his father, whom he had barely known, and we walked to a coffee house on MacDougal Street. He was lively, attractive, likable, a character, a little younger than Julian. I had dinner with Serena Stewart, lunch with John Lucas at Florent, my favorite restaurant, tea and theatre talk

David Brainard and Kinsey Packard in
Fast Forward

with Bob Heide and Irene Fornés. And I wrote my play, sitting cross-legged on my bed in my little room.

Fast Forward zips through forty years of my life in a little less than fifteen minutes. The play is essentially a monologue: an actor representing me recounts each of my filial visits to Santa Barbara through the years, my parents making silent cameo appearances to illustrate the scenes, my sister

Bicky played by a doll. The play starts off charmingly grave but light, then darkens as my parents age, my young, vigorous father slowing, then dying, my clubbable mother ending up in a wheelchair, nibbling a chocolate mint, me behind her, in the present. Maurie directed it with three fine actors, and despite a crisis of confidence halfway through rehearsals, his realization of my little play could hardly have been better. It was unexpectedly touching; audiences liked it very much.

I VISITED MY FRIEND DAVID GURIN and his family in Toronto, and he took me to see a play by George F. Walker, a Canadian playwright, vividly directed by the author. It was one of six plays, collectively titled *Suburban Motel*, all set in the same motel room. They were outrageously funny but also shockingly real, the characters flaky but original and likable, the situations gritty and fantastic. Maurie liked them as much as I did. We decided to do two of these plays in repertory, Maurie directing *Criminal Genius* and me directing *Featuring Loretta*, which I found exquisitely funny and touching. I booked Center Stage Theater for three weeks in January 2000.

I had not directed a substantial play in years. I found a rehearsal space that was free, thankfully, but freezing cold. Nor was it altogether pleasant to rush out night after night after an early dinner, no time to relax after often grueling days at the magazine. But the act of directing was a joy; I was never more alive than in the rehearsal room. Maurie stayed up all night obsessively planning every move. I liked to come to rehearsals essentially blank and discover the staging with the actors. Then I got possessed with getting it just right. I jumped up on the stage, demonstrated my ideas, hovered over the actors, egging them on; or sat back and let them work it out for themselves.

I love actors and had a choice group. I pushed them to make *Featuring Loretta* as ridiculous as it wanted to be, and Maurie's production of *Criminal Genius* was fiendishly noir. The two plays were a hit, the reviews great, and word of mouth brought in audiences. Counting a few thousand dollars in contributions, the production broke even.

In the afterglow of this success Maurie and I decided, rashly, to do another, bigger George F. Walker play, *Escape from Happiness*, at the Lobero the following June.

Every year Dan Denton had given each of the staff of *Santa Barbara Magazine* a $100 gift certificate to Downey's, the best restaurant in town, a Christmas bonus that provided Carol and me with a special dinner on our anniversary. The Smiths gave me a Cartier ballpoint pen and no respect. Dan had kept after me with advice and suggestions, but the actual words were mine, my dignity intact; I could be proud of the magazine I edited for him. Jennifer brought me one dumb, vulgar idea after another. She wanted me to let her friends write for the magazine though they could barely write. She showed me departments in her favorite magazines, suggesting we copy them—glitzy snippets of shopping advice instead of stories. She forced me to run wedding pictures and lined up a fashion spread on her own. She paid no attention to my opinions.

Above, Kinsey Packard and ClaireMarie Mallory; below, Jay Carlander and Ted Harmand in *Featuring Loretta*

I tried to level with her. At a private meeting in my office, my frankness was met, to my surprise, by tears, hurt feelings, and a passion for the magazine that I had not suspected. An hour later Bob phoned to say that the magazine was his, he could do what he wanted with it, Jennifer's word was law.

A couple of weeks later she popped in with more "suggestions," and it was suddenly too much. They were determined to change our nice little magazine into something I was not going to like. It was a matter of taste, which is inarguable. There was no future in fighting them, I would lose every battle. More power to them. The good times for me, such as they were, were over. Not a bad ride.

Carol encouraged me to go ahead and quit, saying it was not worth the anguish. I called Jennifer, asked for a meeting with her and Bob, which was promptly arranged, and resigned. They said they were sorry, but I didn't believe them, although it would cost them much more to get someone else—several people, actually—to do what I had done.

Not far behind me, Kim Kavish quit with two weeks' notice. I hung in for six weeks and finished the big summer issue with a substitute art director, who was much easier to work with, doing whatever Jennifer said.

17

IN FEBRUARY UNCLE AL CALLED to tell me that Maxine had died. He was shattered, unable to hold back his sobs, the love of his life suddenly gone. Al and Max had been partners in life and art for more than sixty years. I was sad too. Maxine had loved me and been very good to me, and I had great esteem for her as an artist. She was a powerfully focused dancer and a deliciously witty choreographer who never won the recognition she deserved.

Aunt Ginny came from Connecticut, and my cousins John and Mary Lucas were in Santa Barbara that weekend for Mother's ninetieth birthday. Al flew out from Denver, grief-stricken, to be with his surviving sisters one more time. Mother never quite knew who he was, which made him even sadder, they had been so fond of each other all their lives. We took turns

John Lucas, Aunt Ginny, Uncle Al, Mother, and Alfred;
below, Mary Lucas with Mother at the piano

playing the piano. Al and Ginny could hardly play anymore, but Mother was herself again: "Moonlight on the Ganges" emerged from the mists of memory to amaze us all.

MARTHA WAS OKAY to ride but not much fun. I wanted another horse of my own. Checking out the horse country near Castaic, Carol and I dropped in on an old man who was closing down his business renting horses to movies and television, to see what he might have. He showed us an older horse named Sparky, who had been standing around in a paddock for a year. He was grayish and scrawny, his coat dull and patchy, his teeth messed up, stiff but willing when I rode him around the ring. I liked the look in his eye, and we took him home. I appreciated his background in show business.

Carol applied all her wiles to bringing Sparky back to health. Steve Goss, her vet, pulled out the teeth that were giving him trouble, leaving him enough to chew with but not to rest his tongue, which subsequently hung out. Carol found hay cubes he could eat, and he gradually recovered from years of neglect. At first he was weak. We avoided hills, then gradually rode farther. His coat came in shiny and

Sparky, my second horse.

black, he regained his strength, after a few months he looked great, and he was happy. Sparky turned out to be a dream horse and a complete pleasure for me.

Escape from Happiness would be the biggest production Genesis West had undertaken: three acts, nine actors, elaborate set, multiple costume changes. Maurie put together a dynamite cast, with several of our favorite actors from previous plays and some outstanding newcomers. I had much more difficulty raising money this time; I would have to pay for most of it myself, make the maximum marketing effort, and hope for the best. It was an appealing play, richly funny and heart-warming, but completely unknown.

I built the set with the designer, Kent Hodgetts, in the multicar garage of the historic mansion he and his wife were restoring. His design was ingenious, and we worked together well. Unfortunately the Hodgetts freaked out before the set was painted. Maurie had been rehearsing in their yet-to-be-restored music room, and Kent's wife decided the actors were too hard on the floor. He abruptly ordered me to take the set away. Too big to assemble inside his garage, it was standing outside in the driveway. I was afraid it would be rained on and ruined. I had to rent a truck and enlist Alfred to help me move it in pieces to the theatre a few days early. Kent disappeared, leaving us a color rendering; Maurie and I went to Home Improvement, matched the colors as best we could, and the Lobero crew painted the set. The colors turned out brighter than he probably intended, vivid pink walls with green, yellow, and blue trim. I loved the effect. The play revolved around an eccentric woman who might well have painted her house in crazy colors like these.

I did the lights, Mary Gibson, the brilliant staff designer at Santa Barbara City College, did the costumes, Kent's set looked terrific, the play was funny and outrageous (if overlong), and the performances were phenomenal. Sadly, far too few people came to see it, an average of fifty a night in a sea of empty seats. I had done all possible publicity: snazzy posters all over town, postcards, radio interviews, a big story in the *News-Press*. Maurie and I stood out front every night expecting the audience to build. I lost $13,000. I had to liquidate one of my mutual funds.

We had learned our lesson. You can't do a play in a theatre as big as the Lobero without big names. The kind of theatre we were interested in doing belonged in a smaller space. We would go back to Center Stage.

David Brainard, Don Stewart, Steven Gonzales, ClaireMarie Mallory, Joel Keeler, and Necar Mohsenzadegan in *Escape from Happiness*

18

I HAD BEEN KNOCKING MYSELF OUT producing so Maurie could direct other people's plays. The next one would be mine; that was the whole point of Genesis West. I wanted to do *Heavy Pockets*, my comedy about three couples putting on plays in Taos, but Maurie didn't get it and didn't like it. I organized a reading at the Lobero rehearsal hall, hoping to convince him. The actors called the play a romp, but Maurie was still not interested. I couldn't direct it myself because I couldn't figure out how to make it work: it called for three different sets. I would have to write a new, more practical play in time for our fall dates.

In the midst of reviewing the Music Academy season—I was still the music critic of the *Independent*—my mind was too cluttered to be able to settle down to writing. I took Mother to a couple of Jerry Lowentthal's master classes, but she was not up to it anymore. I decided to give myself a break, hole up in Taos, visit Julian, and write my play there. I was itching to write, a play ready to be born.

MICHAEL SMITH

I kissed Carol goodbye and drove to Taos. Julian found a room for me with the well-known poet Judson Crews, who lived in a modest house in Talpa, a nearby Spanish village. Judson's daughter had fixed up a neat little room that suited me fine. Now in his eighties, the poet could barely walk and spent his days and nights in his recliner. He could no longer write but could still read and seemed at peace, glad of a little conversation now and again. I closed my door and worked.

I went out for breakfast, came back and wrote, went out to lunch, stopped in at the library for email or walked around, came back and wrote, went out to dinner. Julian was living in his house on the mesa, busy with his own life. I loved being in Taos again, savoring the space, light, air, dust, easy tempo, low-key culture, vibes from the sacred mountain. I was happy without pot. I read *A History of Warfare*, the *New York Review*, the *Nation*, and found myself uncharacteristically politicized, though I could not bear to read about the interminable campaign between good Gore and bad Bush. I wrote about a woman who had been a radical activist in the sixties, gone underground, changing her identity, married, had a son—then was so upset by the Gulf War photos of burning oil fields and the Highway of Death that she could not keep silent any longer, and was arrested for earlier crimes. (Something like this had happened to several real women, but I did not research their stories, just made it up.) I was interested in the effect on her family of learning that she was a different person than they thought.

I loved writing this play, and it went right along. I let myself be direct. For too long I had thought subtlety was all-important, obscurity a marker of profundity, and avoided the obvious at all costs. No more. Writing for Koch had taught me the value of saying the obvious. I went straight at the emotions: the characters said what they thought and felt. My heroine talked straight about politics. Improbably acquitted, she ran for president and articulated issues I had been thinking about in silence: the grotesque inequalities in our deformed democracy, the monstrous evil of nuclear weapons and other armaments, corporate media power corrupting politics and destroying discourse, the ideology of greed eating away our beautiful potential. In a week the play was finished. It was just over an hour long, my favorite length, with four characters, several scenes, a tidy structure. I called it *Dogs Bark All Night*. There were no dogs in the play, but they barked at night in Talpa. The title sounded good and had the right feel.

Julian and I went to Denver to have some time together and visit Uncle Al, stopping for a night at a hot springs in southern Colorado. Theo took us for a hike in Boulder Canyon and a swim in the creek. Jim and Prudence Scarritt included us in a lavish family dinner outing. Al was living alone in the pleasant apartment he had shared with Maxine after they closed The Changing Scene. He'd had a small stroke but was doing well.

With Theo in Boulder Creek

Sid and Lisa were in Santa Barbara with their laughing baby when I got home, Sid working on the phone and at Carol's computer, Lisa shopping and showing off her baby. Carol was delighted with her new granddaughter. I reviewed the Music Academy opera and the last several concerts, enjoying them more because I had missed a few.

Phil Brandes was too distracted by assignments in L.A. to cover Santa Barbara theatre. Tom Jacobs, the arts writer at the *News-Press*, asked me to start reviewing plays for them. I held Tom in high regard, but I was reluctant to review theatre in Santa Barbara, where big-world standards might not apply and a gentler touch was called for. Classical concerts are always good, plays often not. Musicians can always play their instruments, often dazzlingly well; actors may or may not be able to act, may or may not say the lines the author wrote, as I knew too well. But I was flattered to be asked and could ill afford to turn down honest work; I love theatre and wanted to talk it up to the community. I hoped to keep reviewing classical music for the *Independent* as well so Carol and I could keep going to concerts. I would write for both papers, have my cake and eat it too.

Maurie loved *Dogs Bark All Night*. We had also been delving into Irene Fornés's plays. He enthused about *Mud*, and I wanted to direct Irene's beautiful, haunting play *The Danube*. A season brochure took Genesis West a step closer to being a real theatre company. We announced *Dogs Bark All Night* in the fall and a repertory of *Mud* and *The Danube* in March at Center Stage

Lisa and Genevieve

Theater. Irene was a magnificent writer whose plays were not known in Santa Barbara; this was just what Genesis West should be doing. We put together pictures from our previous productions, bios of Maurie and me, a note about the company, blurbs I dashed off about the upcoming plays, and printed and mailed out 1,500 of them—to no effect, so far as I know.

We were lucky to have Laurel Lyle, a very strong actor, to play Janice, the lead in *Dogs Bark All Night*. Laurel connected personally with the political content as well as the family dynamics; she was perfect in the part. The other actors were excellent, and Maurie did his usual meticulous directing. The production was hard work, and cost too much, but everything came out pretty much as I had imagined it, crisply defined on a bare stage in my careful lights, with projections on the backdrop. The run of the play coincided with

David Brainard, Laurel Lyle, Steven Gonzales, and ClaireMarie Mallory
in *Dogs Bark All Night*

the undecided weeks after the Bush-Gore election of 2000—my optimistic idealism was still barely tenable. A number of audience members thanked me for bringing social-political content into the theatre and praised the play's style and fine writing. Not all of my friends bought tickets, many theatre people had to be comped, and a few appreciative theatre-lovers showed up, but there was no way to break through to a general audience. Most people never go to plays, and a surprising number of supposedly devoted theatre-goers in Santa Barbara had never been to Center Stage Theater, which was beneath the notice of the upper crust.

Julian came for a visit in high spirits, fired up about digital video, wanting to make movies. I shared his enthusiasm and was eager to help. How could we use this wonderful new technology to offset the fugitive nature of theatre? Julian orchestrated a memorable father-and-sons day with me and Alfred, including a ping-pong tournament, a walk on a deserted beach, and a spontaneous swim in the ocean, always a thrill. By the end of his stay, coming down from the play, I felt I was falling apart, probably by association with Mother, two of whose front teeth had fallen out. I held my own at ping-pong; otherwise I was not quite up to Julian's strenuous pace.

Putting both sons on the train to New Mexico, I turned my attention to the pitiful box office settlement for *Dogs Bark All Night*. Fewer than 400 people saw the nine performances, 100 of them for free. We went $1,500 over budget; I lost $6,400 after contributions. Without my magazine salary, I could not go on losing money on show after show. Or could I? Carol spent a lot of money on her horses. If theatre was the equivalent in my life, why should I not spend my money on it?

The only way I could eaarn money was by writing. Still reviewing concerts for *The Independent*, I began reviewing dance as well as theatre for the *News-Press*, and also writing interviews and arts features. I talked the new editor of *Santa Barbara Magazine* into letting me write a story about the Chumash Revolt of 1824, a sorry tale.

Carol recovered from a cold in time for Christmas, and we rode Chinita and Sparky up into the hills of Rancho San Julián, leaving all our cares behind. It was a fine, clear day. Picnicking high on a ridge, we could see down into the Santa Ynez Valley on one side, over the rugged coastal mountains to the offshore islands on the other. Then we wandered, pointing our horses down new trails in a landscape that was virtually unchanged since before the Europeans arrived, not wanting the day to end.

IN FEBRUARY MOTHER'S HIP gave way and she fell. In the hospital she looked terribly wan and frail. I gave the go-ahead for blood transfusions, and the next day she was rosy and robust, though flat on her back. She demanded that I take her out to smoke. "You can do it," she insisted, "just do it." One nurse, a smoker, thought I could roll her bed outside, but wiser voices prevailed. Once she was sitting up, I did take her out; but she wanted to go right back in.

Back in her room at the Casa Dorinda, her hip repaired, she lay still with her hands under the covers, not up to the effort it would take to regain her strength. It was hard not to be able to do anything but sit with her. She said, "You're my best friend, I love you."

After that she was in a wheelchair and needed more attention than the Personal Care Unit was set up to provide. One day it was arranged that I would take her out for a ride, then bring her back to her new room on the second floor of the Casa Dorinda's big new Medical Center. We tried to explain it to her, but she didn't want to hear, and when the time came, she was extremely distressed. "Take me home," she pleaded as I inexorably rolled her into the new building. "This is your new home," I said. In fact it was a small hospital-like room, and she knew it was the end of the road. I felt terrible, but it could not be helped. I left her there in the care of the nurses, knowing they would be kind.

19

THE DOUBLE BILL OF *Mud* and *The Danube* was my favorite of all the shows I did with Maurie (not to diminish the others). He directed *Mud*, a stark tragic triangle set in a rude cabin in Appalachia, the set built from the weathered wood of our old fence that Julian had replaced with sticks from New Mexico. I directed *The Danube*, a complicated, subtle, profound play set in Budapest just before World War II. The two long Fornés one-acts would play for three weeks in repertory, with separate tickets.

Once rehearsals began, I was so busy I could hardly think, much less ride with Carol or write anything besides reviews. I gave *The Danube* a richly detailed production. A fine Mexican artist made woodcuts to be rear-projected as the backdrops of the various scenes. A young Polish cellist wrote and recorded a haunting musical score, with me on harpsichord. (We played it live on opening night.) Dolls resembling the actors were made for the puppetry scenes. I had a brilliant cast, a diligent stage manager, Mary Gibson did the costumes, and Center Stage Theater's crack techie, Brad

George Backman, Erica Kylander-Clark, Drew Murphy, and Ken Gilbert in *The Danube*

Spaulding, supported me in lighting the play exquisitely.

The opening gala was a grand success. Tickets for both plays plus dinner were $50, and we sold enough to pay for the party. I wanted a full house for the opening so I invited several people who would not have come otherwise. Our theatrical peers were all there, warmly praising our work and Irene's beautiful plays.

Maurie's production of *Mud* was intense—he won an Indie for his direction. *The Danube* was the best work I had ever done. After the opening, though, audiences were uneven. And I was worn out. Producing and directing was too much. I had rented the theatre, signed the Equity contracts, paid the royalties. I had never worked so hard in my life. The day after we closed, trucking back the platforms, I could hardly walk. I lost $7,000 on it.

DAVID RUBENS AND I had been polishing up Schumann's song cycle *Dichterliebe* and wanted to share its exquisite beauty, so we did a performance for Mother and the other residents of the Casa Dorinda Medical Center. The nurses set up the audience with Mother in the front row and thirty or forty other old people, mostly women, most of them in wheelchairs. I could see Mother as I played, looking distracted and disconsolate. It was too late. Afterwards we were asked to go around and speak to each person individually. Several of them were gracious and appreciative. Mother seemed not to know what it was all about, barely recognizing me in this context.

Concentrated writing was impossible, my time and mind squeezed by distractions. Carol and I had been talking about cleaning out the garage for two years. Now we were hatching plans to remodel the kitchen. I decided to stop complaining about not having time to write and do something about it. Paul McNulty, my piano-builder friend from Stonington, had moved to a village in the Czech Republic and invited me to come stay with him. He worked all the time at his demanding craft. There would be nothing to do but write. I decided to go for two months.

Carol let me go lightly. After months of training, she was beginning to show her new horse, Annie. She was curating an exhibition at the Casa De la Guerra. She was going horse-camping and then back east to visit her children and would not be home half the time anyway.

Paul's house on the square in Divisov, a village fifty kilometers southeast of Prague in central Bohemia, was built sometime after 1721, when the whole center of the village burned. Out back the former barn was a large workshop where Paul and two Czech assistants had three pianos under construction. I had brought music, expecting to play a lot; there were half a dozen historic pianos in pieces but not a one was playable.

Michiko Uchida, the pianist, had lent Paul the money to buy the house; when it was paid off he would fix it up. There was hardly any furniture. I slept and worked in a big corner room on the second floor looking out on the square. We ate at a simple restaurant across the way, or one of us cooked something. Everything was cheap. Paul brought me CDs from his collection to listen to on my Walkman. I explored the area on a bicycle. The village was quiet. I forgot all about the outside world. No one but Paul spoke English. We went into Prague once or twice briefly, went to Vienna for a weekend to look at antique pianos. Later his children came to visit from Amsterdam, and he lent me his car for a day-long outing to southern Bohemia and a visit to a local castle. I relaxed in the deep bathtub beside the window reading big books by Winston Churchill.

I finished a draft of more than half of this book in the Czech Republic, working on it for many hours every day, bringing the story of my life up to the present, until there was nothing more to tell. Paul was good company and a generous host. I loved being in Europe

Paul McNulty with his children

and in his village, but two months was too long to be away from Carol. The last week or ten days I was impatient to get home, and it took me some time to win her attention back

CAROL WAS ENJOYING a flurry of success in the equestrian world, linked into a network of fellow horse-lovers through her column in the *Independent*, leading the effort to save Earl Warren Showgrounds, and winning events on the paint show circuit. Her historical exhibition of bits and spurs at the Casa De la Guerra was a brilliant specialized success. I helped her put together an illustrated chapbook of her findings.

I bowed out of the *Independent* and solidified my position as music and dance critic of the *News-Press*, Phil Brandes having returned and reclaimed the theatre beat. Reviewing concerts gave me considerable satisfaction, not just the pleasure of delicious performances, but renewed confidence and joy in the writing. Procrastination and self-torture were left behind. When the moment came, I went into my study, shut the door, smoked a little pot if I had any, and wrote my review. Carol proofread it before I emailed it in. I could knock out a nicely structured, quietly sparkling piece in as little as an hour. Words could never convey the full flavor of the musical artistry I so admired and enjoyed, but it was uplifting to try. Writing is weird mild agony as the mind floats around attempting to find words for the wisps of thought that tickle at the edge of consciousness, then shape them into something intelligible and fun to read. It feels good when you get it right.

Carol loves opera especially. For our own pleasure we went to the opera together in Los Angeles, San Francisco, and Long Beach, our favorite, where a bold, imaginative impresario staged excitingly experimental productions of neglected gems. We enjoyed it mightily, always glad we made the effort. In summer 2001 we spent a week in Seattle seeing the *Ring* cycle, immersing ourselves in the story, tired of sitting by the end but deeply fulfilled.

Our love life was fine and satisfying, with ups and downs, I suppose, or ebbs and flows, but steady and strong. I had no interest in being gay anymore, so you could hardly call me bisexual, but in the interest of frankness I should also write about my solosexual exploits. Readers who don't want to know should feel free to skip ahead, if you haven't already. The fact is, I spent a lot of time on it over many years. Once internet porn came along, I couldn't get enough of it, pursuing advanced studies of the human penis in arousal and ejaculation, leading to or accompanied by my own self-pleasuring. Then the consumer video camera came along. Carol permanently borrowed one from her father to help with horse dealings; I later upgraded to digital. It was an irresistible if somewhat unaccountable pleasure to shoot video of myself masturbating. If you don't already know, this is something a great many, perhaps all men like to do, especially now that they have cameras in their phones. Countless young men post their wank videos on the internet, which I never did or wanted to do: you won't find any naked pictures of me out there. The internet offers an endless supply of such videos waiting to be watched, which is lucky for me: I much prefer them to scenes of men treating women as objects. I rarely or never did any of this when Carol was at home, but she was often away for days at a time for horse shows or trail rides. The house was all mine. I had only myself to entertain.

I took a train to New Mexico to visit Julian and flew home the day before the attack on the World Trade Center. Oralia, our Mexican cleaning woman, saw the planes crash into the towers on tv and came to tell us, "We are at war." I was not surprised that my country's heavy-handed interference in other countries' affairs had finally provoked vengeance—but had no idea it would lead to such profound, disheartening changes in the coming years.

I usually found Mother in bed nowadays, often asleep, looking soft and peaceful. If it was lunchtime, I took her into the dining room and fed her, bite by bite. She was beyond words and having difficulty swallowing. By late October she was fading away. I met with the doctor to discuss what to do. She could be rehydrated temporarily, he said, and fed through tubes, but there was no evident pleasure left to her in life, and it seemed kinder to let her go. The doctor prescribed morphine, and for several days she was in limbo, often dozing. Sometimes she was awake and seemed to hallucinate, straining and reaching her arms upward in desperation. I tried to calm and comfort her, but she was far away now, except for one extraordinary moment deep in this final agony when she snapped into focus as I leaned over her, looked me in the eye, reached up, and strongly pulled me down, kissing me full on the mouth, a final blast of love. Then she was gone again.

At an early hour on the last day of the month—Alfred's 23rd birthday, as it happened—the nurses called to inform me that Mother had died in the night. By then Bicky had come out from Ithaca. The two of us drove over in the pre-dawn dark, sat with her body, said our farewells more in our hearts than in words, then, in the spirit of Mother's own cheerfulness, went for breakfast down by the beach at sunrise.

Bicky and I organized a memorial gathering a few days later at the Casa Dorinda. Countless people had loved and admired Dot for her many wonderful qualities through the years. Bicky talked about Mother's hard work for good causes and her support of younger women. I talked about how much fun she was, her love of music and talent for friendship, her generosity and energy and buoyant spirit and sense of play. I wanted us to remember all that rather than the sad decline of her last few years. I was happy I had been there for her, relieved that it was over.

20

WITH MONEY COMING from Mother's estate and the wrap-up of Dad's, I figured I could do another show. Maurie wanted to take a break from theatre so I was on my own and could do what I liked. I had written *Turnip Family Secrets*, a musical fairytale, in the attic in Westerly when my children were little, my family in ongoing crisis, and I had always wanted to get it on. Joe Woodard, my jazz/new music colleague from the *Independent*, took on the challenge of writing music for my lyrics. It was too good to be true when he brought along his cool, far-out band, Headless Household, to play in the "pit," plus the soulful trumpeter Nate Birkey. Inspired by the placement of the orchestra for *The Threepenny Opera* in East Berlin, I would raise them up on a platform at the rear of the stage, looking down on the actors from behind.

The set was a special challenge. *Turnip Family Secrets* centers on a turnip that grows to gigantic size before our eyes. The garden-loving family hollow it out and move in. One magical night, when the little boy goes out for a walk, a giant picks the turnip and carries it away with the parents inside. The turnip fairy appears to comfort the abandoned child. Human years later a giant knife cuts the turnip in half with the family inside, and the fairy magically transports them to Venice. Julian came from Taos and pitched in as production manager, building the giant knife, which came down with a thump that made the audience jump, and we realized most of what I had imagined.

Producing was as much as I could handle so I enlisted the director of a youth theatre group to direct. She was used to things being more conventional, but she had some chops and came through with beautiful stagings of the songs. At times I had to insist on my original vision, however peculiar, and it worked out well. We had a glorious cast: a ten-year-old boy with a beautiful voice as both the fairy and the giant, a talented young man as the little boy, and a skilled, ebullient song-and-dance duo as his parents. Joe Woodard's music was expert and distinctive, the musicians masters.

While *Turnip Family Secrets* was in the planning, I was pleased to be asked to design the lighting for *Kiss of the Spider Woman* (the play, not the musical), directed at Center Stage by a smart, hip guy from New York who hypnotized his actors into giving a truthful, obsessive, excruciatingly slow performance of the two characters. With Brad's help I hung stage lights in mid-air unusually close to the actors to express the closeness of the cell. I played the sex scene ultra-dim, at the bare edge of visibility.

That season I also had the opportunity to direct a smart, creative actor, Robert Lesser, in *Krapp's Last Tape*, my second staging of Beckett's beautiful, tender comedy. A mutual friend, D. J. Palladino, had asked Bobby to do the play for his fiftieth birthday party at Center Stage Theater, and the two of them asked me to direct. Bobby and I created a meticulously

Geren Piltz, Fred Lehto, and Paula Re in *Turnip Family Secrets*

detailed production, delving deep into Beckett, with great shared pleasure. Old Krapp celebrates his birthday by moving back and forth through time, playing snatches of tape recordings from earlier birthdays, musing on love and loss. To get the sound cues just right, I ran a second tape recorder hidden in the wings, matching Krapp's operation of the dummy machine on stage, so I had the pleasure of performing without being seen. The show was a gem. (I lit it with two lights.) We revived it in the spring as part of the Lit Moon International Theatre Festival.

Maurie invited me to Hollywood to light his production of *Happiness* by George H. Walker at Sacred Fools. I stayed with my old friend Deborah Lee Lawlor, who acted in the first play I directed in New York and now had a theatre of her own, the Fountain.

I loved practicing the art of lighting, but all this activity was strenuous. My remaining natural hip, the right, was sometimes so sore I could barely

Geoffrey Bell as the singing gondolier in the final scene of "Turnip Family Secrets"

walk even with a cane. Carol steered me to another unconventional chiropractor, and I started taking a deep-water aerobics class in the YMCA pool, which helped.

Robert Lesser in *Krapp's Last Tape*

WHEN SPARKY GOT TO BE as lame as I was, I gave up horseback riding. We gave him to 4-H Hearts, a therapeutic riding program for children with disabilities, where he served happily for several years. Much as I had loved the time on the trail with Carol, in truth I did not miss having a horse. I would be satisfied with our romantic strolls on Goleta Beach every month on the night of the full moon. The sandspit was constantly changing; we never knew what we would find. One March night, the water was unexpectedly warm so we stripped off our clothes and ran in.

I resigned from the Lobero Theatre board once we had stabilized the staff and finances and finished a major technical upgrade. The programming philosophy had to be more populist, we could not take any more chances of losing money, and I was not so interested anymore. Before I left, overriding the theatre's ban on rock music, I helped launch a singer-songwriters series called Sings Like Hell that brought in a new audience and thrived. I slid over to the board of Center Stage Theater, where I belonged.

I itched to go abroad again. Carol wasn't interested in going anywhere except east to visit her children. She was busy with her horses, working with a new trainer, plugged into the paint circuit, winning, racking up points, heading for a championship. In August 2002, I left her to it and went to Britain by myself, scoring a bargain first-class seat on Virgin Air from Los Angeles to London and back, which made the journey almost pleasant. I put up at a bed and breakfast in Chelsea and walked around the neighborhood soaking up the energy and richness of the city, now strikingly more diverse than I remembered. I went to a play every day, then went on to Edinburgh for the Fringe Festival, staying for a week in Glasgow, an hour's train ride distant, with Steve Bottoms, a theatre scholar at Glasgow University. Steve had tracked me down and mined my knowledge and views for his excellent book on Off-Off-Broadway, *Playing Underground*, which thankfully relieved me of the need to write one. Steve and his wife, Paula Rabbit, welcomed me into their comfortable life as I sampled the overwhelming variety of theatre on offer in Edinburgh, wishing I was doing it instead of watching it. Bobby and I could have brought *Krapp*.

MUCH AS I LIKED IT, my little red Honda lacked airbags and cruise control, so I bought myself a new car for the first time ever, a silver VW GTI, like the ones that kept passing us on the highways of Europe. I was at loose ends in Santa Barbara, not up to doing more plays, not sure what to do instead. In October I took off on a 4,000-mile road trip, first to Taos to see Julian, then on to Ottawa, Kansas, to revisit the scene of my early childhood, relishing the long drive across Kansas. Our house at Seventh and Cedar was not smaller but grander than I remembered, beautifully restored. I retraced the short walk to my first school, which I remembered clearly, arriving as the three o'clock bell rang and the children came out. I might have been one of them. The houses were the same, the sidewalks a little more cracked, the streets busier, most children driven away instead of walking home. Stalled in a time warp, Ottawa had sprawled into the fields, the interstate sucking its life out.

On the way back west I stopped in Denver to see Uncle Al, who had taken a fall and was in the hospital. I stayed with Nancy Mangus, a Changing Scene dancer who had acted for me long ago in *A Wedding Party*.

Remembered from childhood: 701 South Cedar Street, Ottawa, Kansas

She welcomed me into her comfortable house in one of Denver's many nice neighborhoods. Nancy was looking after Al's affairs, a thankless and heroic chore. I helped her move him to a rehab facility to recuperate. It was a miserable place, and I was sad to see him laid low. He was stoic and cheerful and would soon recover.

21

WHEN I GOT HOME I was taken aback to find Carol talking about leaving Santa Barbara. I had thought we were stuck there and was making the best of it. She had been thinking about it for a year, but she hadn't mentioned it to me. While I was away she had made up her mind. We couldn't afford to live in Santa Barbara, she said. The crux was the endless difficulty of finding places to stable her horses; now she was having to drive over the pass to Santa Ynez Valley. She wanted her own barn, and horse property anywhere near Santa Barbara was out of her range. This was her issue, not mine: I was doing pretty well there.

In truth, though, I was sick of Santa Barbara, and as soon as I got over the shock, I embraced the idea of moving. We would regret our exuberantly flowering garden and the lemon and orange trees and avocados, but it was a good time to move on. With our parents gone, Alfred on his own, and neither of us seriously employed, there was nothing holding us. Carol was nostalgic for a Santa Barbara that no longer existed. I was proud of Genesis West, but it seemed to be over. I had written for all the major publications in town. After churning out reviews for more than forty years, I longed to go to a play or concert and not have to be formulating verbiage and opinions. I was too old to start another job-job. Fortunately I didn't need to earn money. Having inherited $400,000, I could take $1,000 a month out of investment income without depleting my capital, which I hoped to preserve for my children. On top of social security, and thanks to Carol's outright ownership of our house, I had enough to live on and not worry. Amazing how that worked out!

I had rebooted my life a few times before by making large, more or less sudden moves. I was up for doing it again—another adventure into the unknown.

But where were we to go? Carol hadn't figured that out. I was drawn to the Middle West, where people are friendly. For that matter, the house in Ottawa was for sale. But the winters are too fierce on the plains and also in the Northeast, where Carol's children and grandchildren lived. She suffers when her hands get cold, and she wanted to be able to work with her horses year-round. Neither of us wanted to go back to New York. I suggested France, Italy, or Spain—I always yearned to live in Europe. Carol didn't want to go that far. Or it was too late.

We studied a map of the United States and identified three areas that seemed worth exploring, all new to both of us: the Willamette Valley in Oregon; the hill country around Austin, Texas; and the Great Smokey Mountains in South Carolina. We projected three trips over the next nine months to scope out the possibilities and vibes. It was Carol's call, ultimately. The house was hers, and she would buy the new one. I was along for the ride, happy to be with her. I can write anywhere.

We flew to Portland in January, when it would inevitably be raining, to see how we felt about Oregon at the worst time of year. We stayed in a hotel on the river, watched bicyclists ignore the drizzle, and walked around downtown. It was chilly but not seriously cold.

Renting a car, we set out to explore the towns in the Willamette Valley, famously fertile, well-watered farm land stretching a hundred miles south from Portland to Eugene between the Cascades and the Coast Range. Carol's cousin Ann Smith and family welcomed us to their comfortable house on sweetly isolated acreage near Canby, half horse pasture, half blueberries. Ann's husband, Steve, a fish biologist and hunter, showed me the head of his prize elk. They had two schoolboy sons and heated with wood.

Ann and Steve took us for a drive, Ann extolling the view of Mount Hood across the fields, although it was raining so hard you could barely see past the edge of the road. Steve drove us up the Molalla River into the foothills of the Cascades and south as far as Silverton, a small town with an old-fashioned main street and a movie theatre. The next day Carol and I continued south to try the flavors of Albany, Corvallis, and Eugene. We stayed for a couple of days with my old friends Laurel and Hinrich Müller in South Salem, where Louisa had grown up. I had lost touch with them when they moved to Oregon; I was surprised and pleased to find us together again. Laurel ran her graphic design business out of the basement. Hinrich was playing in a concert band. Louisa, who still didn't know I was her biological father, was at college in Wisconsin, studying to be an opera singer.

On an internet horse site, Carol had connected with Jerry Hinsvark, a real estate guy in Silverton, fifteen miles east of Salem. Jerry drove us around the area in his SUV, pointing out possibilities that ranged from abandoned mobile homes to an attractive modern house with outbuildings up in the hills, where thick fir and spruce forest opened up into wide rolling fields under dramatic skies. It was beautiful but too isolated. I wanted to live closer to town. Carol was concerned about pasture and infrastructure for the horses.

At the Silver Creek Coffee House on the main street of Silverton, a bookshelf held copies of *The American Scholar*. Finding something interesting to read made me think this was a place I could live. Carol felt the same. There was no need to go to Texas and South Carolina; with W. as president, it didn't seem right to move to Texas, and the South would be problematic for Carol's biracial grandchildren and our own values. Oregon was pleasantly laid back, less hectic than California. Silverton was well away from the I-5 corridor, beyond the suburbs and urban sprawl, spared the worst of American hubris and only an hour from downtown Portland. Jerry would see what he could find.

The idea was to wind up our affairs in Santa Barbara and move in six months or so, maybe in the summer. Carol's realtor advised her to go ahead and put the house on the market. Bush, Cheney, and Rumsfeld were preparing to invade Iraq, and the market had been dead for months after the first Gulf War. Buyers immediately offered more than the asking price. The

MICHAEL SMITH

The house at 264 Monson Road, Silverton

first sale fell through; the next people in line, a young family, were eager to move in. We had to be out by the end of March.

Carol and I drove to Oregon for a second visit. Jerry showed us a small farm along Silver Creek just outside the Silverton city limits. The street was a funky, low-density mix of aged bungalows and mobile homes. The house was modest, painted a jarring turquoise, but the interior was bright and clean. The moment we walked into the living room, Carol murmured to me, "This could be our bedroom." We had long wanted a bigger bedroom, with room to do yoga and exercise and read and write as well as sleep.

Behind the house was seven acres of mostly flat land, ideal for Carol's equestrian purposes. It felt like country, open fields stretching east along Silver Creek to a distant grove of cottonwoods; yet it was virtually contiguous to the town, two minutes from Safeway. The owners were hobby farmers, with a small herd of smelly cattle milling about in the mud behind the large metal-clad garage. Another outbuilding was full of bantam chickens, a pen full of ducks. There were a variety of fruit trees.

Carol bought it the next day. The house would need substantial revision

The property stretched down along Silver Creek to the far cottonwoods

before we could move in; we rented a house a mile away to live in until it was ready. We went back to Santa Barbara and packed up the house, filling a very large moving van. We had enjoyed a good run in Santa Barbara and left with no regrets. Many friends came to a farewell party in the empty house where we had enjoyed ten years of love, joy, creativity, and real life. Carol dug up special plants from the garden, encouraged people to take them home, and brought some favorites with us to plant on our farm in Oregon.

Just Life

2003 – 2018

My studio in the former chicken house

MICHAEL SMITH

1

On April 1, 2003, we moved to Silverton, driving up in two cars to meet the movers. Carol flew back to Santa Barbara to fetch her truck, trailer, and two mares, Annie and Chinita, and installed them in a nearby boarding stable. We would live in a rented house for the next nine months while our new house was extensively rebuilt and a horse barn constructed de novo.

Carol and I, both interested in architecture, redesigned the house to suit our tastes and needs, reading *A Pattern Language* and working out the plan together. I drew it up, and a draftsman made working drawings for the builders. We wanted the house to look west toward the fields rather than east onto Monson Road, though this is a blessedly quiet dead-end street with very little motor traffic. After trying more modernistic ideas, we matched the existing hip-roof vernacular style so the house looks virtually the same as it did from the street, though much enlarged at the other end. The former living room became our bedoom, the former master bedroom turned into an office for Carol, dressing rooms and a new bath were carved out of the former dining room and kitchen. We would add on a new front entrance on the side, laundry/mud room, kitchen, dining room, and high-ceilinged living room facing west toward farmland.

It took a few months to plan, organize permits, and find a reliable contractor. Meanwhile, knowing no one in our new hometown, I had time on my hands and wanted to write something. Decades earlier, Paul Sand had told me about *Victor ou les Enfants au Pouvoir*, a play written in 1928 by the surrealist Roger Vitrac, a cohort of Artaud, doubtless envisioning himself as eight-year-old Victor. I couldn't find an English translation and finally read *Victor* by writing it out, puzzling my way through the French line by line. I loved the struggling characters and the play's unique marriage of boulevard realism and absurdity, farce and tragedy. I enjoyed writing my translation but still have not found a way to put it on stage.

Carol's Steinway lived in my lower-level study in the rented house, where

Hinrich Muller, Marya Ursin, me, Louisa Muller, Laurel Muller, and Daniel Potter
came for dinner on our interim back patio

I spent many happy hours at the keyboard reading the great composers. Its lid had been crackled by the hot California sun shining on it through the skylight; the piano would be sent away to be refinished on the way to the new house.

In Santa Barbara I had been swimming for exercise at the YMCA. Three times a week I started driving twenty minutes to Woodburn for a deep-water workout and a few laps in the municipal pool.

We went east for Memorial Day with Carol's family in Vermont. All summer and fall we were busy supervising three separate construction crews. Endless decisions had to be made and errands run. I interfaced with the contractor who was remodeling the house. Carol hired pole-barn experts to construct her enormous, complicated horse barn and covered arena. Meanwhile I had a family crew with its own drama rebuilding the roomy chicken house as my studio. When they took up the floor to replace joists, I shoveled out years of chicken shit that had fallen through the cracks. We brought over a very large window from the former living room and paneled the interior with wide cedar clapboards from the house, which had to be replaced. These were painted bright green on one side. I cleaned up the other side with a wire brush in an electric drill, and the effect is pleasingly rustic, not unlike my cabin in the Berkshires.

We demolished a duck pen and removed a fence to expand the yard. I bought a riding mower; Carol bought a tractor. So much needed to be done. Faustino, a sweet- tempered, hard-working Mexican man, worked for Carol a couple of days a week for the first several years we were here, cleaning up after the construction crews, building fences, helping Carol set up her gardens and horse facility. Faustino, who had been living in the area for twenty years, was undocumented, and the constant threat of deportation eventually drove him to move back to Mexico. We would never find anyone nearly as helpful.

Burning Man had been on my radar for several years. Shannon Dodge, my niece, invited me to join her group, Aguamala, many of them city planners she had met in graduate school at Berkeley. I loaded up my car with jugs of water and camping equipment and drove to the Black Rock Desert in Nevada. Plugging into the group, I helped them set up their camp just off the Esplanade and produced one night's dinner for the whole gang. I had brought a white

With Shannon at Burnng Man, 2003

bicycle and dressed exclusively in white. After dark the Aguamalans dressed up in fanciful rags, took carefully planned drugs, and we went out to dance and party. Shannon gave me Ecstasy, which is aptly named.

The construction crew demolished the existing one-car garage on the back of our new house (above) and addeed on a new front entry, mud room, kitchen, dining room, living room, and veranda (below) facing the open farm land to the west.

MICHAEL SMITH

Carol had a separate crew building her horse barn and arena (above) where she would be able to ride all year. A country carpenter and family helped convert the former chicken house (below with its new front porch) into a writing studio for me.

Jerry Hinsvark, the realtor who found the Silverton property for us, gave Carol invaluable help with permits and the like. Jerry and his wife, Lorin Johnson, had a picturesque farm on Crooked Finger Road above nearby Scotts Mills. Lorin and Carol often rode together until Lorin plunged into the study of Oriental medicine and had no time or headspace for anything else, later setting up an acupuncture practice in town. Jerry brought Carol onto the Pudding River Watershed Council, which proved an exercise in frustration. That would lead to her becoming a director of the Marion County Soil and Water Conversation District, which was even worse, her leadership skills stymied by bureaucracy and entrenched negativity. I noticed that Carol had a pattern of getting into opposition on boards and losing. Jerry and Lorin made us part of their family for Thanksgiving dinner every year. Jerry was a skilled baker and produced three or more gourmet pies and cakes for dessert.

The long stretch of land along Silver Creek had been grazed bare by cattle.

Carol on her tractor

Carol set up a conservation easement for an acre and a half of it. A grant funded a fence to separate it from the horse pasture, and a team of volunteers came to plant 450 seedlings of native trees. These were attacked by deer and beaver and eventually the area had to be entirely fenced in. Enough trees survived and grew that now, fourteen years later, there is a dense forest all along the creek, some of the trees twenty feet high. I keep a walking path mowed to the swimming hole and the end of our property.

We moved into our new place on Christmas Eve. Bicky came from Santa Barbara for New Year's just in time for an ice storm. The house is a great success, bright, comfortable, and well arranged. I am especially proud of the figure-eight floor plan: multiple paths mean you're never stuck anywhere. There are outside doors on both sides and both ends. The rooms are made to order for our picture collection and our inclinations. The piano is at one end of the house, the tv at the other, the skylit kitchen simple and convenient, the bedroom, dressing rooms, and bath just what we wanted, a glassed-in shower with a bench and wand for Carol: she sits, I stand. She has a cozy office, fitted with the workspace we had built to her specifications in Santa Barbara. There's a guest room with its own bath.

NOTICING THE BRUSH CREEK PLAYHOUSE, a former one-room schoolhouse not far down the road to Salem, thinking I might be able to do plays there, I introduced myself to the board—and was immediately put to work lighting *Come Back to the Five and Dime, Jimmy Dean, Jimmy Dean*, a touching comedy by Ed Graczyk. I watched the entire run from the light booth on a platform behind the audience. It was so grotesquely miscast and ineptly acted that it took me half the run to figure out the plot.

I joined the Brush Creek Players board and had a grand time directing Christopher Durang's outrageously humorous play *Beyond Therapy*. I had two talented comic actors, a solid leading man, and a couple of entertaining personalities in the cast. I treated the stage like the Caffè Cino, making a simple set to represent the different locations. Our leading lady was mentally unstable and drinking but otherwise perfect for the role. For all the compromises community theatre entails, the play was funny and enjoyable once the actors got it up to speed.

In the wake of *Beyond Therapy* civic-minded John Burke asked me to direct *A Midsummer Night's Dream* as a benefit for the Silverton Arts Association. I had always wanted to direct Shakespeare and agreed to do it if he would produce. The entire play would have been too hard so I abbreviated it to not much over an hour, focusing on the love stories and Puck and the fairies. I found talented high school kids to play the young lovers, a delightful Puck, and capable grownups for Oberon, Titania, and Bottom. Sitting them down around the big table under the walnut tree in our yard, I helped them pick through the text until everyone understood what they were saying at every moment. The country setting for the show

Betty Ann Prior as Titania and Phil Baker as Bottom in *A Midsummer Night's Dream (Abbreviated)*

was lovely, the audience friendly, kind vounteers helped with costumes, scenery, and music, the weather held, and everything came together for two magical performances.

I am in the zone when I'm directing, maddening though actors can be. An obliviously demanding energy rises in me, everyone is forced to go along, and some are inspired to go beyond. We believe the details of this preposterous thing we are doing are more important than anything else. That's what engages and thrills the audience.

Surprisingly, our little town hosted a significant annual poetry festival. It turned out there is a thriving poetry community in Oregon, unlike Santa Barbara, where poets are few and far between. Steve Slemenda and Kelley Morehouse, both on the faculty at nearby Chemeketa Community College, had started the festival in 2000, when Steve was on sabbatical. They welcomed me onto the board of the Silverton Poetry Association, first as treasurer (succeeding John Burke, an accountant), later as president. It was a fair amount of work, raising money, rounding up poets, running the festival's numerous poetry events over two weekends and other events through the year, bur I have always liked putting on shows. John and Kelley became my good friends.

This was the blog moment, before everyone went on those damn social media, and I started a blog on a whim—saw something I liked on the web and thought I can do that. I had no desire to write for a newspaper or magazine again, but I missed writing in public; this was a way to be published at will, with nothing at stake except my own expression. I didn't initially intend to write poetry, although I had written poems from time to time all my life. Inspired by Oregon poet William Stafford's famous practice of early morning writing, my blog quickly evolved into daily poems, short and written quickly, sometimes at the last minute, just before I went to bed. I continued to offer a new poem every day for the next seventeen years.

Julian was living in Oakland with his lovable musician girlfriend Nina Nilssen. He worked for Peace Action West, fund-raising on the phone and very good at it. Nina was getting ready to go to music school. Carol and I went to the Bay Area for her brother Charlie's birthday and stayed with Julian and Nina, who had moved to a warehouse near Jack London Square. Julian was growing a few marijuana plants under a high-tech light in a hidden, discreetly ventilated room. Upstairs were several little rooms,

Julian and Nina

very bohemian, and an inconspicuous roommate, just the kind of thing I liked when I was their age. They were exquisitely welcoming, giving us their bed. They took me to an anti-nuke demonstration at Livermore Labs and I heard Medea Benjamin speak, one of my heroes.

I went to Denver to see Uncle Al, who was in the hospital with a broken hip. Carol and I went to the Oregon coast for my birthday. We went to Santa Barbara for a weekend and stopped off on the way back to see the Mark Morris Dance Group in Berkeley; Carol liked it so much she wanted to go again but they were sold out.

Carol wanted to spend Christmas with her children, which was complicated enough without me—Tensie and Lora-Faye in Park Slope, Sid and family in their new house in Harlem, a four-hour drive to Danby and back. I flew east with her, and we separated at Newark Airport. I went to Stonington for a delightful Christmas visit with dear friends Dan Potter and Marya Ursin, rejoining Carol in New York for one city day on our own—just right.

2

YEARS BEFORE, GUY J. JACKSON, a young man working in the box office at the Lobero Theatre, had given me his play *The Flight of the Butter Boy.* I loved it, but Maurie wasn't interested, and it would have been costly to produce it in Santa Barbara. It was perfect at Brush Creek and cost me nothing. Alfred, who never expressed interest in being in my plays in Santa Barbara, had started studying acting at SBCC after we left and came up to play Tobyus, the romantic lead. He threw himself into the part with gusto, and it was a kick for me to have him in the cast. I had a perfect kid in the title role and a wonderfully eccentric company. Michele and Joy, Julian, and Alfred's circus friend Peter Perigo came from afar to see it. It was one of my best productions, albeit wildly amateur.

Taylor Bradberry as the
Butter Boy

Irene Fornés came to Seattle to accept an award at the annual Theatre Communications Group convention, accompanied by Michelle Memran, a warm, friendly woman who was making a documentary film about Irene and keeping her on track. I went up to see her for old times' sake. Irene was sliding into Alzheimer's but feisty as ever. It was fun to see her, although anywhere near TCG, I felt painfully invisible in the contemporary theatre world, active as I was.

Maurie Lord revived Genesis West, finally heeding my hard-won advice that if he wanted to direct the plays he wanted to direct, he would have to produce them himself. Maurie flew me down to Santa Barbara to light *Blue Heart,* an exquisite pair of short plays by Caryl Churchill (the English Irene Fornés). I love lighting, and Center Stage Theater was a perfect place for me to do it, thanks to the skills and good work of tech director Brad Spaulding; I designed it, he made it happen. I went three more times in succeeding years, to light Churchill's *Far Away*, Albee's *The Goat*, and Sam Shepard's *The God of Hell*, and won two Indies for my lighting.

I HAD HAND-MADE A NUMBER of books through the years, getting real pleasure out of being a publisher. *Near the End* was the only professionally bound book I had produced, but it was costly: I had to print 500 copies and still had most of them. Print-on-demand made book publishing affordable. John Labovitz, a new friend, helped me publish *Automatic Vaudeville*, a dream-based text I had written in 1970. He designed the book, did the computer work of laying out the pages, gave me a photograph for the cover, and helped me produce it on Lulu. This was the start of a burst of productivity from Fast Books that continues to this day, including the book in your hands.

Kelley asked me if I would read a play by her friend Vere McCarty. Of course! In fact it was not a play but a playful short novel about Elvis Presley and his imaginary twin brother. I thought it was funny and offered to publish it. John Labovitz designed the cover. I threw a book launch party for *Jesse & Elvis* in our yard on a beautiful summer day, but we only managed to sell a few copies. I don't care. I just like producing books.

In connection with the 2007 Silverton Poetry Festival, I had the idea of publishing an anthology of poets who had read at the festivals through the years. I asked Ruth Hudgens to co-edit it with me. John designed the cover and helped me perfect-bind 100 copies on a machine in the basement of the town print shop. I called it *Yes Poetry*.

I have published twenty-four books in the past twelve years, half by me, half by other writers. I get considerable satisfaction from it, other people's books even more than my own. John created a website, fastbookspress.com, with a catalog of the books and links to Amazon, and also wrote special software for my personal website, michaeltownsendsmith.com, which lets me add to and revise it at will. John, a man of many interests, moved to Portland, then West Virginia, and I had to learn to design books myself, which I enjoy. He still hosts my websites. Thank you, John!

Carol on the east side of Steen's Mountain

New to the Pacific Northwest, Carol and I were curious to explore the territory. She was reluctant to leave her horses for more than a day or two except to visit family, but we managed a few trips, amazed by the grandeur and variety of this land, much of it barely marked by human intrusion.

3

Wanting to do a play in New York with Alfred, I decided to produce *Trouble,* my play about the Bess Myerson scandal, at Theater for the New City. I had a good idea how to pay for it. In 1967 Diane Arbus had mailed me a contact print of one of her iconic images—the topless young waitress at the nudist camp—with a note on the reverse about her show at the Museum of Modern Art. I treasured it and kept it sitting around in a double-sided frame for years, unnoticed. I sold it at Sotheby's to fund *Trouble*; they got me $13,000. Donald L. Brooks, who had played Marley's ghost in *Christmas Carol* at the Caffè Cino, kindly let Alfred and me stay in his unused apartment at 43rd and Eighth Avenue for barely any rent. We found a place to play ping-pong in the Village and thoroughly enjoyed our time together in the city.

Alas, it turned out I was too long out of the loop to organize a good physical production of my play; and it needed a big star in the lead role to make sense, which I was unable to get. I liked the cast I had, but the sets were lame, the lighting a nightmare. Alfred and Jimmy Camicia were funny and right-on as Dickie and Sandy Morphol. Kathryn Chilson was good as Tess Byerson but still reeling from death of husband and hard to reach. The

Jimmy Camicia, Kathryn Chilson, and Alfred in *Trouble* at TNC

Siblings: with Bicky, Lewis, and Virginia on MacDougal Street

play bombed: four years after 9/11 no one cared about Bess Myerson and Ed Koch. Virginia came from Santa Fe to see it, Lewis from upstate, Bicky and Carol from Santa Barbara. Kathryn chose that night to come in drunk. The only real critic who came was there that night too and blamed the stumbling pace on my direction.

While I was in New York I hosted two events at La Mama as part of a series called Coffeehouse Chronicles, one on Johnny Dodd and one about myself. Johnny had never had a memorial; many people came who knew and worked with him and spoke about him warmly. I was well known as a former critic, but no one knew the extent of my work as a playwright and director because it was all over the place, more in Denver, Taos, Santa Barbara, and Oregon than in New York. I showed slides and talked about the plays I've done, whether people liked it or not.

Michael Warren Powell, one of Johnny's dearest friends, showed up at the Johnny event, and I went to visit him in his midtown loft. I had known Michael since he acted in Lanford Wilson's first plays at the Caffè Cino. He'd had a stroke that slowed him down, but he was still himself. Johnny had given Michael a thick book of his painstakingly intricate collages; he showed it to me and then spontaneously gave it to me. Back in Oregon, I showed it to Adam Davis, a rare book dealer and specialist in literary ephemera, who found Johnny's collages extraordinarily beautiful. A decade later Adam and I co-published a sumptuous book of them, working with Portland designer Fredrik Averin, under the title *My Funny Valentine*.

I was still in New York when word came than Uncle Alfred had died in Denver, ending a long life of creativity and priceless generosity to any number of aspiring spirits including me. Alfred and I stopped off on our way back from New York to attend his memorial.

The Mount Angel Glockenspiel

Mount Angel, a German Catholic town four miles north of Silverton, was building a glockenspiel as part of a new Bavarian-style senior housing project in the center of town. Wood carvers made two-thirds lifesize figures for a moving display. I was brought in as volunteer "producer." I went to the machine shop that was making a turntable for the figures and found out what it could be programmed to do. There were five historical figures plus a pair of Bavarian children on a swing up above. I worked out a timeline of their movements, and Hinrich recorded and edited music to go with each of the figures as they appeared, composing glockenspiel pieces to transition from one to the next. It was a fun project. The glockenspiel plays four times a day, a major attraction of the town.

Carol had a good time showing Annie in the mountain trail competitions at the Oregon Equestrian Center in Eugene. An elaborate course was set up in the arena, with logs to step over, twisty trails over hills, water-filled ditches, and bridges. I went to watch. Contestants went one at a time, moving slowly and steadily; horse and rider had to be completely focused, perfectly under control. After a few tries and much hard work, Carol won the open championship. She loved getting Annie to do exactly what she wanted her to do, and she was proud of her success, a longtime goal. I was glad she had a horse to control so she didn't try to control me, although I never resisted her suggestions anymore.

She especially enjoyed camping trips in the Cascades with her riding friends, sleeping in the back of her truck and exploring the mountain trails, which took her to beautiful places we would never reach on foot. I envied her but didn't want to go. She liked these horse-camping trips more than anything. She also went to workshops with various advanced horse trainers. She didn't just want to ride, she wanted to improve her skills and those of her horse. So I had the place to myself fairly often.

One sunny summer day Carol left for a workshop across the Columbia in Washington. I went out to my studio, which was very hot, took off all my clothes, and jumped into the hammock, a string hammock like the one in the cabin at Charlemont. Unfortunately I jumped too far, flipped right over it, landed on my head and shoulder, and broke my collarbone. I could have called Carol, I suppose, but I didn't want to ruin her weekend. I got into my clothes somehow, drove to the doctor's office, and was put into an uncomfortable strap affair that I had to wear for weeks. He sent me across the street to the hospital for a scan of my head, which found nothing wrong, but I'm sure I had a concussion, at least a confusion—my mind was out of whack for some time.

MICHAEL SMITH

Carol with Sid, Lisa, Genevieve, and Gabrielle; and with Lora and Edward

Carol was pleased when Lora-Faye, her eldest grandchild, came west to attend Lewis and Clark College, an hour away from us in Portland. Lora-Faye liked Portland but not Lewis and Clark, went home to Brooklyn at Christmas, and did not return. It was sad how far apart our families ended up; I would have liked to be living in a compound with all of them, like Bali. Julian was in Taos, Alfred was in Santa Barbara, and Carol's family were all on the East Coast—Tensie and Lora-Faye in Brooklyn, Sid and Lisa and the girls in Harlem, Lora in Eastport, Maine, the last coastal town before Canada and very hard to get to. Carol went to Eastport for Lora's wedding to Edward French, the editor of the town newspaper. Hating air travel, she went anyway to family get-togethers in Vermont most years, and I sometimes went along. She was glad when they came to visit us on the farm, and so was I. They were all of them interesting in different ways.

I wrote a new play, *Deep in the Woods,* specifically for the Brush Creek stage, which is roughly the size of my cabin in the Berkshires, positing a group of friends who gather there after a catastrophe destroys Manhattan. Despite vigorous efforts, I failed to find a stage manager or fill two key roles, and I was forced to cancel the production the day before the beginning of rehearsals. It was jarring—all that adrenaline andnothing to be done. I felt badly let down by the Brush Creek crowd and was out of sorts for weeks, but it was probably just as well, the play unfixable. The premise is not very plausible, the tone is uncertain, and there really is no place for the story to go.

In Santa Barbara we had hosted an annual open house on New Year's Day. Now that I had met some interesting people through the local arts groups and Carol was starting to have horse connnections, we had enough Oregon friends to resume the tradition. I made chili, pasta al pesto, and a salad, Carol made spiced cider, wine flowed, music was played, and our house was filled with laughter and lively talk.

It gradually became sadly clear that Carol and I could no long have sex together. Her membranes had thinned with age. Fucking, formerly so pleasurable for us both, had become painful. Any touch caused fine breaks and bleeding, and of course that was very uncomfortable in the saddle. She tried everything but nothing helped: we had to stop. This was a serious blow. Our mutual attraction had been the private heart of our relationship, the engine and magnetic bond that made everything else worth the effort. I was afraid we would lose the precious intimacy sex gave us access to, and to some extent we did. We were still affectionate. We kept expressing and feeling our love, holding each other close, letting the electrons mingle, basking in the warmth of each other's touch, kissing and snuggling, true to each other and glad we had fucked so much when we still could. It took a couple of years but I slowly regained my balance. We would be fine. Carol simply forgot about sex, as far as I could tell. I didn't want to give it up, but I didn't want to do it with anyone else. Luckily I have always liked masturbation, good to keep the fluids flowing, and pornography makes it easy.

MICHAEL SMITH

4

A SILVERTON FRIEND, Chris Bradberry, got me started doing tai chi, which I liked right away. After our first teacher drifted away, we found another, Barb Dahlum, who is focused and devoted. When she was out for a spell I did the form every day on my own until I learned it—108 linked movements, forty-five minutes of continuous slow enactment. Doing tai chi is pleasurable and said to be beneficial. Ten years later I still practice it with Barb and a small group every Wednesday at five. On sunny warm days we do it barefoot in the grass in the town park.

Still thinking I needed to get away from home to write anything new, I retreated to the blissfully remote Hotel Diamond near Steen's Mountain for a few days and worked on *Bad Dog*, a sequel to *Dogs Bark All Night*. I had some ideas and got started, and I enjoyed exploring the nearby Malheur National Bird Refuge, but I was too lonely in Diamond and came home a day early. I can write at home, here in my beautiful study or on my laptop in the living room whether Carol is here or not, awake or asleep.

I decided to do *Bad Dog* in Santa Barbara so Alfred wouldn't have to interrupt his life again. That was where I had done *Dogs Bark All Night*, the prequel, and I could have two of the same actors, Laurel Lyle and David Brainard, who had created the principal characters. Laurel has been elected President! *Bad Dog* was not long enough to make a full evening; I combined it with three existing short plays of mine: *More! More! I Want More!* (1965), *Fast Forward* (2000), with Alfred playing me, and *Point Blank*, a whimsical loop play about a family picnic, written in Westerly in the eighties. These were inserted, without explanation, between the four discontinuous scenes of *Bad Dog*, which oddly enough seemed to work—nobody complained that it was totally weird and incoherent. It was certainly unusual and entertaining. I had an ideal cast to work and play with and my favorite costume designer, Mary Gibson. The show was made to order for Center Stage Theater, with practically no set, and I had a very good time doing it, struggles and all, lighting the plays in bold defining colors.

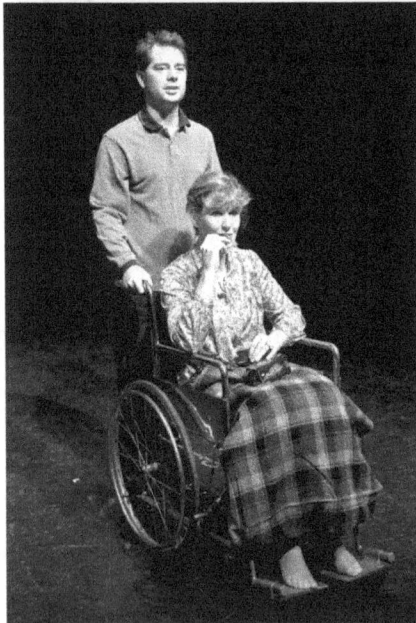

Bad Dog & Other Plays at Center Stage Theater: above, David Brainard, Alfred Smith, Laurel Lyle, Tom Petra, Susan Keller, Melissa Rose Ziemer, Melissa Paper, and Suzanne Bodine in *Point Blank*; left, Alfred and Laurel in *Fast Forward*

Winters are dark this far north—we're on the 45th parallel, the same latitude as Eastport, Maine. I was happy with Carol but bored with Silverton, where there is not much going on—nothing that really interests me. Portland is only an hour away, though, and easy to get in and out of. We went into the city for concerts, plays, and operas. One season I bought myself a subscription to the White Bird dance series, excited most of all by

MICHAEL SMITH

the Merce Cunningham company. Closer to home, I dressed up as Dante and read from the *Divine Comedy* at the Brush Creek talent show and the Poetry Association's Dead Poets event. I worked hard on the poetry festival. I wrote. The best way to fend off depression is to do something.

CHRISTOPHER WICKS, a young organist, composer, pianist, and baritone, was the town's leading musician. We began getting together regularly to read through lieder and piano duets. Christopher was an excellent sight-reader, though not very sensitive or expressive. Christopher and I played at our New Year's parties and gave several well-received public performances over the next couple of years. I liked being motivated to improve, trying to play beautifully and share the pleasure.

Our swan song was Schubert's sublime *Winterreise* for the Poetry Festival and again at a church in Salem. After the latter performance, Christopher, off his meds, turned on me, wrote me an inexcusably insulting email, and that was the end of our friendship.

A violinist named Eadie Anelli had been playing with Christopher. I said I wanted to play with her when she first moved to town, but he chased me off, saying, "She's mine!" When she too broke with Christopher, Eadie and I began playing together every week. She worked as a public school music teacher and played viola as well as violin with a sympathetic musicality if somewhat wobbly intonation at times. I had long wanted to play the Mozart violin sonatas and never had anyone to do it with. There are many of them, with sparkling piano parts Mozart wrote for himself. We had a very good time with them, endlessly challenged and delighted.

Eadie introduced me to another violinist, Nancy Korda, who had bought a historic house in Silverton and opened a bed and breakfast. Nancy studied at Interlaken and played for years in the Pasadena Symphony. We also started playing every week, sometimes with Eadie but more often separately. Nancy encouraged me to tackle music I thought was beyond me, at the outer edge of my ability, and we have had a glorious time working our way through the rich violin-piano repertory: sonatas by Bach, Handel,

Haydn, Beethoven (the best), Brahms (too hard), Schubert, Schumann, Mendelssohn, Debussy, Prokofiev, and Shostakovich. Like me, Nancy likes to work as well as play—practice ahead of time, slow down the hard parts and solve the problems, dig deeper into the inexhaustible subtleties of the greatest musical minds.

Alfred took a fall on his bicycle after a night at Elsie's, his hangout bar in downtown Santa Barbara, and broke his femur. Bicky took him in for the first couple of weeks of his painful recovery, and Michele came from New Mexico. I went down to see him. He was in rehearsal for a melodrama at the Circle Bar B dinner theatre and would have to play it on crutches. He took it as a sign that once he recovered he should change his life.

CAROL WAS READY for a new equestrian challenge. She was interested in dressage, a more formal discipline, but Annie was a quarter horse and not really suited for it. So she bought herself a big, beautiful, fancy horse expressly for dressage competition. Gwynnevere was part thoroughbred, a striking presence, tall and noble looking, with an arched neck and a superior attitude. Carol liked her high spirits. Unfortunately she turned out to be crazy and unpredictable, nervously on guard at all times. Carol spent the next several years trying to calm her down

Louisa had moved on from singing to stage managing operas with an eye to becoming a director. Laurel and Hinrich finally told her she was my biological daughter. Shocked at first, she said, "You mean I'm not German?"

I went to New York by myself to see friends, again staying in Donald Brooks's vacant apartment on 43rd Street. Patti Dodd took me to her storage unit to look for more of Johnny's collages but couldn't find them. I'd heard Sam Shepard was in the city, called him, and met him for lunch at Noho Star; it was great to see him and hear about his big life. I checked out the New Museum on the Bowery and went uptown to the Frick, thrilled by the masterpieces; paid a visit to Jimmy Camicia, whom I was encouraging to expand his book about Hot Peaches into a life-memoir; and had dinner with my good friend Gary Zarr, a lover of literature who had been the press guy

Carol on Gwynnevere

for the Parks Department when I worked for Mayor Koch.

One day I went to visit Judith Malina, who had suffered a terrible blow when Hanon, her much younger husband, suffered a stroke and died. They had opened a new Living Theatre on Clinton Street, and the whole burden of it fell on her. It was more of a challenge than ever to keep a theatre going in New York now that rents had risen to exorbitant heights, but Judith passionately wanted to keep writing and directing plays. She lived in an apartment upstairs from the theatre and showed me her roof garden. That night I saw her radical new play, *Eureka*, completed from a concept of Hanon's, in which the audience was set loose in the middle of the space—no seats—surrounded by and participating in the action, bathed in a wild environment of sound, lights, and projections by Gary Brackett.

Judith on her Clinton Street terrace

As if all that wasn't enough, I then rented a car and drove up into New England, visiting John Lucas, his wife Kathy, and Aunt Ginny in Darien, Dan and Marya in Stonington, and Jean-Claude at Shantigar. It was good timing: I got to see his play *The Tibetan Book of the Dead* in Northhampton. I stopped for dinner with Lewis and Alice, then living in Hurley, New York, on the way back to the city, and attended a Living Theatre board meeting at Elinor Munro's apartment in Manhattan. Whew!

I WROTE A NEW FULL-LENGTH PLAY, whimsically appropriating a Wodehouse title, *Summer Lightning*, making a virtue of the tight confines of the Brush Creek stage, with juicy parts for actors I could actually get. The comedy is set

Alison White, Norman Gouveia, Tavis Evans, and Jacob Dickson in *Summer Lightning*, my play about the Caffè Cino, at the Brush Creek Playhouse

in the Caffè Cino, with my version of *Phèdre* (after Racine) in the middle as a specimen of coffee-house theatre. I designed an ingenious set, with the cafe on the right, complete with lighting booth, the ridiculously crowded dressing room on the left, seen through a lighted makeup mirror, and a tiny thrust stage in between for the Greek tragedy. I went over to the theatre while I was writing it to pace off the stage and make sure it would all fit. I rounded up a lively cast, worked them hard, and by the end of the run the play was getting good. Alfred played Kyle Duette, the critic character, as well as Hippolytus. Michele and Joy came from New Mexico to see it, and Bicky from Santa Barbara. The play embodied my warm feelings about the Caffè Cino and the way we used to do theatre. I was still doing it that way!

Big Sidney, Carol's ex-husband, invited Carol and me and their whole family to Timberlock, a sweetly rustic family resort in the Adirondacks, for a week in late July 2009. I added Julian to the mix so it wouldn't be

Sidney Whelan with family at Timberlock: Patsy, Lora-Faye, Sid, Lisa, Tensie, Carol, Edward, and Lora. Below, with Julian.

just me and Whelans. (Alfred had just been with us for the play and had to work.) The Adirondacks was fully as special as I remembered, blissfully far away from everything but nature and good company. We swam, went on group and duo expeditions in kayaks and canoes, and sailed Hobie cats, exciting in the wind. Julian, who had never sailed before, blew over; I swooped around and saved him. It was very relaxed. Julian had his own cabin. When we weren't with the group, the two of us hid out together in the lodge playing gin rummy.

Michael Smith

5

CAROL AND I, Kelley and Vere, Laurel and Hinrich, and new friends Rosa and William got together to read the play version of Melville's *Billy Budd* out loud, all taking parts, and to share a potluck dinner. Soon after that we did Robert Lowell's *The Old Glory*. With two additional members—Elizabeth Keyser and Steve Slemenda—our play-reading group continues to meet every month to read a play and hang out together. In seven years we have gone through a wide swath of dramatic literature, which satisfies my desire to do plays without actually having to mount a production. Thanks, friends!

Our Silverton play-reading group (clockwise from bottom left): William Naiditch, Kelley Morehouse, Carol, me, Hinrich Muller, Vere McCarty, Laurel Muller, Elizabeth Keyser, and Rosa Waggoner (Steve Slemenda missing)

Julian had broken up with Nina and moved back to Taos. He phoned from Costa Rica, where he was traveling with his new girlfriend, Liane Pellegrini, with the devastating news that Nina had been murdered on the beach in Antigua. A month later Julian came to visit with Liane, who had been Nina's roommate in San Francisco before moving to Taos. Nina's death had been a harsh blow to both of them; it was a wonder their relationship survived it. Liane was sweet to Julian, and he was in fine fettle, fiercely competitive at ping-pong.

Lora-Faye hadn't originally wanted to go to Smith because it was too gay; now she had come out as a lesbian. Carol and I went east for her graduation. The whole family was there for the joyous occasion. Funny how Smith College kept cropping in my life! Carol and I stayed at the Hotel Northampton and walked all over town, enjoying our memories and the sparkling present.

Tensie and Lora-Faye

After the weekend Carol went off with her children, and I took a bus into Boston to meet Dennis Pinette, who came down from Maine to see me. We went to three thrilling art museums and dabbled at mutual wankery in our hotel room (our unspoken intention all along), which was pretty ridiculous. Dennis is even more heterosexual than I am, but we had fooled around together a couple of times in an earlier life and kept in touch by email about art and sex. From Boston I flew to Chicago to visit David Rubens, who had inherited his parents' handsome house in Glencoe. We did a little music together, saw a terrific production of *A Streetcar Named Desire*, he took me to a great eccentric pizza place, and we visited the Chicago Art Institute, which had a new wing I was eager to see.

Ignacio Fernandez, a Cuban-born artist and architect from Los Angeles, was the ex-boyfriend of John Labovitz's friend Patti Battin's sister, if I have that right. Ignacio had gone back to Cuba and done a series of watercolor paintings, wry commentary on the Castro saga, which Patti exhibited at her gallery in Silverton. John was more or less partnering with me in Fast Books at this point; *Azúcar, Tabaco y Café* was his project. I helped Ignacio expand his captions into longer texts that made the book much more substantial, and learned a lot from watching John design it. We published it through Lightning Source, a more professional printer-binder with links to online distribution.

Magie Dominic had the idea of putting together a book of remembrances of our old friend Harry Koutoukas, which we co-edited and I published. I also published *Every Day Arising*, collecting the first five years of my blog posts, a book of 753 pages containing 1,760 brief poems—why not? Some of the poems are good! I did a signing event for it at the Silverton Arts Association gallery.

I LOVE HAMLET, THE CHARACTER, but I hate how the story turns out. It occurred to me that Shakespeare might have got it wrong. What if the Ghost was imaginary, a fantasy, or false and lying? What if Hamlet's father had colluded with Gertrude in her affair with his brother Claudius in a harmonious secret ménage à trois—Claudius was Hamlet's real father, and it finally came out, clearing his mind—he married Ophelia, became king—and nobody died? I was inspired to write my version for Kory Crosen, who had played Lysander for me in *A Midsummer Night's Dream (Abbreviated)* and Theramenes opposite Alfred's Hippolytus in *Summer Lightning*. Kory, twenty-one and the very image of Hamlet, was ill at ease at first with the "Shakespearean" text. Alfred came for an initial read-through in the summer and was appalled. I worked with Kory for two months before full rehearsals started in the fall, and by then he was on top of it.

Hamlet in Love would have looked stupidly amateurish on Brush Creek's rigid little stage so I arranged to do it in the black box theatre at the

Dianne Bates as Ophelia, Kory Cozen as Hamlet, Kelley Morehouse as Gertrude, Vere McCarty as Claudius in *Hamlet in Love*. Right, Norman Gouveia ss Polonius and Alfred as Laertes.

new Silverton High School. I drafted Kelley Morehouse to play Gertrude, opposite her boyfriend Vere McCarty as my non-villainous Claudius. Kelley had never acted before, which was difficult at first; she hung in and became remarkably queenly. Norman Gouveia, my closest thing to a pal from Brush Creek, was born to play Polonius. Kory was forceful and excellent as Hamlet, and Alfred was strong as Laertes and the murderer in Hamlet's "mousetrap" play—which Claudius answers with his own play, correcting Hamlet's misapprehensions.

Karyl Carlson, the invaluable costumer, stepped up as stage manager and was wonderful. Otherwise I had virtually no help putting the production together. I had to focus the lights by myself, climbing up and down to the grid over and over despite my painful hip, Alfred inexplicably refusing to come help me. It was too exhausting. I have not wanted to do another play since.

Alfred was done with Santa Barbara and wanted to move. I was confident that he would like Portland, which I had been quietly promoting for years, and *Hamlet in Love* helped him make the transition. City friends of ours came down to see it and mentioned over dinner that their daughter was looking for someone to do theatre with the clients at Full Life, her day program for developmentally disabled adults. Alfred called her, got the job, and stuck to it for seven or eight years, liking the clients, finding the work rewarding.

Delighted to have Alfred so close, I drove into the city to see him practially every week, checking out the mNY sushi restaurants and small theatres, although he had decided he no longer wanted to act. Sometimes I drove in for a quick visit on his half-hour lunch break, going for a walk in the neighborhood, always happy to be with him. He liked coming to the farm and visited often. If I didn't feel like driving in to fetch him, he would take the train or bus to Salem, sometimes bringing his bicycle. Once he biked all the way from Portland, but the country roads around here are narrow—it felt too dangerous. After a time Julian gave him a car, which died, Michele and Joy gave him another to replace it, and he comes to Silverton to visit every few weekends. I still hold my own with him at ping-pong—nothing more fun except directing plays!

EARLY IN MY EFFORTS to write this account of my life, Dan Potter suggested that my love-work idyll with John P. Dodd in the sixties was the story I most wanted to tell. He was probably right at that point: Johnny and I were lovers from 1963 to 1971, and our bond remained vital until his death in 1991. He was the love of my life. But life went on, I loved again, and Carol is the love who lasted. Johnny still fascinated me; I wanted to

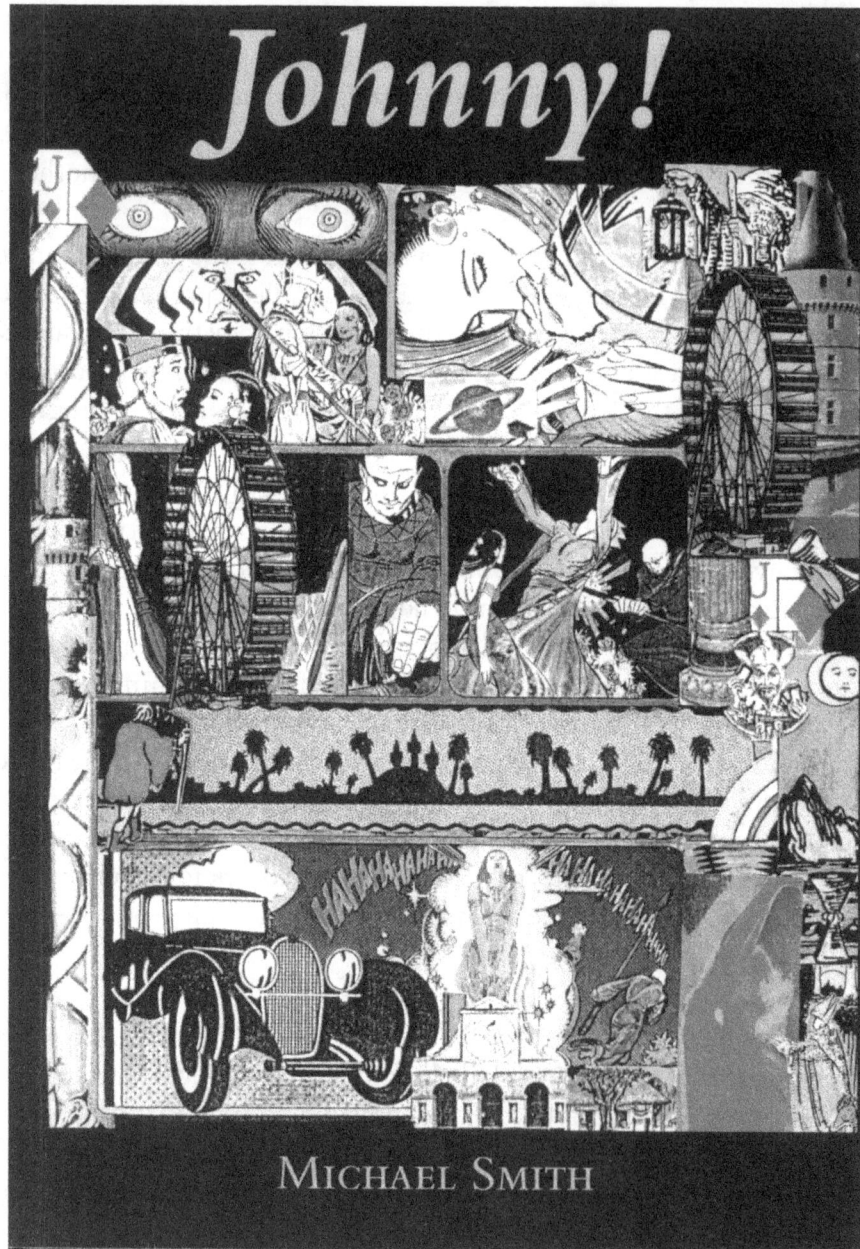

Johnny!

MICHAEL SMITH

tell his story, as much as I knew it, not just his story with me. *Johnny!* is an informal biography as well as a memoir of our love affair. I put one of his exquisite collages on the cover. In retrospect I wish I had done more research instead of being so subjective and hit-or-miss about the facts. I should have spoken to Johnny's mother, but he had kept us apart: I didn't know her. I have subsequently heard from his family and added further material to the book's page on my website.

It was a pleasant surprise at the 2011 Kennedy Center American College Theatre Festival in Ames, Iowa, to find that I had some lingering reputation as a critic among Middle Western theatre academics. It was frigid in Iowa, icy underfoot, fun to be there among so many other theatre maniacs as a V.I.P. Thanks to David Crespy from the University of Missouri for inviting me!

I had long fancied the idea of keeping chickens, which turns out to be extremely easy once you have things set up. Carol helped me build a chicken coop under the shed roof in back of the garage: I did the carpentry and Carol did the footing (gravel and dirt) and the wire to protect them from predators. Traci Dahlberg, who had been stabling her horse in Carol's barn in exchange for feeding and cleaning up after hers, was my partner in the chicken enterprise. We started with six hens, who gave us an abundance of delicious eggs for our two families. We also raised several batches of mighty good meat chickens.

JULIAN URGED ME TO COME TO TAOS and stay a while. Carol was going east to be with her children so I went for two weeks in July, a heavenly time of year in northern New Mexico. Liane was living with Julian in his cozy adobe in El Prado. Michele and Joy came over from San Juan for the day, and Julian's good friend John Kane joined us for a festive dinner on the porch. They put me up in another house they had, isolated on the mesa above Arroyo Hondo, where Julian was running a grow room in an apparently disused outbuilding. I enjoyed my time there alone. Julian took me to Ojo Caliente to see the utility building and land he had bought for his business and we went to the hot springs—a memorably relaxed day together. Julian

John Kane, Michele, me, Joy, Julian, and Liane (with dog under table)
at a dinner party on Julian's front porch

is very interesting, and when things are good we have a bracing rapport. I took them to a string quartet concert at the TCA; Liane, incredibly, had never been to a classical concert before. The space and light in Taos are exhilarating and the people are wild. Silverton is dull by comparison, but I would much rather live here.

6

GERARD FORDE, A YOUNGISH English scholar-curator living in Berlin, came to see me researching a biography of Fred Herko and interested as well in other art people I knew in the sixties, including Søren Agenoux and Peter Hartman. Gerard, a flamboyantly gay, bald bon vivant and a formidable researcher, was stimulating and fun. It was refreshing to be with someone who knew, liked, and cared about the recondite creative milieu I came of age in, which no one in Oregon will ever begin to grasp. We spent a couple of days digging through my archives; then I drove him to a yoga retreat in Grass Valley by way of Arcata "on my way" to visit Bicky in Santa Barbara. She had set herself up in a pretty house on the lower Riviera with a wide ocean view and constructed a fine new life for herself, with tennis, chamber music, and many friends. I practiced tai chi on her terrace every afternoon, gazing at the wide Pacific. I went to Los Angeles for lunch with Paul Sand and dinner with Anne Militello, happy to see them both. On the way back north I stopped in San Francisco, stayed with my cousin and boyhood buddy Bud Foster and his artist wife Nancy in their mansion overlooking the Presidio, visited Shannon, Mark, and their young son Silas, and had sushi with Diane di Prima.

Julian and Liane were married in May 2012 in an exquisite small ceremony in Taos, eloquently presided over by John Kane. Carol and I were happy for them. The wedding was followed by a big, boisterous party in Cañon for a wider circle of family and friends. Dinny came from Santa Fe, and it was fun to see my ex-in-laws. The next day Carol and I had lunch with her Smith friend Lucy Lippard in Galisteo, witnessed an annular eclipse of the sun with Michele and Joy in San Juan, and wandered around Las Vegas (NM) looking for sites from Carol's family history.

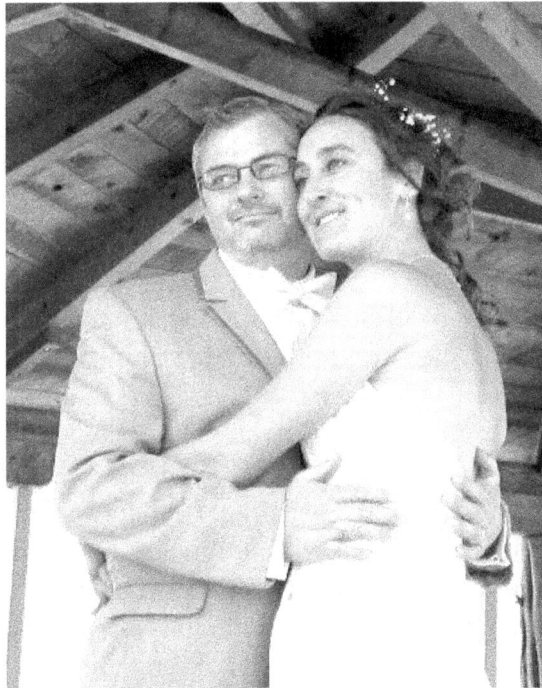

Julian and Liane at their wedding

Ron Tavel had been living in Thailand, whence he had sent me drafts of *Chain*, his ambitious novel about gay goings-on in Bangkok in the 1980s. Ron died of a heart attack in 2009 on a plane flying from Berlin back to Bangkok. The book was still unpublished, and his former agent had ditched it. Ron's brother Harvey was grateful when, through Jimmy Camicia, I offered to publish *Chain*, a densely written, long, difficult, brilliant, important novel, a complex picture of a unique time and scene and a literary tour de force. Earlier editors had pressed Ron to simplify its narrative strategy, which made it hard to follow, but I long ago gave in to his eccentric style and was glad to publish the book as he wrote it. The manuscript was practically error-free. I worked through it closely, discreetly clearing up a few unnecessary obscurities. I bought InDesign, the graphic design software, taught myself to use it, and was proud of the way *Chain* came out. My good-faith but feeble efforts to get reviews and publicity for it came to naught. *Chain* has yet to find the respect and audience it deserves.

Michel Samson, a young Dutch violinist, had my phone number when he arrived in New York in 1964. He and a friend crashed in Johnny's and my living room on Cornelia Street for his first few days in America. I had a reed organ Johnny had bought me, and Michel and I played Bach together. His visit is described in my book *Names and Events*. Michel saw an excerpt on my website five decades later and got in touch. I learned that he had stayed in America from then on, teaching violin at the University of Kentucky in Louisville and dealing in rare violins. He came to Silverton for a visit with his nice wife, Rebecca, and we played music together for hours.

Jimmy Camicia, house-sitting in Amsterdam with his boyfriend, Mark Hannay, for the month of August, invited me to come over for a week. I thought it would be fun to hang out with a couple of urban gay guys, a flavor I miss. They were welcoming but lazy, Mark recovering from a bicycle injury, Jimmy sleeping till noon, so I wandered around the old city, teeming with tourists, and went to museums by myself. I was editing Jimmy's memoir, *My Dear Sweet Self*, and we did a bit of work on it while I was there. I was delighted with the way this book came out, having pressed Jimmy to write about his personal life as well as his theatre company, Hot Peaches.

Jerry Hinsvark died shortly before Thanksgiving. Lorin urged Carol, me, and Alfred to come for Thanksgiving anyway, held this year at Jerry's daughter Amber's boyfriend's mansion in Lake Oswego, lavish and bizarre, with numerous grieving family.

Julian and Liane were overjoyed with the birth of their baby daughter on February 5, 2013. I was tickled to be a grandfather and touched that, after days of suspense, they decided to name her Malina. Judith Malina had been a vital friend and mentor to me; Julian of course was named for Judith's husband, Julian Beck.

Alfred and I went to Taos to meet her. I was happy to see Julian and Liane so happy with their baby, although they were not getting along with each other very well. On our last night they withdrew into the bedroom to hash things out. Alfred and I went to the Outback for pizza by ourselves.

Julian with Malina Sky Pellegrini Smith

On the way back to Oregon I stopped in Boulder to visit Jim and Prudence Scarritt and Theo Ehrhardt and Joani Hinrichs, old friends ever more precious with the passage of time.

7

PUBLICATION OF *Rhapsodic Photography, Selected Poems 1964–2012* was the beginning of an effort to put my writings into the lasting form of books. Too much was languishing on shelves in my file room. I never thought of myself as a poet, but I had written poems all my life, and they had been pouring out since I started my blog. Whatever you think of their quality, they say a lot. Next came *Michael Smith Plays, Volumes I and II*. There they are. Not to scant my work as a theatre critic, still my main claim to fame, I read through all the reviews I could find in Google's *Village Voice* archive, paid a young Living Theatre member to dig out the rest at the New York Public Library, selected the best and organized them into a readable sequence, and published *Theatre Journal: Reviews from The Village Voice, 1960–1974*. Opinions aside, they are an invigorating chronicle of a remarkable period in modern theatre.

Annie, the paint mare with whom Carol had won her greatest equestrian triumphs, knocked her down and struck out at Traci's kids. Deducing a tumor, Carol had her put down, a sad goodbye. She was in New York for Hurricane Sandy—just made it from Syd's house in Harlem to Tensie's in Brooklyn before the subways shut down, and miraculously made it home on time.

My right hip was getting seriously painful: it was time for a second hip replacement surgery. Conveniently, Silverton Hospital had a star orthopedic surgeon, David Thorsett, who fit me into his busy schedule. I was diligent about doing my exercises and made a good recovery.

A few months later, though, my new hip became intensely painful. X-rays showed nothing wrong. Dr. Sanford prescribed Percocet, which knocked down the pain, but after several days of taking it regularly I gradually sank into gloom and misery, nauseous and wiped out, unable to eat or do anything but burrow into the sofa. My friend William identified it as depression; and indeed it was, the hideous, overwhelming black depression I had read about but never experienced before. I recovered when I stopped taking the drug. Fortunately the pain had resolved.

I wrote a novel tracking my life with others for nearly twenty years through the eyes of my beloved feline friend Cat. Cat was named for a character in *Prussian Suite*; in the book he is called Charles, in memory of Charles Stanley. I was a little sheepish about this book, feeling it was too self-involved to keep telling my own self-serving story over and over; but I knew it was a good idea for how to tell it and thought I had carried it off: the book was funny and touching. I had taken to reading books on a Kindle, which is easier to see, and published *A Cat's Tale* as an ebook

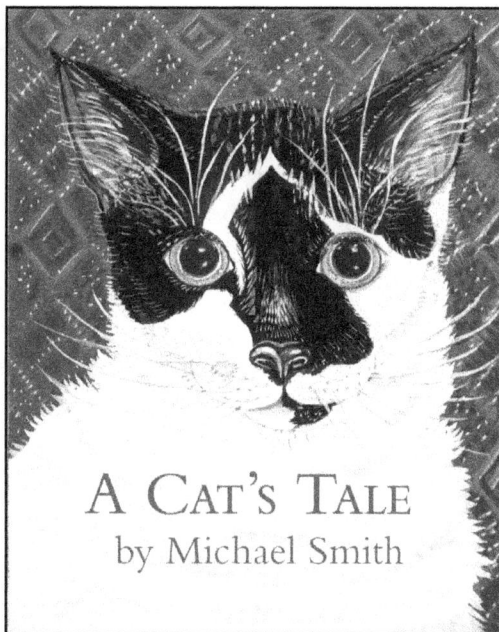

A CAT'S TALE
by Michael Smith

only. It has not been reviewed. Only a handful of copies have been bought. Alfred liked it, but otherwise I have had no response. It is more satisfying to publish real books that I can put into the hands of potential readers. One day I will bring out a paperback edition. The beautiful cover is a faithful egg-tempera portrait by Michele.

My new health insurance came with a free membership at Anytime Fitness so I signed up. Exercise is key to well-being in later years. I do yoga by myself every morning, go to the gym on Monday, Wednesday, and Friday, go to the Silverton pool for a deep-water workout and a few laps on Tuesday, Thursday, and Saturday, and do tai chi every Wednesday at 5.

Liane brought Malina to Oregon to visit her parents. Alfred had the good idea for us to meet Liane and Malina at Laurelhurst Park in Portland for a picnic. Michele was there too. It was a beautiful summer day, the park full of people playing and dancing around—slack rope walking, group contact yoga, hooping—the city at its best. We laid out blankets on the grass, lolled around, and admired baby Malina, utterly adorable and full of fun.

Bicky invited me to join her and her children to celebrate her birthday with dinner at Chez Panisse in Berkeley. How could I resist? The dinner experience was outstanding. This was my first meeting with Ben's girlfriend, Dana Weissman, another planner. Neither Carol nor I had been entirely well. My hip still hurt, her knee was giving her trouble, and we both caught colds, Carol's lingering as an exhausting cough. We thought she was better, but when I arrived home from my weekend in San Francisco, the house was ominously dark. I found Carol in bed, shivering and barely coherent. At Urgent Care, she was diagnosed with pneumonia and started on antibiotics. She was very sick. It took two rounds of antibiotics to turn it around.

I learned just as guests were arriving for our 2014 New Year's party that Julian had gone into rehab in Santa Fe. Apparently he had been medicating his anxiety with opioids and sometimes heroin. After much drama and distress, Liane persuaded him to commit to a month-long residential drug treatment program to break the pattern.

Christopher Storke, the son of Carol's baby brother Paul, brought his Taiwan Chinese girlfriend Szu-Ju to meet us. They had met in law school. He was working in Florida, she in Nevada, and they wanted to get married. Chris's mother, who is Guatemalan, was pushing back. Chris lost his father at an early age, and Carol is his main connection to his Storke family roots. Her approval and support are precious to him and Szu-Ju. I like them.

G ERARD FORDE ORGANIZED four days of events in New York to mark the 50th anniversary of Fred Herko's suicidal leap from Johnny Dodd's fifth-story window, including a proper symposium at NYU, performances at Judson Church and a downtown gallery, a gathering across the street from 5 Cornelia Street on the day and hour, and a conversation with Jean-Claude and me at the 42nd Street library. I was one of a handful of survivors who had actually known Freddie, and I went to everything, not sure how I

With Deborah Lawlor and Robert Heide at the Cornelia Street Café

With Jean-Claude van Itallie backstage at the New York Public Library

felt about the whole Freddie story but enjoying Gerard and old friends.

I had a second aim in going east, which was to get poems from Judith Malina for a book. This involved an hour's bus ride and a walk to the Actors' Home in Englewood, New Jersey. Judith was sharp and vital as ever, though she hated being in the old folks home and out of the city. We had lunch and a good visit, then she said it was time to get to work. I sat down and read through a stack of her poems from the past decade or so and made a selection—she thought about 90 would be good—which Dennis Yueh-Yeh Li kindly xeroxed for me. Judith had a small painting by Julian Beck on the wall of her room; I reproduced it on the cover of her book. She liked the title I proposed, *Having Loved*. I sent her a box of books, and she was pleased to have them to give to her visitors in the last months before she died. I was glad to have realized this fine project in a timely way.

Tensie was out of town; I stayed by myself at her apartment in Park Slope, where for some reason I was never entirely comfortable. Once my obligations were done, I spent a day museum-going and paid a visit to Jean-Claude at his elegant Village pied à terre. Otherwise New York was more tiring than fun. Regrettably, I didn't have the energy to go to Darien to see John Lucas, who was in the late stages of Parkinson's disease and impossible to communicate with by phone. I paid extra to fly home three days early.

My father's macular degeneration made it impossible for him to drive, read, or write in his later years. Now I had it. I embarked on the latest treatment, a course of injections into the left eye, monthly for the first year or so, which stopped the condition from getting worse, although damage had been done. The right eye was still all right, doing most of the work.

Alfred came with me to Taos for Malina's second birthday party. We stayed in a dreary motel the first night, then moved to Julian's house in El Prado, which was much pleasanter. Liane was living in a different house at the other end of town; it was not clear whether they were together or not. The party was at Liane's and a splendid affair, with a forest of balloons and many children frolicking. Julian made a spectacular cake.

8

Carol no longer felt safe on Gwynnevere; after six years she had to go. That was the end of Carol's dressage ambitions. I went with her to southern Oregon to look for a replacement, and she acquired Bella, a pretty white mare (technically gray) with a bit of Arab in her, an ornament to the pasture.

Steve Slemenda is one of my good friends here. His son Kai was a delicate boy, and I was touched by their close relationship as he was growing up. Now a senior in high school, Kai was planning to study music in college but hadn;t had much training. I noticed his slim figure leaning against the counter at a poetry reading in the coffee house and offered, through Steve, to give him piano lessons. Months later I ran into them in the park and talked to Kai directly. He told me he needed to improve his sight-reading; I said I could help with that. In his gap year after high school he came for a lesson every week, and I guided him through the first three books of Bartok's *Mikrokosmos*.

I threw myself an 80th birthday party under the big walnut tree in our yard. Julian came from Taos and made me a cake. Bicky came from Santa Barbara, Alfred from Portland. In addition to family, including Laurel and Hinrich, I invited selected Silverton friends for an afternoon of games: badminton and croquet on the grass and ping-pong in the garage with the doors open. It was a gorgeous Indian summer day, hot in the sun. Now that I was 80, I could start thinking of myself as old.

As a birthday favor I collected a few stories I had written over the years that no one had ever read and made a little book, *Six Stories*, printed 100 copies, and gave or sent them to family and friends. "The King and His Cats," written when I was ten after my first visit to New York, got the most comments.

Shannon and Mark brought Silas for a second visit—they'd been here for Easter when he was three. A delightful kid, he succeeded in catching one of my young chickens.

Ben and Dana staged their wedding in Sonoma. Carol and I flew down for it, staying with her cousin Tom Menzies and wife at their vineyard near Glen Ellen. Bicky hosted a festive party the night before. The simple outdoor marriage ceremony at Sebastiani Winery was lovely, but the high-decibel reception was too much for Carol and me: we fled before the main course. Dana's family's picnic the next day was more relaxed. We miss New York Jews.

By the time we got home, Carol was coming down with the flu. Her new doctor's assistant at the Providence clinic in Canby, forty minutes away, didn't take it seriously and sent her home. Her temperature kept rising. When we went back a couple of days later, she had pneumonia on top of the flu. They called an ambulance, which took her to Silverton Hospital, me following close behind. She was in the hospital during Lora and Edward's long-planned visit, sicker and sicker. Soon after they left, I got a call in the middle of the night that she had been moved into the ICU. Repeated efforts to uncollapse her lung by extracting fluid with a needle and syringe failed. Surgery was required, and she was sent by ambulance at night in the pouring rain to Legacy Emmanuel, a major medical center in Portland. Tensie arrived while she was in transit. The surgery the next day went well, but Carol was desperately ill, tormented with multiple I.V.s, scrutinized by a team of doctors who couldn't think what to do but give her more antibiotics, which she hated. Tensie rented an airbnb for us near the hospital, and I stayed there, making occasional runs home. Tensie left, and Lora-Faye came. Carol

Silas

was profoundly affected and miserable but fought her way back, getting the nurses to take her on walks around the halls day and night. After a week I brought her home. She was on oxygen for weeks and slept with it for months, exercising with my help and gradually recovering her strength. I liked taking care of her, feeling needed and useful.

Following countless difficult trips to the East Coast to see her children, from which she often came home sick, Carol made up her mind not to fly anymore. They finally accepted that they would have to come here.

AFTER I BROUGHT OUT RON TAVEL'S NOVEL *Chain*, Harvey wanted me to publish the screenplays his brother had written for Andy Warhol in the sixties. He sent me the manuscript Ron had left. There were seventeen screenplays in various states of coherence and readability. They were of some interest, certainly, but it seemed like too much for me to take on editing the scripts into publishable condition and rounding up the stills to illustrate them. I tried to persuade the Whitney Museum or the Andy Warhol Museum in Pittsburgh to support the publication or publish it themselves. Harvey died before anything happened. His husband, Norman Glick, called me, saying it was Harvey's dying wish to see this book published, and he would be glad to pay for it. So I looked at it again. I didn't actually like the screenplays themselves, which no one would want to read, but the introductions Ron had written for them comprised an entertaining, insightful narrative about the scene at the legendary Factory and Andy's uniquely effective art-making process. I drew up a budget to cover the hard costs (not charging for my editing and design work, etc.); Norman accepted, sending half in advance. I carefully explained my revised intentions, i.e., not to publish the actual screenplays, but Norman was very sick, and I was not sure he got it. I went ahead with the book, acquiring suitable illustrations. Marc Siegel, a scholar-critic in Berlin, wrote an excellent introduction and thought up the witty title, *Andy Warhol's Ridiculous Screenplays*: Ron is known for originating the post-Absurd "ridiculous" theatrical style. By the time the book came out, Norman had died, leaving his salesman nephew David Glick as Ron's sole heir. David paid the balance of my costs from his brother's estate.

Salem poetry impresario Marc Janssen invited me to read my poems on the Salem Poetry Project series, then meeting incongruously at a yogurt shop in downtown Salem. I put together a retrospective sample and read them to a small audience of friends and young Salem poets. It was pleasant enough, but I was not thrilled to read my poems aloud; they are written more for the eye, for the page, needing thought and reflection. Alfred came down from Portland to hear me. It cheers me that he likes my writing—he is my best reader.

Invited to write an introduction to my late friend Bill Hart's journal of a trip to Ecuador with his Ecuadorian boyfriend, I offered to help put it into print. Gerry Herman, a friend of friends, had discovered and transcibed this charming text. He came to visit, worked closely with me to finalize the design, and paid for the printing. It made a sweet little book, with an extended poetic afterword by Sam Shepard.

9

JULIAN WANTED A BREAK from winter in Taos. I suggested we meet up in Houston; I had never been there and wanted to see the museums. He preferred to go to the ocean. I said why not Santa Barbara, then, we can stay with Bicky, at which point he backed out altogether. I had already told Bicky we were coming so I went anyway. As always we had a good time together—Camerata concert, farmers market, dinner at Downey's, beach walk. Bicky is a graceful host and loads of fun, but it really didn't mean anything to me to be in Santa Barbara anymore.

Julian came here instead for a few days in March. He was in fine fettle but fragile—had a breakdown in the middle of a ping-pong game. He felt a pain in his side and thought it was cancer. I assumed he was joking, but he wasn't and had to go back to the hotel for an Ativan. He stayed at the Garden Resort—needed his own space, he said. I went over the last night and got into the spacious outdoor spa with him, floating on our backs under the dark sky. He and Liane were now "buddies," he said, and thinking of moving to Oregon. I wished they would so I could see more of him and be part of Malina's young life.

The next thing I knew, Julian and Liane had separated, on their way to getting a divorce. When she brought Malina to Parkdale for the Fourth of July, Julian came here, staying at a nearby airbnb; in a couple of days he would go fetch Malina. I would have much preferred that they stay here, but he didn't want to. After a cheery first afternoon together picking blueberries, he underwent a sudden mood-shift midway through dinner, taking offense because Carol thought Malina at three and a half was too young for Legos. (We had a big box of Legos on loan from Carol's cousin and she felt responsible.) It was as if a demon took him over. He seemed to feel we were impugning Malina's intelligence or his parental judgment. Looking frightened and desperate, impervious to reason and appeal, he walked out before dessert and went into a twenty-four-hour tailspin, threatening to leave town and make me come into Portland if I wanted to see Malina. He was angry, willful, insistent on arguing it out, whatever it was. He wouldn't come to the house the next day, saying he didn't feel safe here, and insisted we meet him in the park. I didn't respond particularly well, getting upset myself. By evening he had pulled himself together, came to dinner, and went to fetch Malina the next day as planned. Alfred came for the weekend, and we all had a wonderful time. Malina was energetic, sweet, and loving, her occasional meltdowns quickly passing. I had been scrupulously supportive and noncritical of Julian since he had asked me years before not to judge him. It was distressing that he now felt threatened and attacked by me. I was afraid anything I said might set him off again. I sorely missed our long-standing intimacy and ease.

CAROL ORGANIZED A FAMILY REUNION to celebrate her 80th birthday, and a raft of them came, including Big Sidney, Tensie and her boyfriend, Damon Santostefano, Lora-Faye and her girlfriend, Jordan Kisner, Chris Storke with Szu-Ju, their baby, and Szu-Ju's mother, Pao-Lin. Carol's

Lora-Faye presenting the amazing birthday cake she and Jordan made for Carol

birthday is September 2; she celebrated it in July because that was when people could come. Sid and Damon presided over the barbecue. Croquet and badminton were played. Lora presented Carol with a birthday book I had helped her make. It was a fine party, slightly strange for me to be one of Carol's two husbands, surrounded by the offspring of the other.

I felt the familiar itch to write something. On July 15, the day after the Bastille Day truck massacre in Nice, I started a book called *How to Be Funny* in the morning and another book, ultimately called *Play Work*, in the afternoon. I plugged away on these two texts practically every day for the next six months. Inspiration never flagged.

Bicky came for a visit with her amiable new boyfriend, Bill Goldsmith, who had been her city planning professor at Cornell. She had known his

Michael Smith

late wife. Bill was as lively as she was, interested in everything. I was happy that she had found love again.

Carol lined up a busy season of horse-camping trips with Carole Clinkscales, a friend who lived east of the Cascades. They had fun planning gourmet meals and enjoyed each other's company. Carol's right knee was giving her trouble, which made it hard to do the tasks of saddling, setting up camp, moving hay and water, etc., but once she was in the saddle she was fine. She lived for these interludes in the woods. Her friend was worse off, with limited lung function, and traveled with oxygen, ready to die in the saddle. They tried to get younger horse friends to go along, but it was usually just the two of them

On her horse-camping outings, Carol had been sleeping under the shell in the back of her truck. She had herself set up with a comfortable mattress, abundant padding, a potty, everything she needed, but it was awkward and unsafe getting in and out over the tailgate. In the run-up to knee surgery, she ordered herself a new, longer horse trailer with a gooseneck hitch and a tiny bedroom with a high bunk up front—quite a rig to pilot into the mountains.

She put off knee surgery until after the summer riding season. For the last few months she was painfully limping around. We had confidence in her

Carol's new rig

surgeon, Dr. Puskas, and the surgery went well. I cheerfully took care of her afterwards, keeping her ice machine filled, taking her to physical therapy, helping with her exercises as long as she needed help. She made a good recovery, though the knee remained painful, something about a strained ligament. The other knee was stabilized with injections.

Traci Dahlberg had been here almost every day for ten years, helping Carol look after the horses in exchange for stabling one and then several of her own in Carol's barn and pastures, later partnering with me on the chickens. We watched her become a mother, and her two boys were often around as they were growing up. Her husband Mike hunted deer in the easement with a compound bow. They enriched the life of the farm, and I would miss them. But Traci was getting on Carol's nerves. They had different ideas about how to work with horses, and Carol had started to feel the barn was more Traci's than her own. Traci left, returned, then left for good in late 2016, wanting to have more horses than Carol had room for. Carol took full ownership of Rosie, a mare she been sharing with Traci, not very comfortably.

Traci's depaarture meant the chickens were all mine. I took good care of them, showing up morning and evening to let them out to run around outside and shut them in for the night. The chickens and the blueberries are the extent of my farming, and I get a big kick out of them. Plus eggs.

Several of our favorite friends were going out of town, and we'd both had colds, and we were not sure we wanted to invite the rest of the usual suspects on New Year's Day 2017. People kept dropping off the guest list until there weren't enough left to make it worth doing. So we called it off. Laurel said she and Hinrich would come anyway, so when the time came I invited them to dinner.

Jean-Claude had transformed his peaceful farm in Massachusetts into Shantigar, a foundation and retreat center dedicated to theatre arts, meditation, and healing. Shantigar proposed an online 21-Day Meditation Challenge beginning January 1. Ten minutes a day was all they asked; I

Szu-ju, her mother and brother, and Chris Storke (rear) with baby Paul at PDX

thought why not, adding it onto my morning yoga. Ten minutes turned out to be too short; I upped it to twelve and have been doing it ever since.

Carol and I went to Las Vegas for Chris and Szu-Ju's wedding, everyone very happy and glad to be together. Sid came too. What a weird place! A year later Baby Paul was born, and they took to visiting us twice a year, sometimes accompanied by Szu-Ju's amiable brother and mother, speaking Chinese. They are delightful people, a welcome glimpse into another culture and generation. Baby Paul was the center of attention. We marveled at what young parents go through. How did we do it?!

EAGER TO SEE SHANNON AND MARK in their new house, I flew down to San Francisco for a weekend in April. Silas was now seven, and I hadn't seen Ben and Dana since their wedding. I had a grand time. Shannon and Mark had spent a couple of maddening years remodeling the house, which turned out beautiful and full of light, with roomy guest quarters on the lower level. Silas was under the weather on Saturday so we lay around much of the day and he filled me in about *Hamilton*, infinitely dear. The next day, walking down toward Mission with Shannon and Mark on the way to SFMOMA, I tripped and fell down on the sidewalk. It was scary but no harm was done, the moment redeemed by a concerned neighbor who saw me fall, ran out, and sweetly brought a damp cloth to soothe my scraped palms. We went on to SFMOMA, newly expanded and overcrowded; I didn't like it anymore. Ben and Dana also had a new house, long and narrow with high ceilings. I was happy to see them one and all, touched by their warm welcome.

Desperate for help with the weeding and garden chores that need to be done every spring and were increasingly beyond me, I called a friendly young man who had given me his number in the coffee house months before. Besides the multiple flower beds around the house, all invaded by grass and weeds, the forest we had planted along Silver Creek was overrun with blackberries and vines climbing the trees. Theo was a godsend. Part of a large Russian family, living on his uncle's farm in Woodburn, he was working for his father and uncle framing houses and only erratically available, but he was big and strong and worked hard when he was here, edging beds, getting things reasonably under control around the house, transforming the easement into a beautiful park. I hope he will keep coming—help is needed!

10

CAROL AND I CELEBRATED OUR 25TH ANNIVERSARY with dinner at the Silver Grille, glad there was a good restaurant in town for special occasions. (The other options were not so good.) We thoroughly enjoyed our periodic dinner-dates and the wide-ranging conversations that ensued.

At home on the farm at the end of the road, we had settled into a routine that carried us right along. In the morning Carol went into her office or out to her horses and garden. I had my regular weekly schedule of gym, pool, tai chi, and music-making. William occasionally came over to play ping-pong, or I met Kelley or Steve for coffee. Otherwise I was at my computer in my studio. I came into to the house around one for lunch and a nap. We occasionally crossed paths, exchanged a few words, a kiss, a touch or embrace, shared a chore or ran an errand together; often we hardly saw each other all day. We came together for dinner. Carol had ideas for the menu and sometimes laid out the ingredients, including vegetables from her garden. I loved to cook, now that I dared. At harvest time I made jam, plum, cherry, marionberry, grape, and currant. She worked outside; I cleaned the house, did most of the shopping, took out the trash, mowed the grass, replaced toilet paper rolls, and handled other karmic responsibilities I have taken on. Winter evenings we would read books aloud to each other, taking turns; in summer I liked to go outdoors after dinner and do projects, enjoying the long, delicious twilights of the Pacific Northwest. At bedtime for years we did the *Times* crossword; we built in a special light for it when we remodeled the bedroom. We slept side by side in a comfortable queen-size bed, quite big enough. I loved to be physically close to my beloved, kissing, exchanging warmth and love-currents, pressing our skulls together, feeling the heat of her brain as our souls and circuits harmonized.

CAROL WORKED HARD TO RECOVER from knee surgery and regain the strength to ride. Bella would be too lively to start on, and Rosie wasn't trained or reliable enough. The previous winter, while she was recovering from pneumonia, Carol had borrowed her friend Marti's Toby, a reliable gelding, and wished she had a horse like that. So she sold Rosie and bought Dusty, an older gelding she could ride as she got stronger, a horse her children and grandchildren could ride when they came to visit, and Bella, a more reasonable horse for her to ride on the trail. By the end of March she began going out on rides when weather allowed and planned another eventful summer of horse-camping with Carole Clinkscales.

The first outing with Bella was at Sheep Springs, a favorite campground near Sisters, where Carol and Carole met up with Marti on June 1. The next morning they had barely left camp on their first ride when Carole's large dog came running up the narrow trail from behind and ran right under Bella, who freaked out, spinning and bucking, forcing Carol to bail out into the underbrush. She landed hard on her back and couldn't move. A group of forest volunteers who happened to be nearby helped her up, and Marti drove her to the hospital in Bend. Nothing was broken, but she was badly bruised. She spent that night in her trailer. In the morning Ann and Steve Smith drove over the pass to rescue her; Ann brought Carol home, and Steve drove her rig back with Bella. For a couple of months Carol could hardly do anything. As soon as possible she started exercising again, slowly healing. She was afraid to ride Bella now, sensing that she too had been traumatized by the dog incident, so she sent her away to be sold and bought herself an ostensibly milder horse named Rocky. After all the mares, she now had gelded males.

Grampa and princess

Liane brought Malina here for a few days after the Fourth of July. I was feeling a bit depleted, but Alfred came from Portland, bringing additional energy, and we all had a joyful time. Carol put Malina on Dusty and she lit up. No Julian this year.

My macular degeneration was pretty well under control with continuing injections, but my eyes were losing acuity. Carol and I gave up driving at night after a harrowing near-miss on narrow, curvy 213 on the way back from a chamber music concert at Reed College. This limited our cultural intake, which generally required driving into Portland and home late.

Malina on Dusty with Liane and Carol in the arena

Friends were generous about giving us rides to events in Salem, and we didn't mind too much, happy to stay home.

It was also getting hard for me to read music at speed, sharps and naturals looking too much alike. I didn't want to give up music or reading, God forbid. It was time for cataract surgery. Dr. Farmer referred me to Dr. John Dodd (!) in Salem, who performed the surgery efficiently, the right and then the left three weeks later. Immediately colors were brighter. With new glasses I could see considerably better.

I finished writing my two small books and published them on the same day!

How to Be Funny is poetry-prose, written in the second person in stand-alone sentences, each a paragraph to itself, grouped in stanzas of varying length. Once I had the idea and started, it wrote itself, not exactly easy but not hard and often fun. Every day I sat down, opened the file, and something came, making me think and wonder where I could go with it. It was pure play, nothing like anything I ever wrote before. I had 100 copies printed and bound by a commercial printer in Salem and gave them to friends. I read from it at local poetry readings. The reactions were so positive that I did a trade edition, with blurbs on the back cover, and put it up on Amazon, where it has yet to be discovered. A timeless classic, in my opinion.

Play Work is a straight-ahead chronicle of all my multifaceted adventures in the theatre, an intermittent continuity of intense, short-lived events punctuating and paralleling my love life and ordinary existence, each project self-contained, with its own dramatic cast of characters and arc of relationships. My creative work in theatre, scattered in time and space, meant a lot to me and made a curious story.

Two good books: I was proud of myself.

By the time Carol was riding again, Oregon was ablaze with wildfires, which burned right through some of her favorite campgrounds in the Cascades. Carole Clinkscales was no longer available for her to ride and camp with, unwilling to go without her dog. Carol had two new riding friends, Dorothy Vasquez and her sister Jewel Wallace, who were as avid for trail rides as she was. She went camping with them to Timothy Lake, a relatively clear space between fires when the smoke was thick in Silverton. The smoky conditions persisted for weeks.

August 21, 2017 was an unusually clear day, and Silverton was on the fabled path of totality for the solar eclipse. We had a perfect view from our yard. Rosa and William came over to watch it with us with their little dog Pinkerton, which made it more festive—a beautiful fadeout and amazing two minutes as the brilliant shining halo floated in the darkened summer sky.

Louisa and her husband Eric Melear suddenly had a baby. Louisa's flourishing career as an opera director involves frequent sojourns in different cities; I hadn't been sure she wanted motherhood too. Laurel told me they had tried for some time, then set about adopting, and in August a baby came their way with magical speed. Selected by the birth mother, they flew from

Observing the eclipse with Carol, William, and Pinkerton. Photo by Rosa Waggoner.

Vienna, where Eric had a continuing job at the opera, to Salt Lake City in time to take the baby home from the hospital to their hotel room; it took a week to arrange to take her back to Austria. Laurel and Hinrich hastened to Utah to meet their granddaughter. The proud parents named her Maisie, not realizing this was the name of my beloved grandmother. I was happy for them, though sorry she doesn't have Maisie's excellent genes.

The seven chickens Traci had left me with stopped laying reliably. Frustrated, I put a notice on Craig's List and gave them away to the first caller. I didn't have personal relationships with individual chickens—couldn't tell them apart within the breed—but I liked having chickens, and that night I lay awake feeling unexpectedly bereft. The next day I bought six baby chicks, four Buff Orpingtons and two Welsummers, the first chicks I would raise on my own. Once I had them set up, I realized we wouldn't have any eggs for five or six months. So I bought three six-month-old hens from a friendly farmer and his son, a Leghorn, a Barred Rock, and a Speckled Sussex. They quickly made themselves at home in our coop with its large fenced run, found the laying boxes, and started producing two or three delicious eggs every day for Carol and me. The six chicks thrived, well-feathered in time for cold weather, by the end of the year almost full-grown. I sold four of them to our next door neighbor so we wouldn't be overwhelmed with eggs.

11

I HAVE DECIDED THIS IS THE YEAR to end the story of my life, a book I have been working on sporadically for as long as I can remember. It isn't the end of my life: I will spare readers the decline and actual end—not anytime soon, I hope.

My initial impulse was to write about my friends, lovers, and collaborators, who have given me so much. Eventually I had to admit that it was my own story I wanted to tell: love, work, music, place. An earlier draft began when I went away to school, ending when I left New York and moved to the West Coast, and grew to more than 800 pages (without pictures). I gave copies to Julian and Alfred when I thought they were old enough, wanting them to know their father (and mother) in a way I never knew mine, who left no record of their lives, thoughts, and friendships. The boys were a bit shaken but took it well.

Meanwhile life went on. That wasn't the whole story; I wanted to tell the rest of it. I wrote about my childhood, so typical and expressive of my class and time, now utterly gone, but it seemed too boring, delaying the juicy parts; I reduced it to a pictorial prologue. I whittled the earlier sections down to a manageable size and wrote up my busy years in Santa Barbara, where I found myself again as editor, critic, playwright, director, producer, lighting designer, musician, son, lover, and father.

Less happens now—just life. Carol and I started fresh again on our farm in Oregon, setting ourselves up with everything we need, constructung a life here that suits and gratifies us in an increasingly less dynamic phase, well aware that this is a dreadful time for our country and the planet, with worse to come, glad to be out of the center we once relished. I found new friends and had a good time doing a few more plays. Finally I was not up to that anymore; publishing books is easier. I have solved my problems and had my career, if you want to call it that. I never was rich and famous, never got much recognition for my creative endeavors, but I did a lot of honest work, had a good time doing it, and made some beautiful art.

Carol and I have been happy together, encouraging each other to do what we love. I like recalling the amazing people I have known, so generous with themselves, and the serious fun we had together. I wouldn't want to be young again: I want to be authentically old. I think of all the places I've been and don't want to go back or elsewhere. This is fine.

I wanted to tell my story, and here it is. A life in parts and all one, like anyone's.

MICHAEL SMITH

Notes on Illustrations

Holy Memory

3 — My father at Culver Military Academy, c. 1918; my mother c. 1930 (Strauss-Peyton photo); Mother and Dad on their honeymoon in Nassau; baby Michael

6 — Photo of my father's family by Ken Neumann

8 — With Bicky on my bike and at the pony ride in the Country Club Plaza, Kansas City, Missouri

11 — At Remuda Ranch, Wickenburg, Arizona: practicing rope tricks; competing in the junior rodeo; with my mother; with my father (loved that Buick)

12 — On the beach at Small Point, Maine, summer 1946; on the beach at La Jolla, California, 1947; with Bicky and Dinny at C Lazy U Ranch, Granby, Colorado, summer 1950; Dad and Dinny; with Bill Evans

13 — At Big Wolf Lake, summer 1949; my boat; at the Lawrence camp's tennis court, 1951

115 — As Queen Guinevere in *A Connecticut Yankee* at Hotchkiss

18 — Photo of my family on the patio at 210 San Ysidro Road by Hal Boucher

When I Was Gay

20, 31, 71, 79, 105 — *Village Voice* photos by Fred W. McDarrah

28 — Photo by the author

37 — Jerry Tallmer receiving George Jean Nathan Award from Julie Harris

39 — Drawing by Paul Cadmus

42 — Photo by Helen Merrill

45 — Photo by the author

63 — Photo by Ben Martin, 1961: Shirley Stoler in *The Gypsy*

69 — Photo by Billy Name

71 — Søren on the way to the 1965 Obies

88 — Photo by Phill Niblock

107 —Photo by Billy Name

172 — Photo by the author

175 — Patricia Madsen, John Simcox, and Nancy Mangus at the table, Dennis Stull and Melanie Kern upstage of them, musician Erica Bramesco in the background

Early Music

Return to New York

Reset West

Just Life

www.ingramcontent.com/pod-product-compliance
Lightning Source LLC
Chambersburg PA
CBHW080041280326
41935CB00014B/1752